A User-friendly PL 280 Resource Guide

Alex Tortes & Cindy Pierce

A USER-FRIENDLY PL 280 RESOURCE GUIDE

A User-Friendly PL 280 Resource Guide Team:

TECHNICAL & PRODUCTION EDITOR
Wendy Olson

TECHNICAL INPUT
Alex Tortes
Cindy Pierce

PRODUCTION MANAGER, COVER DESIGN & ALL CREATIVE CONCEPTS
Cindy Pierce

THIRD EDITION: July 2013

Much of this publication contains compiled information from a variety of sources. Each source has been clearly cited and we encourage the purchase (where applicable) of these books, articles, etc. for the purpose of further study.

Every effort has been made to ensure the information in this resource guide is complete and accurate. Discovery of any errors or omissions will be updated/changed in future editions of this guide. Any trademarks, service marks, or product names are assumed to be the property of their respective owners and are used only for reference.

ISBN-13: 978-0615683645
ISBN-10: 0615683649

Printed and bound in the United States of America.

Attention: Seminars for "A User-Friendly PL 280" are presented by the authors and available to those interested. Quantity discounts of this guide are also available for resale.

www.nexuscommunitysolutions.com

DEDICATIONS

This book is dedicated to:

The tribal communities who graciously taught us many things along the way and provided support for building partnerships;

and

Riverside County Sheriff-Coroner, Stan Sniff, who had the vision and commitment to improve relationships between the tribes and law enforcement.

- ALEX TORTES & CINDY PIERCE

ACKNOWLEDGEMENTS

I would like to personally acknowledge ...

The Tribal Nations -- who shared their history, culture and support with the Riverside County Sheriff's Department, Tribal Liaison Unit. I am thankful for their willingness to put the past behind them and build relationships for the future.

Riverside County Sheriff-Coroner, Stan Sniff -- whose vision and commitment to building relationships and improving services to the Riverside County Tribal Nations was the inspiration for writing this book.

My family -- who supported my decision to return to work and follow my dream of finding tribal family members I lost contact with because I had been assimilated, and to continue my passion for teaching.

Joely Proudfit, Ph.D. -- who took the time to meet with the Tribal Liaison Unit and provide information and guidance for becoming an effective bridge in building relationships between the Riverside County Sheriff's Department and the Tribal Nations of Riverside County.

- ALEX TORTES

I would like to personally acknowledge ...

My parents – who have greatly impacted my life in a positive way: my mother for her creative and "think-outside-the-box" ways and my father whose kind and humble demeanor I have always admired.

My daughters, Joy and Abbie – who encouraged me time after time during this project.

My sister, Wendy – my best friend. Her support specifically for this project translated to literally hundreds of hours of roll-up-the-sleeves, nitty-gritty hard work edit after edit.

Riverside County Sheriff-Coroner, Stan Sniff – whose desire to lead an agency that professionally serves all its communities, provided the environment of giving – with no expectation of return other than building good working partnerships.

The Tribal Nations – first, the Morongo Band of Mission Indians Indian Reservation – which was the first community I had the opportunity to work with. So many from this reservation helped me understand crucial things along the way. Additionally, the other eleven tribal communities in Riverside County – whose willingness to reach out in partnerships inspired me.

Two who were instrumental during my humble beginnings in learning about Public Law 280 (more than they probably realize) – George Forman – upon my first eye-opening experience of responding to a call as a deputy sheriff regarding a dispute over trust land on an Indian reservation, George patiently guided me to several court cases that helped me understand the circumstances I was dealing with. Also, Captain Ed Harvey – who understood the importance of building strong working relationships, therefore, allowing me the freedom to have flexibility in my schedule to participate in the various events on the reservation I was assigned to.

Thank you also to the many whose input in this project was invaluable – Lori, Daniel and Bill. And, of course, Rosie, who was always checking to make sure I had a good meal (she said it was the "Mexican Mother" in her).

I must end by acknowledging my business partner, fellow tribal liaison, co-collaborator in this book, and, most of all, friend, Alex Tortes. I have learned so much from him. It has been an honor to work with him in creating a user-friendly resource on Public Law 280.

- CINDY PIERCE

ABOUT THE AUTHORS

ALEX TORTES

Alex Tortes *is a tribal member of the Torres-Martinez Desert Cahuilla Indian Tribe. Alex was born at the Soboba Indian Hospital in southern California. He is a very active member of his community. He is a father of four children, and proud grandfather of twelve grandchildren.*

Alex has over 35 years of law enforcement experience. He served on the Riverside Police Department where he promoted to the rank of Lieutenant/Area Commander. Some of his assignments included patrol, traffic, detective bureau, narcotics unit, special enforcement (SWAT), gangs, and special operations.

Alex has a Bachelor's Degree and has earned a Vocational Teaching Credential. He is an instructor for the State of California's Peace Officer Standards and Training (POST), teaching both classes on "Policing Native American Communities" and "Domestic Violence & Sexual Assault for First Responders on Tribal Lands". Alex has also served as a consultant for the US Department of Justice, Community Policing Consortium.

Alex was the founding member of the Tribal Liaison Unit for the Riverside County Sheriff's Department. Alex also serves as the Executive Director of Nexus Community Solutions.

CINDY PIERCE

Cindy Pierce *has a successful graphics/design business. She has two daughters and one granddaughter. Cindy worked with the Riverside County Sheriff's Department as a Deputy Sheriff where she began her involvement working with tribal communities, focusing on community oriented policing. Cindy is presently a member of the Tribal Liaison Unit for the Riverside County Sheriff's Department. This position has given her valuable experience working in Indian country as well as with local, state and federal agencies. As part of the Tribal Liaison Unit, she assists the team in providing inter-departmental training along with facilitating educational orientations for the Tribal communities that focus on community policing/collaboration and safety awareness. She helped to develop the State of California's Peace Officer Standards and Training (POST) curriculum for "Policing Native American Communities" of which she is a POST certified trainer. She serves, together with Alex, as an instructor and consultant with Nexus Community Solutions, a business dedicated to connecting tribal communities with public safety and service providers.*

TABLE OF CONTENTS

TABLE OF CONTENTS

A Word From The Authors

We would like to welcome you as you begin your adventure through these pages about a law that greatly impacts many tribal communities. We feel confident that when you complete this resource guide, you will have a good understanding of what Public Law 280 is all about. Although *A User-Friendly PL 280 Resource Guide* is not an exhaustive source, by the end of this guide you should be able to navigate easily through PL 280 and the U.S. Attorneys' jurisdictional charts for Indian country with a clearer understanding. For areas that simply go beyond the scope of what is covered in this resource guide, we will offer direction on where to dig deeper regarding such information.

Many of you are fully aware that Public Law 280 has not been very easy to get acquainted with and has often been a frustrating piece of legislation for those who are connected, one way or another, in Indian country. Both Native Americans and the myriad of individuals who work or interact within tribal communities have been forced to make sense of this convoluted law.

Our goal through this guide is to take the "mystery" out of Public Law 280 and help unravel the tangled jurisdictional maze that is seen in Indian country today. PL 280 became a law quite a long time ago, yet has managed to remain elusive for over half a century. We say, "No more hiding in the shadows or being camouflaged in highbrowed legalese!" Let's grab Public Law 280 by the collar and confront it face-to-face.

Allow us to present you with *A User-Friendly PL 280 Resource Guide . . .*

Symbols Used in this Manual:

SAY IT SIMPLY!

Defines the meaning of a word in plain, simple terms.

DIG DEEPER

For areas where there is more that can be looked into, but not included in this book, suggestions will be given where you can go into greater depth on the subject.

KEY POINT

Learning points that are key to understanding PL 280.

QUOTES

Goes to the source to see what was actually said.

NERDY STUFF

Sections dedicated to the guys and gals who just love to know more details.

How To Read A Case Citation

Case Citation is the system used to identify the decisions in past court cases. Although case citations are formatted differently in different jurisdictions, they generally contain the same key information. The following are a few examples of case citation with explanation:

Roe v. Wade is the abbreviated name of the case. The first name *Roe* is the name of the **plaintiff** and *Wade* is the name of the **defendant**.

410 is the volume number of the "reporter" in which the court's written opinion in the Roe v. Wade is published.

(1973) is the year in which the court rendered its decision. The abbreviated name of the court will be included inside the parenthesis before the year if the name of the court is not obvious from the reporter.

Roe v. Wade, 410 US 113 (1973)

US is the abbreviation of the reporter, here "US" stands for *United States Reports.*

113 is the page number (in volume 410 of *United States Reports*) where the opinion begins.

Worcester v. Georgia is the abbreviated name of the case.

31 is the volume number of the "reporter" in which the court's written opinion is published.

(1832) is the year in which the court rendered its decision.

Worcester v. Georgia, 31 US 515, 520 (1832)

US is the abbreviation of the reporter, *United States Reports.*

515 is the page number where the opinion can be found, sub-section 520.

US v. Young is the abbreviated name of the case.

936 is the volume number of the "reporter" in which the court's written opinion is published.

(9th Cir. 1991) is the abbreviated name of the court, the 9th Circuit Court of Appeals, and the year the decision was rendered.

US v. Young, 936 F. 2d 1050 (9th Cir. 1991)

F. 2d is the abbreviation of the reporter, the *Federal Reporter*, second series or edition.

1050 is the page number (in volume 936 of the *Federal Reporter*) where the opinion is.

The Term "Indian"

We have used the term *"Indian"* throughout this resource guide in referring collectively to all indigenous people in North America. This use of the term Indian is consistent with the majority of federal and state laws.

With this said, we do acknowledge the fact that the label "Indian" was designated because of the mistaken belief by the European explorers that they were encountering people from the Indies.

Chapter One

This chapter will cover:

- *Reading the text of PL 280*
- *Defining "Legislative History"*
- *The confusion of Public Law 280*

Chapter One

Getting Started

First Things First

The first thing to do to understand Public Law 280 (PL 280) is to actually read it – completely through in its entirety. If you haven't done this yet, we encourage you to stop right now and jump to the Appendix section of this book (Appendix A, pgs. 346-349) where you will find the complete text of PL 280.

It doesn't take very long to read – and you'll be glad that you did.

(Pause)

What did you think? Not too long, eh? The text is rather simple and straightforward . . . PL 280 doesn't even use cumbersome vocabulary or fancy words. So, what's the big deal about PL 280 anyways?

What's the Big Deal?

The very fact that you are reading this book shows that you know there is much more to understand about PL 280 beyond simply reading the text.

Truth be told, Public Law 280 is very difficult to understand without knowing the context of when and why it was written. In other words, to understand PL 280, one needs to know its *"legislative history."*

Say it Simply!

"legislative history" -- the historical background of a law

Legislative History

When a law is created, the events leading up to it are kept as historical records. These records can be things such as: various committee reports and hearings, analysis from data that was compiled, and debates and comments made during the process.

Say it Simply!

All of this comprises what is called the "legislative history" of a law. This is important stuff because it helps us understand the contemporary concerns and issues surrounding the law, and why it was enacted. In fact, sometimes it gets quite interesting to read the debates of the legislators as they hash things out before a law is approved or *amended*.

"amended" -- to add to or change in some way

Courts look into the legislative history of a law when they interpret the law during a court case. They will look at why a law was passed (intent of the law) in order to know how it should be applied.

Clear As Mud

PL 280 has been used and abused for years. It has frustrated and confused many a law enforcement officer and baffled even the most seasoned of judges. If there is one area of law that has been all over the place, it would be in the area of Indian law. If you have ever used the expression, "It's as clear as mud," when commenting about Indian legislation, you are actually in good company! One US Supreme Court Justice, when reaching a decision about a case involving Indians, put it this way:

Quotes "Q"

> *"Federal Indian policy is, to say the least, schizophrenic. And this confusion continues to infuse federal Indian law and our cases."*
>
> *US Supreme Court Justice, Clarence Thomas – 2004 United States v. Lara*

This Dr. Jekyll and Mr. Hyde way of doing business in Indian country has created a messy situation when it comes to understanding laws relating to Native Americans. And so, we are compelled to look at the legislative history of PL 280.

In order to properly display the main feature of this book, PL 280, a sequential historical unfolding of events will be helpful. If you were one who just cringed when you read the word "historical," have no fear! This account of events will not get bogged down with an overload of historical information. However, the history buffs out there will be given ample direction where they can dig deeper on their own (follow the Dig Deeper symbol).

Historical background (legislative history) is necessary for understanding PL 280.

Sovereignty Blooper

Right away it must be pointed out that we won't get too far digging into the background of Public Law 280 without knowing about "tribal sovereignty." A lack of understanding in this area would be like learning to fly without having any concept about gravity. Tribal sovereignty is a foundational key component in PL 280. Here are things you will need to know:

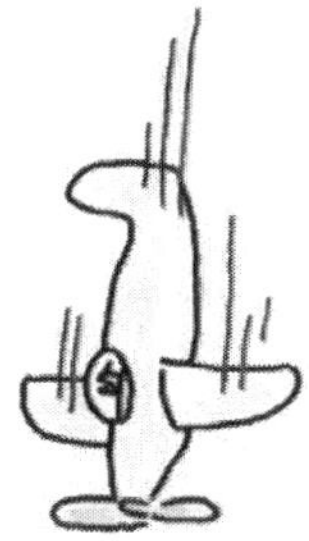

- What does tribal sovereignty mean?
- Where did tribal sovereignty come from?
- Does tribal sovereignty still exist?
- If so, what does it mean to me?

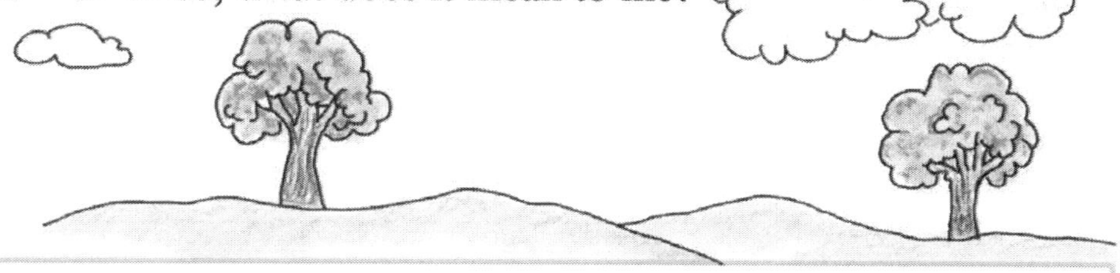

> *"Tribal sovereignty means that, it's sovereign. I mean, you're a – you've been given sovereignty, and you're viewed as a sovereign entity. And therefore the relationship between the federal government and tribes is one between sovereign entities."*
>
> *Former President Bush's response when asked to define "tribal sovereignty" by Mark Trahant, Seattle Post Intelligencer at Unity: Journalists of Color 2004 Convention in Washington, D.C.*

Unfortunately, the former president found out too late that he was not prepared to articulate the definition of "tribal sovereignty." How many of us would be prepared to give an accurate definition on the spot, if asked?

In spite of the humor of that presidential blooper, there was something said that was completely on target: *"[T]he relationship between the federal government and tribes is one between sovereign entities."*

Key Point

PL 280 will not be understood apart from a knowledge of tribal sovereignty.

Since it is crucial to understand tribal sovereignty as we delve into PL 280, let's take a closer look to see what it is all about . . .

Chapter Two ~ Part 1

This chapter will cover:

- *What does tribal sovereignty mean?*
- *Treaties, sovereignty and tribal self-rule*
- *The uniqueness of tribal sovereignty*

Chapter Two ~ Part 1

What Is Tribal Sovereignty?

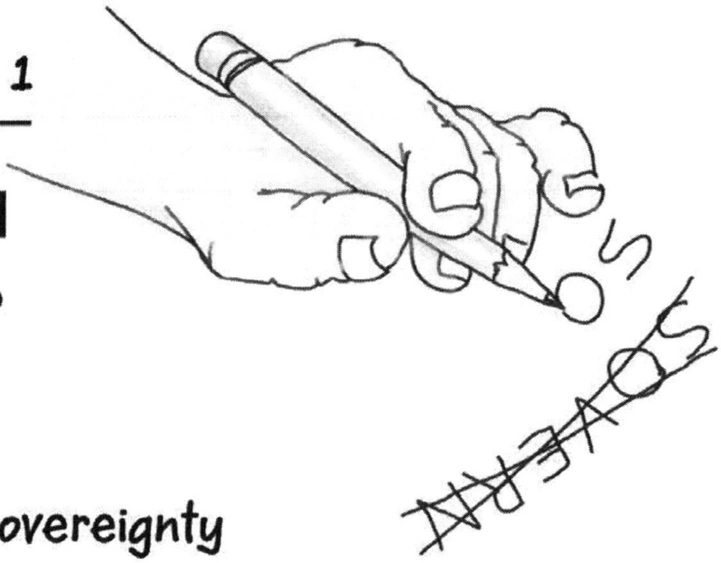

Defining Sovereignty

For most people, the word "sovereignty" is not part of their everyday vocabulary. In fact, many of us, if we looked away from this page, would struggle to spell the word correctly on our first attempt.

Since we have established that knowing the basics of tribal sovereignty is the first step toward understanding PL 280, let's start by defining "sovereignty."

▶ *Sovereignty* = exercising independent and self-governing power, status or authority.

Sovereignty is used to describe governments who are self-ruling and independent. A sovereign nation is self-governing and is its own *political* unit or governmental entity.

Say it Simply!

"political" -- of or relating to a government; concerned with the policies and strategies of a system of government.

Dissolving Political Connections

We have only to look at the birth of the United States of America to get a picture of sovereignty. Today we speak of the USA as a sovereign nation, but this was not always so. At the beginning of the North American settlement, only colonies existed under British authority. The governments of the colonies were directly connected to their Motherland, with whom they were politically tied.

The self-ruling independence the United States exercises today was initially only a hope and a dream for the American colonists. It was only when the thirteen colonies united together and, figuratively speaking, cut the *umbilical cord* with Great Britain, that they became their own sovereign nation.

Cutting the umbilical cord is what the American revolutionists believed was necessary and was the only way they would become a self-governing people. In declaring their independence they chose the word "dissolve" which comes from Latin, meaning, "to make loose and release from."

Quotes

> *"When, in the course of human events, it becomes necessary for one people to* ***dissolve the political bands which have connected them with another*** *..."*
>
> *Declaration of Independence*
> *The Continental Congress, July 4, 1776*

Key Point

> **Self-governing means self-rule;**
> **A government with jurisdiction over its own people and territory.**
>
> **Independent and free from any other sovereign (although a sovereign nation may certainly choose to make an alliance or partnership with another sovereign).**

Family Feud

During the time of the American Revolutionary War, the thirteen colonies that stood united were surrounded by many tribal nations. There were also other foreign nations that had staked their claims on the continent. The tribal and foreign nations watched as the children of Great Britain dissolved the political band connecting them to their motherland. The American colonists collectively sought their own unique political status: to be *an independent, self-ruling sovereign nation*.

Initially, tribal nations wondered what was to become of this feud between Mother England and her children. Many Indians believed this spat between America and Britain was a "family quarrel." [1] The Congress of the Revolution was resolved to maintain a continuance of friendship with the Indian tribes, seeking their neutrality during the colonists' "unhappy dispute with Great Britain." [2]

Say it Simply!

"nebulous" -- confusing, hazy, vauge or indistinct

Many of the Indian tribes had already made formal, government-to-government treaties with Great Britain. (Over 100 Indian treaties had been signed with the British government and colonial governments between 1607 – 1776.) [3] These treaties had been negotiated for various land cessations and for an allegiance of friendship to the Crown.

Quotes

"(T)he actual political status of the American colonists was nebulous. Were they a nation or merely a handful of rebellious subjects? What was their relationship with European nations or with the Indian nations in the interior of the continent? Would problems with England be resolved, or would a colonial civil war continue? If Americans did not know, neither did the Indians, and most of the larger tribes remained loyal to the king."

Deloria, Vine and DeMallie, Raymond J., Documents of American Indian Diplomacy: Treaties, Agreements, and Conventions, University of Oklahoma Press 1999, p.12

Dig Deeper

Deloria, Vine and Raymond J. DeMallie, *Documents of American Indian Diplomacy: Treaties, Agreements, and Conventions*, University of Oklahoma Press 1999 – This book provides great detail about Indian treaties, explaining important facts and you'll be intrigued with the historical documents many know little about.

WHAT IS A TREATY?

"Treaties would be worth no more than the blank paper upon which they were written, if either party could discharge itself from their obligations at pleasure, and without responsibility."

Speech of Hon. James W. Bradbury of Maine, delivered in the US Senate (April 15, 1852)

EXPLAINED	EXAMPLE(S)	QUOTE(S)
A treaty is a binding contract between two or more independent sovereign governments.	If a US state makes a formal agreement with another US state, or even with the US federal government, this is *not* a treaty because it was not between two independent sovereign governments. US state governments are political entities that fall under the umbrella of the sovereignty of the United States of America. The very words, *"United States,"* speaks of the connection of the individual states to form a federal government which governs them collectively in areas that branch out further than state-specific issues. For this same reason, no US state can make treaties with foreign nations. This is clarified and spelled out in the US Constitution, Article 1, Sec. 10, Clause 1: "No State shall enter into any treaty ..." Power to make treaties with foreign nations is vested in the federal government only (see US Constitution, Article 2, Sec. 2, Clause 2).	*". . . the General (Federal) Government, only, has the power to treat with the Indian nations, and any treaty formed, and held without its authority, will not be binding . . . No State, nor person, can purchase your (Indian) lands unless as some public treaty held under the authority of the United States. The General Government will never consent to your being defrauded, but it will protect you in all your just rights."* President George Washington, Dec. 29, 1790, regarding Indian Affairs *"A treaty, including one between the United States and an Indian tribe, is essentially a contract between two sovereign nations."* Washington v. Fishing Vessel Assn., 443 US 658, 675 (1979)
A treaty is not made with individuals, but only with governments of an independent sovereign nation.	If individual citizen, John Smith, wants to make a treaty with another nation, he has no authority to do this. This was also the case historically regarding individuals within tribal communities. Only those representing a tribal government could make *legitimate* treaties.	*"Indian tribes or nations of North America . . . held their respective lands and territories each in common . . . their sole method of selling, granting, and conveying their lands . . . always has been from time immemorial and now is for certain chiefs of the tribe selling to represent the whole tribe in every part of the transaction . . ."* Johnson & Graham's Lessee v. McIntosh, 21 US 543, 549, 550 (1823)
A treaty obligates each party by the terms of the contract they have agreed to and legally signed into law. CH-2A	Governmental officials do not simply decide one day, "Hey, let's make a treaty today!" Treaties are not flippant arrangements between nations. Much goes into the making of a treaty and it is for very specific purposes. The language of a treaty is solemn, representing a formal oath and commitment on behalf of the signing parties.	*"Great nations, like great men, should keep their word."* US Supreme Court Justice, Hugo Black in Federal Power Com'n v. Tuscarora Indian Nation, 362 US 99, 142 (1960) *"The treaty agreements, which were struck in solemn councils between official representatives of the negotiating parties, guided formal political relationships in Indian affairs throughout most of the nineteenth century. Indeed, the treaties were the only legal means for dealing with Indian tribes during much of the nation's early history."* Echo-Hawk, Walter R., *In the Courts of the Conqueror*, Fulcrum Publishing 2010, p. 165

A Treaty Makes It Official

It was not until the end of the American Revolutionary War in 1783, through a treaty, that Great Britain actually recognized the United States of America as a sovereign nation. A treaty was the formal way self-governing nations made agreements between each other. Through the official signing of the Treaty of Paris, the United States of America was now internationally recognized, for the first time, as part of the sovereign nations at-large.

Sovereignty + Tribes = Tribal Sovereignty

Tribal sovereignty has all the attributes of sovereignty as we have so far discussed. However, tribal sovereignty also has *unique* characteristics that are important to recognize.

Say it Simply!

"indigenous" -- native, original inhabitants

During the time of early America, when the states, now united, were making baby steps in their new form of government they recognized the existing governments of the *indigenous* people. These indigenous governments were independent of each other. Some had alliances with other indigenous tribal nations or other foreign nations. Each tribal government exercised sovereignty over their people and their territories.

The inhabitants of the North American continent were not simply one huge tribal unit. Although some had similarities, the tribal communities were individual in their system of government, culture, language and traditions – and had existed as far back as anyone could remember.

Quotes

"Q"

". . . the discovery of the continent of North America by the Europeans . . . was held, occupied, and possessed in full sovereignty by various independent tribes or nations of Indians, who were sovereigns of their respective portions of the territory and the absolute owners and proprietors of the soil and who neither acknowledged nor owed any allegiance or obedience to any European sovereign or state whatever."

Johnson & Graham's Lessee v. McIntosh, 21 US 543, 545 (1823)

Say it Simply!

"proprietors" -- property owners, landowners, administrators

Quotes

"Q"

"America, separated from Europe by a wide ocean, was inhabited by a distinct people, divided into separate nations, independent of each other and of the rest of the world, having institutions of their own, and governing themselves by their own laws. . .The Indian nations had always been considered as distinct, independent political communities, retaining their original natural rights, as the undisputed possessors of the soil, from time immemorial . . ."

Worcester v. Georgia, 31 U.S. 515, 543, 559 (1832)

Tribal Sovereignty Is Unique

"immemorial" -- long past; beyond the limits of memory, tradition or recorded history.

"inherent" -- natural, true, real, an intrinsic part of

The quotes on the previous page illustrate how the sovereignty of the tribal nations is uniquely different than the sovereignty of the United States. Tribal sovereignty is distinctive from most other sovereigns in two ways:

- It has existed since time *immemorial*.
- Tribal sovereignty is *inherent*, not given.

The tribal nations, which predate the United States of America by a long shot, had their own communities and governments (albeit, very different from European norms). They were independent of any other sovereign and made alliances with whom they chose to associate. [4]

In recognition of the unique status of Indian tribes, one US Senator commented during a speech before the United States Senate that "God, in his providence, planted these tribes on the Western continent, so far as we know, before Great Britain herself had a political existence." [5]

When Great Britain became a "political existence" she explored the Western continent and claimed, through "discovery," the exclusive right to purchase lands from the tribes that occupied territory that eventually became part of the United States. This became known as the *Doctrine of Discovery*. We will cover more on this later, but basically this doctrine established that Great Britain had a title to the lands she "discovered," subject to the *tribe's legal and just right of occupancy*.

Senator Frelinghuysen's whole speech is archived in the book: *Documents of U.S. Indian Policy*, Compiled by Prucha, Francis Paul, University of Nebraska Press (3rd ed.) 2000, p. 49.

Recognizing Tribal Sovereignty

A tribe's sovereignty was *never* given to them by the federal government. No law created the Indians' power to govern themselves. The various treaties, agreements and statutes the US government made with, or regarding Indians, have simply *recognized* the fact that Indian tribes already had such power.

"The very term 'nation,' so generally applied to them (Indians), means 'a people distinct from others.' The constitution, by declaring treaties already made, as well as those to be made, to be the supreme law of the land, has adopted and sanctioned the previous treaties with the Indian nations, and consequently admits their rank among those powers who are capable of making treaties. The words 'treaty' and 'nation' are words of our own language, selected in our diplomatic and legislative proceedings, by ourselves, having each a definite and well understood meaning. We have applied them to Indians, as we have applied them to the other nations of the earth. They are applied to all in the same sense."

Worcester v. Georgia, 31 U.S. 515, 559 (1832)

Key Point

Tribal sovereignty dates back to time immemorial. It is an inherent sovereignty and was *not given* to the tribes by any government.

A Subject of Displeasure

The tribal nations, in making alliances with the various European countries, viewed it as a partnership of loyalty that they were bound to. By doing so, they continued to govern themselves and claimed the "protection of a powerful friend and neighbor." [6] There was no thought that being under the protection of a strong ally would strip them of their individual sovereignty. "Protection does not imply the destruction of the protected." [7]

Independence and self-governance was definitely recognized in the Indian nations by the Europeans. Such an observation caused one British commander to privately remark about one tribal group to the British Superintendent for Northern Indian Affairs, "As for the six nations having acknowledged themselves subjects of the English, that I conclude must be a very gross mistake, and am well satisfied – were they told so, they would not be pleased." [8]

Dear King . . .

One powerful Indian chief, Chief Brant of the Mohawks, wrote a letter to his political ally, the King of England (via the Governor of Quebec), reminding the king how his tribe and another tribe "took you by the hand like friends and brothers . . . treating you with kindness . . . We were a great people . . . and you but a handful, after which you increased by degrees and we continued your friends and allies." [9]

This same Indian chief, while visiting in England in 1785, refused to kiss the hand of King George III or bow his knee. He saw himself an equal as he was a ruler of his own people. However, he must have been quite the ladies' man as he made it known he would be very pleased to kiss the hand of the queen. [10]

It is also interesting to see that the Iroquois (an alliance of several Indian tribes, including the Mohawks) referred to themselves as "the older people" and the white man "our younger brother." [11]

Know, But Don't Know

Many of us became aware of Indian treaties during our elementary education. We learned that the US government made agreements with Indian tribes through these formal documents. Yet, even though we are familiar with what Indian treaties are, how many reading this book have actually read a US – Indian treaty?

We have included a few treaties in this book, in the Appendix section (Appendix B, pgs. 350-363) so you can see for yourself the solemn tone of the treaties and the things each side desired and agreed to through these negotiations.

What Did the Tribes Negotiate for?

You will find it very interesting as you read the treaties. It soon becomes evident that the individual tribal nations were negotiating terms for the protection of:

- Their lands
- Their people
- Their future livelihood and prosperity

Say it Simply!

"integrity" -- adhering to ethical, moral and honorable principles

They wanted to be self-sufficient independent communities. This is why they struggled so hard against the encroachment of their lands and for treaty *integrity* in respect to their boundaries. When stipulations were not honored by certain individuals, they wanted treaty violations enforced as defined in the contract.

Native Americans, through treaties and other agreements, sought to protect their land, resources and culture, along with all the various aspects of their way of life. Generally, what the different tribes wanted was to protect their independence and self-governance. One Indian chief explained, "We have plenty of buffalo, beaver and other wild animals – we have also an abundance of horse – we have everything we want – we have plenty of land, *if* you will keep your people off it." [12]

Dig Deeper

The book, *In the Courts of the Conqueror*, by Walter Echo-Hawk, discusses what he categorizes as the ten worst Indian law cases ever decided. This book provides a unique and thought provoking presentation, showing the historical struggles Indians faced (and continue to face today).

Chief Joseph

The story of Chief Joseph of the Nez Perce Indian tribe is one example, among many, of how Indian nations sought their inherent right of self-rule:

Quotes "Q"

> *"(Chief) Joseph replied that he 'asked nothing of the President. He was able to take care of himself. He did not desire Wallowa Valley as a reservation, for that would subject him and his band to the will of, and dependence on, another, and to laws not of their own making. He was disposed to live peacefully. He and his band had suffered wrong rather than do wrong.'"*
>
> *Helen Hunt Jackson, A Century of Dishonor, Dover Publications (reprint) 2003, p. 126*

What Did the US Negotiate for?

The US government generally wanted alliances of peace through the early agreements. Only one of these agreements became an official treaty between the US and Indians during the Revolutionary War: *The Treaty with the Delaware Tribe* (see Appendix B, pgs. 350-351). After the American Revolution, the main thing the United States wanted from the tribes was their land. When tribes agreed to *cede* land, they were promised very specific things by the United States. This was accomplished through the Indian commissioners, who were authorized to conduct treaty-making. In the treaties, the United States promised, expressly or by implication, to provide the following things which the tribes negotiated for in exchange for their lands:

- Food
- Various supplies
- Training and education
- Justice
- Protection from their enemies

Say it Simply!

"cede" -- surrender, give up

As Understood

Treaties were to be interpreted according to the way they were expressed to the Indian tribe at the time of the negotiations. Legally, when a question arises about a term in a contract, the question is asked, "What was the original understanding between the involved parties signing the contract?" [13]

"legalese" -- the specialized language of the trained legal professional

Great care should be given to this question, especially when the contract is written in the language of one negotiating party, while it is being translated (verbally, not in written form) into the language of the other negotiating party. It should be a question of the *clear* meaning versus the *technical* meaning of the word. The nation whose language is being used (superior negotiating) has the responsibility to avoid taking advantage, in any way, of the other party through any type of misrepresentation or legalese.

"The language used in treaties with the Indians should never be construed to their (the Indians') prejudice . . . How the words of the treaty were understood by this unlettered people, rather than their critical meaning, should form the rule of construction."

Federal Power Com'n v. Tuscarora Indian Nation, 362 US 99, footnote 2/1 (1960)

"When Indians are involved . . . the United States, as the party with the presumptively superior negotiating skills and superior knowledge of the language in which the treaty is recorded, has a responsibility to avoid taking advantage of the other side. '[T]he treaty must therefore be construed, not according to the technical meaning of its words to learned lawyers, but in the sense in which they would naturally be understood by the Indians.'"

Washington v. Fishing Vessel Assn., 443 US 658,675,676 (1979)

Treaties Were Cheaper Than Fighting

After the American Revolution, the war-torn United States did not want to continue incessant fighting. A report made to the Continental Congress on Oct. 15, 1783, by a committee on Indian Affairs sheds light on the contemporary concerns with Indian tribes just one month after the end of the American Revolutionary War: [14]

- Indians were "not in a temper to relinquish their territorial claims, without further struggles."
- An Indian war would be far too expensive (loss of lives and money).
- The British government in Canada would love to gain the friendship of the Indians and secure a monopoly on the fur trading (a crucial part of the economy of the time).

Say it Simply!

"equilibrium" -- sense of balance, stability

These concerns gave Indian nations some temporary balance to negotiations, but the *equilibrium* of the scale would soon change. When Indian tribes negotiated the terms of a treaty from a position of strength (generally prior to the early 1800's), the treaty had more favorable elements for the tribe. "After the War of 1812 . . . the relaxing of the European threat against the United States, and the weakening position of the tribes, led to more one-sided treaty negotiations in favor of the United States." [15]

You may want to read Robert J. Miller's article entitled, *History Commentary - Indian Treaties as Contracts*, Columbia Magazine. 20.1 (2006). The archived article can be found online at: *http://columbia.washingtonhistory.org/anthology/government/historyCommentary.aspx.* Robert J. Miller serves as Associate Professor of Law at Lewis & Clark School in Portland and Chief Justice of the Court of Appeals for the Confederate Tribes of Grand Ronde Community of Oregon.

Outrageous

Say it Simply!

"digression" -- departure from the standard

"flagitiously" -- shamefully wicked, flagrant, atrociously wicked

"rhetorical question" a question posed without expectation of an answer but merely as a way to make a point

"exploitation" -- taking advantage of, manipulation

Many accounts tell of the *digression* and abuse of the powers during negotiations with the tribes. A report dated July 18, 1788, from Secretary of War, Henry Knox, is very telling of the situation Indians found themselves in while trying to coexist on the American frontier. Knox told how certain "white inhabitants on the frontiers . . . had frequently committed the most unprovoked and direct outrages" against the Indians. He explained how the problem had gotten so huge that it amounted "to an actual, although informal, war" on the Indians. Knox clearly stated that the conduct of the non-Indians was unjustified. He appealed to the Continental Congress to honor the Indian treaties and enforce punishment against those who have "so *flagitiously* stained the American name." [16] From this context, "Congress became concerned with providing effective protection for the Indians 'from the violence of the lawless part of our frontier inhabitants. Without such protection … all the exertions of the Government to prevent destructive retaliations by the Indians'" would prove fruitless. [17]

The Indian tribes could not understand how the United States, who had defeated the mighty British, was unable to enforce its own treaties. When the Indian tribes looked to the United States to stop the encroachment of their lands, they were told the settlers were too numerous for them to control. This response prompted one Indian chief's *rhetorical question*, "Are Congress, who conquered the King of Great Britain, unable to remove those people?" [18]

The seemingly unrestrained *exploitation* and treaty violations made yet another Indian chief conclude: "I admit that there are good white men, but they bear no proportion to the bad; the bad must be the strongest, for they rule. They do what they please." [19]

No American Humble Pie

One of the US Supreme Court cases we quoted earlier gives some historical background about Indian treaties. It points out how things changed for the Indians in America, explaining that, initially, the various European nations competed for the Indians' alliances:

Quotes "Q"

> *"[T]heir (Indian tribes) alliance was sought by flattering professions, and purchased by rich presents. The English, the French, and the Spaniards, were equally competitors for their friendship and their aid."*
>
> *Worcester v. Georgia, 31 US 515,547 (1832)*

We see that when the nations were in need of the Indians' aid, there was humility and even "flattering" words along with gifts in the negotiations. Gift-giving was a way many nations honored the highest authority of another sovereign nation. However, as the balance of power eventually shifted to the new nation of the United States of America, and the US grew in power, there was a "higher tone" in the verbiage of the treaty negotiations. [20]

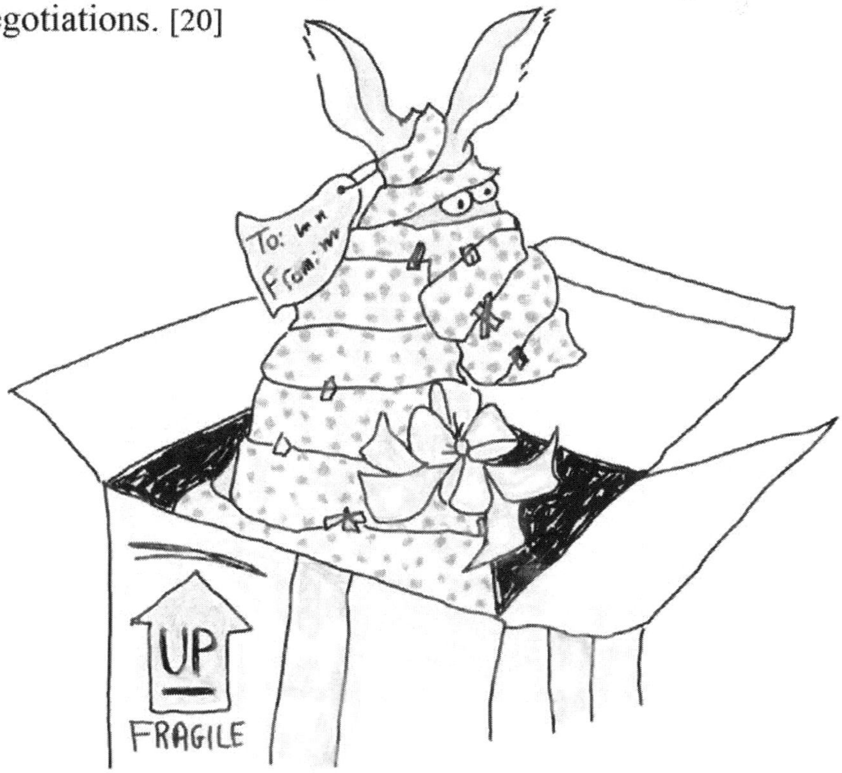

Gift-Giving

Gift-giving in diplomatic interactions between sovereign nations was historically a very customary form of showing honor and respect to the recipient. A gift can surpass many a language barrier, and its purpose is to please and impress. An appropriate gift will show the giving country's:

- Strength
- Wealth
- The state-of-the-art technological know-how

For example, it could be a weapon that is formed from a material not readily available to the country receiving the gift. Or, the gift may be something highly valued due to its uniqueness, beauty or craftsmanship.

The fact that the European nations were giving gifts to the Indian tribes shows that it was initiated by the Europeans. They were the ones approaching the indigenous peoples, wanting to wheel-and-deal, not the other way around. It is also important to note that in many cultures, rejecting a gift can be a sign of disrespect to the giver of the gift.

To illustrate how common gift-giving was, we can look at two examples that the first US president wrote about. In the first example, we read in one of President Washington's correspondences, that he had been trying to purchase a "Jack" (donkey) of "good size and breed" from Spain. Apparently the King of Spain became aware of this inquiry and, unbeknown to the president, ordered two donkeys to be exported and presented to the US president "as a mark of his esteem". Washington noted he had wanted to buy such a fine animal for some time, "but had little expectation of receiving two as a royal gift." [21]

The second example does not involve a gift to President Washington from a foreign nation, but rather from his fellow countrymen. Washington was the recipient of a very generous gift that was to commemorate his exemplary service and express to him the gratitude of his country. The actual gift was in the form of fifty shares in the Potomac Company and one hundred shares in the James River Company for him and his heirs.

Say it Simply!

"declination" -- to decline, a polite refusal

Washington responded to the offering of this substantial gift with "surprise and gratitude." He noted how "customary these gratuitous gifts are made in other countries," however, he graciously declined their offer. President Washington was very concerned his *declination* would not be misunderstood as a sign of disrespect. In this situation, the president believed if he took such a gift from his countrymen, it would appear as though he was using his position for personal gain. Therefore, he refused to accept the gift as it was "incompatible with (his) principles, and contrary to (his) declarations." [22]

One More Word About Gift-Giving

One last, but very important thing to mention about gift-giving …

When we see the US government giving supplies and items to an Indian tribe which they promised in a treaty or other type of agreement, this is *not* a gift. Rather, it is actually a barter; something given in exchange for another. In treaty agreements, the tribes gave up that of great value in exchange for other things of value. Items negotiated in a treaty are not gifts of benevolence, but are obligations of binding legal agreements.

The Indian tribes sought treaty integrity for the protection of their people, lands and future livelihood.

100 Years In The Making

One woman who was born in the 1830s, Helen Hunt Jackson, created quite a stir when, in 1881, she published documentation about the US government's violations of Indian treaties in her book entitled, *A Century of Dishonor*. She had been moved to action after hearing a first-hand account of one Indian tribe's struggles by Chief Standing Bear.

The story of Chief Standing Bear and his people's struggle is told in part in the *Standing Bear v. Crook* (1879) case. In this case the judge declares an Indian is a "person" within the meaning of the laws of the United States.

As Ms. Jackson dug deeper, she felt duty-bound to do something about the revealed abuse and corruption by governmental officials. She was an established poet and author, so it was natural for her to use her writing skills to expose the issues at hand.

Searching through official reports of the War Department and the Department of the Interior she gathered documentation. She also collected other witnessed accounts of the US government's dealings with Indian tribes. This she compiled into a book that passionately cried out for US governmental leaders to bring about change in policies toward Native Americans.

Guts & Blood

This gutsy woman carefully packaged up her hot-off-the-press book and mailed a copy to every member in Congress. With her book she included a personal note which read:

> *"Look upon your hands: they are stained with the blood of your relations."*

Although Ms. Jackson wrote, in the beginning of her book, she believed, "the American people, as a people, are not at heart unjust," not everyone appreciated her call for reform. For many, this information was a hard pill to swallow! One member of the US Board of Indian Commissioners in a document prepared for the US House of Representatives, had some powerful things to say:

"Like many another man who loves his country, I once felt inclined to believe that the friends of the Indian were guilty of exaggeration when they made such sweeping charges. Helen Hunt Jackson . . . A Century of Dishonor, I resented, as did many of you, perhaps, as an unjust reflection upon our country's good name. But, my friends, we cannot change the sad facts of history which that eloquent protest (her book) rehearses. Let us not try to ignore them.

Let us recognize this, frankly. We shall gain nothing by shutting our eyes to facts. Broken treaties are matters of record. Shuffling with the accounts of amounts due to Indians can be shown from the books. The shameful instructions issued to special commissioners and agents to deceive Indians as to the value of lands the Government wished to purchase, and to take by show of force for a few cents an acre vast tracts known to be worth from twenty to a hundred times the price paid – all this is in the letter books and the published reports. The money promised but not paid for education and for instruction in farming is still in our hands, a foul blot upon the nation's ledger. The broken pledges of the United States toward the Indians are so numerous that a monotony of shame wearies you at their recital. Let us like honest patriots recognize clearly our country's disgrace in this matter, and then resolve to do what we can to remove it by our fair treatment of these men in the future."

Merrill Edwards Gates, LL. D.,
President of Rutgers College, Member U.S. Board of Indian Commissioners,
Executive Documents of the House of Representatives
for the First Session of the Forty-Ninth Congress, 1885-'86

Example of the Delawares

One example Helen Hunt Jackson used in her book, to illustrate the United States' broken promises with the Indian tribes, was the case of the Delaware Tribe. In Chapter Two of her book, she articulates the progression of the US government's dealings with this tribal nation.

To summarize the story:

- ▶ The United States first treaty was with the Delawares. (see Appendix B, pgs. 350-351)
- ▶ The treaty even opened up the possibility of an Indian confederation of many tribes which would be headed by the Delawares, with a representative in Congress.
- ▶ The treaty was soon broken and compromised.
- ▶ The Indians sent messages to Congress about their displeasure.
- ▶ They begged Congress to stop surveyors and other people from coming into their lands.
- ▶ Years went by as their requests for the US to honor the treaties fell on deaf ears.

In final desperation, the Indian chiefs suggested to the United States commissioners that the money they were offering to pay them to move off their ancestral lands could be given instead to the white settlers to help them move elsewhere. [23] One Indian chief put it this way: "Money to us is of no value, and to most of us unknown; and as no consideration whatever can induce us to sell the lands on which we get sustenance for our women and children . . . Divide, therefore, this large sum of money which you have offered us among these people (white settlers)." [24]

When everything was said and done, the commissioners failed to get the Indians to agree to move off their land. Therefore, a notice was sent out saying the Indians refused to make peace. Soon after, outright war was waged against the *hostile* Indians. [25]

Endnotes - Chapter Two, Part 1:

[1] Letter from Philip John Schuyler, Major General of the Continental Army, to Commander-In-Chief George Washington, Aug. 27, 1775 about a meeting with a large body of Indians of the Six Nations. "Being apprehensive that we should request them to take up arms in our cause, they explicitly declared, that, as it was a family quarrel, they would not interfere, but remain neuter, and hoped we would not desire more of them."

[2] Resolution of the Continental Congress, June 30, 1775; The following month another Resolution of the Continental Congress, July 12, 1775 stated that securing and preserving the friendship of the Indian nations was of utmost concern to the united colonies and they wanted them to refrain from "taking any part in the present commotions."

[3] 1607 marked the first British colony (Jamestown); 1776 marked the Declaration of Independence beginning the American Revolution.

[4] Deloria, Vine and DeMallie, Raymond J., *Documents of American Indian Diplomacy: Treaties, Agreements, and Conventions*, University of Oklahoma Press 1999, Volume 1, p. 103; "It may come as a surprise to the layperson and perhaps to many attorneys that treaty making by Indian nations with foreign nations, primarily England and Spain and later Mexico, continued long after the American Revolution. Not until after the War of 1812 did Great Britain curtail its treaty making with tribes living on the American side of the Canadian border." See also: Bennett, Elmer, *Federal Indian Law*, The Lawbook Exchange 2008, p. 152 ..." During the first few decades of the Republic, the political relations of many of the Indian tribes were not confined to the United States. As late as 1835, the 'friendly relations' existing between some Indian tribes and the Republic of Mexico, the Republic of Texas, and among several Indian tribes were formally recognized by the United States."

[5] Speech by Theodore Frelinghuysen,United States Senator of New Jersey, April 9, 1830, from Register of Debates in Congress, 6:311-16, Compiled by Prucha, Francis Paul, *Documents of U.S. Indian Policy*, University of Nebraska Press (3rd ed.), 2000, p. 49

[6] *Worcester v. State of Georgia*, 31 U.S. 515, 552, 549 (1832)

[7] Id. at 552

[8] Preston, David, *The Texture of Contact: European and Indian Settler Communities on the Frontiers of Iroquoia 1667-1783*, University of Nebraska Press 2009, p. 11

[9] Letter of Chief Joseph Brant to Governor Frederick Haldimand of Quebec in 1783. Johnston, Charles M., *Valley of Six Nations*, University of Toronto Press 1964, p. 39; See also: William Penn, Perkins and Marvin 1829, *Essays on the Present Crisis in the Condition of the American Indians*, pp. 27-28. The writer of these essays, a strong and ethical leader of early America, explained the Cherokee would never have signed a treaty in 1791 if they did not believe the US would uphold the clear stipulations of the treaty. In the early years of America the Cherokee were sufficiently strong enough, "a formidable force," to drive off the white settlers. "The people of the United States wanted a peace. We invited the Cherokee to lay down their arms. We spoke kindly to them; called them our brothers, at the beginning of every sentence; treated them as equals; spoke largely of our future kindness and friendship . . ."

[10] Wood, Louis Aubrey, *The War Chief of the Six Nations: A Chronicle of Joseph Brant*, Glasgow Brook Publication 1914, pp. 110 - 111.

[11] Preston, David, *The Texture of Contact: European and Indian Settler Communities on the Frontiers of Iroquoia 1667-1783*, University of Nebraska Press 2009, p. 11

[12] Echo-Hawk, Walter, *In the Courts of the Conqueror*, Fulcrum Publishing 2010, p. 181, (quoting Pawnee Chief to President Monroe in 1822)

[13] "[T]he basic rule for interpreting Indian treaties is to determine what was the intent of the parties." *State v. Lemieux*, 110 Wis. 2d 158 (1983) citing *State v. Gurnoe*, 53 Wis. 2d 390, 403, 192 N.W. 2d 892 (1972) "... they must be construed not according to their technical meaning but in the sense in which they would naturally be understood by the Indians." *Jones v. Mecham*, 175 US1, 11 (1899)

[14] Journals of the Continental Congress, 25:681-83, 693, Compiled by Prucha, Francis Paul, *Documents of U.S. Indian Policy*, University of Nebraska Press (3rd ed.), 2000, pp. 3-4

[15] Robert J. Miller serves as Associate Professor of Law at Lewis & Clark School in Portland and Chief Justice of the Court of Appeals for the Confederate Tribes of Grand Ronde Community of Oregon, Miller, Robert J., *History Commentary - Indian Treaties as Contracts*, Columbia Magazine. 20.1 (Spring 2006): http://columbia.washingtonhistory.org/anthology/government/historyCommentary.aspx.

[16] Journals of the Continental Congress, 34:342-44, Compiled by Prucha, Francis Paul, *Documents of U.S. Indian Policy*, University of Nebraska Press (3rd ed.), 2000, pp. 11-12

[17] *Oliphant v. Suquamish Indian Tribe*, 435 US 191, 201 (1978) quoting from President George Washington's Seventh Annual Address. President Washington also spoke of the need to stop non-Indian abuses against the Indians in his Seventh Annual Address to Congress.

[18] Jackson, Helen Hunt, *A Century of Dishonor*, Dover Publications (reprint) 2003, p. 263 "The chiefs complained bitterly of the encroachments of white settlers upon lands which had been by old treaties distinctly reserved to the Cherokees. They demanded that some of these settlers should be removed; and when the commissioners said that the settlers were too numerous for the Government to remove, one of the chiefs asked, satirically, 'Are Congress, who conquered the King of Great Britain unable to remove those people?'"

[19] Jackson, Helen Hunt, *A Century of Dishonor*, Dover Publications (reprint) 2003, pg. 32. See also: Bennett, Elmer, *Federal Indian Law*, The Lawbook Exchange 2008, p. 144. "The legal standing of Indian Treaties did not assure necessarily, their actual enforcement. Some important treaties were negotiated but never ratified by the Senate, or ratified only after a long delay. Treaties were sometimes consummated, it is said, by methods amounting to bribery, or signed by representatives of only a small part of the signatory tribes. The Federal Government has failed at times to fulfill the terms of treaties, and is said to have been unable or unwilling in some instances to prevent states, or white people, from violating treaty rights of the Indians."

[20] *Worcester v. State of Georgia*, 31 U.S. 515, 551 (1832). The competition over land and power on the continent from other European powers lessened through the years as the US population greatly increased.

[21] Ford, Worthington Chauncey, *The Writings of George Washington*, Vol. X, 1782-1785, G.P. Putman's Sons 1890, p. 479, Letter to Marquis De LaFayette, July 25, 1785

[22] Id. at p. 454, Letter to Major-General Greene, May 20, 1785

[23] Jackson, Helen Hunt, *A Century of Dishonor*, Dover Publications (reprint) 2003, pg. 41

[24] Id. at 42

[25] See also: Cohen, Felix S., *Handbook of Federal Indian Law*, Washington, United States Government Printing Office 1945, p. 38 – An Office of Indian Affairs archive tells of the Osages who did not want to give up their land but "had no choice; they must either sign the treaty or be declared enemies of the United States."

Chapter Two ~ Part 2

This chapter will cover:

- *Sovereignty is not individual*
- *Federal trust responsibility*
- *Self-government and jurisdiction*

Chapter Two - Part 2

What Is Tribal Sovereignty?

Two "I"s in Indian

Say it Simply!

"ethnicity" -- relating to or characteristic of a human group having racial, cultural, religious, linguistic, and other common traits

One can't say, "I'm a sovereign Indian." But, what can be said is, "*WE* are a sovereign Indian tribe/nation."

Think about that for a minute . . . Do you see the difference?

This is an important concept in understanding PL 280 (and Indian law in general). Tribal sovereignty is the basis for a tribe's political relationship with the United States. A tribe's government-to-government relationship is *not* based on individual ethnicity. Rather, it is based on the historical dealings of the United States government with sovereign tribal governments. Tribal governments represent their communities who collectively share a form of government, culture, tradition and values.

Treaty-making, an expression and exercise of sovereignty, was never individual. A treaty could only be made through governmental authorities representing their tribe as a whole. When you think about it, this is also true regarding the United States' political relationship with other nations. For example, the US has a government-to-government relationship with many countries (e.g. Sweden, Japan, China, Germany, etc.). The US government does not ever deal with an individual from any of these countries regarding international policies based on a person's ethnicity. If the federal government has formal dealings with individuals from another country it is because that person is representing their country in an official capacity.

Key Point

Tribal sovereignty is never individual and is not based on an individual's ethnicity.

A Political Relationship

Say it Simply!

"**conciliate**" -- to win over, gain the favor of

From the very beginning of the history of the United States, the federal government has acknowledged the sovereignty of Indian tribes. As the states stood united in their common cause, with full intention of declaring their own sovereignty, they pursued government-to-government negotiations with the tribes by establishing three Indian departments. On June 30, 1775, the Congress of the Confederation created three departments of Indian Affairs: a northern department, a middle department, and a southern department. Commissioners were appointed to make treaties of peace with the Indians "in the name of and on the behalf of the United Colonies." Congress showed the importance they gave to these departments by choosing well-respected men, such as Benjamin Franklin and Patrick Henry, to serve as Indian Commissioners. "The early journals of congress exhibit the most anxious desire to conciliate the Indian nations. Three Indian departments were established; and commissioners appointed in each, 'to treat with the Indians in their respective departments, in the name and on the behalf of the United Colonies, in order to preserve peace and friendship with the said Indians, and to prevent their taking any part in the present commotions.'" [1]

From the United States' first treaty with an Indian nation until the official ending of such treaty-making in 1871, roughly 370 treaties were negotiated with the Indian tribes by the US government. However, not all tribes have treaties. Other sources of the United States political involvement with the tribes are through various historical events, court decisions, statutes, Acts of Congress, and Executive Orders. We will be discussing more on the various ways the US government interacted with tribal governments as we move along in this book.

Code for "Indian"

When federal laws are enacted, they are compiled into the United States Code (USC), the codification of all general and permanent federal laws in the United States. The USC is arranged by subject matter called "titles." The various laws are categorized and placed within the appropriate title.

There are more than fifty subject matters (or titles) that United States laws are categorized into. Did you know that one title is specifically for Indians? That's right – USC Title 25 is entitled "Indians."

If you choose to look further at USC Title 25, you will find all sorts of laws relating the US government and tribes, revealing the unique political status between the federal government and the Indians.

Dig Deeper

The US Code is found online on several sites. One that is set up well is provided by the Cornell University Law School at: *www.law.cornell.edu/uscode/text/25*

A Special Relationship

> *"The special relationship between Indians and the federal government is a result . . . of solemn obligations which have been entered into by the United States government.*
>
> *Down through the years through written treaties and through formal and informal agreements, our government has made specific commitments to the Indian people. For their part, the Indians have often surrendered claims to vast tracts of land and have accepted life on government reservations. In exchange, the government has agreed to provide community services such as health, education and public safety; services which would presumably allow Indian communities to enjoy a standard of living comparable to that of other Americans.*
>
> *This goal, of course, has never been achieved. But the special relationship between the Indian tribes and the Federal government which arises from these agreements continues to carry immense moral and legal force. To terminate this relationship would be no more appropriate than to terminate the citizenship rights of any other American."*
>
> *President Nixon, Special Message on Indian Affairs, July 8, 1970*

Say it Simply!

"gratuitous" -- something received without duty to return or reciprocate in value

"cession" -- the act of yielding or formally surrendering, relinquishing a right to property

This special message to Congress by the 37th US president recognized tribal sovereignty and the responsibility of government-to-government commitments. He pointed out that just as the US government cannot haphazardly stop rights of US citizens that are spelled out in the US Constitution, neither would it be appropriate to cut off at will, legal obligations made with the Indian tribes.

> *"The treaties made with this (Indian) Nation purport to secure to it certain rights. These are not gratuitous obligations assumed on the part of the United States. They are obligations founded upon a consideration paid by the Indians by cession of part of their territory."*
>
> *Cherokee Nation v. Georgia, 30 US 1, 58, 59 (1831)*

It's a Matter of Trust

Say it Simply!

"trust" -- confidence in; reliance on the integrity, character and ability of another

"responsibility" -- infers being accountable, acting with good judgment, fulfilling obligations of the duty or trust

"engagements" -- a fancy way of saying, "contracts" or "promises"

"benevolence" -- an act of kindness, a charitable gift

"The Congress finds and declares that –

(1) There is a government-to-government relationship between the United States and each Indian tribe;

(2) The United States has a *trust responsibility* to each tribal government that includes the protection of the sovereignty of Indian tribes."

(The Indian Tribal Justice Act, 25 USC 3601)

We can get a glimpse into the federal trust responsibility starting with the first president of the United States, President George Washington. In one of his letters he wrote to several key individuals of an Indian tribe. He spoke of being "truly brothers, promoting each other's prosperity by acts of mutual justice and friendship." [2] Washington was very happy to tell these Indians of a law that had just been enacted by Congress that was created to protect them from being taken advantage of by non-Indians. [3] In President Washington's own words, this showed "the *fatherly care* the United States intended to take of the Indians." He then wraps up his letter by telling them they may rely upon the kindness and protection of the US, finishing his correspondence with: "If any man brings you evil reports of the intentions of the United States, mark that man as your enemy, for he will mean to deceive you, and lead you into trouble. The United States will be true and faithful to their *engagements*." [4]

Wow! Let's look again at the first president's last phrase because it really captures what the trust responsibility is all about:

"The United States will be true and faithful to their engagements."

Certainly, the United States' trust responsibility involves national honor along with the moral and ethical reasons for having integrity as a nation. Yet, the trust goes far deeper than federal *benevolence*. It is based on legal transactions between political entities. The federal trust responsibility is not based on how the Nation feels or is disposed about Indian tribes at a certain time, but it's grounded in actual historical government-to-government events that took place between the United States and Indian tribes. The Federal government's trusteeship responsibility for Indian communities is not an "act of generosity toward a disadvantaged people" that can be discontinued or disregarded "whenever it sees fit." [5]

Throughout the years, the US courts have recognized the federal trust responsibility – as seen in the following quotes:

> *"[T]his Court (US Supreme Court) has recognized the distinctive obligation of trust incumbent upon the Government in its dealings . . . in carrying out its treaty obligations with the Indian tribes, the Government is something more than a mere contracting party. Under a humane and self-imposed policy which has found expression in many acts of Congress and numerous decisions of this Court, it has charged itself with moral obligations of the highest responsibility and trust."*
>
> *Seminole Nation v. US, 316 US 286 (1942)*

> *"[T]he government's dealings with the Indians . . . (is) the undisputed existence of a general trust relationship between the United States and the Indian people."*
>
> *US v. Mitchell, 463 US 206, 225 (1983)*

Quotes

"Q"

"The United States, as the Tribes' fiduciary, is held to strict standards and is required to exercise the greatest care in administering its trust obligations."

Assiniboine and Sioux Tribes v. Bd. Of Oil and Gas, 792 F.2d 782 (US Court of Appeals, Ninth Circuit 1986)

Say it Simply!

"fiduciary" -- legally authorized to hold something of value in trust for another; infers that another has placed trust and confidence in another to manage and protect their money or property; legal authority and duty to make wise decisions regarding financial matters on behalf of another

No Instructions

Over two hundred years of dealing with Indian tribes through treaties, agreements, statutes, and executive orders has left no doubt that the federal government has, in fact, made specific commitments to the Indian tribes. These have established a trust responsibility on the part of the United States towards the tribal communities. *How* that responsibility can best be fulfilled, however, is open to interpretation. [6]

Although the trust responsibility is recognized by all three branches of government: the executive branch, congress and the courts, it is not clearly defined or outlined in one particular way on *"how"* to exactly fulfill it. There is no box to open up, complete with instructions and a schematic showing how everything fits together regarding the administration of the federal trust responsibility.

Therefore, the *"how"* will always be subject to debate. When everything is said and done, the application, or fulfillment of the United States' trust responsibility will be seen through either a *broad* interpretation, or a more *narrow* interpretation.

Broad v. Narrow

A broad interpretation construes the federal trust responsibility as an obligation of general support and promotion of tribal interests (i.e. tribal self-governance and economic development). It looks beyond just the specific commitments outlined in treaties and statutes and sees its trustee role of federal resources as extending broadly in the same vein as the first US president expressed it.

A narrow interpretation views the federal trust responsibility being only obligated to those things explicitly detailed in the treaties and statutes. The federal government, through its federal agencies, may go above and beyond the call of duty – but they are not required to do so. "[A]n Indian tribe cannot force the government to take a specific action unless a treaty, statute or agreement imposes, expressly or by implication, that duty." [7]

The book, *The Rights of American Indians and Their Tribes* (New York University Press 2004) by Stephen L. Pevar, explains the broad interpretation versus the narrow interpretation of the federal trust responsibility in greater detail. Pevar has also written an article entitled: *The Federal-Tribal Trust Relationship: Its Origin, Nature, and Scope (2008).*

One-sided Obligations

"unilaterally" -- involving only one side; not mutual

One point about *narrow interpretation*, where the government will only obligate itself to specific commitments clearly spelled out in "a treaty, statute or agreement," is that it disregards the fact that Congress unilaterally stopped the government-to-government treaty-making process in 1871. [8] Essentially, through this policy change, the Indian tribes significantly lost their voice regarding their specific issues and interests while legislation was passed with very little, if any, input from those who were most affected by the statute. This point is significant and we will spend more time on this in Chapter Three, Part 4.

Presidential Legacy of Trust

As we saw earlier in this chapter, it was the very first president who wrote about "the fatherly care the United States intended to take of the Indians." Congress also wrote during this same time that the "utmost good faith shall always be observed towards Indians." [9] Both President Washington and Congress emphasized to the Indians their land and property, which the tribes were very concerned about, would never be taken from them without their consent.

If our first president, along with many in the early Congress, would have travelled in a time-machine and stepped off at various time periods, they may not have believed the state of affairs with the Indians. Certainly, many US policies did not show "care" or "good faith" as the indigenous people at times literally faced the possibility of extinction. While governmental actions were not the only reason for such bleak statistics, they played a huge contributing factor in the equation.

Through the years, US policy toward its indigenous peoples has worked both for their ill and for their good. Two examples of good US policy toward Native Americans are found in the Indian Reorganization Act of 1934 and the Indian Self-Determination and Education Assistance Act of 1975. Under the Roosevelt administration, a move was made to work at major policy changes regarding Indians. The Indian Reorganization Act (IRA) was a response to a report that revealed the absolutely deplorable conditions on the government-run Indian reservations. [10]

A great hurdle was championed during President Nixon's tenure. His *Special Message to Congress on Indian Affairs, July 8, 1970*, has been recognized as a pivotal point where US governmental policy began to turn toward a positive direction for tribal governments and their communities. The new policy encouraged Indian self-determination *without* cutting off legal obligations on the part of the US government. Nixon's predecessor, Lyndon B. Johnson, also spoke about erasing "old attitudes" to promote "partnership self-help" between the federal government and the Indian tribes. [11]

Every US president since Nixon, has officially acknowledged the United States' unique political relationship with the sovereign tribal nations and the government's corresponding trust relationship. To show the consistency given in acknowledging and encouraging US-Indian government-to-government relations, see the following chart (CH-2B) listing actions each president since Nixon has done to promote this political relationship:

PRESIDENTIAL FEDERAL TRUST ACTIONS (1975 - Present)

CH-2B

YEAR	PRESIDENT	FEDERAL TRUST ACTION
1975	**President Gerald Ford**	Signed into law the *"Indian Self-Determination and Education Assistance Act"* (Jan. 4, 1975)
1978 1979	**President Jimmy Carter**	Signed into law the *"American Indian Religious Freedom Act"* (Aug. 12, 1978) *"Indian Child Welfare Act"* signed into law (1978) The *"State of the Union Annual Message to the Congress, 'Native Americans'"* (Jan. 25, 1979)
1983	**President Ronald Reagan**	*"Statement on Indian Policy"* (Jan. 24, 1983)
1991	**President George H. W. Bush**	*"Government-to-Government Relationship of the United States with Indian Tribal Governments"* (June 14, 1991)
1994 1998 2000	**President Bill Clinton**	*"Government-to-Government Relations with Native American Tribal Governments"* (April 29, 1994) *"Executive Order 13084: Consultation & Cooperation with Indian Tribal Governments"* (May 14, 1998) *"Executive Order 13175: Consultation & Cooperation with Indian Tribal Governments"* (Nov. 6, 2000)
2004	**President George W. Bush**	*"Executive Order 13336: American Indian & Alaska Native Education"* (May 5, 2004) *"Memorandum for the Heads of Executive Departments and Agencies: Government-to-Government Relationship with Tribal Governments"* (Sept. 23, 2004)
2010	**President Barack Obama**	Signed into law the *"Tribal Law and Order Act"* (July 29, 2010)

Key Point

> **The United States' trust responsibility with Indian tribes is based on actual historical events and commitments.**

Sovereignty & Jurisdiction

Earlier we mentioned how the Indian Tribal Justice Act (25 USC, section 3601) recognizes the US government's trust responsibility. We will quote from it again to show the connection between tribal sovereignty and tribal jurisdiction:

"Congressional findings:

- Congress, through statutes, treaties, and the exercise of administrative authorities, has recognized the self-determination, self-reliance, and inherent sovereignty of Indian tribes.

- Indian tribes possess the inherent authority to establish their own form of government, including tribal justice systems.

- Tribal justice systems are an essential part of tribal governments and serve as important forums for ensuring public health and safety and the political integrity of tribal governments."

As we have discussed in length, sovereignty equals self-government. With this fact in mind, let's take it to the next step: Self-government equals authority over one's own area. This is called *"having jurisdiction."* There is little point in saying that a nation is a sovereign nation, if they do not have the authority to govern their territory. The article, *Concurrent Tribal and State Jurisdiction Under Public Law 280*, explains how "jurisdiction is an integral" part of sovereignty which involves "the power to make and enforce rules, resolve disputes and conflict . . . and maintain a stable and safe environment." [12] This applies to tribal sovereignty. Tribes have the inherent and fundamental ability, as sovereign nations, to govern their people and territories. [13]

Quotes

> *"Before the coming of the Europeans, the tribes were self-governing sovereign political communities. Like all sovereign bodies, they then had the inherent power to prescribe laws for their members and to punish infractions of those laws."*
>
> *U.S. v. Wheeler, 435 U.S. 313, 323 (1978)*

Fundamental Right

In 1939, during the era of Indian Reorganization, [14] a document was sent to the Commissioner of Indian Affairs. It was from a small Southern California tribe that detailed a "businesslike and workable program or plan for the handling of their tribal affairs." [15] Within this document are found words that express the *very essence* of tribal sovereignty: "It is contrary to all tribal history and tradition that Indians should be separated among themselves. What strength they have mustered in the past has come from unity of thought and effort. We wish to request a continuation to our Tribe of that *fundamental right of self-management* . . ."

Key Point

> **Tribal sovereignty gives a tribe authority to manage their territories and their people. This includes the ability to make and enforce laws within their jurisdiction.**

Jurisdictional Complexity

Things get quite interesting – and complex – as we begin to examine jurisdiction in Indian country, specifically, *criminal* jurisdiction. As we move into the next chapter, you will see for yourself how the evolution of criminal jurisdiction in Indian country has created a web of intersecting jurisdictions between tribal, federal and state governments.

> *"For more than two centuries, the Federal Government has recognized Indian tribes as domestic sovereigns that have unique government-to-government relationships with the United States. Congress has broad authority to legislate with respect to Indian tribes, however, and has exercised this authority to establish a* ***complex jurisdictional scheme*** *for the prosecution of crimes committed in Indian country."*
>
> *Office of the Attorney General, Department of Justice, Assumption of Concurrent Federal Criminal Jurisdiction in Certain Areas of Indian Country, Federal Register / Vol. 76, No. 234, Dec. 6, 2011.*

Public Law 280 & Jurisdiction

State criminal jurisdiction under the authority of PL 280 must be understood in light of how criminal jurisdiction evolved over the years within Indian country. In fact, this evolution is exactly what Chapter Three is dedicated to. We have broken it up into several bite-size pieces for you (parts 1 thru 5), so that you can easily follow the path of criminal jurisdiction in Indian country.

Where, then, do we begin telling the story of criminal jurisdiction in Indian country? We will start at the very beginning – When tribes had *complete internal and external sovereignty . . .*

"... the discovery of the continent of North America by the Europeans ... was held, occupied, and possessed in full sovereignty by various tribes or nations of Indians, who were sovereigns of their respective portions of the territory ... who neither acknowledged nor owed any allegiance or obedience to any European sovereign or state whatsoever."

Johnson & Graham's Lessee v. McIntosh, 21 US 543, 545 (1823)

"As we have often noted, Indian tribes occupy a unique status under our law. At one time they exercised virtually unlimited power over their own members as well as those who were permitted to join their communities."

National Farmers Union Ins. Cos v. Crow Tribe,
471 US 845, 851 (1985)

Endnotes - Chapter Two, Part 2:

[1] *Worcester v. State of Georgia*, 31 U.S. 515, 549 (1832)

[2] Sparks, Jared, *The Writing of George Washington; Being his Correspondence, Addresses, Messages and Other Papers, Official and Private, Selected and Published from the Original Manuscripts*, Ferdinand Andrews, Publisher 1839, Part IV, pp. 210-214

[3] The Trade and Intercourse Act of 1790 was enacted into law in response to abuse against Indians by non-Indians. The act required a valid license for non-Indians to trade with Indians and provided protection and justice against abuse. See also: Bennett, Elmer, *Federal Indian Law*, The Lawbook Exchange 2008, p. 151 "Frequently treaties prohibited the trespass or settlement of American citizens on Indian territory, unless licensed to trade. Such provisions were supplemented by statutes. Additional evidence of recognition of the national character of Indian tribes during the early periods appears in the provision requiring passports for citizens or inhabitants of the United States to enter the domain of an Indian tribe."

[4] Sparks, Jared, *The Writing of George Washington; Being his Correspondence, Addresses, Messages and Other Papers, Official and Private, Selected and Published from the Original Manuscripts*, Ferdinand Andrews, Publisher 1839, Part IV, pp. 210-214

[5] President Richard Nixon's *Special Message to the Congress on Indian Affairs, July 8, 1970*

[6] Id.

[7] *Shosone-Bannock Tribes v. Reno*, 56 F.3d 1476, 1482 (D.C. Cir. 1995)

[8] Congress passed the Indian Appropriations Act on March 3, 1871

[9] The Northwest Ordinance, July 13, 1787

[10] Institute for Government Research, Studies in Administration, *The Problem of Indian Administration (Meriam report)*, The Johns Hopkins Press 1928

[11] President Lyndon B. Johnson's Special Message to the Congress on the Problems of the American Indian: *The Forgotten American*, March 6, 1968

[12] "In the context of a government's sovereignty, jurisdiction is an integral, inherent aspect of authority, involving the power to make and enforce rules, resolve disputes and conflict within the community, and maintain a stable and safe environment through the application of criminal laws." Jimenez, Vanessa J. and Song, Soo C., *Concurrent Tribal and State Jurisdiction Under Public Law 280*, American University Law Review (1998)

[13] *Iowa Mut. Ins. Co. v. LaPlante*, 480 US 9 (1987), "We have repeatedly recognized the Federal Government's longstanding policy of encouraging tribal self-government. This policy reflects the fact that Indian tribes retain 'attributes of sovereignty over both their members and their territory,' to the extent that sovereignty has not been withdrawn by federal statute or treaty."

[14] The Indian Reorganization Act of June 18, 1934, was designed to restore self-government and self-management to the Indian tribal communities. It also prevented further depletion of reservation resources.

[15] Agua Caliente Band of Cahuilla Indians, document received in Washington, D.C. by Commissioner of Indian Affairs, John Collier, on May 4, 1939; Approved by the Secretary of Interior on June 2, 1939; Approved by the Band on June 22, 1939

Chapter Three ~ Part 1

This chapter will cover:

- *The complexity of jurisdiction in Indian country*
- *The Doctrine of Discovery*
- *"Indian country" beginnings*

Chapter Three - Part 1

Evolution of Jurisdiction in Indian Country

Quick & Easy Reference Chart

Wouldn't it be fantastic if everyone working in Indian country could simply grab a quick and easy reference chart that clearly spells out how jurisdiction works on Indian lands? Actually – there is such a chart – well, sort of. This quick reference chart is found in the US Attorneys' Manual, Title 9, Section 20.000 at 689, *Indian Country Jurisdictional Summary*. [1] Even though it is the best jurisdictional chart available, it certainly cannot be labeled "easy."

To illustrate the complexity of this quick reference jurisdictional chart, the following is a small selection:

> **Offender:** Indian
>
> **Victim:** Non-Indian
>
> **Jurisdiction:** If listed in 18 U.S.C. at 1153, there is federal jurisdiction, exclusive of the state, but probably not of the tribe. If the listed offense is not otherwise defined and punished by federal law applicable in the special maritime and territorial jurisdiction of the U.S., state law is assimilated. If not listed in 18 U.S.C. 1153, there is federal jurisdiction, exclusive of the state, but not of the tribe, under 18 U.S.C. at 1152. If the offense is not defined and punished by a statute applicable within the special maritime and territorial jurisdiction of the U.S., state law is assimilated under 18 U.S.C. at 13. [2]

Whew! That's enough to aggravate anyone … it begins to sound like doubletalk as it seems you are reading words without meaning! Believe it or not, though, what you just read will make a lot of sense once you understand the history of what has taken place in Indian country.

Key Point

The legal framework that exists in Indian country has been built piece-by-piece through the years and PL 280 is just one of those pieces which added to the complexity of jurisdiction.

All Tangled Up

With the multitude of individuals involved on Indian lands today, it can appear as though tribal, federal and state officials are playing a game of Twister ™! Indeed, one US court called the existing statutory framework for Indian country jurisdiction "tangled." [3] Yet another US court pointed out how jurisdiction on Indian lands is a "complex patchwork of federal, state, and tribal law." [4]

Having covered the foundational concept of tribal sovereignty, we can now move toward an understanding of jurisdiction in Indian country. In this chapter, we will follow the historical path in the development of Indian country jurisdiction, and in so doing we can begin to make sense of why the tangled and complicated jurisdictional web exists as it does today.

So, let's get started untangling this jumbled web, one knot at a time . . .

Beginning Point

The beginning point in discussing the evolution of criminal jurisdiction in Indian country starts with self-governing tribal communities. We have spent a good amount of time discussing this point as we looked at tribal sovereignty, so we will not linger here too long.

> *"America, separated from Europe by a wide ocean, was inhabited by a distinct people, divided into separate nations, independent of each other and of the rest of the world, having institutions of their own, and governing themselves by their own laws . . .The Indian nations had always been considered as distinct, independent political communities . . . from time immemorial . . ."*
>
> *Worcester v. State of Georgia, 31 US 515, 543, 559 (1832)*

Not One Big Tribe

All too often, non-Indians fail to recognize that Indian tribes are, as mentioned in the quote above, "divided into separate nations, independent of each other . . ." The tribes are individual sovereign entities, each with their own governments, and not just clumped into one big tribe. This has been true historically, and is *still* true today.

The fact that tribal self-governments have existed "from time immemorial" is the legal basis for tribal jurisdiction in Indian country. As we have previously discussed, this jurisdiction is inherent and not given to the tribes. Tribes have governed themselves from the very beginning.

Quotes

"It must always be remembered that the various Indian tribes were once independent and sovereign nations, and that their claim to sovereignty long predates that of our own Government."

McClanahan v. Arizona State Tax Commission, 411 U.S. 164, 172 (1973)

Key Point

Recognize that the Indian tribes are each individual sovereign entities, having governments with their own priorities.

Ahoy There!

A nation does not have to reside across an ocean for it to be a separate political entity from another nation. Having a sovereign government does not depend upon where that government sits on a map. The United States, Mexico and Canada are a good example of this as they all share one continent. Although these three nations exist on the same land mass, they are separate sovereigns, each with independent governments.

The fact that the tribes were eventually encompassed by the United States does not change the fact they are separate political entities from the US. As one Supreme Court Justice pointed out, "It is the political relation in which one government or country stands to another which constitutes it foreign to the other." [5]

Dig Deeper

> You may find it interesting to read Justice Thompson's discussion about the "national capacity" of Indian nations in *Cherokee Nation v. Georgia*, 30 US 1, 55-56 (1831)

Something New

Originally, the tribes were *autonomous* and completely self-governing. The eventual arrival of the European explorers brought something brand new – something that would, in time, greatly affect jurisdiction in Indian country. This new thing, or concept, was called the "Doctrine of Discovery." Without realizing it, you have actually been introduced to it through the small sample from the US Attorneys' jurisdictional charting which you read earlier (you know, the one that sounded like double-talk). Within that brief section, the word "*exclusive*" was used twice to describe federal jurisdiction. It was specifically stated this way because of historical events stemming all the way back to the Doctrine of Discovery.

Say it Simply!

"autonomous" -- self-governing; independent; subject to its own laws only; not subject to control from outside

"exclusive" -- having the only right to something; shutting out all others from a part or a share

Doctrine of Discovery

A doctrine is a set of rules or regulations people follow – an established policy. The Doctrine of Discovery was a set of rules established between the European nations who were equally competing for new land *"discoveries."* The European nations set up a type of regulation amongst themselves. The Indian nations did not acknowledge or adhere to these rules, but they found themselves indirectly affected by these international regulations.

Essentially, the Doctrine of Discovery was like a big game of Monopoly ™ – only the players played for keeps! US Supreme Court Chief Justice, John Marshall, shed much light on this doctrine. He himself said it was a difficult thing to understand how nations from another part of the globe could actually make such claims. [6]

Another justice agreed: "It may not be easy upon general reasoning to establish the doctrine, that priority of discovery confers any exclusive right to territory. . . In respect to countries, then inhabited by the natives, it is not easy to perceive how, in point of justice, or humanity. . . it (the Doctrine of Discovery) can be successfully vindicated." [7]

But, alas, this was simply the way it was, as Chief Justice Marshall explained [8]:

- ► The powers of Europe *discovered* different parts of the American continent at nearly the same time.
- ► The continent was too immense for one European power to singularly grasp it for themselves.
- ► Also, none of the European powers would have allowed one nation to have the monopoly.
- ► In an attempt to avoid bloody conflicts they established a rule they each agreed to follow.

The rule was: Whichever European nation got to the land first and claimed it, won the *"right of title."* The right of title meant no other European nation could intrude on claimed land, either for settlement or to purchase land from the natives. The European nation having the right of title was the only nation who could settle on the claimed area and purchase land from the indigenous residents (original possessors). A purchase of land could *only* take place if the native inhabitants wanted to sell their land.

Cut Up the Pie

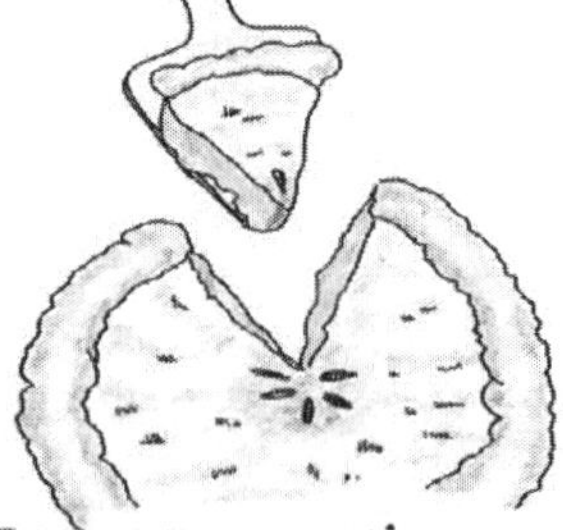

Of course, all of the European nations agreed to this doctrine, because they all got a piece of the pie. They set up "feeble settlements," [9] but did not interfere with the Indian's tribal territories or self-government. The only thing regulated was between the European nations – they *themselves* were not allowed to break the rules and do business with the Indians that were in an area claimed by the other.

Quotes "Q"

> *"Certain it is, that our history furnishes no example, from the first settlement of our country, of any attempt on the part of the crown to interfere with the internal affairs of the Indians, farther than to keep out the agents of foreign powers, who, as traders or otherwise, might seduce them into foreign alliances. The king purchased their (lands) when they were willing to sell, at a price they were willing to take; but never intruded into the interior of their affairs, or interfered with their self-government, so far as respected themselves only."*
>
> *Worcester v. State of Georgia, 31 US 547 (1832)*

Monopoly Fight

The Doctrine of Discovery was intended to keep everything civilized among the European powers, but it was not long before the players were fighting and contesting each others' claims. As simplistic as it sounds, it went something like this:

European Nation #1: "You can't go there – that's exclusively mine!"

European Nation #2: "No! It's mine! . . . make me stay out!"

European Nation #1: "Ok, I will."

That's pretty much how it was for years. Bloody conflicts after bloody conflicts continued as the imperial wars played out on the American continent. Native Americans were caught up in the mess, fighting for their own territories and also with those whom they had aligned themselves. "The English, the French, and the Spaniards, were equally competitors for their (Indian's) friendship and their aid." Tribal nations chose what they deemed prudent – "so long as their actual independence was untouched, and their right to self-government was acknowledged." [10]

The Doctrine of Discovery did not interfere with tribal governments or the Indian's right to occupy their territories. It did establish the regulation between European sovereigns as to who could claim exclusive rights to deal with the Indians in discovered areas.

Aliens from Outer Space

Many have lauded the creator of the sci-fi hit *Star Trek*, Gene Roddenberry, as a great visionary and a man before his time. NASA even named the first space shuttle after his literary spaceship, the USS Enterprise, and the Smithsonian National Air and Space Museum proudly displays an impressive 11 foot, 200 pound scale model of the spaceship.

Another writer and man before his time was known more for his stories about a bearded old man with the curious name of "Rip Van Winkle" and a haunting headless horseman riding about, than his tale about aliens from outer space. This author, often referred to as the "Father of American Literature," is none other than Washington Irving. He was born the same year the American Revolutionary War ended, therefore, he had the opportunity to observe everyday life in early America.

Irving was a clever and witty writer who used his skills of *satire* to get his readers to think about serious matters. He had the unique ability to address sensitive and controversial issues through tongue-and-cheek humor. He was especially known for exposing *paradoxes*. One such paradox he challenged, with creative flair, was the European Powers' claim of exclusive title to Indian land through the Doctrine of Discovery. With able pen in hand, he created a world filled with hippogriff spaceships and pea-green aliens who carry their one-eyed heads under their arms.

This intriguing story is sandwiched within chapter 5 of Irving's book, *A History of New York*, which he wrote under the *pseudonym* of "Diedrich Knickerbocker." Writing in star-trekish fashion, Irving asks his readers to suppose aliens from outer space have invaded the little planet called "Earth." He describes these aliens as vastly superior in knowledge and power. They are also superior in their mode of transport, as they move about in spaceships called "hippogriffs." Earthlings are at their mercy as they have no defense against the alien's concentrated sunbeams and enormous moonstones. These foreign conquerors easily overpower and subdue earth's inhabitants.

As the aliens take inventory of their victory, they disappointedly find this planet is nothing but a howling wilderness filled with poor savages and wild beasts. Yet, they claim it in the name of the honorable and excellent Man in the Moon.

Say it Simply!

"satire" --
the use of sarcasm to expose human folly or vice

"paradoxes" --
inconsistencies, contradictions, absurdities

"pseudonym" --
fictitious name, pen name, or stage name

"potentate" --
a person who possesses great power, such as a sovereign, monarch, or ruler

"allegory" --
a symbolic narrative; figurative treatment of one subject under the guise of another subject

In order to at least have something to show for their efforts, they snatch up the American president, the King of England, the Emperor of Hayti, the mighty Bonaparte, and the great King of Bantam. These prizes they parade before their courts "as were the Indian chiefs led about as spectacles in the courts of Europe."

As the alien victors stand before their mighty potentate, the Man in the Moon, they bow low before him, presenting him with the gift of "the five uncouth monsters" they captured from the "obscure little dirty planet." They assure the Man in the Moon that these five *really* are considered important chiefs among their fellow savages. The aliens find it hard not to gawk at these captive creatures who are destitute of the common attributes of humanity:

- They carry their heads upon their shoulders instead of under their arms!
- They have two eyes instead of one!
- They are destitute of tails!
- They have a variety of unseemly complexions, particularly of horrible whiteness instead of pea-green!

Then, the Man in the Moon declares the inhabitants of earth incapable of possessing any property on the planet they infest. Right of title goes to the aliens who discovered the planet Earth. With right of title, the aliens invade earth's lands; seizing the most fertile territories.

And then, Earthlings do something unbelievable – they actually complain about their treatment! The superior aliens scold the Earthlings:

> *"Miserable barbarians! Ungrateful wretches! Have we not come thousands of miles to improve your worthless planet?"*

Not only are the Earthlings ungrateful, they go so far as to daringly defend their property. Therefore, completely exhausted of patience for the Earth-savages, the conquerors pour out their wrath, hunting the rebellious Earth dwellers in their highly superior hippogriffs and demolish the Earth cities with crushing moonstones.

Diedrich Knickerbocker, *A History of New York (Volume 1)*,The Knickerbocker Press 1894. Book I, Chapter V, pp. 100-109

Certainly, Washington Irving presented a powerful allegory. Perhaps this story should also become part of the reading in American literature classes along with his other literary works.

If you appreciated Irving's allegory, you may want to read the entire chapter, Chapter V, pages 84 – 109, of the Washington Irving's book, *A History of New York*. You can view his book online at the following link:
http://books.google.com/books?id=RQQhAAAAMAAJ&printsec=frontcover&source=gbs_ge_summary_r&cad=0#v=onepage&q&f=false

Indian Country

The term "Indian country" is a legal term which is very important in determining jurisdiction for tribal, federal and state governments. This definition is codified today at 18 USC § 1151. It is written in such a way as to clearly include all reservation lands whether created by treaty, an act of Congress, or by an executive order.

18 USC § 1151 reads:

(a) all land within the limits of any Indian reservation under the jurisdiction of the United States Government, notwithstanding the issuance of any patent, and, including rights-of-way running through the reservation,

(b) all dependent Indian communities within the borders of the United States whether within the original or subsequently acquired territory thereof, and whether within or without the limits of a state, and

(c) all Indian allotments, the Indian titles to which have not been extinguished, including rights-of-way running through the same.

The first time land was specifically set aside by a European nation for Indian use was back in 1763. When the British won the French and Indian War, the French ceded lands. These lands, which had been under French control, had restricted the British colonists from western expansion. Many of the war-torn British colonists believed they had won the right, through their blood, sweat and tears to begin new settlements on these newly ceded lands. However, the British government had different ideas, and the king and his council made it clear to the colonists through the Proclamation of 1763.

This proclamation clearly stated that large sections of Britain's newly acquired lands were *not* to be accessible to the colonists. The British colonists, whom the king referred to as "loving subjects under parental care of the crown," were to stay within the boundaries established through the proclamation. Anyone who settled outside of the areas prescribed by the king would be considered rebellious to the crown.

So, what was to become of all this coveted land that had just opened up? The colonists were shocked when the King declared it as separate and protected area for the Indians. That did not sit well with many of the colonists! They had fought for these rich lands. How could they be deprived of the land and be hemmed into only selective areas? And above all, how could the King favor the Indians over them? To the British government, this arrangement made a lot of sense. They wanted to have good control and regulation over their colonies and having them in specified areas served this purpose. Also, from an economic point of view, it was beneficial "to leave the Indians unmolested so as to maximize the benefits of the fur trade." [11]

The King's proclamation also established:

- Regulation for purchasing land and trading with Indians, required non-Indians to obtain an official license from a representative of the British government.

- There was a provision for apprehending a criminal who fled into Indian territory (extradition).

The proclamation's restrictions were quickly violated as colonists knew the British parliament lacked the manpower and resources to effectively enforce these laws. As westward movement increased, so also an increase occurred in the connection between the European settlers with the Indian tribes.

Key Point

> **Indian country was labeled as territory specifically designated for Indian tribes. From a legal point of view "Indian country" is a vital element in establishing whether tribal, federal and/or state jurisdiction exists.**

Endnotes - Chapter Three, Part 1:

[1] United States Attorneys' Manual, Title 9 – Criminal, Section 20.000 – Maritime, Territorial and Indian Jurisdiction, at 689 – Jurisdictional Summary. This charting is found on the U.S. Department of Justice's website at: *http://www.justice.gov/usao/eousa/foia_reading_room/usam/title9/crm00689.htm* See also Chapter Six, part 2 of this book on pp. 299-309 where we have reviewed the criminal jurisdiction in Indian country summary charts.

[2] This selection is taken from the chart "Where Jurisdiction has not been Conferred." PL 280 will fall under the chart "Where Jurisdiction has been Conferred by Public Law 280, 18 USC at 1162." For this same scenario of Indian offender and Non-Indian victim, the jurisdiction will read: "'Mandatory' state has jurisdiction exclusive of federal government but not necessarily of the tribe. 'Option' state has concurrent jurisdiction with the federal courts." In order to understand PL 280, it is important to first understand how jurisdiction works outside of PL 280 areas since this is the jurisdiction that was transferred.

[3] *United States v. Markiewicz*, 978 F.2d 786, 50 (2nd Cir.1992) ". . . we must first explore the admittedly tangled statutory framework that governs the application of federal criminal laws to offenses committed on Indian territory."

[4] *Duro v. Reina*, 495 US 676, footnote 1 (1990) "Jurisdiction in 'Indian country,' . . . is governed by a complex patchwork of federal, state, and tribal law."

[5] Justice Thompson in Cherokee Nation v. Georgia, 30 US 1, 55 (1831). In the case of *Cherokee Nation v. Georgia* the court did not decide on the case due to a supposed technicality in jurisdiction to hear such a case. The Supreme Court recognized Indian tribes as separate and distinct political entities but were hung up on labeling them as "foreign" nations and thus denying them a forum for their case to be decided. Justice Thompson explained in his opinion (see 30 US 55-56) how the Cherokee Nation was a separate sovereign in spite of the fact their territory was within the US, specifically, within the charted limits of the state of Georgia: "Suppose the Cherokee territory had been occupied by Spaniards or any other civilized people, instead of Indians, and they had from time to time ceded to the United States portion of their lands precisely in the same manner as the Indians have done, and in like manner retained and occupied the part now held by the Cherokees, and having a regular government established there; would it not only be considered a separate and distinct nation or state, but a foreign nation, with reference to the State of Georgia or the United States?"

[6] Worcester v. State of Georgia, 31 U.S. 515, 543 (1832)

[7] Story LL.D., Joseph, *Commentaries on the Constitution of the U.S. (1833)*, Lonang Institute 2003, 2005 electronic edition, Book I, p. 17, § 2

[8] *Worcester v. State of Georgia*, 31 U.S. 515, 544 (1832)

[9]Id.

[10] Id.

[11] Dolin, Eric Jay, *Fur, Fortune, and Empire*, W.W. Norton & Company (2010), p. 121

Chapter Three - Part 2

This chapter will cover:

- *The American Revolution*
- *The Pennsylvania Mutiny of 1783*
- *Indians and the US Constitution*

Chapter Three - Part 2

Evolution of Jurisdiction in Indian Country

The American Revolution

As mentioned in the previous section, many of the British colonists viewed America's western lands very differently than the British government viewed it. The fact that the king had declared a specific area as *Indian territory* did not stop many non-Indians from settling on these lands. Great tensions existed between the colonists of America with their long-distance government. The conflict about western lands was only a small part of the tension.

Within thirteen years of the king's Proclamation of 1763, the American colonists declared their independence. During the American Revolutionary War, both the British government and the American Continental Congress made it a priority to preserve peace and friendship with the Indians. [1] They reasoned that, even if the Indians chose not to assist them in their cause, they at least wanted to ensure the Indians would remain *neutral*. However, as things progressed, neutrality became a virtual impossibility for some of the tribes and history shows that Indians fought on both sides of the revolution.

Say it Simply!

"neutral" -- impartial, not taking sides

In 1772, another proclamation was issued addressing the problem of persons violating the king's order by establishing illegal settlements on Indian lands. The new proclamation demanded "many persons contrary to the positive orders of the king" to remove themselves off these lands "without delay." See *Worcester v. Georgia*, 31 US 515, 548 (1832)

When the American colonists won their independence, Great Britain acknowledged the new sovereign government of the United States through the Treaty of Paris and ceded their lands in North America (except for their territories in Canada). Therefore, America gained right of title to the land – making the US government the sovereign who could now *exclusively* deal with the Indians (within US territory). This exclusive title meant that no other government other than the United States held the right to buy land from the Indians who were willing to sell their lands. And so, the concept of the Doctrine of Discovery was passed to the United States through the international law of that time period, laying the foundation for government-to-government relationships and *exclusive jurisdiction* with the various Indian tribes.

Quotes "Q"

"By the treaty, which concluded the war of our revolution, Great Britain relinquished all claim, not only to the government, but to the 'propriety and territorial right of the United States,' whose boundaries were fixed in the second article. By this treaty, the powers of government, and the right to soil, which had previously been in Great Britain, passed definitively to these States. We had before possession of them, by declaring independence; but neither the declaration of independence, nor the treaty confirming it, could give us more than that which we before possessed, or to which Great Britain was before entitled. It has never been doubted, that either the United States, or the several States, had a clear title to all the lands within the boundary lines described in the treaty, subject only to the Indian right of occupancy, and that the exclusive power to extinguish that right was vested in that government, which might constitutionally exercise it."

Johnson v. McIntosh, 21 US 543, 585 (1823)

Key Point

> **The concept of *exclusive* governmental authority to deal with Indian tribes in America was passed from Great Britain to the new United States.**

Preserving Peace & Friendship

The intent of the United States government for its western territories was expansion through new settlements. This is clearly seen through the Continental Congress' enactment of the *Land Ordinance*. This ordinance provided a system for surveying and selling land. Soon after, Congress also passed the *Northwest Ordinance* in 1787, creating a method for admitting new states into the union of the USA. The surveying and selling of land along with the establishment of towns, and eventually states, into the Union was to be in the most orderly fashion. There were drawings and descriptions of how the lands would be divided according to neat and tidy rectangular township grids. In *theory,* these new lands were to be carefully sold and parceled out without disturbing the Indians.

Quotes

> *"The utmost good faith shall always be observed towards the Indians, their lands and property shall never be taken from them without their consent; and in their property, rights and liberty, they never shall be invaded or disturbed, unless in just and lawful wars authorized by Congress; but laws founded in justice and humanity shall from time to time be made, for preventing wrongs being done to them, and for preserving peace and friendship with them . . ."*
>
> *Northwest Ordinance, July 13, 1787*

Golden Land

A major purpose of the *Northwest Ordinance* was to raise money for the new federal government of the United States. Prior to the US Constitution, which was not *ratified* until 1788, the laws of the land (The Articles of Confederation) did not allow for taxes to raise the federal revenue. The recent war had created a national debt that the US government wanted to be clear of. Also, federal revenue would strengthen the independence of the new nation. Therefore, this new land was seen as a gold mine.

Say it Simply!

"ratified" -- confirmed, approved

"augmented" -- increased, enlarged, improved

An early report to the Continental Congress from the Committee on Indian Affairs stated that the increase in the US population, along with continual immigration, made it extremely important "to make speedy provision for extending the settlement of the territories of the United States; and because the public creditors have been led to believe and have a right to expect that those (western) territories will be speedily improved into a fund towards the security and payment of the national debt." [2]

Congress passed a resolution showing their strong and determined intent to sell the "intermediate lands," even using US troops to make it happen:

Quotes

> *". . . It (is) highly necessary that the troops in the service of the United States be immediately augmented, not only for the protection and support of the frontiers of the states bordering on the western territory and the valuable settlements on and near the margin of the Mississippi, but to establish the possession and facilitate the surveying and selling of those intermediate lands, which have been* ***so much relied on for the reduction of the debts*** *of the United States."*
>
> *Report to Congress, October 20, 1786 from the War Office containing intelligence of the hostile intentions of the Indians in the Western Country.*

Between the years 1787 through 1788, two contemporary newspapers of the day published a series of articles called *The Federalist*. One of the 1788 articles made this statement, "It is now no longer a point of speculation and hope, that the western territory is a mine of vast wealth to the United States." [3] Also, while acknowledging the government's view of western lands, one US Supreme Court judge stated matter-of-factly that the general policy of the United States has "always looked to . . Indian lands as a certain future acquisition." [4]

A Flood

The US government may have designed and outlined an orderly and systematic way of settling the new frontiers, but *reality* was quite a different story. Independent-minded settlers, in search of land, gold or other profit, along with their desire for freedom, flooded into this new territory. "Irrespective of good intentions, settlers flooded into Indian lands." [5]

- By the year 1790, Kentucky had a white population of 74,000.
- Tennessee and other frontier regions had a white population of 36,000.
- Around 300,000 people had passed through the *Cumberland Gap* by the year 1800.

"Between 1784 and 1789, government officials pressured Indian leaders into land cession treaties, forcing Native Americans into small reservations. The means of acquiring land were decidedly dubious, and most Indians denounced the agreements." [6]

Dig Deeper

International scholar, Dr. Ian Barnes' wrote a book, *The Historical Atlas of Native Americans*, Chartwell Books, Inc. (2010), which chronicles the history of North America's indigenous peoples. This book contains over 150 maps plus illustrations.

Sable Colors

In 1794, the first Secretary of War, Henry Knox, wrote a reflective letter to his friend, President George Washington, two days prior to officially retiring from his prestigious assignment. After years of in-the-field experience, this seasoned administrator made several observations. One of his responsibilities as Secretary of War was to oversee Indian affairs, therefore, he was directly involved in what was happening on the frontier. Knox made the remark that non-Indians have generally "grown to hate" the Indians and many "were eager to pounce upon them and their lands." Knox also told how, especially the younger Indians, sought revenge and often hurt innocent non-Indians. [7]

In continuing his reflections, he lamented the "modes of population" by the United States. He believed the settlement of the frontier lands had been "more destructive to the Indian natives than the conduct of the conquerors of Mexico and Peru." Keep in mind, this was the Secretary of War speaking – a man well acquainted with war and human conflict. He certainly was not one to over-exaggerate as the success of his life work, as both a General of the United States Army and then the Secretary of War, depended on coolness and clarity of thought. In wrapping up his reflections he wrote that he believed ". . . a future historian may mark the causes of this destruction of the human race in *sable* colors." [8]

Say it Simply!

"sable" --
very dark, black

Paint a True Picture

One man who had extensive experience interacting with Indian tribes on the frontier was a man named George Catlin. He is known most for his many pictures that now hang in the Smithsonian American Art Museum. All his pictures are connected, one way or another, to life on the frontier. As an artist, his goal was to preserve the life and culture of the Indians on painted canvas before these things would inevitably be destroyed by western expansion.

In his many travels he saw first-hand the effects "civilization" had on the Indians. The following is an excerpt from one of his books written in the mid 1800's:

> "The combined causes of border *emigration* moving on faster than the government can purchase the lands of the Indians – the unemployed hunters, and trappers, and whisky sellers, whose business is declining, and a headlong stampedo of half-crazy adventurers flying to the gold fields of the Rocky Mountains, form a *phalanx* of the most desperate men, who take possession of the Indians' country – claim it, and hold it – pronounce the Indians all 'brutes, who can hold no title' – build towns of log huts, and call them 'cities' – publish newspapers, and announce 'Indian murders! Indian murders of white men!' (whether perpetrated or not), call upon the government for regiments and armies of soldiers to protect them, and these soldiers in their country openly advocate 'extermination' – offer rewards of twenty dollars for every Indian's scalp that can be taken (with the civil condition annexed), 'provided that both ears are attached to them!' Here, my young readers, we are upon facts, and I am ashamed for the character and honor of my country to acknowledge them as such; and I now put the question which I promised to ask, 'Who is the savage, and which the brute?' My heart bleeds at this, but I cannot prevent it."

Catlin, George, Last rambles amongst the Indians of the Rocky Mountains and the Andes, Sampson Low, son, and Marston 1868 (digitized from public domain by BiblioLife, LLC) p. 348

Say it Simply!

"emigration" -- the act of leaving one country or region to settle in another

"phalanx" -- a group of people united for a common purpose

Confirmed by the Court

This sad portrayal of life in some areas of the western frontier was also referred to by the US Supreme Court in the case of *US v. Kagama* in 1886. The court in this case recognized the "local ill feeling" of the non-Indians towards the Indians. It was explained that the federal government had a duty to protect the Indians due to the fact that "the people of the States" where the Indians live "are often their deadliest enemies." [9]

Dig Deeper

In his book, *Flyboys*, author James Bradley includes a section in the first part of Chapter Six discussing how Japan saw the US as hypocritical in its condemnation of their killing innocent people, (many whom were women and children), when they bombed the capital of China, Nanking, on September 21, 1937. "To the Japanese, the depth of the western Christians' hypocrisy was breathtaking. Japan was taming her own Wild West as the Americans had theirs." Bradley, James, *Flyboys*, Little, Brown and Company 2003, p. 66.

Key Point

Federal protection of Indians against non-Indian abuse became necessary and therefore a responsibility that fell under federal exclusive jurisdiction.

Just & Lawful Wars

Say it Simply!

"charters" -- contract, agreement, deed

"defensive" -- protecting, defending, guarding against or resisting attack

"offensive" -- attitude or position of aggression, starting the attack

"squatted" -- settled on and occupied without a legal right, and without payment

The Northwest Ordinance, which you read just a few pages ago, mentioned "just and lawful wars authorized by Congress." Historically, the verbiage of "just wars" was also seen in many of the *charters* of the British colonies. These charters recognized the right of the colonies to defend themselves against an enemy. But clearly, it was to be against an enemy who gave them just reason to fight *defensively*, rather than *offensively*. "The power of war" was only given for "defense, not for conquest."[10]

Congress intentionally put in the *Northwest Ordinance* the fact that they can always authorize a "just and lawful war" against hostile Indian nations. They made it very clear they could, *and would*, defend themselves against any hostilities. Every nation must provide for its own defense, right?

Yes, of course, but Dr. Ian Barnes, in his book, *The Historical Atlas of Native Americans*, explains how many Indian wars were not truly defensive in nature. [11] He explains how settlers illegally *squatted* on Indian land, provoking the Indians to drive off the settlers. In response, the US military forces would then come to protect the settlers. Eventually, as great damages and losses were sustained by the tribe, it was pretty easy to coerce them to sign treaties that gave up much of their lands. It is noted by one author that the Indian tribes "never fought a battle . . . excepting on their own ground." [12]

In spite of the corrupt dealings with Indian tribes, the US Government never claimed Indian lands by right of conquest. Even though methods of obtaining Indian lands were, to say the least, questionable, they were technically all gained legally. Over 100 years after the birth of America, the Commissioner of Indian Affairs in his annual report for 1890 stated: "[T]he United States has pursued a uniform course in extinguishing the Indian title only with the consent of those tribes . . . Except in the case of the Sioux Indians in Minnesota after the outbreak of 1862, the Government has never extinguished an Indian title as by right of conquest; and in this case the Indians were provided with another reservation, and subsequently were paid the net proceeds arising from the sale of the land vacated."

Kappler, Charles J., *Indian Affairs: Laws and Treaties*, Washinton: Government Printing Office 1929, p.1154

Say it Simply!

"impetus" -- motion forward, drive, thrust, energy

The Pennsylvania Mutiny

The same year the American Revolutionary War officially ended, an event occurred that gave the *impetus* for something unique on American soil. The event became known as *"The Pennsylvania Mutiny of 1783,"* and the unique thing which was created was called a "federal enclave."

You may be thinking that we are getting way off track from PL 280. However, understanding what a federal enclave is will help you tremendously as we follow the path of jurisdiction in Indian country. Instead of giving you the dull and tedious task of memorizing the definition of a *"federal enclave,"* we are going to give you the background story -- which is actually quite interesting *and even* a little suspenseful . . .

Here's the skinny on what happened at The Pennsylvania Mutiny of 1783:

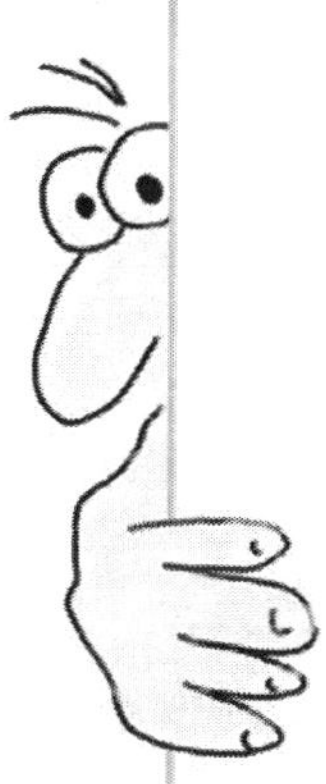

- The Congress of the Confederation were working on important congressional matters at Independence Hall, which was located in Philadelphia, Pennsylvania.

- They received a message that a large group of soldiers were upset about not getting paid for their service during the American Revolutionary War and were demanding payment.

- Congress did not listen to their demands and kept working on their important congressional matters.

- Three days later, Independence Hall was taken over by hundreds of armed soldiers. They blocked the door and would not allow the Congress to leave until Alexander Hamilton negotiated with them.

- Congress asked the Pennsylvania Council to have their state protect them (federal government) from such treatment. Congress, at that time, was at the mercy of the state to enforce laws and maintain peace.

- ▶ Unfortunately for the Congress, the state of Pennsylvania did not activate their state militia to protect them.

- ▶ Congress went off to a safer location (Princeton, New Jersey) to do their important congressional work.

After this hair-raising incident Congress decided they needed to create a special area – a *seat of government* -- that was totally separate from state control. That way, if anything threatened the federal government again, they could provide their own protection. [13]

When General George Washington heard about the mutiny in Pennsylvania, he "instantly ordered three complete regiments of infantry and a detachment of artillery to be put in motion" to deal with the distant situation. He was obviously angered by the incident, calling it an "outrageous mutiny of a part of the Pennsylvania troops . . . not worthy to be called soldiers." See the *Writings of George Washington*, Vol. X, 1782-1785, Collected and edited by Worthington Chauncey Ford, The Knickerbocker Press 1891, pp. 270-273.

"seat of government" -- location of the government for a political entity, usually located in the capital city

"enclave" -- isolated, foreign, separate areas

Congress wrote into the US Constitution the authority to have such an area under their sole and exclusive jurisdiction in Article 1, section 8, clause 17. This section gave them power to create a federal *enclave* for the seat of government and any other enclaves / districts necessary for federal purposes.

> "To exercise exclusive legislation in all cases whatsoever, over such District (not exceeding 10 miles square) as may, by cession of particular states, and the acceptance of Congress, become the seat of the government of the United States, and to exercise like Authority over all Places purchased by the Consent of the Legislature of the State in which the Same shall be, for the Erection of Forts, Magazines, Arsenals, dock-Yards, and other needful Buildings."
>
> *US Constitution, Article 1, Section 8, Clause 17*

Washington, D.C.

And so it was that the states of Maryland and Virginia ceded land on the banks of the Potomac River to the United States, creating a new seat of government that was totally separate from any US state jurisdiction. This district was initially called the "City of Washington" in honor of the newly elected US President, George Washington. Later, when Congress incorporated the city into a larger area, it was referred to as the *"District of Columbia" (D.C.)* with the capital called *"Washington."*

"maritime" -- pertaining to the sea, related to navigation or shipping

The fact that Congress had the power to create these special areas under the authority of the Constitution, gave them the subsequent right to enforce any laws they deemed necessary within these areas. [14] During the early days of our nation, other than Washington, D.C., the other types of federal enclaves Congress established were forts, arsenals, dock yards (including military ships, whether docked at port or on the high seas), various federal buildings, etc. The current formal list of US jurisdictional enclave areas is found in 18 USC 7, *Special Maritime and Territorial Jurisdiction of the United States.*

A specific set of federal enclave laws were enacted by Congress to deal with crimes within these special areas. Interestingly, these same set of laws apply on Indian lands today. There is a reason for this and we will discuss more on the application of federal enclave laws within Indian country in part 4 of this Chapter. For the time being, the important thing to remember is that an enclave is an area completely *separate from state jurisdiction*, even though it may be situated within a state's boundaries.

In the US Attorneys' jurisdictional charts for Indian country, you will see the phrase *"federal law applicable in the special maritime and territorial jurisdiction of the US,"* which is simply the official way of referring to the federal enclave laws.

Key Point

Federal enclaves were specifically designed to be under the sole and exclusive jurisdiction of the federal government.

The US Constitution (1788)

The United States Constitution begins with these words:

> *"We the people of the United States . . ."*
>
> *~ Preamble of the US Constitution*

Say it Simply!

"domestic nations" -- a nation within the boundaries of another nation

We have made it abundantly clear throughout this book, that from the very beginning of European contact the Indian tribes were recognized as independent sovereign nations. This is why, when the US Constitution was ratified in 1788, the phrase contained in its preamble, "We the people of the United States" did not include the Indians. [15] However, Indians are specifically mentioned within the Constitution, not as being part of the people of the United States, but as people whom the US deals with as detached *domestic nations*. There are three sections within the US Constitution involving Indians. (Two sections were in the original document of the Constitution and one was added, via an amendment, eighty years later.)

1) Article 1, Section 8, clause 3 – *The Commerce Clause* - Congress regulates trade with Indian tribes

2) Article 2, Section 2, clause 2 – *The Treaty Clause* - Regarding constitutional treaty-making (not specific to Indian treaties only)

3) The 14th Amendment (added in 1868) – *"Indians not taxed"*

Let's briefly cover each of these sections . . .

The Commerce Clause

> "Congress shall . . . have power to regulate commerce with foreign nations, and among the several States, and with the Indian tribes."
>
> *US Constitution, Article 1, Section 8, Clause 3*

This section established that it was the federal government who *exclusively* dealt with Indian tribes. According to a leading commentary on the US Constitution written in1833, the phrase "and with the Indian tribes," was not included in the first draft of the Constitution. Later it was suggested that the Constitution should read that Congress had the power "to regulate affairs with the Indians, as well within, as without the limits of the United States." Of course, the final draft that was approved gave Congress the power, exclusive of the individual states, to regulate commerce with the Indian tribes. It was believed it was unnecessary to spell out the fact that Congress had the power to regulate commerce with Indian tribes that resided outside the territorial limits of the US as well as with those living within the boundaries of a state. All regulation was to be from one source – the federal government – which incidentally also solved the problem of previously conflicting Indian trade regulations between the several states. [16]

Over time, the Commerce Clause has been used to justify and provide legal authority for numerous laws regarding Indian affairs. This clause has been the apparent *catch-all* authorization for Congress to legally implement its will over Indian nations. "The Constitution of the United States is almost silent in regard to the relations of the government which was established by it to the numerous tribes of Indians within its borders." [17]

Although the US Constitution outlines very little regarding Indians, "The mention of Indians in the Constitution which has received most attention is that found in the clause which gives Congress' power to regulate commerce with foreign nations and among the several States, and with the Indian tribes." [18] Yet, to rely on this clause to create a whole "system of criminal laws for Indians living peaceably in their reservations," the Supreme Court, at one time found this to "be a very strained construction of (that) clause." [19]

Say it Simply!

"implausibility" -- not having the appearance of truth or credibility

In a more recent US Supreme Court case, *US v. Lara* (2004), [20] one Supreme Court Justice stated in his opinion that he "cannot locate . . . congressional authority in . . . the Indian Commerce Clause" for "regulating virtually every aspect of the tribes." He recalled how "At one time, the *implausibility* of the assertion at least troubled the Court ... (considering such a construction of the Indian Commerce Clause to be 'very strained.')"

Treaty-making

> "The President shall . . . have power, by and with the advice and consent of the Senate, to make treaties, provided two-thirds of the Senators present concur."
>
> *US Constitution, Article 2, Section 2, Clause 2*

We will be spending some time on this section when we discuss Congress' ending of Indian treaty-making, so we will only point out here that there was a very specific method incorporated into the Constitution for negotiating formal contracts with foreign nations, which included the Indian nations. For almost a century the United States formally recognized Indian tribes as among those capable of treaty-making. At least three hundred and seventy treaties were made and ratified between the United States and the various Indian tribes. [21] The first treaty was September 17, 1778, with the Delawares. Treaty-making with Indian nations continued for nearly one hundred years until it was officially stopped in 1871.

Indians Not Taxed

> "All persons born or naturalized in the United States, *and subject to the jurisdiction thereof*, are citizens of the United States . . . Representatives shall be apportioned among the several States according to their respective numbers, counting the whole number of persons in each State, *excluding Indians not taxed*."
>
> *US Constitution, 14th Amendment (1868)*

The 14th Amendment to the US Constitution was added in 1868, at the end of the Civil War. The congressional debates prior to this amendment's ratification, documented in the Congressional *Globe*, [22] are quite interesting and revealing regarding the various views the legislators of that time had about Native Americans. For our discussion here, the two things to point out are:

- ► Indians were not "subject to the jurisdiction" of the US, therefore, not made citizens under the 14th Amendment. [23]

- ► Indians, as belonging to a foreign nation, were not responsible to pay taxes and, therefore, they did not have representation in Congress. [24]

On Nov. 7, 1940, the Department of Interior documented, "Since all Indians are today subject to Federal taxation, there are no more "Indians not taxed" within the meaning of that phrase as it is used in the Constitution and Fourteenth Amendment." See *Opinions of the Solicitor of the Department of the Interior Relating to Indian Affairs 1917-1974, Washington, United States Government Printing Office, Vol. 1, page 990; See also Do Indians Pay Taxes?*

Native American Rights Fund (NARF) Answers to Frequently Asked Questions about Native Peoples at:
http://www.narf.org/pubs/misc/faqs.html
(It explains how Indians do pay federal income taxes today along with other taxes.)

Supreme Law

The authors of the US Constitution made certain to establish the fact that this historic document would be supreme – above *all* other laws of the land. The new constitution replaced the existing constitution, the Articles of Confederation, as a stronger, more empowered law of the land that provided for administration of effective government.

The US Constitution is the supreme law of the United States of America, with the states being united under its authority. Therefore, any laws or treaties made under the authority of the Constitution carry the same weight of supremacy over individual state laws and state constitutions. We read in Article VI, clause 2:

> "This Constitution, and the laws of the United States, which shall be made in pursuance thereof, and all treaties made, or which shall be made, under the authority of the United States, shall be the supreme law of the land. And the judges in every state shall be bound thereby, anything in the constitution or laws of any state to the contrary notwithstanding."

Essentially, this means that federal law and US treaties that are made according to the US Constitution must be observed by the whole nation. If a state has a law to the contrary, federal law will always supersede that law. If this were not the case, it would be like the saying, "The tail is wagging the dog." Or, as one of the founding fathers explained, it would be like "a monster, in which the head was under the direction of the members." [25]

Angry Brits & Careless States

An example of US law/treaties being supreme over the states is seen in a letter Congress wrote to British officials in 1787. Apparently, the British were upset the Americans had broken a section of the Treaty of Paris by not paying a debt promised (each state was required to contribute funds). Congress responded in a letter to British authorities stating:

- Treaties are binding on the whole nation regardless of the fact that some of the states paid "too little attention" to the requirements of the treaty.
- State authority is not superior over federal authority; otherwise there would be anarchy and confusion.
- Broken treaties would result in hostilities and war with nations.

Needless to say, in spite of some opposition from the states, Congress made sure the United States fulfilled the treaty stipulations and paid the debt. [26]

Endnotes - Chapter Three, Part 2:

[1] *Worcester v. State of Georgia*, 31 U.S. 515, 549 (1832) ". . . when the war of our revolution commenced . . . the colonists had much cause for the apprehension that the Indian nations would, as the allies of Great Britain, add their arms to hers. This, as was to be expected, became an object of great solicitude to congress. Far from advancing a claim to their lands, or asserting any right of dominion over them, congress resolved 'that the securing and preserving the friendship of the Indian nations appears to be a subject of the utmost moment to these colonies.' The early journals of congress exhibit the most anxious desire to conciliate the Indian nations."

[2] Congress passed the Land Ordinance on May 8, 1785 (each lot sold for no less than $640) Journals of the Continental Congress, 25:681-83, 693, Compiled by Prucha, Francis Paul, *Documents of U.S. Indian Policy*, University of Nebraska Press (3rd ed.), 2000, p. 4

[3] Quoting from the Federalist, Story LL.D., Joseph, *Commentaries on the Constitution of the U.S. (1833)*, Lonang Institute 2003, 2005 electronic edition, Book III, pp. 589 - 590; The Federalist was published in both The Independent Journal and The New York Packet

[4] *Cherokee Nation v. Georgia*, 30 US 1, 26 (1831)

[5] Dr.Barnes, Ian, *The Historical Atlas of Native Americans*, Chartwell Books, Inc. 2010, p. 226

[6] Id.; The "Cumberland Gap" was considered the first great gateway to the west. It was a path that had long been used by Native Americans as a passage through the lower central Appalachian Mountains. In 1775, a team of loggers led by Daniel Boone, made the pathway wide and level enough for horse-driven wagons to travel on. This opened up the western frontier for greater settlement, especially in Kentucky and Tennessee.

[7] Callahan, North, *General Washington's General*, A.S. Barnes and Co. 1958, p. 336, Knox also grieved the fact that "the United States did not treat the murderers of Indians with the same severity as the murderers of whites."

[8] Id. at 337

[9] *US v. Kagama*, 118 US 375, 384 (1886)

[10] See the discussion in *Worcester v. State of Georgia*, 31 U.S. 515, 545-546 (1832) "The power of making war is conferred by these charters on the colonies, but defensive war alone seems to have been contemplated . . . The power of war is given only for defense, not for conquest;" See also Echo-Hawk, Walter R., *In the Courts of the Conqueror*, Fulcrum Publishing 2010, p.3 "In the very first case to come before the United States Supreme Court involving a significant Native American issue, Chief Justice John Marshall ominously described the American judicial system as 'the Courts of the conqueror.'" This case, Johnson v. McIntosh, 21 US 543 (1823), discusses the Doctrine of Discovery which gave a European nation absolute and exclusive title which ultimately meant that title could not be shared with another. "An absolute title to lands cannot exist at the same time in different persons or in different governments. An absolute must be an exclusive title, or at least a title which excludes all others . . ." (21 US 543, 588) "The British government, which was then our government and whose rights have passed to the United States, asserted title to all the lands occupied by Indians within the chartered limits of the British colonies. It asserted also a limited sovereignty over them (the Indian tribes) and the exclusive right of extinguishing the title which occupancy gave to them." *Id.* Therefore, the United States as "conqueror" is in reference to the Doctrine of Discovery which was passed from Great Britain to the US after the American Revolution through the Treaty of Paris in 1783. The "conquered" refers to those capable of holding a conflicting title – European nations. The inhabitants of the conquered areas included the Indians. When Indian tribes fought for their lands, the title-bearing conqueror held their ground: "Frequent and bloody wars, in which the whites were not always the aggressors, unavoidably ensued. European policy, numbers, and skill prevailed. As the white population advanced, that of the Indians necessarily receded. The country in the immediate neighborhood of agriculturists became unfit for them. The game fled into thicker and more unbroken forests, and the Indians followed. The soil to which the Crown originally

claimed title, being no longer occupied by its ancient inhabitants, was parceled out according to the will of the sovereign power and taken possession of . . ." (21 US 543, 590-591) Although there is a fine line, the wars amongst the European nations were outright imperialistic, while combat with the Indian tribes themselves was technically seen as defensive in nature.

[11] Dr. Barnes, Ian, *The Historical Atlas of Native Americans*, Chartwell Books, Inc. 2010, p. 226

[12] Catlin, George, *Last rambles amongst the Indians of the Rocky Mountains and the Andes*, Sampson Low, son, and Marston 1868 (digitized from public domain by BiblioLife, LLC) p. 356; Catlin also states, "Every battle which the whites have lost has been a *'massacre,'* and every battle by the Indians lost, a *'glorious victory!'*"

[13] See *The Federalist Papers No. 43*, James Madison discusses the need for such a district with exclusive federal jurisdiction.

[14] Story LL.D., Joseph, *Commentaries on the Constitution of the U.S. (1833)*, Lonang Institute 2003, 2005 electronic edition, Book III, pp. 550 - 551, § 1229 – 1230; This commentator also tells the story of the Pennsylvania Mutiny in § 1214, p.546 ". . . the congress, then sitting at Philadelphia, was surrounded and insulted by a small, but insolent body of mutineers of the continental army. Congress applied to the executive authority of Pennsylvania for defense; but, under the ill-conceived constitution of the state at that time, the executive power was vested in a council consisting of thirteen members; and they possessed, or exhibited so little energy, and such apparent intimidation, that congress indignantly removed to New Jersey, whose inhabitants welcomed them with promises of defending them. Congress remained for some time at Princeton without being again insulted, till, for the sake of greater convenience, they adjourned to Annapolis. The general dissatisfaction with the proceedings of Pennsylvania, and the degrading spectacle of a fugitive congress, were sufficiently striking to produce this remedy (Art. 1, sec. 8, cl. 17)."

[15] Indians were not part of "we the people" when the United States was originally formed. A New York Chancellor (who had previously been the Chief Justice of New York's Supreme Court), made these remarks about Indians in a court case during the early 1820s:
"Do our laws, even at this day, allow these Indians to participate equally with us, in our civil and political privileges? Do they vote at our elections, or are they represented in our legislature, or have they any concern, as jurors or magistrates, in the administration of Justice? Are they, on the other hand, charged with the duties and burdens of citizens? Do they pay taxes, or serve in the militia, or are they required to take a share in any of the details of our local institutions? Do we interfere with the disposition, or descent, or tenure of their property, as between themselves? Do we provide their wills, or grant letters of administration upon their estates? Do our Sunday laws, our school laws, our poor laws, our laws concerning infants and apprentices, or concerning idiots, lunatics, or habitual drunkards apply to them? Are they subject to our laws, or the laws of the United States, against high treason; and do we treat and punish them as traitors, instead of public enemies when they make war upon us? Are they subject to our laws of marriage and divorce, and would we sustain a criminal prosecution for bigamy, if they should change their wives or husbands at their own pleasure and according to their own customs, and contract new matrimonial alliances? I apprehend, that every one of these questions must be answered in the negative, and that on all these points they are regarded as dependent allies, and alien communities." Extract from the opinion of Chancellor Kent in Goodell v. Jackson, recorded in Penn, William, *Essays on the Present crisis in the Condition of the American Indians*, 1829 p. 108

[16] Story LL.D., Joseph, *Commentaries on the Constitution of the U.S. (1833)*, Lonang Institute 2003, 2005 electronic edition, Book III, p. 489, § 1092 – 1096

[17] *US v. Kagama*, 118 US 375, 378 (1886)

[18] Id.

[19] Id.

[20] *US v. Lara*, 541 US 193 (2004) Justice Thomas, J., concurring in judgment on writ of certiorari to the United States Court of Appeals for the Eighth Circuit

[21] Kappler, Charles J., *Indian Affairs: Laws and Treaties*, Washington: Government Printing Office 1929, p.1154

[22] The *Globe* contains the congressional debates of the 23rd through the 42nd Congresses from 1833 through 1873.

[23] Senator Johnson commented during the debate regarding the 14th Amendment, "Now all this amendment provides is, that all persons born in the United States *and not subject to some foreign Power* – for that, no doubt, is the meaning of the committee who have brought the matter before us – shall be considered as citizens of the United States." See Congressional Globe, 1st Session, 39th Congress, pg. 2893

[24] "[A]t the time of the adoption of the Constitution these Indians were not subject to taxation, so too were they not subject to taxation at the time of the adoption of the Fourteenth Amendment. This attribute of their status remained the same and it was retained as descriptive of a status which likewise had remained the same. Though the States may have desired to tax the Indians within their borders and though they did, on more than one occasion, attempt it, they were effectively precluded from doing so by decisions of the Supreme Court. *The Kansas Indians*, 5 Wall. 737; *The New York Indians*, 5 Wall. 761. The effect of these decisions and of other decisions which enunciated the doctrine that Indian affairs are subject to the control of the Federal Government rather than that of the States (*Worcester v. Georgia*, 6 Pet. 515), has been to exclude Indians while in their separate communities or on reservations from the application of State laws except as the Federal Government may confer upon the States power over certain subjects." See *Opinions of the Solicitor of the Department of the Interior Relating to Indian Affairs 1917-1974*, Washington, United States Government Printing Office, Vol. 1, page 992

[25] *The Federalist Papers*, number 44; Although all 85 essays were signed "Publius," the 44th paper is attributed to James Madison's authorship; Federal law, especially criminal law, was purposely limited to issues involving direct federal interest and to its areas of exclusive jurisdiction (enclaves) during the early years of America. Everyday law and order was generally left up to the individual states to enforce. After the Civil War (1861-1865) there was a shift towards enacting increasingly more federal criminal laws. See article by Nikhil Bhagat, J.D. Candidate 2011, Columbia Law School, *Filling the Gap? Non-Abrogation Provisions and the Assimilative Crimes Act*, Columbia Law Review, Vol. 111:77, p. 86

[26] Documents from the Continental Congress and the Constitutional Convention, 1774 – 1789, Letter of Congress, April 13, 1787, responding to "facts and matters urged by Britain as infractions of the treaty of peace on the part of America." This document can be found on the Library of Congress, American Memory website at: http://memory.loc.gov/cgi-bin/query/r?ammem/bdsdcc:@field(DOCID+@lit(bdsdcc21701)).
At this site you can select the option to actually see the handwritten document for yourself. Included in Congress' response is "[w]hen therefore a treaty is constitutionally made, ratified and published by us, it immediately becomes binding on the whole nation, and superadded to the laws of the land, without the intervention of state legislatures. Treaties derive their obligation from being compacts between the sovereign of this and the sovereign of another nation; whereas laws or statutes derive their force from being the acts of a legislature competent to the passing of them. Hence it is clear that treaties must be implicitly received and observed by every member of the nation; for as state legislatures are not competent to the making of such compacts or treaties, so neither are they competent in that capacity, authoritatively to decide on, or ascertain the construction and sense of them. When doubts arise respecting the construction of state laws, it is not unusual nor improper for the state legislatures, by explanatory or declaratory acts, to remove those doubts: but the case between laws and compacts or treaties is in this widely different; for when doubts arise respecting the sense and meaning of a treaty, they are so far from being cognizable by a state legislature, that the United States in Congress assembled have no authority to settle and determine them: for as the legislature only, which constitutionally passes a law, has power to revise and amend it, so the sovereigns only, who are parties to the treaty, have power by mutual consent and posterior articles, to correct or explain it."

Chapter Three ~ Part 3

This chapter will cover:

- *Federal Indian Affairs*
- *Trading with Indians*
- *Vanishing Lands*

Chapter Three - Part 3

Evolution of Jurisdiction in Indian Country

"succession" -- in sequence, one after the other

Indians - A Federal Affair

One of the first federal departments established by Congress, under the new US Constitution, was the War Department (1789). Congress gave high priority to the formation of this new department, creating it a few weeks prior to the Treasury Department. Congress' establishment of the War Department outlined the position of the Secretary of War who would administer the duties they defined. One of the responsibilities placed under this department was *"Indian Affairs."*

During the American Revolutionary War, the Confederate Congress controlled military affairs through acts of Continental Congress, having it administered by a Board of War. Two individuals served in *succession* as Secretary of War under the Articles of Confederation: General Benjamin Lincoln and then, General Henry Knox. When the US Constitution became the law of the land, it recognized the President of the United States as the Commander-in-Chief of the Army and Navy. The newly elected and first president, George Washington, appointed Henry Knox to serve as Secretary of War, and the Senate immediately confirmed this appointment. Knox, who had previously held large executive power in military affairs under the Articles of Confederation, continued under the authority of the president, in accordance with the US Constitution. [1]

"Indian affairs" was officially made a *federal* affair and responsibility by an act of Congress. Henry Knox, now appointed as the Secretary of War, was already familiar with Indian affairs through his involvement in the field during the American Revolution. The goal of the federal government regarding Indian affairs, which was placed on the shoulders of the Secretary of War, was for the peace of the Union and gaining land for growth of the nation.

As head of the War Department, Henry Knox stressed to Congress that peace on the frontier would require laws that would regulate how non-Indians conducted business (i.e. trading, etc.) with the Indians. He hoped that even if all fraudulent conduct could not be completely prevented, at least it could be restrained and regulated. His concern was echoed by many others who did not want to stifle the trade business with Indians, yet protect the industry from known abuses.

What Were "Indian affairs"?

You may be asking, "What exactly were the War Department's duties when it came to Indian affairs?" This department held the responsibility of Indian affairs for 60 years (from 1789 – 1849) until it was transferred to the newly created Department of Interior. Official documentation of the 60-year history of the War Department published in 1880, stated the responsibility for Indian affairs over the years had been two-fold:

1) The duties of the War Department with Indians involved bargaining for Indian land through federal treaties. The War Department actively pursued initiating and negotiating treaties with the Indian tribes time and time again. These negotiations created a tremendous increase of landholdings for the United States. [2]

2) The second duty of the War Department was to ensure the enforcement of the federal laws for trading with Indians. This was important to the federal government because it was stated at the time, "there has always been considerable profit in Indian trade." [3]

Key Point

"Indian affairs" was officially categorized within a *federal* department.

Trading with the Indians

Many are familiar with the story of the Pilgrims who came to the Americas in 1620 seeking religious freedom. Very little is ever mentioned about the arrangement of how they purposed to accomplish this goal – which was through a binding contract with their sponsoring company, "Merchant Adventures." Essentially, the contract the Pilgrims had with this company stipulated that, in order to pay their bills, they were required to devote seven years of full-time work for the company's profit.

Quotes "Q"

> *"Everyone on that ship (the Mayflower) was expected to earn their keep and generate dividends for the company one way or another. If the Pilgrims failed to achieve this goal, the colony would likely fail as well."*
>
> *Dolin, Eric Jay, Fur, Fortune, and Empire, W. N. Norton & Company, Inc. 2010 p. 37*

What ended up sustaining these early colonists was trading with the Indians. For the Pilgrims it was specifically trading for beaver pelts. The beaver had been extinct in England for at least one hundred years, therefore its fur was highly valued. [4] By the late 1600's the southern colonies, in addition to beaver pelts, traded deerskins. As a matter of fact, for purchasing various manufactured products, deerskins became the "standard of measurement." [5]

Nerdy Stuff

One author attributes the fact that deerskins became the standard of measurement to the reason why the slang name for the American dollar is – a "buck." See the book, *Chronology of Native Americans* by Greg O'Brien (Amber Books Ltd. 2011) p. 114.

Dig Deeper

The book *Fur, Fortune, and Empire* tells the epic history of the fur trade in America. Author Eric Jay Dolin illustrates the critical part fur trading played in early America. Dolin, Eric Jay, *Fur, Fortune, and Empire*, W.N. Norton & Company, Inc. 2010. Another book with excellent illustrations and photography with a running timeline on each page is the *Chronology of Native Americans*, by Greg O'Brien, Amber Books Ltd. 2011.

Fur Fortunes

Many groups sought out ways to trade with the Indians for economic gain. The competition was tremendous as the various European nations fought for the monopoly on trading with the Indians. Wars were fought between Indian tribes over hunting grounds, with much support and backing of European nations who were pitted against each other for the cutting edge on European fur markets.

Fur trading played a huge role in the economy of the Americas. To give you an idea of how voluminous the North American fur exportation was, during the mid-eighteenth century, South Carolina shipped a total of 150,000 deerskins (per year) to England while nearly 500,000 deerskins were collectively exported out of New Orleans, Savannah, Mobile, Pensacola, and St. Augustine during this same time. [6]

Say it Simply!

"intercourse" -- mutual dealings or communications between individuals

Trading Laws

Trading with Indians was very much alive and well in America during its early years. Indian trading that had begun long before the establishment of the United States of America, continued after the USA was a nation. Of course, this brought various degrees of interaction between non-Indians and Indians. A word used, especially during that time period, that described the business connection or interaction between people, was the word *"intercourse."* Therefore, when Congress took steps to make laws specific to the trade business transactions between non-Indians with Indians, these laws were called *Trade and Intercourse Acts*.

A Federal First

The very first federal law made under the authority of the new US Constitution regarding Indians was the *Act to Regulate Trade and Intercourse with the Indian Tribes*, enacted on July 22, 1790. This law was created in light of great concern over "providing effective protection for the Indians" from what President Washington called "the violences of the lawless part of our frontier inhabitants." [7] It was believed, if Congress did not enact these laws, the hope for peace with the Indians would be *"illusory."* Through this first federal Indian law, "Congress assumed federal jurisdiction over offenses by non-Indians against Indians."

Say it Simply!

"illusory" -- unreal, false, imaginary

This new law stated:

- A license was required for anyone making transactions with Indians, having a punishment of $1,000 for failure to obey the rules and forfeiture of all merchandise offered to Indians if one attempted to trade without a license.

- Government officials had full power and authority to recall a license.

- No sale of Indian lands could take place except through an authorized US government treaty that was open to the public.

- Any US citizen or inhabitant who committed a crime against an Indian within Indian territory would be punished exactly as if the crime had happen off Indian territory against a non-Indian.

After the passage of the first *Trade and Intercourse Act*, President Washington, in a speech to the Chiefs and Counselors of the Seneca Indian Nation on December 29, 1790, said:

> "I am not uninformed that the Six Nations have been led into some difficulties with respect to the sale of their lands since the peace (end of the Revolutionary War). But I must inform you that these evils arose before the present government of the United States was established, when the separate States and individuals under their authority, undertook to treat with the Indian tribes respecting the sale of their lands.
>
> But the case is now entirely altered. The general Government only has the power, to treat with the Indian Nations, and any treaty formed and held without its authority will not be binding.
>
> Here then is the security for the remainder of your lands. No State nor person can purchase your lands, unless at some public treaty held *under the authority of the United States*. The general government will never consent to your being defrauded. But it will protect you in all your just rights."

The first president had earlier recognized that the main thing Indians were fighting against were abuses regarding their lands. In his third annual message to Congress he had acknowledged land issues as "the main source of discontent and war" and he called for clearly defined regulations to be outlined and authorized by Congress. [8] He believed this was the best way to alleviate the abuse and provide that "commerce with them (the Indians) should be promoted under regulations." He viewed those who violated the rights of Indians and broke treaties as those who "endanger the peace of the Union." He asked Congress to make effective and adequate penalties against such individuals.

One influential Indian chief during this time period also explained that the "cause of war" was due to broken treaties and encroachment on their lands. Many promises were made during treaty-making, especially the guarantee that the tribes' reserved lands would be free from illegal settlements. Broken treaty contracts were, "the sole cause of the abrupt termination of the negotiations for peace," the Indian chief explained. "Thus, you see that claims upon our lands always have been, and still continue to be, *the cause of the war*." [9]

Key Point

The first federal Indian law enacted by Congress made offenses by non-Indians against Indians a federal crime.

Benjamin Franklin's Story

In one of his papers, Benjamin Franklin shared a conversation his Indian interpreter, Conrad Weiser, had with an Indian friend. This Indian friend told Conrad he noticed how, once in seven days, the white people shut up their shops and assemble in the great house. Since he knew Conrad was familiar with the customs of the white people, he asked him for the truth of why they do this. Conrad answered . . .

"They meet there, to hear and learn good Things. I do not doubt says the Indian, that they tell you so: They have told me the same; But I doubt the Truth of what they say, and I will tell you my Reasons. I was lately to Albany to sell my Skins, & buy Blankets, Knives, Powder & Rum and You know I us'd generally to deal with Hans Hanson, but I was a little inclin'd this time to try some other Merchant; however, I call'd first upon Hans, & ask'd him what he would give for Beaver. He said he could not give more than four Shillings a Pound; but says he I cannot talk on Business now; this is the Day when we meet together to learn good Things, and I am going to the Meeting. So I thought to my self, since we cannot do any Business to day, I may as well go to the Meeting too; and I went with him.

There stood up a Man in Black, and began to talk to the People very angrily. I did not understand what he said; but perceiving that he look'd much at me, and at Hanson, I imagin'd he was angry at seeing me there, so I went out, sat down near the House, struck Fire and lit my Pipe, waiting till the Meeting should break up. I thought too that the Man had mention'd something of Beaver, & I suspected it might be the Subject of their Making. so when they came out, I accosted my Merchant, Well, Hans, says I, I hope you have agreed to give more than four Shillings a Pound. No, says he, I cannot give so much; I cannot give more than three shillings & sixpence. I then spoke to several other Dealers, but they all sung the same Song. Three & sixpence, Three & sixpence. This made it clear to me that my Suspicion was right; and that whatever they pretended of meeting to learn Good Things, the real purpose was to consult how to cheat Indians on the Price of Beaver.

Consider but a little, Conrad, and you must be of my Opinion. If they met so often to learn Good Things, they would certainly have learnt some before this time. But they are still ignorant. You know our Practice. If a white Man in travelling thro' our Country, enters one of our Cabins, we all treat him as I treat you; we dry him if he is wet, we warm him if he is cold, we give him Meat & Drinks that he may allay his Thirst and Hunger, and spread soft Furs for him to rest & sleep on: We demand nothing in return. But if I go into a white Man's House at Albany, and ask for Victuals & Drink, they say, where is your Money? and if I have none; they say, Get out you Indian Dog. You see they have not yet learnt those little Good Things, that we need no Meetings to be instructed in, because our Mothers taught them to us when we were Children: And therefore, it is impossible their Meeting, Should be as they say, for any such purpose, or have any such Effect. They are only to contrive the Cheating of Indians in the Price of Beaver."

The Papers of Benjamin Franklin: Remarks concerning the Savages of North America, Sponsored by The American Philosophical Society and Yale University (Digital Edition by The Packard Humanities Institute) at: http://www.franklinpapers.org/franklin/framedNames.jsp

Building Tensions

During the early years of the United States of America, various levels of tension existed between non-Indians, Indians and foreign nations. These tensions continued to build throughout the years and many dynamics were involved such as:

- Encroaching settlers on Indian lands
- Fur trading crucial to the economy
- Military outposts
- Foreign influences

President Washington shared a concern before Congress in 1794 that "some encroachment was about to be made on our (US) territory by an officer and party of British troops." Communication to Congress, May 21, 1794, *Indian Affairs: Laws and Treaties*, Compiled and Edited by Charles J. Kappler; see also [10]

"**contravention**" -- breaking

As stress and apprehension increased, so did the rules and regulations. By 1800, Congress' enactment of the *Act for the Preservation of Peace with the Indian Tribes*, threatened to slap a $2,000 fine, along with a two-year prison sentence on anyone who "shall send any talk, speech, message or letter to any Indian nation, tribe, or chief, with an intent to produce a *contravention* or infraction of any treaty or other law of the United States, or to disturb the peace and tranquility of the United States." [11]

In fact, just three years prior to this Act, US Senator William Blount had been expelled from Congress due to a charge of a high misdemeanor. Blount's alleged crime was that he tried to influence a US Indian agent to turn Indians from their trust in the United States. [12]

New and Improved Rules

The Trade and Intercourse Acts were updated by Congress from time to time with minor adjustments. By 1802, Congress was ready to enact the new and improved Trade and Intercourse Act. This Act strongly clarified the line between Indian territory and non-Indian territory – a line that was not to be crossed. In fact, no one was to go on Indian lands without a passport. [13] A few other things to make note of in this Act:

- It addressed the issue of *reciprocal* revenge between Indians and non-Indians. No attempting of private satisfaction or revenge on either side was allowed.
- If a non-Indian was a victim of a crime by an Indian, he (or his representative) would have to make an application, through the US government agent, to the tribal nation for justice.

Say it Simply!

"reciprocal" -- given or done in return

"diminution" -- diminishing, chipping away

"perturbations" -- agitations, irritations

Vanishing Land

The third president of the United States, Thomas Jefferson, was well aware of land losses for the Indians. Their land cessations, along with the large settled areas surrounding their increasingly smaller borders, threatened their ability to provide for their very livelihood. [14] Jefferson sent this message to Congress on January 18, 1803:

Quotes "Q"

> *"The Indian tribes residing within the limits of the United States have for a considerable time been growing more and more uneasy at the constant diminution of the territory they occupy, although effected by their own voluntary sales, and the policy has long been gaining strength with them of refusing absolutely all further sale on any conditions, insomuch that at this time it hazards their friendship and excited dangerous jealousies and perturbations in their minds to make any overture for the purchase of the smallest portions of their land."*
>
> *Richardson, James D., comp., Messages and Papers of the Presidents, 1:340-41, Compiled & Edited by Francis Paul Prucha, Documents of U.S. Indian Policy, pg. 21*

Say it Simply!

"assimilate" -- absorb into or conform to another's customs, attitudes and way of life; to resemble another

Jefferson continued his speech, stating that the United States needed to quickly extend its territory because of the "rapid increase" in population. He believed he had a win-win solution to the Indian problem. His solution was two-fold:

1) Have the Indians give up hunting and become farmers. He reasoned that farmers did not need as much land, so then the Indians would have surplus land which they could exchange for things to improve their farms.

2) Build many trading houses that are more easily accessible that would encourage Indians to get used to "domestic comforts" and *assimilate* into the civilized culture.

Land Concerns

To say Indian nations had concerns about their land would be an understatement! They wondered how they would survive, as a people and as a culture, apart from their lands. They were willing to cede large areas, but not to the point of extinction.

Agriculture was not totally unknown amongst the Indian tribes. Certain tribal chiefs had even written to the president with their concerns about tilling the ground. However, they posed a fundamental question to the president which they needed answered before they could discuss any more about changing to farming as a way of life.

The president's response to these tribal chiefs reveals the question they posed:

> *"You have said in your speech, 'That the game is going away from among you, and that you thought it the design of the great Spirit, that you should till the ground, but before you speak upon this subject, you want to know whether the United States meant to leave you any land to till?'"* [15]

Endnotes - Chapter Three, Part 3:

[1] "The President shall be Commander in Chief of the Army and Navy of the United States, and of the Militia of the several States, when called into the actual Service of the United States; he may require the Opinion, in writing, of the principal Officer in each of the executive Departments, upon any Subject relating to the Duties of their respective Offices . . ." US Constitution, Art. 2, Sec. 2, cl. 1

[2] See Ingersoll, Lurton Dunham, *A History of the War Department of the United States*, Washington, D.C.: Francis B. Mohun 1880, p.122; The author of this historic documentation of the War Department described the Indian tribes as "obstacles in the way of national development and of the progress of civilization." The author says it was the duty of the War Department to remove these obstacles and "it was impossible always to avoid misunderstandings and wars." (p.130)

[3] Id. at p. 131

[4] Dolin, Eric Jay, *Fur, Fortune, and Empire*, W. N. Norton & Company, Inc. 2010, p. 38

[5] O'Brien, Greg, *Chronology of Native Americans*, Amber Books Ltd. 2011, p. 114

[6]Id. at p. 115

[7] *Oliphant v Suquamish Indian Tribe*, 435 U.S. 191, 201 (1978) "Congress' concern was with providing effective protection for the Indians "from the violences of the lawless part of our frontier inhabitants . . . Without such protection, it was felt that 'all the exertions of the Government to prevent destructive retaliations by the Indians will prove fruitless and all our present agreeable prospects illusory' . . . Beginning with the Trade and Intercourse Act of 1790 . . . Congress assumed federal jurisdiction over offenses by non-Indians against Indians ."

[8] President George Washington's Third Annual Message, Oct. 25, 1791

[9] Chief Brandt at the proceedings of a council held at Buffalo Creek, October 10th, 1793

[10] In southern regions there were tensions between the U.S. and Spain over territorial rights of Spanish Florida and New Spain. Foreign policy embodied in the Monroe Doctrine was rooted in concerns about sovereign foreign powers gaining dominance.

[11] An Act for the Preservation of Peace with the Indian Tribes, Enacted by Congress on January 17, 1800

[12] Story LL.D., Joseph, *Commentaries on the Constitution of the U.S. (1833)*, Lonang Institute 2003, 2005 electronic edition, Book III, p. 383, § 836

[13] An Act to Regulate Trade and Intercourse with the Indian Tribes, and to Preserve Peace on the Frontiers, Enacted by Congress on March 30, 1802

[14]"As the settlements of the whites shall approach near to the Indian boundaries established by treaties, the game will be diminished, and the lands being valuable to the Indians only as hunting grounds, they will be willing to sell further tracts for small considerations . . . Indians will . . . in their intercourse with the whites, be reduced to a very small number . . ." *American State Papers: Indian Affairs*, 1:13-14, Compiled & Edited by Francis Paul Prucha, *Documents of U.S. Indian Policy*, pg. 13

[15] Letter written to chiefs and counselors of the Seneca Nation by President George Washington, Philadelphia, Dec. 29,1790

Chapter Three - Part 4

This chapter will cover:

- *Enclave Laws*
- *The Marshall Trilogy*
- *Treaties v. Legislation*

Chapter Three - Part 4

Evolution of Jurisdiction in Indian Country

Federal Jurisdiction

In the previous section, we discussed how federal jurisdiction in Indian country began through the enactment of the Trade and Intercourse Act of 1790. We saw how this Act made crime by a non-Indian against an Indian within Indian territory a federal crime. Through this act (and subsequent Trade and Intercourse Acts), Congress clarified that *all* dealings with Indians would be under *federal* jurisdiction, *not state* jurisdiction.

It'll Take an Act of Congress

Stepping away from Indian country for a minute . . . During this same time, Congress was beginning to address criminal concerns on its federal enclaves. Because the enclaves were under the *sole and exclusive jurisdiction* of the United States, state law did not apply to crimes committed in these areas even though they were often within the boundaries of a state. Indeed, this had been the whole purpose for creating the federal enclaves – to be totally separate from state control. However, this also meant that Congress would have to create its own laws for these areas. The saying, "It'll take an act of Congress!" was literally true for laws to exist for the federal enclaves. If Congress did not create criminal laws, crimes would virtually go unpunished.

Congress certainly did not want criminal actions to go unpunished in the areas under their control. Keep in mind, though, the early enclaves consisted of only a small population of individuals who were assigned to or interacted with the special federal areas (i.e. forts, arsenals and dockyards). For this reason, the first federal penal code developed for the enclaves concentrated on only the most serious crimes and their corresponding punishments. This was accomplished by Congress' enactment of the Federal Crimes Act of 1790.

Nerdy Stuff

Interestingly, the first penal code authorized judges "at their discretion" to intensify the punishment of a convicted murderer by adding to the death sentence that the body "be delivered to a surgeon for dissection."

Gaps in Jurisdiction

The first federal penal code was an attempt to address criminal issues, but remained an insufficient body of law. The problem was there were gaps in criminal jurisdiction. If someone on a federal enclave committed a crime not covered by the crimes specifically listed in the Federal Crimes Act, there would be no authority to punish the act. There was great concern about these enclaves becoming a criminal's paradise. One individual who worked hard at trying to correct this problem wrote in 1816 about his concern that at the federal naval yards, arsenals, forts, dockyards, and the high seas "[r]apes, arsons, batteries and a host of other crimes, may in these places be now committed with *impunity*." [FN1]

Say it Simply!

"impunity" -- without punishment or consequences

Meanwhile ... Back in Indian Country

Jumping back to Indian country, in 1817 Congress decided to make the same laws they had created for the federal enclaves also apply on Indian lands.

Quotes

"Beginning with the Trade and Intercourse Act of 1790 . . . Congress assumed federal jurisdiction over offenses by non-Indians against Indians which 'would be punishable by the laws of [the] state or district . . . (as) if the offense had been committed against a citizen or white inhabitant thereof.' ***In 1817, Congress went one step further and extended federal enclave law to the Indian country."***

Oliphant v. Suquamish Indian Tribe, 435 U.S. 191, 201(1978)

This expanded jurisdiction was established through the *Act of March 3, 1817*. Through this Act, Congress extended federal jurisdiction in a greater way than they had ever done before in Indian country. The earlier Trade and Intercourse Acts had addressed the issue of interracial crime within Indian country only one way: Non-Indian (offender) versus Indian (victim). However, now in 1817 federal jurisdiction over interracial crime that occurred on Indian land was covered *both* ways:

- ► Non-Indian (offender) v. Indian (victim); and
- ► Indian (offender) v. Non-Indian (victim).

Alike - But Different

Although Indian territory was not technically a federal enclave, Congress applied federal enclave law because they saw the similarities between these two unique areas:

- ► Similar to the federal enclaves, Indian country was its own separate area free from state jurisdiction, even though residing within a state's boundaries.
- ► And, in a similar fashion to Congress' sole and exclusive right in dealing on the enclaves, the federal government claimed *sole and exclusive right* in dealing with the Indians and their lands.

Congress, however, also recognized the significant and distinctive difference between the federal enclaves and Indian country . . . *tribal sovereignty*. Because of tribal sovereignty, federal enclave laws were applied in a *limited* manner. [2] The enclave laws did *not* apply to Indian country under these three circumstances:

1. If it was an Indian against Indian crime (The tribe had exclusive jurisdiction). [3]

2. If a treaty stipulated that the tribe had jurisdiction over the offense.

3. If an Indian had already been punished by the local law of the tribe (stipulation added later in 1854). [4]

The Act of March 3, 1817, is nowadays codified under 18 USC 1152, and reads as follows:

> "Except as otherwise expressly provided by law, the general laws of the United States as to the punishment of offenses committed in any place within the sole and exclusive jurisdiction of the United States, except the District of Columbia, *shall extend to the Indian country.*
>
> This section shall not extend to offenses committed by one Indian against the person or property of another Indian, nor to any Indian committing any offense in the Indian country who has been punished by the local law of the tribe, or to any case where, by treaty stipulations, the exclusive jurisdiction over such offenses is or may be secured to the Indian tribes respectively."

The wording of the original law, The Act of March 3, 1817, is a bit different, but its goal is essentially the same as the wording seen today codified in 18 USC 1152.

Inherent Jurisdiction Untouched

The purpose of the Act of March 3, 1817, was to accomplish the same goal Congress had for its federal enclaves – no gaps in criminal jurisdiction. With the increase of interaction between non-Indians and Indians, more situations naturally arose that had never existed before in the new and evolving world of early America. This law, however, was never intended to do away with tribal self-government. Rather, quite the opposite as it clearly acknowledged the sovereignty of the tribes through its three specific exceptions. Congress recognized Indian versus Indian crime to be exclusively under the jurisdiction of the

These specific exceptions to federal law only apply to the federal enclave laws, not to all federal law. This is why general federal law that *applies throughout the United States* (no matter where) applies equally to Indians as to anyone else who breaks these laws. If general federal crimes such as bank robbery, counterfeiting, drug sales, and assault on a federal officer are committed anywhere – *on* or *off* Indian lands – none of the three stipulations in 18 USC §1152 would apply.

tribe. Also, Congress respected treaty contracts and confirmed the validity of the local law of a tribe to punish the criminal behavior of their members. [5]

Federal criminal laws were applied in limited fashion while the civil and criminal laws of the tribes regarding their people and territories were left untouched. It was recognized, in light of inherent tribal sovereignty, the individual tribal governments had long-established rules and regulations which were guided by their traditions and cultures. (We will spend more time on the inherent authority of tribal government in Chapter 6.)

Generally Confusing

As mentioned already, the Act of March 3, 1817, is today codified in 18 USC §1152. Through the years this law has also been referred to by other names – but it is the same law. Most commonly it is referred to as the *General Crimes Act* or simply, *1152*. You may also see this law referred to as:

- Indian Country Crimes Act (ICCA)
- Enclave Laws on Indian Territory
- Inter-racial Crimes Act

Federal criminal jurisdiction stretched further into Indian country through the General Crimes Act, but respected the tribes' inherent jurisdiction over their own people and territories.

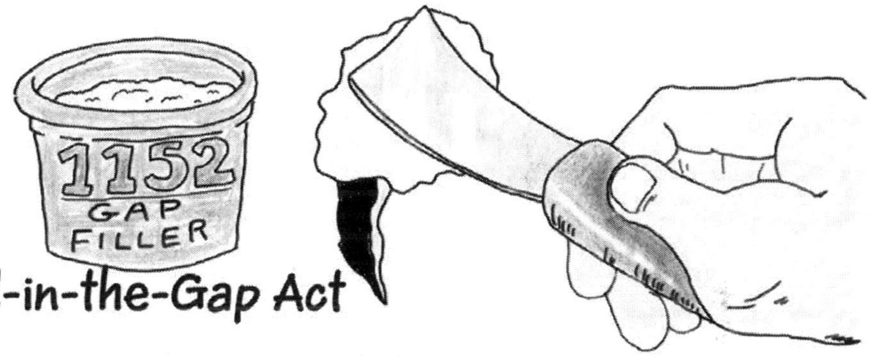

Fill-in-the-Gap Act

The gaps in criminal jurisdiction on federal enclaves increasingly became a larger issue for Congress. Although certain laws had been enacted to deal with crime on lands under the sole and exclusive jurisdiction of the United States, this body of law was still not sufficient. Truth be told, Congress did not want to create a substantially large penal code for federal lands. So this was how a solution was found in the form of a *fill-in-the-gap act.*

In 1825, Daniel Webster, then serving in the House of Representatives, sponsored this fill-in-the-gap act – the *Assimilative Crimes Act (ACA)*. [6] With the ACA in place, crimes would no longer go unpunished because it allowed state criminal laws to *fill in* where no federal criminal law existed for the offense committed.

This was how it worked:

- ► John Doe commits a crime on a federal enclave.
- ► There is no federal enclave law to cover that specific crime.
- ► But, the state where the federal enclave is situated has state law against that action with penalties.
- ► John Doe, under the Assimilative Crimes Act (ACA), is then *federally* prosecuted using the State's penal code.

The Assimilative Crimes Act (ACA) is today codified at 18 USC § 13:

> "Whoever within or upon any of the places now existing or hereafter reserved or acquired as provided in section 7 of this title, or on, above, or below any portion of the territorial sea of the United States not within the jurisdiction of any State, Commonwealth, territory, possession, or district is guilty of any act or omission which, although not made punishable by any enactment of Congress, would be punishable if committed or omitted within the jurisdiction of the State, Territory, Possession, or District in which such place is situated, by the laws thereof in force at the time of such act or omission, shall be guilty of a like offense and subject to a like punishment."

Nerdy Stuff

The original ACA – the Act of March 3, 1825, 4 Stat. 115, varies in the wording, but is the same in essence. We have included the original wording in the Appendix section.
(See Appendix C, p. 364)

Crawls into the Skin

Under the federal statute of the ACA, a state's criminal law is *not* enforced, rather, *federal law crawls into the skin* of state law and is enforced as *federal* law. Pretty tricky, huh? It certainly saved Congress lots of work and also helped the public see that the laws within the federal enclaves were similar to the laws of the state in which they lived. [7] "In essence, then, the ACA is a vehicle that gives US Attorneys the ability to federalize state criminal law." [8] The ACA became applicable to all federal enclaves, which then meant that, because of the Act of Congress eight years earlier, the Act of March 3, 1817 (18 USC §1152), the ACA also applied to Indian territory. [9]

Nerdy Stuff

The concept of incorporating state laws to prosecute crimes on Indian lands was not a totally new concept. The earliest Trade and Intercourse Act with the Indian Tribes used state/district law to determine the crime and punishment of non-Indians who committed crimes against the person or property of an Indian. [10]

Key Point

> **The Assimilative Crimes Act did not give the states jurisdiction on Indian lands, rather, it was federal law crawling into the skin of state law. Federal jurisdiction over Indian territory remained the sole responsibility of the federal government.**

No State Regulation

ACA's legislative history shows that the intention of this law was for the specific purpose of eliminating jurisdictional gaps that had alarmingly opened up the door for crimes to go unpunished. However, this law was never intended to enforce any individual state's laws designed for controlling their state-specific regulations. [11] As we saw earlier in the application of the General Crimes Act (18 USC §1152), Congress applied this law in a *limited* way, recognizing tribal sovereignty. So also, the ACA, as an extension of the General Crimes Act, was to be applied in the same vein.

Key Point

> **The Assimilative Crimes Act (ACA) federally enforced a state's prohibitory (criminal) laws, not state regulatory laws.**

A Trusty Sidekick

The Assimilative Crimes Act only works in conjunction with the federal enclave laws. If there is a federal law in place, there is *no* need for the ACA and it will remain dormant. But, whenever federal law needs its trusty sidekick – the ACA will never disappoint. Able and ready to fill-in-the-gap, the ACA will help get the job done!

Quotes "Q"

"Congress' purpose in enacting the ACA was to fill in the gaps in the criminal law applicable to federal enclaves created by a failure of Congress to pass specific criminal statutes."

US v. Marcyes, 557 F. 2d 1361 (9th Cir. 1977)

It is quite interesting to see the issue of *jurisdictional gaps* come to the surface during this early date in time. As we move closer to the enactment of PL 280, the terminology of jurisdictional gaps will present itself again.

Marshall Trilogy

"trilogy" --
a set or sequence of three related things

During the early years of the United States its newly established "Supreme Court" [12] was growing and evolving as it grappled with issues that required interpretation of the Constitution and US law. The various decisions of the court impacted US policy in many political fields. Early on, in the political arena of Indian law, there were three significant US Supreme Court cases that shaped US policy toward Native Americans. These court cases, referred to as the *Marshall Trilogy*, greatly impacted subsequent court cases – and, in fact, continue to impact court cases and Indian policy today.

The three cases of the Marshall Trilogy span a time period of nine years. The first case was in 1823 and the last case was heard in 1832. These three cases are:

- *Johnson v. M'Intosh*, 21 US 543 (1823)
- *Cherokee Nation v. Georgia*, 30 US 1 (1831)
- *Worcester v. Georgia*, 31 US 515 (1832)

Because of the importance of these cases in reference to US - Indian policy, we will give you a brief overview of each one.

These cases were called the "Marshall Trilogy" because John Marshall was the Chief Justice of the US Supreme Court during all three of these cases. John Marshall served from 1801-1835 and during his tenure the court grew in power and prestige.

Case One of Three:
Johnson v. M'Intosh, 21 US 543 (1823)

Neither of the two individuals this case is named after were Indians, but their case indirectly involved Indians. The issue presented to the court was that William M'Intosh had obtained a land *patent* from the United States for the very same piece of land that Thomas Johnson had purchased from Piankeshaw Indians many years earlier. Johnson's relatives had inherited the land, and were fighting to keep it. Amid lengthy historical facts, Chief Justice Marshall laid out the *Doctrine of Discovery*. It is explained that, because of this doctrine, Johnson's land grant could not be recognized by the court. Johnson, as a private individual, could not legally purchase land from the Indians. Rather, according to the rules of the Doctrine of Discovery, the right to purchase lands from the Indians could only be done by the sovereign who held the right of title through discovery. Since M'Intosh held a government issued land patent, his right to the land was valid and recognized by the court.

Say it Simply!

"patent" -- governmental grant, exclusive right

As previously discussed, the Doctrine of Discovery, along with its rules, was only acknowledged between the European sovereigns themselves. [13] Although the Indian tribes did not adhere to such a doctrine, it "necessarily diminished" their ability to sell their lands to whomever they chose.

Quotes

"[T]he rights of the original inhabitants were in no instance entirely disregarded, but were ***necessarily to a considerable extent impaired****. . . their rights to complete sovereignty as independent nations were* ***necessarily diminished****, and their power to dispose of the soil at their own will to whomsoever they pleased was denied by the original fundamental principle that discovery gave exclusive title to those who made it."*

Johnson v. M'Intosh, 21US 543, 574 (1823)

This case, and many more to follow, paved the way for US policy regarding Native American land holdings: *the federal government holds title to Indian lands, in trust and on behalf of federally recognized tribes*. This Indian land is therefore referred to as "trust land." The following is a current quote from the federal bureau that administers and manages Indian trust land, the Bureau of Indian Affairs (BIA):

Quotes

> *"A federal Indian reservation is an area of land reserved for a tribe or tribes under treaty or other agreement with the United States, executive order, or federal statue or administrative action as permanent tribal homelands, and where the federal government holds title to the land in trust on behalf of the tribe. . . Some reservations are the remnants of a tribe's original land base. Others were created by the federal government for the resettling of Indian people forcibly relocated from their homelands."*
>
> *Dept. of Interior, Bureau of Indian Affairs official website, Frequently Asked Questions at:http://www.bia.gov/FAQs/index.htm*

Due to the nature of *trust lands*, Indian tribal communities have felt the yoke of management in almost every area of their existence. Everything from home ownership to essential utilities on their lands is filtered through governmental bureaucracy. Most communities would find this very frustrating, and Indian communities are no exception. Keep this thought in the back of your mind as, in Chapter Four, we will discuss something called the *Termination Period*. A multitude of things were happening during that time period, but one main issue being addressed by the tribes was their desire to rid themselves of the *over-management* of their affairs.

Key Point

Indian trust lands are lands reserved for the Indian tribes, held in trust by the federal government.

Case Two of Three:
Cherokee Nation v. Georgia, 30 US 1 (1831)

This next US Supreme Court case involved the State of Georgia and the tribal nation of the Cherokees. This Indian nation found themselves in a situation where treaty stipulations and their unique political relationship with the federal government was completely ignored by the state within whose boundaries their reservation resided.

"injunction" -- an order by a court commanding a person or persons to either do a particular action, or refrain from doing a particular action

The Cherokee Nation appealed to the US president to enforce the legal obligations stipulated in the treaties, but found the executive branch unwilling to enforce treaty obligations. When it was clear the president, Andrew Jackson, was unwilling to intervene on behalf of the Cherokees, Daniel Webster and other members of Congress who were sympathetic to treaty violations gave their advice to the Cherokee Nation to file "an *injunction* to restrain the State of Georgia, the Governor, Attorney General, judges, justices of the peace, sheriffs, deputy sheriffs, constables, and other officers, agents, and servants of that State from executing and enforcing the laws of Georgia or any of these laws, or serving process, or doing anything towards the execution or enforcement of those laws, within the Cherokee territory, as designated by treaty between the United States and the Cherokee Nation." [14]

The ancestral lands of the Cherokee fell within the charted limits of the northwest corner of Georgia when King George II made it a British colony.

A Cold Political Climate

In order to understand the dynamics surrounding the *Cherokee Nation v. Georgia* case, it will be helpful to take a quick look at the bigger picture of the state of the Union during that time period. The relationship of the national government, especially with its southern states was, to say the least, politically charged. Questions as to how far the general government of the United States could limit the sovereignty of the individual states of the Union were heatedly questioned. Such questions manifested as challenges in the courtroom of the United States highest court. The rationale that an individual state's sovereignty was superior to the authority of the federal government under the US Constitution had been clearly rejected by the high court in three different cases. [15]

Say it Simply!

"secession" -- withdrawal, move away from

Tremendous political tensions were building like a time bomb waiting to explode. Given this political climate, it was not too surprising that the State of Georgia thumbed their nose at the Cherokee Nation. Georgia and many of the other southern states favored the idea that each state had the right to ignore and make void or null a federal law if they saw fit. They also held the belief that they could discretionarily withdraw themselves from the union of the United States. In light of these facts, if the State of Georgia did not believe the federal government could tell them what to do, well, certainly, neither could an Indian tribe! As we know, eventually, this political time bomb did explode years later – in the form of the American Civil War (1861-1865), where eleven of the thirty-four states broke away from the United States declaring their secession. (Georgia was one of the eleven states.)

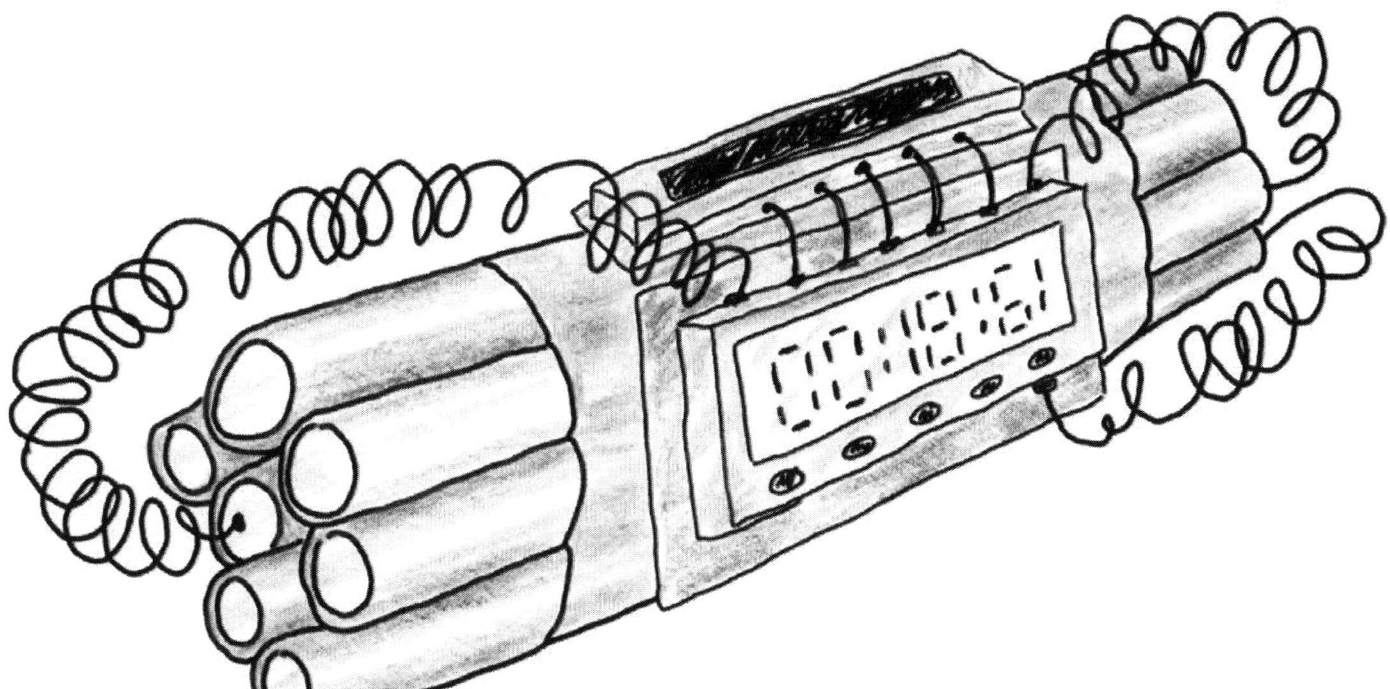

When Chief Justice Marshall began his opinion in *Cherokee Nation v. Georgia*, he started out:

> *"This bill is brought by the Cherokee Nation, praying an injunction to restrain the State of Georgia from the execution of certain laws of that State which, as is alleged, go directly to annihilate the Cherokees as a political society and to seize, for the use of Georgia, the lands of the Nation which have been assured to them by the United States in solemn treaties repeatedly made and still in force."*
>
> *Cherokee Nation v. Georgia, 30 US 1, 15 (1831)*

Instead of this court case serving to uphold the Constitutional authority of the several treaties between the United States and the Cherokees, the majority of the Supreme Court *deflected* the whole issue by focusing on an alleged technicality. Chief Justice Marshall clearly recognized the Cherokee Nation as having "a distinct political society, separated from others, capable of managing its own affairs and governing itself." But the technicality he was hung up on was labeling the Cherokee Nation a "foreign" nation. If the Cherokee could be considered or labeled a *foreign* nation, the high court could hear and rule on their case. If not, the Cherokee were out of luck.

"annihilate" -- destroy, wipe out, make void

"deflected" -- swerved away from, turned aside

The majority of the court decided that Indian tribes did not precisely constitute *foreign* nations. And so it was that the abuses of the State of Georgia were not even addressed. Emboldened with success, the State of Georgia continued their violent actions against the Cherokees – which soon led to yet another case before the Supreme Court. (However, this next case would have quite a different outcome.)

Although the *Cherokee Nation v. Georgia* case was not officially decided upon, there was a new phrase introduced – which Chief Justice Marshall believed was the most accurate description of the status of the Indian nations. This phrase, *"domestic dependent nations,"* was for the first time expressed in this case, and continued to be used from this point on to legally define the status of Indian tribes.

"Though the Indians are acknowledged to have an unquestionable, and heretofore unquestioned right to the lands they occupy, until that right shall be extinguished by a voluntary cession to our government, yet it may well be doubted whether those tribes which reside within the acknowledged boundaries of the United States can, with strict accuracy, be denominated foreign nations. They may, more correctly, perhaps, be denominated ***domestic dependent nations****. They occupy a territory to which we assert a title independent of their will, which must take effect in point of possession when their right of possession ceases. Meanwhile they are in a state of pupilage. Their relation to the United States resembles that of a* ***ward to his guardian****.*

They look to our government for protection; rely upon its kindness and its power; appeal to it for relief to their wants; and address the President as their Great Father. They and their country are considered by foreign nations, as well as by ourselves, as being so completely under the sovereignty and dominion of the United States that any attempt to acquire their lands, or to form a political connexion with them, would be considered by all as an invasion of our territory and an act of hostility."

Cherokee Nation v. Georgia, 30 US 1, 17-18 (1831)

Say it Simply!

"connexion" -- connection, link

Remember King George III's Proclamation of 1763 where he called the British colonists his "loving subjects" under his "paternal care"? Yet, we know the British colonists cast off the paternalism which their government used abusively. How was it that the United States would follow a pattern of paternalism towards the Indian tribes? When the Indians referred to the President as "their Great Father" and did not object to being called "children" either by European governments or the United States, they did not have any thought of relinquishing their internal self-governance and independence. This very fact is clearly stated in the next case we will look at, *Worcester v. Georgia*, where Chief Justice Marshall clarifies his position regarding the political status of the Indian tribes.

Quotes

"Not well acquainted with the exact meaning of words, nor supposing it to be material whether they were called the subjects, or the children of their father in Europe . . . so long as their actual independence was untouched, and their right to self-government acknowledged, they were willing to profess dependence on the power which furnished supplies of which they were in absolute need, and restrained dangerous intruders from entering their country: and this was probably the sense in which the term was understood by them . . . The Indians perceived in this protection only what was beneficial to themselves – an engagement to punish aggressions on them. It involved, practically, no claim to their lands, no dominion over their persons. It merely bound the nation to the British crown, as a dependent ally, claiming the protection of a powerful friend and neighbour, and receiving the advantages of that protection, without involving a surrender of their national character."

Worcester v. Georgia, 31 US 515, 546-547,552 (1832)

Nerdy Stuff

The word *paternal* gives a picture of a father caring affectionately for his child. When the phrase, "a ward to a guardian" is used, this too implies one who is responsible to take good care of another. We discussed the implication of responsible guardianship as we looked at the United States trust relationship with the tribes.

Case Three of Three:
Worcester v. Georgia, 31 US 515 (1832)

Many years prior to this US Supreme Court case, the President of the United States, Thomas Jefferson, wrote to the Secretary of War, identifying that the US government's Indian policy was to respect the right of the Indian's occupation of their lands "independent of the States within whose chartered lines they happen to be." President Jefferson stated the government was "determined to exert all its energy" to protect the "rights of the Indians." [16]

Yet, approximately twenty years after the president's statement of the government's clear policy towards the Indians, *Worcester v. Georgia* was being presented before the US Supreme Court. In this case, not only do you have an Indian tribe desperately struggling for their legal rights, [17] you also have two courageous non-Indians who stood up for their friends, the Cherokee. These two non-Indians, Samuel Worcester and Elizur Butler, were actually arrested by the state of Georgia and sentenced to hard labor in the state penitentiary for four years for their stand against abusive and illegal state actions. Through *Worcester v. Georgia*, the US Supreme Court upheld the sovereignty of the Indian tribes and the supremacy of the treaties over an individual state's law. Chief Justice Marshall declared the actions of the state of Georgia "as being *repugnant* to the constitution, treaties, and the laws of the United States." [18]

Say it Simply!

"repugnant" -- distasteful, foul-smelling

In this case, the US Supreme Court did not sidestep the issue at hand, but rather dealt squarely with abusive state power. But, alas, much damage had been done. After this case was decided, one of the Justices, who had formally disagreed with the majority in the *Cherokee Nation v. Georgia* decision, [19] wrote a letter to his wife. His words expressed relief for the honorable decision of the court, "Thanks be to God, the Court can wash their hands of the iniquity of oppressing the Indians and disregarding their rights." [20]

The Cherokee had won the case decisively, but the State of Georgia, along with a sympathetic US president, paid no attention to the high court's decree. In fact, there is a document dated April 7, 1832, where President Jackson refers to the

Worcester v. Georgia case in a letter to Brigadier General John Coffee. Jackson explained that one influential leader of the Cherokees, Major Ridge, had "expressed despair" because "the decision of the Supreme Court has fell still born, and they find it cannot coerce Georgia to yield to its mandate." Therefore, there was a small delegation of Cherokees who believed the best possible option for the safety and welfare of their nation was to sign a treaty relinquishing their ancestral lands in exchange for other lands far away. President Jackson agreed with their surmise of the situation stating that even if orders to enforce the court's mandate "were issued tomorrow one regiment of militia could not be got to march to save them from destruction and this the opposition know, and if a collision was to take place between them and the Georgians, the arm of the government is not sufficiently strong to preserve them from destruction . . ." [21]

Nerdy Stuff

Samuel Worcester's last name is pronounced differently than one may think. If you are from the east coast you may have heard the name, but for anyone else, it is pronounced [woos-ter].

Dig Deeper

The 1835 treaty signed by only a small delegation of Cherokee was the *Treaty of New Echota*. This treaty was extremely controversial and actually cost these men their lives. The treaty was not negotiated and signed by the majority of the Cherokee and its legality was contested to the very end. Several members of congress strongly opposed this treaty's ratification, however, Congress did ratify it. The final eviction of the Cherokee from their homelands was accomplished by military force. It is estimated that over 4,000 deaths resulted from this removal due to lack of food, water, shoes, clothing and other necessary supplies, along with exposure to severe weather. This removal from the Cherokee and other tribal ancestral homelands to present day Oklahoma is known as the "Trail of Tears." Many good articles and books have been written about their story.

Indian Removal

Contrary to common belief, the Congressional act known as the Indian Removal Act (1830) did *not* authorize the President of the United States to forcibly remove the Indians from their ancestral homelands. The actual title of this act reads: *"An Act to provide for an exchange of lands with the Indians residing in any of the states or territories, and for their removal west of the river Mississippi."* Only those Indian tribes who chose to exchange their lands were to be voluntarily removed. We know from history, though, that this is not exactly how things played out.

During the time of the writing of this book, the official website for the US Department of State, Office of the Historian, has a page called, *"Indian Treaties and the Removal Act of 1830"* where it states:

> "When Andrew Jackson became president (1829–1837), he . . . encouraged Congress to adopt the Removal Act of 1830. The Act established a process whereby the President could grant land west of the Mississippi River to Indian tribes that agreed to give up their homelands. As incentives, the law allowed the Indians financial and material assistance to travel to their new locations and start new lives and guaranteed that the Indians would live on their new property under the protection of the United States Government forever. With the Act in place, Jackson and his followers were free to persuade, bribe, and threaten tribes into signing removal treaties and leaving the Southeast.
>
> In general terms, Jackson's government succeeded. By the end of his presidency, he had signed into law almost seventy removal treaties, the result of which was to move nearly 50,000 eastern Indians to Indian Territory." [22]

Clear Intentions

From the very beginning of his presidency, Andrew Jackson made it clear that he intended to remove the Indian tribes west of the Mississippi River. [23] The Indian Removal Act was passed in Congress only by a narrow margin and in spite of notable opposition by certain members in Congress. New Jersey Senator, Theodore Frelinghuysen, Representative John Test from Indiana, and Edward Everett, Representative from Massachusetts delivered strong arguments against Indian removal. [24] The congressmen's protests were not quick and wimpy speeches before their peers -- they boldly pointed out the injustices they saw. Senator Frelinghuysen asked these pointed questions:

Quotes "Q"

"Do the obligations of justice change with the color of the skin? Is it one of the prerogatives of the white man, that he may disregard the dictates of moral principles, when an Indian shall be concerned?"

Prucha, Paul F., Documents of United States Indian Policy, 1990, University of Nebraska Press p. 50

Humiliating

Say it Simply!

"cumulative" -- formed by or resulting from the addition of successive parts

The year prior to the Indian Removal Act, a series of 24 essays were published in the *National Intelligencer* from August 1829 through December of the same year. The articles were copied in hundreds of newspapers, having extensive circulation. The title of the *cumulative* essays was the "Present Crisis in the Condition of the American Indians." The author, Jeremiah Evarts, wrote under the name of William Penn (in honor of the "upright legislator").

In submitting his papers to the editors, he said he believed the controversy between the United States and the Indians would be the most contested business of the 21st Congress. He explained how literally thousands of Indians could be negatively affected by Congress' decision, yet unfortunately, very few people had clear understanding of the involved issues. Evarts stressed the importance of the treaty contracts as he detailed and discussed the sixteen treaties the US had specifically made with the Cherokee nation. He anticipated the Indian Removal Act would be a vehicle to break treaties with the Cherokee and other Indian tribes. He told his readers that he thought it should be unnecessary to explain that treaty obligations were legally binding: "It is humiliating to be obliged to prove, that parties to a treaty are bound by it." [25]

Dig Deeper

> The entire collection of 24 essays are very insightful and definitely worth reading. See Tracy, E. C., *Memoir of the Life of Jeremiah Evarts*, Crocker and Brewster 1845.

A Status Change

By 1871, the Indian tribes were dealt another blow when Congress passed the *Indian Appropriations Act*. This Act essentially excluded Indian nations from the treaty-making process prescribed in the US Constitution. Congress had no intention of amending the Constitution to eliminate the power to make treaties, but the desired effect of this 1871 law was to cut out a specific group, the Indian tribes, from their ability to make treaties with the United States.

Say it Simply!

"status" -- position, rank, category

As you will remember, treaties had always been the formal way – the only legal way -- of dealing with the Indian nations. Treaties were government-to-government contracts between two sovereign governments, in which over 370 of these legally binding agreements had been negotiated with the tribes by the US federal government. The way Congress was able to eliminate Indian tribes from making future treaties, was to simply change the *status* of Indian nations. The new law stated the US would no longer acknowledge an Indian tribe as being in the category of contracting with the President and the Senate as spelled out in article 2, section 2, clause 2 of the Constitution. [26]

The Indian Appropriations Act reads:

> "No Indian nation or tribe within the territory of the United States shall be acknowledged or recognized as an independent nation, tribe, or power with whom the United States may contract by treaty; but no obligation of any treaty lawfully made and ratified with any such Indian nation or tribe prior to March 3, 1871, shall be hereby invalidated or impaired."
>
> *Codified in 25 USC Section 71 – Future Treaties with Indian Tribes*

Through this law, Congress declared that Indians were no longer recognized as independent nations capable of treaty-making. If the sovereignty of Indian tribes had been based on it being given to them by the US government, this would have been the death of tribal sovereignty. Yet we know that a tribe's sovereignty has not been given to them, but it is inherent and has existed since time immemorial. (See Chapter Two if you need a refresher on tribal sovereignty.)

Say it Simply!

"obliterated" -- demolished, wiped out, eliminated

From March 3, 1871, and onward, Congress said they would deal with Indian tribes through legislation instead of through treaties. Hmmm…. Okay, *so what's the big deal?* At first glance, it really doesn't seem like anything to make a fuss over. But we invite you to take a closer look at this law that, by the stroke of a pen, obliterated the time honored method of dealing with tribes since the earliest American settlement. To understand the significance of this law, we must analyze: *What really is the difference between treaties and legislation?*

Background of the Issue

"The Act of 1871 resulted from the opposition of the House of Representatives to its practical exclusion from any policy role in Indian affairs. For nearly a century, the Executive Branch made treaty arrangements with the Indians 'by and with the Advice and Consent of the Senate,' Art. 2, Sec. 2, Cl. 2. Although the House *appropriated* money to carry out these treaties, it had no voice in the development of substantive Indian policy reflected in them. House resentment first resulted in legislation in 1867 repealing 'all laws allowing the President, the Secretary of the Interior, or the commissioner of Indian affairs to enter into treaties with any Indian tribes,'. . . but was repealed a few months later . . After further unsuccessful House attempts to enter the field of federal Indian policy, the House refused to grant funds to carry out new treaties . . . Finally, the Senate *capitulated* and joined the House in passage of the 1871 Act as a rider to the Indian Appropriation Act of 1871 . . . This meant . . . relations with Indians would be governed by Acts of Congress, and not by treaty."

Antoine v. Washington, 420 US 194, 202-203 (1975)

Say it Simply!

"appropriated" -- set apart, authorize for a specific use

"capitulated" -- yielded, surrendered, gave into

Growing Jealousy

In 1871, there was friction in Congress between the House of Representatives and the Senate regarding the Senate's role in endorsing Indian treaties. When the President authorized a treaty with concurrence from two-thirds of the Senate, in accordance to the US Constitution, the treaty stipulations were to be honored by the whole nation. Many in the House of Representatives did not like this arrangement and there was a "growing jealousy" toward the Senate. [27] They wanted an equal role when it came to Indian policy, especially when it came to anything involving money. The House was involved when it came to setting the money aside to honor the United States' side of the contract, but this was always *after* the fact.

Certainly legislators felt the burden of the financial debt during this time (at the conclusion of the Civil War). In fact, President Grant, in his first Inaugural Address (1869) had made the reduction of the "great debt" a high priority. Yet, the reasoning behind *why* the framers of the Constitution uniquely created the specific arrangement of the executive branch working together with one part of the legislative branch in treaty-making must not be overlooked.

The framers of the US Constitution had very specific reasons for writing Art. 2, Sec. 2, Cl. 2. We can read their strong arguments for this arrangement because they are documented in several of the *Federalist Papers*. [28] Joseph Story, in his Commentaries on the Constitution of the United States (1833), summarized the line of reasoning presented by the Founding Fathers: [29]

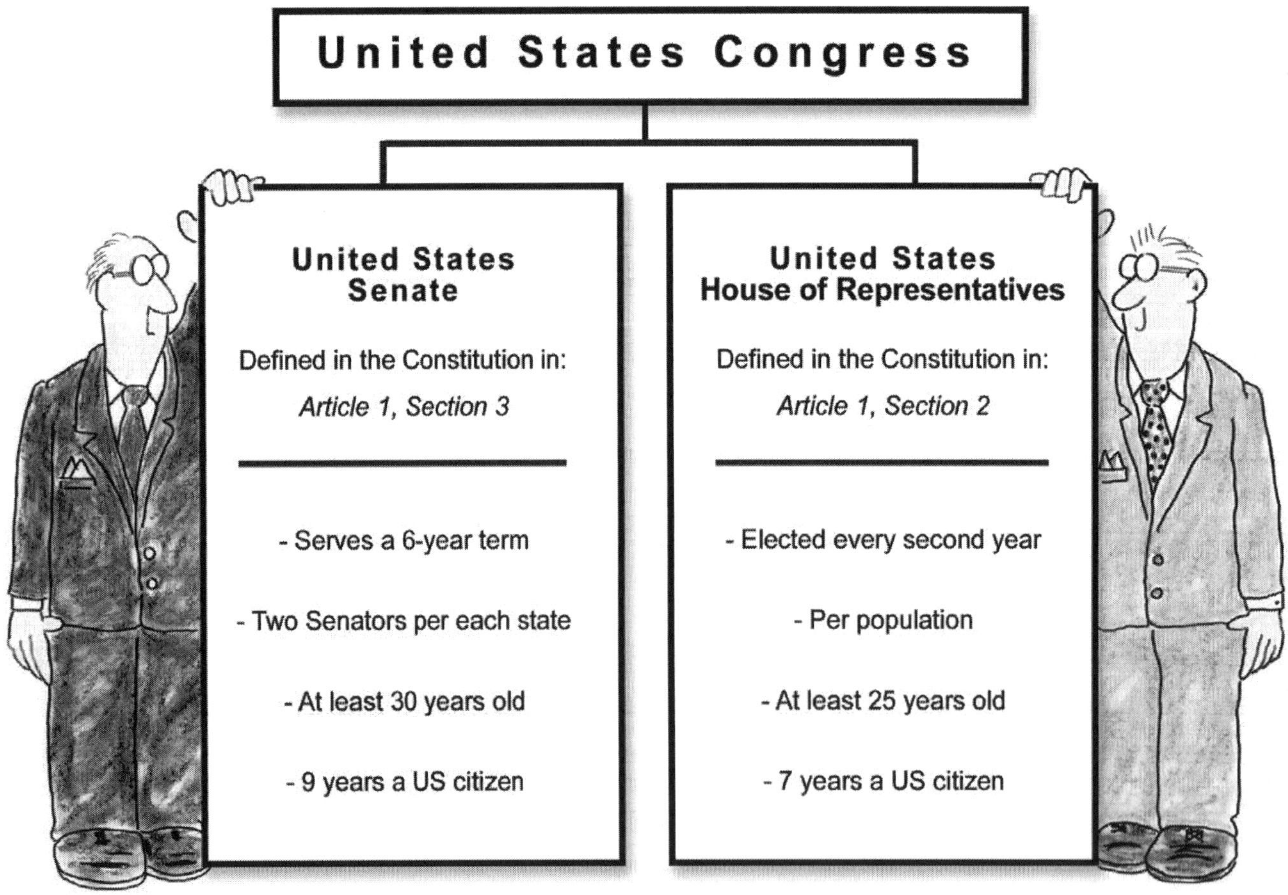

- The President as Commander-in-Chief must have the ability to make treaties for the good of the nation, while having a balance of power, not sole power

- Crucial timing may be lost if the agreement had to be made by the whole of Congress

- The Senate represents all states equally

- A Senator's longer duration of appointment is important for such major contracts

- The older age (maturity) of a Senator is significant

Treaties v. Legislation

Say it Simply!

"precedent" -- standard, model, pattern

With the passing of the 1871 Indian Appropriations Act, Congress changed a legal *precedent* of nearly 100 years. Although this law conveniently relieved tensions between the House and the Senate, this change was extremely significant to the tribal communities. In order to understand why, let's take a look into both treaties and legislation to evaluate the difference between the two.

Treaties – are binding contracts that are only enforceable if parties equally and completely agree to the stipulations. Treaties were signed because they were mutually beneficial and important to each nation. [30]

Quotes "Q"

> *"The treaty agreements, which were struck in solemn councils between official representatives of the negotiating parties, guided formal political relationships in Indian affairs . . . Indeed, the treaties were the only legal means for dealing with Indian tribes during much of the nation's early history."*
>
> *Echo-Hawk, Walter, In the Courts of the Conqueror, Fulcrum Publishing 2010, p. 165*

Legislation – is one-sided, not requiring mutual or specific consent. When legislation is enacted, it becomes *enforceable*.

Say it Simply!

"mutating" -- changing, altering

"metamorphose" -- transform into something else, change

By *mutating* from treaty-making mutual power to one-sided legislative power, Congress essentially gave itself the "power to govern tribes without their consent." [31] It is important to make note that Indians as a whole group did not have the right to vote during this time period. It appeared the representatives of the United States had forgotten so quickly America's fight for life, liberty and the pursuit of happiness, "finding it abhorrent that individuals be forced against their wills to submit to political societies of which they did not approve." [32] Through legislation, Congress could make decisions regarding Indians without having even one Indian's voice heard.

One example, of many, showing this policy *metamorphose* negatively affecting the tribes is in the case of the Colville Indian Reservation. Their story is told in the Washington Supreme Court case of *Antoine v. Washington*, 420 US 194 (1975) . . .

The Colville Indians' original reservation was established on July 2, 1872, by President Grant's Executive Order. The Colville Indian Reservation was located within the boundaries of what later became the State of Washington in 1889. A congressional commission was set up to negotiate an *agreement* (remember no more treaties) with this Indian tribe in 1891. In this agreement, the tribes of the Colville Indian Reservation relinquished the northern half of their reservation in exchange for that which would benefit them. One of the promises in the agreement was that the United States would pay the tribe $1,500,000 in five separate installments.

So far, so good . . . The United States had gained land, and the Indians were promised compensation according to the agreement. After this point, we see legislation (and its negative effect) at work:

- The above mentioned agreement was only to be effective "from and after its approval by Congress."
- Congress approved this agreement through enacting a statute on July 2, 1892.
- The money was not paid and Congress again enacted a statute *14 years later* on June 21, 1906, that authorized the payment of the money promised for the acquired land.

Sixteen lawyers from four different states had to get involved in the Colville claims before things turned favorable for the tribe and some payment was made.

- The money was still not paid and protests were made regarding Congress having "failed to live up to the terms of the Agreement."

- Five more statutes were enacted by Congress: in 1907, 1908, 1909, 1910 and 1911.

One of the protesters against Congress' failure to honor the terms of the Agreement was Mark A. Fullerton. He had been the Chairman of the original committee to negotiate the agreement with the tribe. During Congress' delay in fulfilling the Agreement, Fullerton had become the Chief Justice of the Supreme Court of the State of Washington. He had some powerful things to say to Congress which are documented in the *Antoine v. Washington* court case:

> *"I can not understand why the right of the Indians to this land is not just as sacred as it would have been had it been awarded to them under the most solemn treaty. When they entered upon the reservation they gave up forever land to which they had title as absolute as any band of Indians ever had to any land; and even though the exchange was a forced one, yet exchange it was, and the Government was, under its promise, as I believe, in all honor and right bound to respect it as an exchange and protect the Indians in their title accordingly. Legally, therefore, I can see no difference between the rights of these Indians to compensation for the land taken and the rights of the Puyallup, the Wyakimas, and the Nez Perces to the lands on their reservations which the Government has taken, and which the right to compensation was not even questioned; and, morally, certainly it would be hard to make a distinction.*
>
> *It may be that my relations to this transaction have somewhat warped my judgment, but when I recall the impassioned appeals made by some of the aged members of these remnant bands, calling upon their people and upon the heads of the tribes not to sign away their lands, even though the compensation offered was ample, on the ground that it was their last heritage and their last tie to earth, I can not help a feeling of bitterness when I remember that the Government, whom we represented to them as being just and honorable, took away their land without even the solace of compensation."*
>
> *Antoine v. Washington, 420 US 194 (1975)*

As you can see, with the barrier of mutual consent removed, the way was paved for seemingly endless legislation, far removed from the human element of the people it affected. This major policy change paved the way for various future acts of Congress, such as the Major Crimes Act and the General Allotment Act, that we will soon look at.

Endnotes - Chapter Three, Part 4:

[1] Story, William W., *Life and Letters of Joseph Story: Associate Justice of the Supreme Court of the United States and Dane Professor of Law at Harvard University*, Charles C. Little and James Brown 1851, pp. 293, 297

[2] *United States v. Marcyes*, 557 F. 2d 1361 (9th Cir. 1977) " … federal enclave laws, which congress has applied to Indian territories in a limited manner."

[3] *United States v. Wheeler*, 435 U.S. 313, 324, 325 (1978) "In 1817 federal criminal jurisdiction was extended to crimes committed within the Indian country by 'any Indian, or other person or persons,' but 'any offence committed by one Indian against another, within any Indian boundary' was excluded . . . because 'the tribes have exclusive jurisdiction' of such offenses and 'we can[not] with any justice or propriety extend our laws to' them. H. R. Rep. No. 474, 23d Cong., 1st Sess., 13 (1834)." See also United States v. Quiver, 241 U.S. 602, 604 (1916)

[4] Id. at 325 ". . . in 1854 Congress expressly recognized the jurisdiction of tribal courts when it added another exception to the General Crimes Act, providing that federal courts would not try an Indian 'who has been punished by the local law of the tribe.' Act of Mar. 27, 1854, 3, 10 Stat. 270. 22 Thus, far from depriving Indian tribes of their sovereign power to punish offenses against tribal law by members of a tribe, Congress has repeatedly recognized that power and declined to disturb it."

[5] Id. at 324 "[F]ederal criminal jurisdiction over crimes involving Indians have recognized an Indian tribe's jurisdiction over its members. The first Indian Trade and Intercourse Act, Act of July 22, 1790, 5, 1 Stat. 138, provided only that the Federal Government would punish offenses committed against Indians by 'any citizen or inhabitant of the United States'; it did not mention crimes committed by Indians. In 1817 federal criminal jurisdiction was extended to crimes committed within the Indian country by 'any Indian, or other person or persons,' but 'any offence committed by one Indian against another, within any Indian boundary' was excluded." See also *US v. Marcyes*, 557 F. 2d 1361 (9th Cir. 1977) " … federal enclave laws, which congress has applied to Indian territories in a limited manner." See also US DOJ, Office of Tribal Justice, *Concurrent Tribal Authority Under Public Law 83-280*, November 9, 2000, "The General Crimes Act preserved important components of tribal self-government by providing that crimes between Indians remain with the exclusive jurisdiction of tribal governments and by accepting Indian offenders whom tribal government had tried and punished, ensuring that tribes retained concurrent – indeed pre-emptive – jurisdiction over crimes by Indians."

[6] See *US v. Sharpnack*, 355 US 286, 290 (1958) "In the Act of 1825, sponsored by Daniel Webster in the House of Representatives, Congress expressly adopted the fundamental policy of conformity to local law . . . Congress thereby made it clear that, with the exception of the enlarged list of offenses specifically proscribed by it, the federal offenses in each enclave were to be identical with those proscribed by the State in which the enclave was situated."

[7] See article by Nikhil Bhagat, J.D. Candidate 2011, Columbia Law School, *Filling the Gap? Non-Abrogation Provisions and the Assimilative Crimes Act*, Columbia Law Review, Vol. 111:77, p. 83, footnote 30 "Then-Representative Daniel Webster, the principal author of the measure, noted that in smaller areas which were ceded to the jurisdiction of the United States, rather than creating a comprehensive penal scheme, it was sufficient to 'leave the residue [i.e., those crimes that were not punished by federal law] to be punished by the laws of the state'. . . that 'the people would not view it as any hardship, that the great class of minor offences should continue to be punished in the same manner as they had before the cession.'"

[8] Id. at p. 83

[9] "[T]he ACA is a general law of the United States made applicable to Indian reservations by 18 USC 1152." *US v. Marcyes*, 557 F. 2d 1361 (9th Cir. 1977) *Hopland Band of Pomo Indians v. Norton*, 2004 WL 1529306 (N. D. Cal.) " . . . the federal government through Public Law 280 ceded its authority to enforce certain federal criminal statutes, eg. The Major Crimes Act, General Crimes Act and Assimilative Crimes Act on Indian lands in certain states."

[10] The Trade and Intercourse Act of 1790 authorized the use of the state's laws for "apprehending, imprisoning or bailing the offender." The non-Indian who committed a crime against an Indian was "subject to the same punishment, and shall be proceeded against in the same manner as if the offense had been committed within the jurisdiction of the state or district to which he or they may belong, against a citizen or white inhabitant thereof."

[11] Id. "[T]he ACA only incorporates the general criminal code or prohibitory laws of a state and cannot be utilized to enforce the penal provision of state regulatory laws..."

[12] "The judicial power of the United States, shall be vested in one Supreme Court, and in such inferior courts as the Congress may from time to time ordain and establish." US Constitution, Art. 3, Sec. 1

[13] "The potentates of the old world found no difficulty in convincing themselves that they made ample compensation to the inhabitants of the new by bestowing on them civilization and Christianity in exchange for unlimited independence . . . [I]t was necessary, in order to avoid conflicting settlements and consequent war with each other, to establish a principle which all should acknowledge as law . . . which they all asserted should be regulated as between themselves." *Johnson v. M'Intosh*, 21US 543, 573; See also Echo-Hawk, Walter R., *In the Courts of the Conqueror*, Fulcrum Publishing 2010, p.193, quoting from Desmond M. Tutu, preface in John Witte Jr. and Johan D. van der Vyver (eds.), *Religious Human Rights in Global Perspective* (Boston: Martinus Nuhoff Publishers, 1996), p. ix. Showing the European mindset of the day regarding the lands of the indigenous: "There is a story, which is fairly well known, about when the missionaries came to Africa. They had the Bible and we, the natives, had the land. They said, 'Let us pray,' and we dutifully shut our eyes. When we opened them, why, they now had the land and we had the Bible."

[14] *Cherokee Nation v. Georgia*, 30 US 1, 2 (1831); See Barsh, Russel L. & Henderson, James Youngblood, *The Road*, University of California Press 1980, footnote 8, p. 52

[15] See *Chisholm v. Georgia*, 2 US 419 (1793), *Martin v. Hunter's Lessee*, 14 US 304 (1816), and *McCulloch v. Maryland*, 17 US 316 (1819)

[16] Jackson, Helen Hunt, *A Century of Dishonor*, Dover Publications 2003 (originally published by Harper & Brothers in 1881) Chapt. VIII, pp. 273-274

[17] Address to the People of the United States, by the General Council of the Cherokee Nation, July 1830: "More than a year ago, we were officially given to understand by the Secretary of War, that the President could not protect us against the laws of Georgia. This information was entirely unexpected; as it went upon the principle, that treaties made between the United States and the Cherokee nation have no power to withstand the legislation of separate States; and, of course, that they have no efficacy whatever." Tracy, E. C., *Memoir of the Life of Jeremiah Evarts*, Crocker and Brewster 1845, p. 442; See also *US v. John*, 437 US 634,640,

"In Washington, Congress debated whether the States had power to assert such jurisdiction and whether such assertions were wise. But the only message heard by the Choctaws in Mississippi was that the Federal Government no longer would stand between the States and the Indians."

[18] *Worcester v. Georgia*, 31 US 515, 563 (1832)

[19] Barsh, Russel L. & Henderson, James Youngblood, *The Road*, University of California Press 1980, p. 56 "Justice Thompson wrote a vigorous dissent, in which Joseph Story concurred."

[20] *US v. Forness*, 125 F. Supp 928, 941-942 (2nd Cir. 1942) quoting C. Warren, The Supreme Court in United States History (2d ed. 1926) 756. "It is of interest that, after the decision in *Worcester v. Georgia* was rendered, Mr. Justice Story wrote to his wife, on March 4, 1832, "Thanks be to God, the Court can wash their hands of the iniquity of oppressing the Indians and disregarding their rights."

[21] Andrew Jackson to Brig. Gen. John Coffee, 7 April 1832, in John S. Bassett, ed., Correspondence of Andrew Jackson vol. 4 (Washington: Carnegie Institute, 1929), 429-430 "The Cherokee delegation are still here, and it is now believed before they leave here will propose to treat with us for their intire (entire) removal. The decision of the supreme court has fell still born, and they find it cannot coerce Georgia to yield to its mandate, and I believe Ridge has expressed despair, and that it is better for them to treat and move. In this he is right, for if orders were issued tomorrow one regiment of militia could not be got to march to save them from destruction and this the opposition know, and if a collision was to take place between them and the Georgians, the arm of the government is not sufficiently strong to preserve them from destruction . . ."

[22] Official website for the US Department of State, Office of the Historian, Indian Treaties and the Removal Act of 1830 found at: *http://history.state.gov/milestones/1830-1860/IndianTreaties*

[23] *US v. John*, 437 US 634,640 "In his first annual address to Congress on December 8, 1829, President Jackson made known his position on the Indian question and his support of immediate removal. S.Doc. No. 1, 21st Cong., 1st Sess., 116 (1829)

[24] Jackson, Helen Hunt, *A Century of Dishonor*, Dover Publications 2003 (originally published by Harper & Brothers in 1881) Chapt. VIII, p. 277, "And their cause was not without eloquent advocates. When the bill for their removal was before Congress, Frelinghuysen, Sprague, Robbins, Storrs, Ellsworth, Evans, Huntington, Johns, Bates, Crockett, Everett, Test – all spoke warmly against it."

[25] Tracy, E. C., *Memoir of the Life of Jeremiah Evarts*, Crocker and Brewster 1845, "Address to the People of the United States, by the General Council of the Cherokee Nation, July 1830," p. 443

[26] "The President . . . shall have power, by and with the advice and consent of the Senate, to make treaties." US Constitution, Art. 2, Sec. 2, Cl. 2

[27] *Antoine v. Washington*, 420 US 194, 202 (1975)

[28] Federalist Papers #64 – authored by John Jay; and #75 – authored by Alexander Hamilton, both discuss the power to the President "by and with the advice and consent of the Senate, to make treaties, provided two thirds of the senators present concur."

[29] Joseph Story, *Commentaries on the Constitution of the US (1833)*, Chapter 37: Executive Powers and Duties, pg 663

[30] Barsh, Russel L. & Henderson, James Youngblood, *The Road*, University of California Press 1980, p. 69; See also Echo-Hawk, Walter R., *In the Courts of the Conqueror*, Fulcrum Publishing 2010, p. 165

[31] Barsh, Russel L. & Henderson, James Youngblood, *The Road*, University of California Press 1980, p. 69

[32] Id. at 71

Chapter Three ~ Part 5

This chapter will cover:

- *Non-Indian v. Non-Indian Crime*
- *Major Crimes Act*
- *General Allotment Act*

Chapter Three - Part 5

Evolution of Jurisdiction in Indian Country

Rose-colored Glasses

A tremendous influx of the western frontier settlement occurred during the 1880's, as Congress created new legislation to legalize the taking of land and resources from the Indians. The philosophy of assimilation served as the *rose-colored glasses* legislators looked through as they determined Indian policy. It seemed apparent that all government administrative actions could be justified if, in the end result, it brought the Indian closer to being "civilized."

"philosophy of assimilation" - There was government policy based on the belief and expectation that Indians become identical, or similar to the European culture, (conform into another's way - assumed to be the superior - or "civilized" way.)

"The decade of the 1880's was marked by the rapid settlement and development of the West. As an incident to this process, legislation providing for acquisition of lands and resources from the Indians was demanded. Ethical justification for this was found in the theory of assimilation. If the Indian would only adopt the habits of civilized life he would not need so much land, and the surplus would be available for white settlers. The process of allotment and civilization was deemed as important for Indian welfare as for the welfare of non-Indians."

Cohen, Felix S., Handbook of Federal Indian Law, Washington, United States Government Printing Office, 1945, p.78

Say it Simply!

"conducive" -- favorable towards, tends to produce

"morals" -- principles or beliefs with respect to right and wrong conduct

"epitome" -- perfect example

"condoned" -- approved, supported, sanctioned

By the end of the 1880's, all Indian tribes were located on assigned reservations or in isolated areas. The last of the Indians to be corralled, the band of Chiricahua Apaches, took place on September 8, 1886. The reservations were under the administration and oversight of non-Indian agents of the Indian Office. The reservation system was *conducive* to the implementation of the assimilation policy (i.e. forced religion, boarding schools, break down of cultural norms and traditional social *morals*.) [1]

Indian Off-Reservation Boarding Schools

The *epitome* of the Assimilation Policy was seen through the government *condoned* off-reservation boarding schools. The individual who chiefly conceived the idea of these boarding schools, Richard Pratt, stated that by removing children from their culture and educating them in "civilized" ways, he could "kill the Indian and save the man." Indian children were often taken far away from their parents and familiar settings and placed into strict military-style boarding schools. The children's hair was cut short, uniforms replaced their traditional clothes, and speaking in their native tongue would invite painful discipline from the school's staff. A successful student would be an Indian child who conformed as closely as possible to a white child.

There are many good books available dedicated to the history of the Indian boarding schools. Here are a few to get you started:

- Trafzer, Clifford E., Jean A. Keller and Lorene Sisquoc, *Boarding School Blues*, University of Nebraska Press 2006
- Adams, David Wallace, *Education for Extinction*, University Press of Kansas 1995
- Child, Brenda J., *Boarding School Seasons*, University of Nebraska Press 2006

The Missing Scenario

As we have discussed so far regarding criminal jurisdiction *within Indian country*, a tribe's internal criminal issues were always handled by the tribe and fell under their jurisdiction:

Indian v. Indian crime on Indian land = tribal jurisdiction

Also, beginning in 1790, inter-racial crime was federally addressed:

- ▶ Non-Indian v. Indian, or
- ▶ Indian v. Non-Indian, on Indian land = federal jurisdiction *(except for treaty stipulations or in the case where an Indian was already punished through tribal court)*

So, the missing scenario that we haven't discussed yet is:

Non-Indian v. Non-Indian crime on Indian land

Who had jurisdiction for crimes in Indian country *not* involving or injuring the person or property of an Indian?

Say it Simply!

"nexus" -- connection, link

This question was answered in 1882 through a court case, *US v. McBratney*, 104 US 621 (1182), involving a white man who was murdered by another white man on an Indian reservation. It was determined the state would have "criminal jurisdiction over its own citizens and other white persons" for crimes committed within the boundaries of a reservation. The only exception to this would be if the federal government had a specific interest or *nexus* involved in the case. [2]

Quotes "Q"

> *". . . the Court has consistently and clearly held that federal jurisdiction over crimes in Indian country is contingent upon the existence of either an Indian victim or perpetrator. This rule was first articulated in United States v. McBratney . . . Absent a specific treaty provision . . . the United States stipulating for 'the punishment of offences committed by white men against white men' the federal courts lacked jurisdiction to punish such crimes within the reservation."*
>
> *United States v. Langford, 641 F.3d 1195 (10th Cir. 2011)*

Therefore, it was established that crimes in Indian country which do not involve an Indian(s), or their property, fall under state jurisdiction. "Not all crimes committed within Indian country are subject to federal or tribal jurisdiction . . . [u]nder *McBratney*, a non-Indian charged with committing crimes against other non-Indians in Indian country is subject to prosecution under state law." [3]

This is why, as a general rule, *victimless crimes* also fall under state jurisdiction. [4] Using the same rationale as McBratney, if an Indian is not directly involved or injured, the state retains jurisdiction over their citizens.

"victimless crimes" --
crimes not specifically directed at violating or threatening the rights of another person or persons. Rather they are crimes against the general public and go against societal morals and values. (e.g. individual drug use, illegal gambling, prostitution, vagrancy, speeding, public drunkenness, etc.)

Early Treaties

You may be surprised to know that some of the early treaties included provisions for Indian tribes to address the issue of non-Indians committing offenses against them, by making non-Indian offenders subject to tribal punishment. [5] Felix Cohen in his *Handbook of Federal Indian Law* explains the scope of tribal criminal jurisdiction reflected in the early US and Indian treaties:

> *"Many treaties deal with the difficult political problems created by offenses of Indians against whites or whites against Indians. Some of the earliest treaties adopt the rule usual in treaties between equals. Whites committing offenses within the Indian country against Indian laws are subjected to punishment by the Indian tribe, just as Indians committing offenses against state or federal laws outside the Indian country are subjected to punishment by the state or federal courts."*
>
> *Felix S. Cohen, Handbook of Federal Indian Law, Washington, United States Government Printing Office, 1945, p. 45*

Later, the United States negotiated with the Indian tribes for a grant of jurisdiction over their US citizens who committed offenses while on tribal lands. This was consistent with the way the United States negotiated treaties with the non-European foreign nations. During the 1800's the US was involved in foreign commercial trade, establishing government-to-government working relationships via treaties with the various non-European foreign countries. Again, Felix Cohen discusses the nature of how the Indian treaties evolved with the US:

> *"A number of treaties adopt a modified rule, similar to that found in treaties between the United States and various Oriental nations, whereby the United States is granted jurisdiction over its citizens in the Indian country, to punish them for offenses they may commit, and the Indian tribe undertakes to deliver such offenders to agents of the Federal Government."*
>
> *Felix S. Cohen, Handbook of Federal Indian Law, Washington, United States Government Printing Office, 1945, p. 45*

A Matter of Perspective

Say it Simply!

"conversely" -- on the other hand, on the flip side

US treaties frequently used terms "non-Christian, barbarous/semi-civilized" when describing the judicial systems of the non-European foreign countries. Apparently, this was a matter of perspective between the involved countries because, *conversely*, the foreign nations also, with the exception of the term "non-Christian," used similar terms when referring to the judicial system of the western nations. [6] These foreign treaties included sections that guarded United States citizens from foreign and unfamiliar jurisdiction by specifying that US citizens, who were accused of crimes while in foreign lands, would present their case before US consular officers. [7]

Without a treaty to spell out criminal jurisdiction, a US civilian citizen on foreign soil would be subject to the jurisdiction of the foreign nation where the crime was committed. [8] Along with treaty stipulations, the Revised Statutes of the United States (the forerunner to the United States Code) included statutes authorizing American consuls to try American citizens charged with committing crimes in certain "non-Christian" countries.

Alien Jurisdiction

Just as the United States viewed the non-European justice systems as foreign, so also the tribal nations' justice systems were seen as alien – even characterized by a "want of fixed laws (and) of competent tribunals of justice." [9] Indeed, the tribal justice systems were very *different* than the European format, and could only be fully understood through knowledge of tribal history, norms and culture. Again, though, it's a matter of perspective. The European justice system was also foreign to the Indians, who were "a community separated by race, (and) by tradition." The criminal justice system of America was an "unknown code" [10] which required comprehension of European history, norms and culture in order to understand it.

Recognizing Sovereignty

Although some legislators remarked about the "rude fashion" of the tribal justice systems, the United States, recognizing tribal sovereignty (the tribe's jurisdiction over their own people and territories) did not interfere with these systems. [11] On the other hand, the United States generally guarded against any foreign jurisdiction over its citizens, especially, as noted earlier, when it came to the jurisdiction of nations in the category of "non-Christian" nations.

Say it Simply!

"vignettes" -- small illustrations

A New Frontier

Let's take a few minutes to look at the following excerpts from historical documents and accounts about a group of people who were labeled *"barbarians."* These barbaric tribal nations were part of the new frontier that civilization was now entering. As the *civilized* interacted with this yet unknown world, they would sometimes document their observations. For the most part, the people of this new world were seen as savage, rude and inferior. Read the small *vignettes* of documented history below. As you do, try to envision how this uncertain frontier, filled with *barbarians*, was seen through the eyes of the *civilized world* . . .

". . . the valleys and forests echoed with their **savage** shoutings and jubilant chants."

"Living in **astonishing barbarism** and disgusting misery, eating wild plants, wearing skins and sleeping on the ground . . . **men's faces but beasts' bodies**. . ."

". . . **so wild and backward** that they have nothing in common with us but voice and limbs."

". . . **wild** to look at, **terrifyingly** noisy, coarse and boorish of speech."

". . . **barbarian** world in which all had learned to be warriors from childhood."

". . . **incapable of rational thought** and ready to dash into danger, however hopeless."

". . . **wild** of eye . . ."

"Their manner of living is so **rude and savage**."

These barbarians were generally viewed as treacherous, dishonest, lethargic and untrustworthy. When portrayed in artwork they were obviously the wild and dangerous sort, with scowling looks and long matted hair. They were believed to be on a low moral plane, with beast-like instincts. On the other hand, those of the superior, civilized race were illustrated as ones with whom divine providence had bestowed the earth's fairest portion in courage, intelligence and farsightedness.

Historical documentation tells how the civilized race traded metalwork and household goods with these barbaric savages for skins. As the civilized interacted with the barbarians, it was interestingly noted, "women were respected . . . chiefs were elected . . . tribal decisions were collectively reached . . . military service was governed not by compulsion but by honor . . . and they had a form of democracy." Another account tells of the tribal government of these people: "Their kings have not an absolute or unlimited power; and their generals command less through the force of authority, than of example. If they are daring, adventurous, and conspicuous in action, they procure obedience from the admiration they inspire."

One historian documented how certain barbarian tribes liked to drink in excess, which was sometimes taken advantage of and used to exploit them to alter their decision-making. It was noted: "Their foods are simple: wild fruits, fresh game and sour milk. Though moderate in eating, drinking is quite another matter. Ply them with booze and you may win them more easily than by fighting them."

You may be thinking these observations and quotes are referring to the Europeans who came to the New World.

However . . . ***None*** of these accounts and descriptions had to do with the Europeans' view of the indigenous of the Americas.

So, *who* were these *barbarians*? It may surprise you that all of these accounts were written by ancient Roman historians about the people they encountered in their new and unknown frontier. These *barbaric* tribal people were actually those who generally resided in areas we know today as Western Europe and the British Isles. [12]

Interesting, huh? You may even want to read the quotes again with this in mind . . .

We would venture to guess that many reading this book can trace your heritage from these very people, and – perhaps, will look at the word *"barbarian"* a little bit different from this point on!

Uncertain Justice

The US Constitution's first ten amendments (called the *Bill of Rights*) were put in place to ensure very specific rights for every United States citizen. One such right is found in the 6th Amendment:

> *"In all criminal prosecutions, the accused shall enjoy the right to a speedy and public trial, by an impartial jury . . ."*

This was a protection early American citizens wanted to make utterly *bullet-proof*, especially in light of the not-so-distant experiences with a *tyrannical* government where vindictive prosecutions were common. [13] *Embedding* the right of trial by jury into the US Constitution served as a safeguard for that right, making it impossible for the government to violate it without violating the law of the land. [14]

Say it Simply!

"tyrannical" -- domineering, unjustly cruel and harsh, oppressive

"embedding" -- fixed firmly and deeply in surrounding solid mass, cemented in

When US citizens looked at foreign justice systems, there was uncertainty and anxiety regarding the unfamiliar procedures. An 1880 book, *Philosophy of Criminal Law*, while discussing the need for US jurisdiction outside the boundaries of the United States, stated there are "countries of such imperfect civilization, penal justice is uncertain." [15] Also, around the mid 1800's, congressional records show that some legislators voiced concerns, from their perspectives, about the Indian tribal justice systems as seen in the quote below:

Quotes

"Q"

> *"It will be seen that we cannot, consistently with the provisions of some (of) our treaties, and of the territorial act, extend our criminal laws to offences committed by or against Indians, of which the tribes have exclusive jurisdiction; and it is rather of courtesy than of right that we undertake to punish crimes committed in that territory by and against our own citizens. And this provision is retained principally on the ground that* ***it may be unsafe to trust to Indian law in the early stages of their Government****. It is not perceived that we can with any justice or propriety extend our laws to offences committed by Indians against Indians, at any place within their own limits."*
>
> *H.R. Rep. No. 474, 23d Cong., 1st Sess. 13 (1834)*

A tribe's internal system of dispensing justice generally received little attention from non-Indians. After all, it was the business of the tribe how things were handled amongst themselves. It didn't matter to anyone else – because it really didn't affect anyone else.

At least this was the feeling until the infamous case of *Spotted Tail.*

Spotted Who?

Spotted Tail was a Brule Sioux war chief. He had earned this distinction by his bravery during an attack against his people by another Indian tribe. Spotted Tail's quick and decisive action during that attack made the enemy retreat. He also fought strongly with his people against the encroachment of their lands, believing "it was unwise to allow the white man so much freedom" in their country. [16] His fears about allowing the white man too much access into Indian territory were confirmed when a treaty made in 1851 was quickly broken. The thousands of Indians, representing many different tribal groups who had assembled for the signing of this peace treaty, understood they were agreeing to give safe passage through their lands. However, they never agreed to non-Indian settlements within their territory or the killing of thousands of highly valued bison by trappers. Spotted Tail, along with the other leaders of the tribe, fought against the US army over these lands.

Spotted Tail appeared quite determined to stand his ground against the white man, yet, only seventeen years later, he was involved in negotiating a new treaty for peace (the 1868 Fort Laramie Treaty). This treaty gave away Sioux land, but secured the Great Sioux Reservation, which included the sacred land of the Black Hills.

What had happened to change Spotted Tail's perspective?

A Captive Audience

A major event occurred in Spotted Tail's life to change his view on how to effectively relate to the white man. During a conflict between the Sioux and the United States military, Spotted Tail voluntarily surrendered himself to General Harney in order to protect his people from harm. His brave actions won him "the admiration of his own people" and "the confidence and respect of the military." [17] As a prisoner he was moved to an area of the country where he witnessed first-hand the immense population of the whites. Seeing this reality with his own eyes impressed on him the enormity of his enemy. Carefully he watched and learned as much as he could about the white man's ways.

He was eventually released from prison and he returned to his people. Spotted Tail acted as a type of liaison between the military and his people. "He was in constant communication with the military; but the other chiefs did not understand his views and seemed to have been suspicious of his motives." [18] Spotted Tail believed he was doing what was in the best interests of the tribe. His peers were not so sure, calling him "the white man's friend." [19] One US Indian agent said Spotted Tail was "a great leader in spite of the fact that he was rather inclined to treat diplomatically with the whites than to take the warpath." [20]

The peace treaty Spotted Tail helped negotiate, the 1868 Fort Laramie Treaty, was broken when gold was found in the Black Hills in 1874. The US government took back this land and in 1875 ordered the Sioux onto reservations. If the Indians refused, they were considered hostile. This was the case with Crazy Horse, who fought desperately against those he perceived as invaders of his country. Spotted Tail helped negotiate Crazy Horse's eventual surrender. Before Crazy Horse surrendered, he "rebuked Spotted Tail for signing away the freedom of his people," considering him as a "traitor." [21]

"I'm No Spotted Tail"

Oglala Sioux Chief, Red Cloud, fought against the relinquishing of Sioux land that was supposed to be protected by treaty. He vigorously resisted being funneled onto small plots of land known as reservations. He asked, "Shall we permit ourselves to be driven to and fro – to be herded like the cattle of the white man?" [22] He said he had "listened patiently to the promises of the Great Father, but his memory is short." Therefore, he concluded, "I am now done with him." [23]

Red Cloud was angered by Chief Spotted Tail's submission to the demands for more and more of their lands. He labeled Spotted Tail *"the Beggars' Chief"* because he had allowed himself to be enticed by the white man's riches instead of fighting for the cause of his people. [24] On June 16, 1870, Red Cloud gave a speech before a large audience at the Cooper Union Institute in New York City.

The following is a small part of his speech:

> "When I reached Washington the Great Father explained to me what the treaty was, and showed me that the interpreters had deceived me. All I want is right and justice. I have tried to get from the Great Father what is right and just. I have not altogether succeeded. I want you to help me to get what is right and just. I represent the whole Sioux nation, and they will be bound by what I say. *I am no Spotted Tail*, to say one thing one day and be bought for a pin the next. Look at me. I am poor and naked, but I am the Chief of the nation. We do not want riches, but we want to train our children right. Riches would do us no good. We could not take them with us to the other world. We do not want riches, we want peace and love."

Blaisdell, Bob, *Great Speeches by Native Americans*,
Dover Publications, Inc. 2000, p.132 quoting the New York Times, June 17, 1870

Not by the Will of the Tribe

When the US military had subdued all the hostiles of the Sioux, the military leaders named Spotted Tail as Chief of the Sioux. Culturally, this was a great humiliation to the Sioux leadership and an inappropriate way of designating a chief. However, Spotted Tail became haughty and conceited because of this appointment and his attitude of negotiation turned to manipulation and self-preservation. [25]

Because of this, he was scorned by many, but especially by one named *Crow Dog* who "more than once taunted Spotted Tail with the fact that he was chief not *by the will of the tribe*, but by the help of the white soldiers." [26] It was this very individual who on August 5, 1881, shot and killed Spotted Tail on the day before his trip to Washington, D.C. Many believed Spotted Tail's purpose for that trip was to sign away more of their tribal lands.

Business as Usual

As the tribe always did, they dealt with their internal matters amongst themselves. The killing of Spotted Tail was taken care of according the tribe's culture and tradition. However, because of the importance of Spotted Tail's position to certain non-Indian leaders, they were now paying attention to an Indian v. Indian crime. This interest and awareness was out of the ordinary. Even the local press reported on the situation, providing details that Crow Dog's restitution to Spotted Tail's family was in the form of eight horses, one blanket and $600. A US Indian agent familiar with the circumstances explained, "Crow Dog went into hiding until his friends had made compensation to the family of Spotted Tail for his murder. The adjustment was made according to tribal custom, *the affair was settled so far as the Indians were concerned*; but Spotted Tail was of too much importance for the authorities to permit his assassin to go unpunished." [27]

Things were apparently settled with the Indian community – but *not* with the non-Indians. Spotted Tail was the only one among the great Indian chiefs "to be remembered with more honor by the white man, perhaps, than by his own people." [28] His death would become the *pivotal point* for greatly expanded federal jurisdiction in Indian country.

Say it Simply!

"pivotal point" -- the place where something moves from or rotates around

"ex parte" -- legal term for one side only, without the other party present

Scrambling for Justice

The acting US Indian agent for the region ordered the arrest of Crow Dog a few days after the incident. Before a jury trial in Deadwood, South Dakota, Crow Dog was found guilty for the murder of Spotted Tail. He was sentenced to death by hanging. Yet, through some twists and turns of events, Crow Dog's case was appealed and eventually heard before the US Supreme Court in the 1883 case, *Ex Parte Crow Dog*.

In this case, the United States high court concluded that the lower court had absolutely *no jurisdiction* to hear the case because the jurisdiction of Indian v. Indian crime was exclusively that of the tribe:

> *"[O]ur government has always recognized as exempt from our laws, whether within or without the limits of an organized state or territory, and, in regard to their (Indian's) domestic government, left to their own rules and traditions."*
>
> *Ex Parte Crow Dog, 109 US 556,572 (1883)*

The US Supreme Court made the clear determination that Crow Dog was to be released because his conviction and sentencing were heard in a court without jurisdiction and his subsequent imprisonment was illegal. "The Court reasoned that, in the absence of *explicit* congressional direction, the Indian tribe retained exclusive jurisdiction to punish the offense." [29]

Say it Simply!

"exempt" -- free from an obligation others are subject to

"explicit" -- precise, exact, specific and clear

This Can't Be!

Many in Congress were shocked by the decision of the US Supreme Court. One congressman, Representative Cutcheon, expressed his disbelief and indignation by saying,

> *"Crow Dog went free. He returned to his reservation, feeling . . . a great deal more important than any of the chiefs of his tribe . . . If . . . an Indian commits a crime against an Indian on an Indian reservation, there is now no law to punish the offense except, as I have said, the law of the tribe, which is just no law at all."*
>
> *Keeble v. US, 412 US 205, 210, 211 (1973); Representative Cutcheon sponsored the Major Crimes Act*

The feeling in Congress was strong as they moved toward enacting a law that would give them jurisdiction in Indian country when serious crimes occurred between Indians. In 1885, the Major Crimes Act became law in response to the *Ex Parte Crow Dog* decision:

> *"That immediately upon and after the date of the passage of this act, all Indians committing against the person or property of another Indian or other person any of the following crimes, namely, murder, manslaughter, rape, assault with intent to kill, arson, burglary, and larceny, be subject therefore to the laws of said territory relating to said crimes, and shall be tried therefore in the same courts, and in the same manner, and shall be subject to the same penalties, as are all other persons charged with the commission of the said crimes respectively; and said courts are hereby given jurisdiction in all such cases; and all such Indians committing any of the above-described crimes against the person or property of another Indian or other person, within the boundaries of any State of the United States, and within the limits of any Indian reservation, shall be subject to the same laws, tried in the same courts, and in the same manner, and subject to the same penalties, as are all other persons committing any of the above crimes within the exclusive jurisdiction of the United States."*
>
> *The Original Major Crimes Act (Act of March 3, 1885)*
> *See US v. Kaagma, 118 US 375, 376, 377 (1886);*
> *The Major Crimes Act is now codified at 18 USC 1153.*

Worst Class of Crimes

Congress wanted the same jurisdiction over serious crimes in Indian country as they had over all areas of exclusive federal jurisdiction (federal enclaves). They wanted no restrictions in dealing with major crimes involving Indians. Congress' decision to enact the Major Crimes Act revealed their view of tribal law not being "competent to deal with serious issues of crime and punishment." [30] Therefore, through this congressional act, the "worst class of crimes known to civilized life" [31] were now under US territorial and federal jurisdiction. Nothing in this law eliminated the concurrent jurisdiction of the tribe as a separate sovereign, yet it added, for the very first time, federal cross-jurisdiction into Indian territory over certain Indian v. Indian crimes.

The Major Crimes Act of 1885 introduced, for the very first time, federal jurisdiction over Indian v. Indian crimes. Jurisdiction was limited to only those crimes listed in the Act.

Competent or Not?

In order to touch on the question of whether tribal law was *competent* to deal with serious issues of crime and punishment, we will take some liberty here to break out of the time period we have been discussing and zoom ahead – just a bit– about fifty years or so, to the year 1934. This year introduced what became known as the *Indian Reorganization*. We will explain more on Indian Reorganization later, but what we want to emphasize at this point is that during this time, many tribes developed *written* tribal justice codes for their jurisdictions.

Also during this time period, the legal manual *Handbook of Federal Indian Law* was written and published by the US Department of the Interior, Office of the Solicitor, outlining and clarifying US law and policy involving Native Americans. In the section of this handbook entitled *"Tribal Powers in the Administration of Justice"* it reads (see next page):

Quotes "Q"

"Today the administration of law and order is being taken over as a local responsibility by most of the tribes . . . (they) have adopted constitutions for self-government . . . the Indian tribes have done an admirable job of maintaining law and order, whenever they have been permitted to function."

Cohen, Felix S., Handbook of Federal Indian Law, Washington, United States Government Printing Office, 1945, p. 149

The author of this manual continued in this section to make some very interesting comparisons between tribal penal codes and state penal codes. He pointed out that the main differences he observed were:

- *In the quantity* – Tribal codes generally had between 40 to 50 listed offenses, compared to state penal codes having generally 800 to 2,000 listed offenses.
- *Maximum punishment* – Tribal punishment seldom exceeded six months imprisonment, compared to a state punishment for something such as kidnapping possibly having a 20-year sentence.
- *Large discretion* – Tribal courts were given the ability to adjust the penalty after looking closely at the circumstances involved in the offense and the offender.
- *Typical punishment* – Tribal communities preferred punishment in the form of forced labor for the benefit of the tribe or the victim, rather than imprisonment.
- *No "catch all" crimes* – Tribal offenses did not include crimes with "catch all" provisions, such as vagrancy, where "almost any unpopular individual may be convicted of crime."
- *Put in the hands of members* – Tribal penal codes were widely read and discussed amongst their tribal community, which rarely was the case with state penal codes.

Say it Simply!

"vagrancy" -- wandering from place to place without a permanent home or place of employment

> *"On the basis of this comparison it seems fair to say that the confidence which the US Court indicated in the Crow Dog case, in the ability of Indian tribes to master 'the highest and best of all – the arts of civilized life – that of self-government – the maintenance of order and peace among their own members by administration of their own laws and customs' has been amply justified in the half century that has passed since the case was heard."*
>
> *Cohen, Felix S., Handbook of Federal Indian Law, Washington, United States Government Printing Office, 1945, p. 149*

Proof in the Pudding

The differences between the tribal and non-tribal European judicial processes were between what was viewed as *formal* versus *informal*. The 1978 court case, *Oliphant v. Suquamish Indian Tribe* explains it this way:

> *"Until the middle of this century, few Indian tribes maintained any semblance of a **formal** court system. Offenses by one Indian against another were usually handled by social and religious pressure and not by formal judicial processes; emphasis on restitution rather than on punishment."*
>
> *Oliphant v. Suquamish Indian Tribe, 435 US 191, 197 (1978)*

Clearly, we see there were major differences in the two justice systems. Yet, to say one judicial process was less formal, certainly does not mean it was an inferior or a less effective process. The important question to ask is, *"How well did the laws and justice system work?"* Or, as the saying goes, "The proof is in the pudding."

One source indicates informal tribal law (based on social pressure) was extremely effective . . .

Quotes "Q"

"I have found my way into and through 120 different tribes, in North, South, and Central Americas, and the reader who has got thus far in the book, will easily imagine that my life and my property have been, much of the time, at their (Indians) mercy; and will here learn that, not only have I found it unnecessary ever to raise my hand against one of them, but that they have everywhere treated me with hospitality and kindness; and nowhere, to my knowledge, stolen a six-pence worth of my property, though in their countries there is universal poverty to stimulate to crime, and no law to punish for theft, and where travelers carry no trunks with locks and keys!"

Catlin, George, Last rambles amongst the Indians of the Rocky Mountains and the Andes, Sampson Low, Son, and Marston 1868 (digitized from public domain by BiblioLife, LLC) p. 345

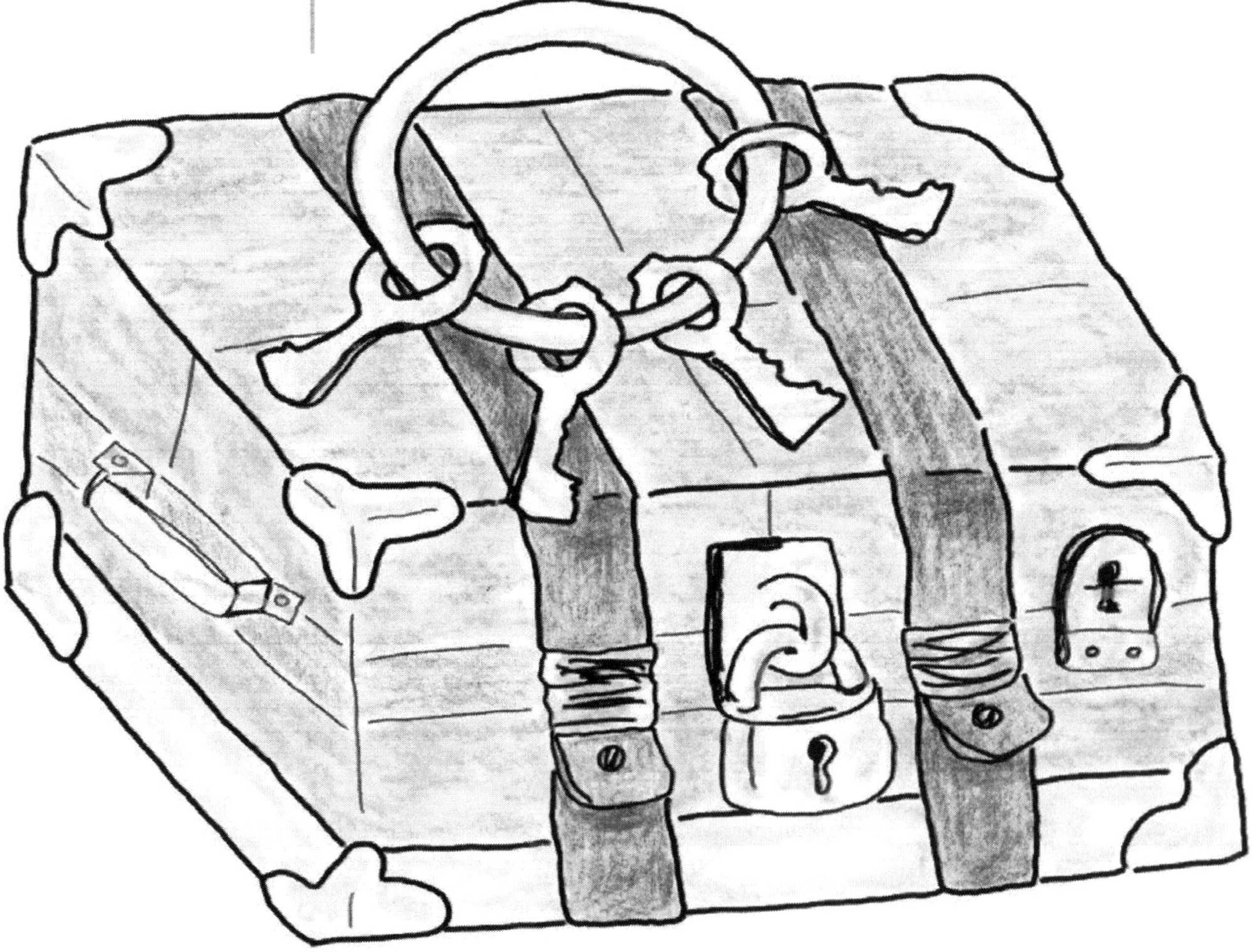

George Catlin wrote a poem about his personal experiences with those he encountered during his travels . . .

"I love the people who have always made me welcome
to the best they had.

I love a people who are honest without laws,
who have no jails and no poor-houses.

I love a people who keep the commandments without ever having
read them or heard them preached from the pulpit.

I love a people who never swear, who never take the name
of God in vain.

I love a people who 'love their neighbours as they love themselves.'

I love a people who worship God without a Bible,
for I believe that God loves them also.

I love the people whose religion is all the same,
and who are free from religious animosities.

I love the people who never have raised a hand against me,
or stolen my property, where there was no law to punish for either.

I love the people who never have fought a battle with white man,
except on their own ground.

I love and don't fear mankind where God has made and left them,
for there they are children.

I love a people who live and keep what is their own
without locks and keys.

I love all people who do the best they can. And oh,
how I love a people who don't live for the love of money!

Catlin, George, Last rambles amongst the Indians of the Rocky Mountains and the Andes, Sampson Low, Son, and Marston 1868 (digitized from public domain by BiblioLife, LLC) pp. 354-355

No Church Wanted

Some observant Indians were not convinced the white man's way was a more civilized way. The following conversation between US Indian Commissioners and Chief Joseph of the Nez Perces reveals a logical line of reasoning on the part of this Indian chief . . .

The US Indian Commissioners asked Chief Joseph,

"Do you want schools and school-houses on the Wallowa Reservation?"

Chief Joseph:

"No, we do not want schools or school-houses on the Wallowa Reservation."

Commissioners:

"Why do you not want schools?"

Chief Joseph:

"They will teach us to have churches."

Commissioners:

"Do you not want churches?"

Chief Joseph:

"No, we do not want churches."

Commissioners:

"Why do you not want churches?"

Chief Joseph:

"They will teach us to quarrel about God, as the Catholics and Protestants do on the Nez Perce Reservation, and at other places. We do not want to learn that. We may quarrel with men some times about things on this earth, but we never quarrel about God. We do not want to learn that."

See this story in Helen Hunt Jackson's book,
A Century of Dishonor, Dover Publications, Inc./ Harper & Brothers 1881, p.124

General Allotment Act (1887)

Say it Simply!

"allotment" -- an assignment of a portion, a divided and distributed section, set apart, dedicated for a specific purpose

"allottee" -- person receiving an assigned portion of land (an allotment)

We have earlier indicated how the 1871 Act of Congress which stopped treaty-making drastically changed the way the federal government dealt with tribes and paved the way for Indian land *allotment*. The General Allotment Act (also known as the Dawes Allotment Act) was the official legislation which authorized the dividing up of tribal lands into individually owned parcels of property. One authoritative source called it "[t]he most important statute of the decade" of 1880 through 1889. [32] The General Allotment Act was touted as an improvement for tribal communities, but its eventual effects were devastating to the Indian tribes.

In two annual messages to Congress, the President of the United States strongly advocated for this policy. [33] Also, the Lieutenant General of the Army pushed for allotment of the reservations in a report to the Secretary of War. [34] Basically, the terms of the General Allotment Act were: [35]

- A grant of 160 acres to each family head, or 80 acres to each single person over 18 years old, or 80 acres to orphans under 18 years old, or 40 acres to each single person under 18 years old.
- Every *allottee* would be issued a "patent in fee" but it would be held in trust by the Government for 25 years, and it could not be sold by the allottee.
- Indians had 4 years to make their decisions. If they did not decide by 4 years, the Secretary of the Interior would choose for them.
- American citizenship would be eventually granted to allottees who "abandoned their tribes and adopted the habits of civilized life."

The General Allotment Act is also known as the Dawes Allotment Act because US Senator Henry Dawes was the one who sponsored the bill.

Radical Change of Policy

This law was enacted during the time when the last of the tribal groups had been subdued and corralled onto reservations. The Indians were required to remain within the boundaries of these assigned areas.

Quotes "Q"

> *"The United States peace policy attempted to place all Native Americans on reservations, to separate them geographically from white settlements, trails, and railroad construction. The reservations would be the forum for a white civilizing mission of Indians. During and after the Civil War, every military campaign in the West and Southwest forced the Indians onto reservations, or made them return there if they fled."*
>
> *Dr. Ian Barnes, The Historical Atlas of Native Americans, Chartwell Books, Inc. 2009, p. 324*

Dig Deeper

> To get a fuller understanding of the interaction between the US military and the Indian tribes during the mid to late 1880's, read Dr. Ian Barnes' book: *The Historical Atlas of Native Americans*, (Chartwell Books, Inc. 2009)

As non-Indian communities quickly populated and spread out, they surrounded the reservations. (Prior Indian lands opened up as the Indians were moved onto the reservations.) Federal policy had, through Indian removal and the forced reservation system, generated poverty, despondency and a dependence on the government for assistance. Although this dire outcome was not the intention of most government legislators, it was the result none the less. The surrounding non-Indian communities looked upon the tribal communities as undesirable and unwanted neighboring *welfare* communities.

There became an evident "growing feeling in the country against the continued appropriations for the care and comfort of the Indians." Therefore, in 1879, the Indian Commissioner recommended the enactment of the General Allotment Act because of "the necessity for a radical change of policy in affairs connected with their (Indians') lands." [36] It was believed that individual land ownership would finally civilize the Indian and assimilate him into the dominant society. One individual expressed what many concurred with: "the enjoyment and pride of the individual ownership of property being one of the most effective civilizing agencies." [37]

Communism

Western thought and mentality differed in many ways from Indian thought and perspective. This is interestingly seen when legislators, while describing tribal cooperativeness and strong sense of being part of their community, incorrectly used the term *"communism"* to describe it. According to one source, this label of communism by both "friends and enemies of allotment alike showed no clear understanding of Indian agricultural economy." [38]

There was also a general lack of understanding regarding *tribal law and order.*

Tribal Law & Order

Land allotment cut the reservations up into smaller, individual-sized pieces. Many involved in supporting the General Allotment Act, saw the world only through their eyes, expressing confidence that individual land ownership was far superior to land ownership by the whole tribe. "[A]llotment was counted on to break up tribal life . . . the cooperativeness and clannishness – the strong communal sense – of barbaric life . . . allotment was calculated to disrupt." [39]

Disrupt it did. With the breaking up of the land there was an opening up of *"surplus lands"* that "belong to the reservations, but not used by the Indians." [40] This new-found extra land was sold by the federal government to non-Indians for settlement, making many of the Indian reservations consist of checkerboard, Indian and non-Indian lands. On some reservations, non-Indian landholdings became greater than Indian landholdings. This negatively impacted a tribal government's ability to adequately enforce law and order on their reservation. "The lack of territorial isolation that reduced a tribe's ability to self-govern is especially due to allotment." [41]

> *"There are some reservations in which the moral sanctions of an integrated community are so strong that apart from occasional drunkenness and accompanying violence, crime is unknown. Crime is more of a problem on reservations where the social sanctions based on tribal control of property have been broken down through the allotment system, and the efforts of these tribes to meet their law and order problem through tribal codes, tribal courts, and tribal police, are worthy of Serious attention."*
>
> *Felix S. Cohen, Handbook of Federal Indian Law, Washington, United States Government Printing Office, 1945, p. 149*

The authors of the book, *The Oneida Indian Experience, Two Perspectives*, also shed light on how the culture of a tribe is interconnected with its land base, and when tribal land is broken up it is a matter of time until it has a "debilitating effect on tribal government." [42]

A Magical Transformation

One may ask, "Exactly what were the Indians expected to do with their individual parcels of land?" In 1886, if we had posed that very question to the supporters of the Allotment Act, we probably would have received glaring scowls and the gruff answer, "Well, farm the land of course!"

The minority of the House Committee on Indian Affairs doubted that creating private property out of the reservations would suddenly change all Indians into farmers:

Quotes "Q"

> *"[I]t does not make a farmer out of an Indian to give him a quarter-section of land. There are hundreds of thousands of white men, rich with the experiences of centuries of Anglo-Saxon civilization, who cannot be transformed into cultivators of land by any such gift."*
>
> *H. Report No. 1576, May 28, 1880, 46th Congress, 2d Sess. 8 quoted in Felix S. Cohen, Handbook of Federal Indian Law, Washington, United States Government Printing Office, 1945, p. 208*

Nerdy Stuff

Anglo-Saxons were known farmers, land and farms were passed on generation after generation.

One US Indian agent stated his belief that the only way the Indians would be able to "begin their real and permanent progress" in becoming civilized was through the creation of individual farm lands. His expression was the sentiment of the majority of the US policy makers. He attributed the Indians' lack of progress to "old and injurious habits" such as "frequent feasts, community in food, heathen ceremonies and dances, and constant visiting." [43] Basically, the thought was to replace the Indian culture for white *civilization*.

Say it Simply!

"despoil" -- to strip of possessions or things of value, rob, plunder, pillage

"vagabonds" -- tramps, beggars, drifters

A Bill to Despoil

US Senator Henry Teller of Colorado stood quite alone when he spoke against the allotment policy. He saw it for what it really was – "a bill to *despoil* the Indians of their lands and to make them *vagabonds* on the face of the earth." [44]

> *"If I stand alone in the Senate, I want to put upon the record my prophecy in this matter, that when 30 or 40 years shall have passed and these Indians shall have parted with their title, they will curse the hand that was raised professedly in their defense to secure this kind of legislation and if the people who are clamoring for it understood Indian character, and Indian laws, and Indian morals, and Indian religion, they would not be here clamoring for this at all."*
>
> *Congressional Record, Jan. 20, 1881 quoted in Felix S. Cohen, Handbook of Federal Indian Law, Washington, United States Government Printing Office, 1945, p. 209*

Say it Simply!

"rhetoric" -- words, speech

"ulterior" -- beyond what is seen, hidden, intentionally concealed or undisclosed

"coincidental" -- by chance, totally unplanned

"ethnocide" -- intentional and systematic destruction of an ethnic culture

The *rhetoric* spoken promised the benefits of civilization to the Indians, yet so many other things indicated *ulterior* motives behind this legislation. One apparent motivation for passing this law was to make way for the "feverish railroad building" that was taking place during the 1880s. It probably was *not coincidental* that the very same session of the Congress which had passed the General Allotment Act also made decisions regarding an increase in grants of railroad rights-of-way through Indian lands. [45] (With the Allotment Act in place, the granting of railroad rights-of-way was a much easier process.)

Nationwide reduction in Indian landholdings, between 1887 until the end of the allotment period in 1934, resulted in the loss of 90 million acres. [46] One justice from the Ninth Circuit Court of Appeals, while discussing the allotment period, quotes from a book about the Yakima Indians to explain the effects of this law:

> *"For 12,000 years, the Yakima Indians have lived on their lands in Eastern Washington . . . Because of the allotment policies, non-Indians today (1990) own more than a quarter million acres, more than half the land originally allotted to individual members of the Yakimas. Allotment and the subsequent sale or lease of Indian lands accomplished what the 'genocide' of epidemics, war, and bootlegged alcohol had not been able to do: a systematic 'ethnocide' brought about by a loss of Indian identity with the loss of land."*
>
> *County of Yakima v. Confederated Tribes and Bands of Yakima Nation, 502 U.S. 251, 276 (9th Cir.1992) Also see:* [47]

Early 1900's

World War I (1914 – 1918), although centralized in Europe, had an impact around the world. The global effects brought the United States into this war about three years after its inception. Native Americans were among those who joined to protect their homeland. It must be remembered that the vast majority of Indians who served were actually volunteers. This was because, at this point in time, Native Americans as a whole were not recognized as United States citizens under the US Constitution. The heroic contribution of Native Americans during this war had a bearing on changing this fact.

"During World War I over 8,000 American Indian soldiers, of whom 6,000 were volunteers, served. Their patriotism motivated Congress to pass the Indian Citizenship Act of 1924." [48] The Indian "code talkers" saved many lives by "use of their tribal languages as a military code that could not be broken by the enemy." [49] At least 600 Native Americans were assigned to the 142nd Infantry of the 36th Texas-Oklahoma National Guard Division – a military unit widely recognized and honored for their efforts in France. [50]

Say it Simply!

"suffrage" -- the right to vote

Many Indian women supported the war effort along with the general population of women in the United States. Although Native American women would not immediately benefit from the 19th Amendment to the US Constitution, which gave women the right to vote, it cannot be denied they too had a part in this change. [51] President Woodrow Wilson, who had not always been a supporter of women's *suffrage*, made note of the undeniable contribution of women to efforts of the WWI, earning them the right to vote as partners in the trauma and sacrifice of war. [52]

Quotes

"Q"

> *"We have made partners of the women in this war . . . shall we admit them only to a partnership of suffering and sacrifice and toil and not to a partnership of privilege and right?"*
>
> *Speech by President Woodrow Wilson before Congress, September 30, 1918*

Indian Citizenship

The same year Congress endorsed the amendment to the constitution allowing women to vote, *An Act Granting Citizenship to Certain Indians* was also endorsed. This Act stated "every American Indian who served in the Military or Naval Establishments of the United States during the war" could become "a citizen . . . if he so desires." Later, the 1924 *Indian Citizenship Act* superseded any of the other Indian citizenship authorizations and granted citizenship to all Indians born in the United States.

The Meriam Report

Say it Simply!

"think tank" -- An institution in which scholars pursue research in public policy. Such research is funded by grants or endowments. The work of a think tank is to provide research based on diverse points of view and remain non-partisan (not supported or controlled by any political or special interest group) and through its reports and publications to raise public awareness and to influence positive governmental action on an issue.

The US Secretary of the Interior during the time of the enactment of the 1924 Indian Citizenship Act was a man named Hubert Work. He was a doctor by profession, serving many years with distinction in this profession, including in the Army medical Corps during WWI as a Lieutenant Colonel. Because of his background, it was probably very natural for him to request a thorough analysis of the government's administrative work with Indian affairs upon accepting the position of Secretary of the Interior under President Coolidge's tenure.

And so it was that Hubert Work requested a survey regarding Indian affairs by a private organization, the Institute for Government Research, which was privately funded. This arrangement, also in line with the purpose of this *think tank*, allowed research to be free from governmental influence. The ultimate hope was to gain feedback that was as impartial as possible.

Lewis Meriam was chosen as the one who would head up this survey – therefore, the report is often referred to as the Meriam Report. Meriam and his team worked very hard on this huge project. They conducted hands-on field work in 23 states, visiting in total 95 reservations, agencies, hospitals and schools. Having started their work in June of 1926, they compiled a massive 847-page document, submitting it to the Secretary of Interior in February of 1928 with the title, *"The Problem of Indian Administration."*

Through their extensive research they found great deficiencies in the general health and welfare of the Indian people. They found basic necessities were lacking and disease was widespread. The existing deplorable conditions on the reservations were detailed in the report and it was noted that the conditions at the Indian boarding schools were "grossly inadequate" (i.e. overcrowding, disease, medical services and attention lacking, student labor, poor diet and lack of food). The *Meriam Report* clearly opposed the Allotment Act and revealed how Indian monies were being used for things which the Indians never requested or did not benefit them. [53]

Lewis Meriam was highly educated having degrees in economics and government from Harvard and two law degrees. His research team was specifically hand-picked as "persons highly qualified as specialists in their respective fields, scientific in their approach, not sensationalists, and free from preconceived views and opinions that would interfere with their impartiality and fairness in gathering and interpreting the facts."(See p. 57 of the Meriam Report) Over five pages are dedicated to the credentials of the researchers. (Id. at pp. 79-85) These highly trained, non-sensationalist professionals stated in their report, "Several past policies adopted by the government in dealing with the Indians have been of a type which, if long continued, would tend to pauperize any race." (Id. at p. 7)

"pragmatic" -- practical, realistic, sensible

The Meriam Report did contain overtones of the assimilation policy of the day. Keep in mind, the whole approach to this survey was that of a scientific approach – a *pragmatic*, just-the-facts approach. Truly, looking at Indian tribes during this time period, from purely this scientific perspective, Indian survival – let alone the survival of tribal government – would accurately be given an extremely low probability rate.

The scientific Meriam Report shows that Indians and their governments have survived against the odds. Tribal extinction was predicted way back in the 1800's, yet Indian tribes have amazingly endured.

The Meriam Report pointed out the *human element* of dealing with the Indians. For example, in one part of the report it is stated, "The Indian is like the white man in his affection for his children and he feels keenly the sickness and the loss of his off-spring." Another section directs those who work with Indians to demonstrate "courtesy and consideration" toward the Indians and encouraged workers to recognize the fact that, "Indians have much to contribute." *(See the following quote.)*

". . . scrupulous care must be exercised to respect the rights of the Indian. This phrase 'rights of the Indian' is often used solely to apply to his property rights. Here it is used in a much broader sense to cover his rights as a human being living in a free country. Indians are entitled to unfailing courtesy and consideration from all government employees. They should not be subjected to arbitrary action. Recognition of the educational nature of the whole task of dealing with them will result in taking the time to discuss with them in detail their own affairs and to lead rather than force them to sound conclusions. The effort to substitute educational leadership for the more dictatorial methods now used in some places will necessitate more understanding of and sympathy for the Indian point of view. Leadership will recognize the good in the economic and social life of the Indians in their religion and ethics, and will seek to develop it and build on it rather than to crush out all that is Indian. The Indians have much to contribute to the dominant civilization, and the efforts should be made to secure this contribution, in part because of the good it will do the Indians in stimulating a proper race pride and self-respect."

Institute for Government Research, Studies in Administration, The Problem of Indian Administration (Meriam report), The Johns Hopkins Press, p. 22-23

Although the report emphasized the need for governmental officials to show respect to individual Indians, it was largely silent when it came to tribal government as a whole. The Meriam report dedicated an entire chapter (Chapter 13) to *Legal Aspects of the Indian Problem*. However, in the only place where it briefly discusses inter-tribal maintenance of law and order and administration of justice it concludes that the tribes cannot effectively manage this. They attribute this inability to "the intrusion of white settlements, the breaking-down of tribal organization, and the subsequent entry of the Indians into the economic and social life of the surrounding white communities." [54] With this assumption, the survey recommends solutions through state-level, state-run government agencies to replace the majority of poorly-run federal programs. Tribal government was not considered a viable *long-term* option or solution.

Moved to Action

Once Meriam and his survey team had accomplished their part, it was handed off to legislators and government administrators. This was the stated purpose from the beginning as the report indicated in its first pages:

> *"The accomplishment of specific reforms the Institute recognizes to be the task of those who are charged with the responsibility of legislation and administration; but it seeks to assist, by scientific study and research, in laying a solid foundation of information and experience upon which such reforms may be successfully built."*
>
> *Institute for Government Research, Studies in Administration, The Problem of Indian Administration (Meriam report), The Johns Hopkins Press, 1928, front pages*

The results of the Meriam Report provided direction for governmental action. Some positive action did take place and the *plethora* of information provided in this report gave policy makers ample data for many years to come. One of the greatest legislative actions taken, largely in response to the Meriam Report, was embodied in the 1934 Indian Reorganization Act. This Act immediately stopped the selling of Indian lands and provided land for landless Indians. [55] Also, tribal organization and government was to have support from the federal government, instead of tearing down and seeking to eliminate indigenous tribal culture. The Act established a system of financial credit and doors were opened for attendance to college or technical training schools as well as job positions in the Federal Indian Service.

Say it Simply!

"plethora" -- an overabundance, excess

This was a complete 180 degree change in government policy toward Native Americans. The concept of acknowledging tribal self-government was certainly not a novel idea, but government policies had *governed without the consent of the governed* for so long, it seems like a brand new thing.

Quotes

"One significant change in the direction of Indian self-government can best be put in negative terms. During the century from 1833 to 1933 hundreds of laws affecting Indian tribes were enacted and a great part of these laws, perhaps a majority of them, in some way deprived the Indian tribes of rights or possessions they had once enjoyed."

Felix S. Cohen, Handbook of Federal Indian Law, Washington, United States Government Printing Office, 1945, p. 86

Your Dusty Shoes

Congratulations!
Take a minute to dust off your shoes . . .

Say it Simply!

"genesis" -- beginning, origin

"dogma" -- belief proclaimed as unquestionably true or right by a certain group

You have now traveled quite a distance along the path of the evolution of jurisdiction in Indian country. Starting at the *genesis* of this evolution, you saw the Indian tribes as completely self-governing sovereign entities. The path then led to interaction between the various tribal nations and the Europeans – the Doctrine of Discovery . . . the battles for land titles . . . and eventually the Revolutionary War. The new sovereign nation of the United States continued the government-to-government treaty contracts with the Indian tribes, in recognition of their inherent sovereignty. The US also continued the concept of the Doctrine of Discovery: claiming the right of title to lands and having the exclusive right to deal with the Indians and purchase their lands.

You saw the role trading with Indians played during the early years, and how laws were put in place to maximize this industry and to protect the Indians from criminal acts by non-Indians. Criminal jurisdiction eventually increased through the General Crimes Act and the Major Crimes Act. Yet, even with these increases in federal criminal jurisdiction, a tribe's ability to govern their own people and territories was acknowledged. Throughout the course of these defining jurisdictional events in Indian country, the federal government made it utterly clear that they had *exclusive* jurisdiction, not the individual states.

We will now tread toward the enactment of PL 280. In order to do this, we must walk through a period of time called the *Termination Period*. As we look at this time period it will serve you well to remember the historical and political relationship that had developed between the Indian tribes and the United States of America. Your understanding of this historical and political relationship will help you grasp the enormity of what took place when the termination policy became the political *dogma* of the day.

Endnotes - Chapter Three, Part 5:

[1] One individual who served many years as a US Indian agent to the Sioux at Devils Lake and Standing Rock Agencies in North Dakota, James McLaughlin, wrote a book entitled, *"My Friend the Indian."* As he begins his book he writes in the preface, "For thirty-eight years I have lived among, or had official dealings with a race of people little understood by the whites who have displaced them in carrying out the immutable law of the survival of the fittest . . . I know of the Indian, of his losing struggle for an existence according to his own ideas, of his manner of living, mode of thought, habit in action and repose . . ." McLaughlin, James, *My Friend the Indian*, The Riverside Press Cambridge, 1910, p. vii; See also Barsh, Russel L. & Henderson, James Youngblood, The Road, University of California Press 1980, p. 63, the authors tell how one Indian commissioner referred to the reservations as "penal" institutions where the tactic of reward and punishment would be used to "civilize" Indians.

[2] "The principle that tangible Indian interests – in the preservation of person and property – should be protected dates from the earliest days of the republic when it was embodied in the Trade and Intercourse Acts. To say that these tangible interests should be protected is not, however, necessarily to say that a generalized interest in peace and tranquility is sufficient to trigger continuing federal jurisdiction." *Memorandum for Benjamin R. Civiletti Re Jurisdiction Over "Victimless" Crimes Committed by Non-Indians on Indian Reservations*, archived in the US Attorneys, Title 9, Criminal Resource Manual at 684, sec. II

[3] *United States v. Antelope*, 430 US 641, 643 footnote 2 (1977)

[4] See *United States v. Langford*, 641 F.3d 1195 (10th Cir. 2011) "The Supreme Court has not directly considered the issue of whether the federal courts possess jurisdiction over victimless crimes committed by non- Indians on Indian land. However, the Court has suggested in dicta that the *McBratney* rule applies to victimless crimes as well. The Court summarized the delimitation of state and federal jurisdiction over crimes in Indian country in *Solem v. Bartlett*, 465 U.S. 463 (1984). 'Within Indian country, State jurisdiction is limited to crimes by non-Indians against non-Indians, and victimless crimes by non-Indians' . . . (noting the 'Supreme Court has expressly stated that state criminal jurisdiction in Indian country is limited to crimes committed 'by non-Indians against non-Indians . . . and victimless crimes by non-Indians') . . . The absence of federal jurisdiction over victimless crimes perpetrated by a non-Indian in Indian country is explicit in the dicta of *Solem* and implicit in the holding of *McBratney*."

[5] Cohen, Felix S., *Handbook of Federal Indian Law*, Washington, United States Government Printing Office, 1945, p. 364

[6] "In explaining the necessity of consular extraterritorial jurisdiction in the middle of the nineteenth century, when so large a number of treaties providing for it were made, the treaties frequently employed the terms 'non-Christian,' 'semi-civilized,' and 'barbarous,' in relation to the oriental states; and the language of official documents of the oriental governments contained similar expressions in regard to the western nations." Hinckley, Frank E., *American Consular Jurisdiction in the Orient*, The Moody-Barton Press 1906, p. 195; The Appendix section (pp. 197-203) of Hinckley's book lists various treaties the United States had with non-European foreign nations. Some listed are: China (1844), Borneo (1850), Korea (1882), Muskat (1833), Morocco (1787), Persia (1856), Siam (1856, Tripoli (1796), Turkey (1830), Zanzibar (1886)

[7] One example is the 1844 Cushing Treaty made with China. In this treaty there is a provision that states U.S. citizens could only be tried by U.S. consular officers; See also *Reid v. Covert*, 354 US at 1, 11 (1957) "At that time, statutes authorized American consuls to try American citizens charged with committing crimes in Japan and certain other "non-Christian" countries." Footnote 14, Rev. Stat. 4083-4130

[8] Crawford, G.D., *Indian Jurisdiction Policies*, Marquette Law Review, Vol. 76:401, p. 416, footnote 112 quoting Reid v. Covert, 354 US 1, 10 (1957) "Such jurisdiction (of American consuls) was a grant of power from the foreign nation to the United States pursuant to treaty. Absent treaty provisions, U.S. citizens were subject to the plenary jurisdiction of the foreign nation where an offense occurred."

[9] *Oliphant v. Suquamish Indian Tribe*, 435 US 191, 210 (9th Cir. 1978) quoting H.R. Rep. No. 474, 23d Cong., 1st Sess., 18 (1834)

[10] *Ex Parte Crow Dog*, 109 US 556, 571 (1883)

[11] *United States v. Wheeler*, 435 U.S. 313, 325 (9th Cir. 1978) footnote 23 quoting S. Rep. No. 268, 41st Cong., 3d Sess., 10 (1870) "Their (Indians) right of self government, and to administer justice among themselves, after their rude fashion, even to the extent of inflicting the death penalty, has never been questioned; and . . . the Government has carefully abstained from attempting to regulate their domestic affairs, and from punishing crime committed by one Indian against another in the Indian country."

[12] Williams, Derik, *Romans and Barbarians*, St. Martin's Press 1998, pp. 10, 22, 23, 26, 76, 79,80, 86, 98, 106, 208. See also Janson, H.W.; Janson, Anthony F., *History of Art: A Survey of the Major Visual Arts from the Dawn of History to the Present Day*, Prentice-Hall 1987, pp. 117-118 depicting the bronze statue of the Dying Gaul. "The statues commemorating their (Galls) defeat were reproduced in marble for the Romans (who may have had a special interest in them because of their troubles with Celtic tribes in northwestern Europe), and a number of these copies have survived, including the famous Dying Gaul. . . Clearly, the Gauls were not considered unworthy foes. 'They knew how to die, barbarians though they were,' is the thought conveyed by the statue."

[13] Story LL.D., Joseph, *Commentaries on the Constitution of the U.S. (1833)*, Lonang Institute 2003, 2005 electronic edition, Book III, p. 831, § 1856, " . . . bill of rights . . . prohibits any tyrannical measures, and vindictive prosecutions."

[14] *Reid v. Covert*, 354 US 1, 13 (1957) "Trial by jury in court of law . . . remains one of our most vital barriers to governmental arbitrariness. These elemental procedural safeguards were embedded in our Constitution to secure the inviolateness and sanctity against passing demands of expediency or convenience."

[15] Wharton, Francis, *Philosophy of Criminal Law*, Kay & Brother, Booksellers, Publishers, and Importers 1880, p. 301

[16] Eastman, Charles A. (Ohiyesa), *Indian Heroes and Great Chieftains*, Dover Publications, Inc. 1997 (reprint of original work 1918), p. 12

[17] Id. at p. 14

[18] Id. at p. 15

[19] Id. at p. 16

[20] McLaughlin, James, *My Friend the Indian*, The Riverside Press Cambridge, 1910, p. 70; Also, earlier in his book, McLaughlin compared the difference between Sioux Chief Red Cloud and Spotted Tail noting Red Cloud, "had been the ideal chief, warlike and of abounding spirit," but he believed "lacking altogether in the qualities of mind that made Spotted Tail a diplomat and agency Indian. Spotted Tail, who had been a warrior of renown in his youth, came to understand that nothing was to be gained in a substantial way from fighting the whites."(p.20)

[21] Eastman, Charles A. (Ohiyesa), *Indian Heroes and Great Chieftains*, Dover Publications, Inc. 1997 (reprint of original work 1918), p. 17

[22] Blaisdell, Bob, *Great Speeches by Native Americans*, Dover Publications, Inc. 2000, p.130

[23] Id.

[24] Id.

[25] Eastman, Charles A. (Ohiyesa), *Indian Heroes and Great Chieftains*, Dover Publications, Inc. 1997 (reprint of original work 1918), p. 17-18 "The famous treaty was signed, and from this time on Spotted Tail never again took up arms against the whites. On the contrary, it was mainly attributed to his influence that the hostiles were subdued much sooner than might have been expected. He came into the reservation with his band, urged his young men to enlist as government scouts, and assisted materially in all negotiations. The hostile chiefs no longer influenced his action, and as soon as they had all been brough under military control, General Crook named Spotted Tail head chief of the Sioux, thus humiliating Red Cloud and arousing jealousy and ill-feeling among the Ogallalas . . . He became a good manipulator, and was made conceited and overbearing by the attentions of the military and of the general public."

[26] Id. at p. 18

[27] McLaughlin, James, *My Friend the Indian*, The Riverside Press Cambridge, 1910, p. 74

[28] Eastman, Charles A. (Ohiyesa), *Indian Heroes and Great Chieftains*, Dover Publications, Inc. 1997 (reprint of original work 1918), p. 18

[29] *Keeble v. US*, 412 US 205, 210 (1973)

[30] Prygoski, Philip J., *"The Supreme Court's Treatment of Tribal Sovereignty From Marshall to Marshall,"* COMPLEAT LAWYER (ABA) (Fall,1995).

[31] *United States v. Kagama*, 118 US 375, 375, 379 (1886)

[32] Cohen, Felix S., *Handbook of Federal Indian Law*, Washington, United States Government Printing Office, 1945, p. 78; Many quotes will be used from this source for explanation regarding the General Allotment Act of 1887. Felix Cohen begins his *"Background of the Allotment System"* by telling his readers that he found "a wealth of detail in J.P. Kinney's study, A Continent Lost – A Civilization Won (1937) and more briefly, in a '*History of the Allotment Policy*' by D.S. Otis." (Id. at p. 206)

[33] Id. at 207 "President Cleveland in his annual messages in 1885 and 1886 advocated the (allotment) policy."

[34] Id. "In 1886 General Sheridan, reporting as lieutenant general of the Army to the Secretary of War, likewise urged an allotment scheme."

[35] Id. at p. 207 - 208

[36] Id. at p. 208

[37] Id. at p. 207

[38] Id. at p. 208; See also Id. at p. 86 ". . . a people whose economy was rooted in the soil, whose reverence for the soil was so deep that they never fully grasped the white man's concept of buying and selling land."

[39] Id. "They were confident that if every Indian had his own strip of land, guaranteed by a patent from the Government, he would enjoy a security which no tribal possession could afford him."

[40] Id. at pp. 208 - 209

[41] Cranford, G.D., *Looking again at Tribal Justice*, Marquette Law Review pg. 422

[42] Campisi, Jack and Hauptman, Laurence M., *The Oneida Indian Experience, Two Perspectives*, Syracuse University Press 1988, pg. 85

[43] Cohen, Felix S., *Handbook of Federal Indian Law*, Washington, United States Government Printing Office, 1945, p. 208

[44] Id. at p. 209, quoting the Congressional Record, Jan. 26, 1881

[45] Id. at p. 209

[46] *County of Yakima v. Confederated Tribes and Bands of Yakima Nation*, 502 U.S. 251, 276 (1992); See also Felix S. Cohen, *Handbook of Federal Indian Law*, Washington, United States Government Printing Office, 1945, pp. 86, 216 "Of the area that remained in Indian ownership a large part was desert or mountainside . . . on many reservations the Indian-owned parcels are mere islands within a sea of white-owned property."

[47] Id., Book: H. Schuster, *The Yakimas*; Justice Blackmun continues by also expressing, "It is little wonder that, as Congress moved toward repudiating the allotment system in 1934, the Commissioner of Indian Affairs informed Congress: "It is difficult to imagine any other system which with equal effectiveness would pauperize the Indian while impoverishing him, and sicken and kill his soul while pauperizing him, and cast him in so ruined a condition into the final status of a nonward dependent upon the States and counties."

[48] See the Bureau of Indian Affairs' official website on the FAQS page under "Do American Indians and Alaska Natives serve in the Armed Forces?" at: *http://www.bia.gov/FAQs/index.htm*

[49] Id.

[50] Naval History & Heritage website / Native Americans and the US Military / Contributions in Combat at: www.history.navy.mil/faqs/faq61-1.htm

[51] "The right of citizens of the United States to vote shall not be denied or abridged by the United States or by any State on account of sex. Congress shall have power to enforce this article by appropriate legislation." 19th Amendment to the US Constitution (added in 1920)

[52] See the United States Senate's official website/ Art & History / Historical Minute Essays / 1878-1920 at: *http://www.senate.gov/artandhistory/history/minute/A_Vote_For_Women.htm* "By 1918, President Wilson had dropped his previously indifferent attitude and fully supported the constitutional amendment. In his September 30th speech to the Senate, he cited the role of women in supporting the nation's involvement in World War I. "We have made partners of the women in this war," he said, "Shall we admit them only to a partnership of suffering and sacrifice and toil, and not to a partnership of privilege and right?" Despite his oratory, the president failed to pry loose the needed two votes and the amendment again died. Finally, in 1919, a new Congress brought an increase in the ranks of the amendment's supporters, permitting adoption of what would become the Constitution's 19th Amendment—52 years after it was first introduced in the Senate."

[53] "In justice to the Indians it should be said that many of them are living on lands from which a trained and experienced white man could scarcely wrest a reasonable living. In some instances the land originally set apart for the Indians was of little value for agricultural operations other than grazing. In other instances part of the land was excellent but the Indians did not appreciate its value. Often when individual allotments were made, they chose for themselves the poorer parts, because those parts were near a domestic water supply or a source of firewood, or because they furnished some native product important to the Indians in their primitive life. Frequently the better sections of the land originally set apart for the Indians have fallen into the hands of the whites, and the Indians have retreated to the poorer lands remote from markets." Institute for Government Research, Studies in Administration, *The Problem of Indian Administration (Meriam report)*, The Johns Hopkins Press, p. 5; See also Felix S. Cohen, *Handbook of Federal Indian Law*, Washington, United States Government Printing Office, 1945, p. 83 "Both the Meriam report and the special subcommittee of the Senate Committee on Indian Affairs had made it clear that in the development of irrigation projects on Indian reservations, Indians had been charged with tremendous costs for construction work which they had never requested and which brought them little or no benefit."

[54] Institute for Government Research, Studies in Administration, *The Problem of Indian Administration (Meriam report)*, The Johns Hopkins Press, p. 757

[55] "Section 1 prohibits further allotment of Indian lands. This provision embodied a considered judgment that the allotment system was incapable of contributing to the economic advancement of the Indians. As was stated in the House report, 'The bill now under consideration definitely puts an end to the allotment system through the operation of which the Indians have parted with 90,000,000 acres of their land in the last 50 years.'" Felix S. Cohen, *Handbook of Federal Indian Law*, Washington, United States Government Printing Office, 1945, p. 84

Chapter Four

This chapter will cover:

- *Indian Emancipation Proclamation*
- *HCR 108*
- *The 83rd Congress*

Chapter Four

The Termination Period

Incongruent Law?

For the purpose of this book, the history we have covered was intended to put PL 280 and jurisdiction of Indian country into perspective. We will now look at a point in time known as the *Termination Period* (a time where the federal government sought to terminate its federal trust relationship with Indian tribes). It is very important for us to spend some time discussing this period, because PL 280 was a direct result of the philosophy behind termination. Through this chapter you will gain valuable insight into the background of termination . . . and therefore, also PL 280.

Say it Simply!

"incongruent" -- inconsistent, contrastingly different

"tenaciously" -- persistently, stubbornly, not easily pulled apart

The end result of the enactment of PL 280 was that it allowed the federal government to transfer some of its jurisdiction to the states. *Stop*, for just a minute, and consider that fact . . .

When you contemplate the historical evolution we have looked at so far regarding jurisdiction in Indian country, PL 280 seems an odd and rather *incongruent* law. It had been clearly established over the years that the federal government held exclusive jurisdiction over Indian territory, excluding only the tribe's jurisdiction over their internal matters. "Because of their sovereign status, tribes and their reservation lands are insulated in some respects by a 'historic immunity from state and local control.'" [1] The federal government had *tenaciously* guarded its jurisdiction in Indian country for one hundred and thirty years, only to now give the individual states jurisdiction on Indian lands.

> *"The courts have* ***repeatedly*** *held that federal jurisdiction over offenses, either felonies or misdemeanors, committed by an Indian in Indian country is* ***exclusive*** *and not concurrent with state jurisdiction."*
>
> *Application of Denetclaw, 83 Ariz. 299, 303 (1958)*

It seems like PL 280 appeared from out of nowhere. Upon closer inspection, though, we will see that PL 280 was actually a manifestation of a policy that had been around for quite some time – but now it had its own unique twist.

Indian Emancipation Proclamation

The termination period, which PL 280 resulted from, was actually a continuation of the federal policy of assimilation. The reservation system, boarding schools and the Allotment Act were natural results of the US government's assimilation policy toward Native Americans. This policy had been briefly interrupted, for about ten years, during the *Indian Reorganization period* [2], but it reappeared cloaked in *euphemistic verbiage*.

Say it Simply!

"euphemistic verbiage" -- to replace or substitute harsher sounding words or phrases for more pleasant and appealing sounding words or phrases

An individual considered as one of the major driving forces behind the termination policy and its implementation, Senator Arthur Watkins of Utah, explained how the assimilation process encountered a brief "delay" by the Indian Reorganization Act of 1934, but the intention of Congress was to get back on track and continue the federal policy of assimilation in Indian affairs.

Say it Simply!

"ideology" -- a guiding belief

"paternalism" -- an attitude or policy of governing a people as a father looks after his children; an adult and child relationship in decision making

Senator Watkins wrote that the Indian is "a fellow American citizen" and his concern was the "freeing of the Indians from special federal restrictions." He went so far as to say that this "historic policy of Congress favoring freedom for the Indians" was "following in the footsteps of the *Emancipation Proclamation*." [3]

Such an *ideology* was embraced by the legislators of the time seen through the enactment of House Concurrent Resolution 108, where the 83rd Congress declared that the United States' policy toward Native Americans was withdrawal of federal supervision over the Indians "as rapidly as possible." Its declaration proclaimed that Indians would "assume their full responsibilities as American citizens."

House Concurrent Resolution 108 reads:

> Whereas it is the policy of Congress, as rapidly as possible, to make the Indians within the territorial limits of the United States subject to the same laws and entitled to the same privileges and responsibilities as are applicable to other citizens of the United States, to end their status as wards of the United States, and to grant them all of the rights and prerogatives pertaining to American citizenship; and
>
> Whereas the Indians within the territorial limits of the United States should assume their full responsibilities as American citizens.
>
> *(See the complete text of HCR 108 US Statutes at Large, Aug. 1, 1953, 67 Stat. B123, with the specific terminations mentioned, Appendix D, p. 365)*

The terminology of Senator Watkins and Congress' resolution actually sounded pretty good – certainly nothing to be alarmed about, right? Most Indians did want to be free from the federal *paternalism* over their lives. The words, "to end their status as *wards* of the United States," were welcoming words. Many Indian tribes felt the restrictive governmental controls, in seemingly every area of their life, were quite suffocating.

What Happened to the IRA?

The Indian Reorganization Act (IRA) had been making headway by stopping the selling of Indian lands and even creating an increase to Indian landholdings. The IRA also helped many tribal governments with their written constitutions and taking control of their own resources, setting up true economic development on tribal lands. Certainly, though, the IRA was *not* a cure-all for the multitude of problematic issues the Indians faced and it was not without its critics. Not all Indian tribes supported this legislation. When it came to the point where the individual tribes needed to vote on its implementation for their government, a minority of the tribes rejected it. [4]

The votes against the IRA were for various reasons, but there certainly were grave concerns and suspicions about trusting yet another law that was intended "for their benefit." The tribes were still reeling from the last piece of legislation that was enacted for their good, which had devastatingly stripped them of much of their valuable land and resources, along with debilitating their cultural norms. [5] Also, the IRA was not totally Indian-friendly. Although it was a tremendous move in the right direction, it had pieces either eliminated because "it was felt that the Indians were not yet ready" [6] or kept governmental control over things which many tribes recognized as another infringement of their tribal sovereignty.

The IRA was put in place during the post WWI era, and was just starting to take root when it felt the impact of WWII. Of course, monies and resources were necessarily diverted to the war effort, but there were other factors that affected the IRA's development because of the war. As seen in the previous war, Native Americans were quick to defend their homeland. Now US citizens (since 1924), Native Americans would fall under the draft requirements, yet many enlisted prior to being drafted. The Indian tribes had many of their leaders involved in the war effort while managing on the home front with only a core group.

Dr. Ian Barnes' book, *The Historical Atlas of Native Americans*, (Chartwell Books, Inc. 2009, p. 368-369) gives statistical information and great examples of Native American's involvement in WWII:

- ► The scale of Native American enlistment during World War II was greater as a percentage of their total number than any other ethnic group.
- ► Of 350,000 Native Americans, 44,000 saw military service.
- ► The Pueblos provided 213 men, 10 percent of their 2,205 population.
- ► Nearly all able-bodied Ojibwa at the Grand Portage Reservation enlisted.
- ► The Navajo contributed 3,600 men.
- ► One quarter of the New Mexico Mescalero Apache enlisted, rather than wait for their draft cards.
- ► Several hundred Indian women also served in the Women's Army Corps (WAC), Women Accepted for Volunteer Emergency Service (WAVE), and Army Medical Corps nurses.
- ► Native Americans in the Army often hit the headlines, but three times as many served in the Navy.
- ► One, Oklahoma Cherokee Joseph (Jocko) Clark, an Annapolis graduate, made the rank of admiral.
- ► The Air Corps generally took Indians from the more assimilated tribes in Oklahoma, Texas, and Wisconsin.
- ► Over 40,000 Indian men and women left their lands to take up war-related work.

As war veterans returned to their reservations, their global experiences gave them a new perspective. Many worked toward a better life for their people. But what were the steps needed to change things for the better? At the very least, it seemed that freedom from the federal yoke must take place. Various leaders, both Indian and non-Indian, talked about freedom and liberty from federal supervision. Many looked at termination as the way to stop federal ward-ship of the Native Americans. Although it seemed Indians and non-Indians were saying similar things initially, the common ground quickly eroded as governmental actions revealed what was meant by the words "freedom" and "liberty."

Actions Speak Louder Than Words

The policy of termination, lasting a decade and a half, involved a multitude of people – yet termination was certainly driven and directed by some key players. Of these *key players*, two strong personalities emerged to the forefront. This duo generally allowed the true issues to remain clouded or oversimplified. Each held a position of influence to significantly promote the policy of termination: Senator Arthur V. Watkins of Utah and Commissioner of Indian Affairs, Dillon S. Myer.

The purpose of showing a brief characterization of these two men is not to vilify individuals, but rather, to show the underlying ethnocentric beliefs these men demonstrated. Both Watkins and Myer, as representative of many others of the time, believed all Americans should be alike. Termination was equivalent to assimilation – throwing the Indian into the cultural melting pot to become the one-American ideal. To these men, preserving any culture different than the one-American ideal was unnecessary and simply slowed down the process of assimilation. Therefore, the termination policy was very rigid and narrow in determining how to *free the Indian*.

Say it Simply!

"ethnocentric" -- seeing all others through one's own culture; belief that one's own culture is superior to others and is the standard by which all other cultures are to be measured.

Arthur V. Watkins was a self-made man. Starting from humble beginnings, he worked hard to establish himself as a farmer, a lawyer and prestigious member of his community. He had never received any handouts or special privileges from the government – so why should the Indians? He was "convinced . . . that Indians had it too easy." [7]

He also believed the Indians simply wanted to take advantage of the system, but he told them they needed to "grow up" and not act as "children." [8] He was not unknown to use manipulative tactics to accomplish his agenda toward Native Americans. His position as a US Senator and acting chairman of the Senate's Indian subcommittee, allowed him to be directly involved in many discussions and negotiations with Indian tribes and their members. Senator Watkins did not believe the United States had a responsibility to uphold its treaty obligations with Indian tribes, because Indians became US citizens, and "the United States did not enter into treaties with any of its citizens." [9]

A crowning moment for Indians nation-wide, in Senator Watkin's opinion, was when, on June 17, 1954, the Menomiee of Wisconsin's property and individual members were terminated from federal supervision. He called the Menomiee termination "a landmark in Indian legislative history." [10] Yes, it ultimately was a landmark – but not for positive results as the Senator indicated.

The Menomiee tribe, who operated their own lumber industry, were no burden on the federal government. They were self-sufficient through their tribal business. Not only did they cover their own expenses, they also supported a hospital, utility company and even paid the salaries for the Bureau of Indian Affairs staff working with them. [11] The Menomiees were not, by national standards, rich, but they were one of the richest of the Indian tribes. The effects of the Menominee Indian Termination Act [12] brought this formally self-sufficient tribe quickly into a $300,000 deficit at the beginning of its termination.

Dillon S. Myer also was a man who started life of simple means, as a farm boy from Ohio. He eventually worked for the US Department of Agriculture. Later in 1942 through 1946, he worked for the Department of the Interior as director of the War Relocation Authority. In this position he oversaw the WWII Japanese Internment Camps.

Dig Deeper

Read Richard Drinnon's, *Keeper of the Concentration Camps: Dillon S. Myer and American Racisim*, 1987 University of California Press.

A few years later, Myer was asked to serve as the Commissioner of Indian Affairs, Bureau of Indian Affairs. Myer was known as a man who could get things done. He was also known to run a forceful, my-way-or-the-highway administration. Those who did not agree with him in the bureau, he simply removed. His determined goal as Commissioner was "to dissolve the Bureau of Indian Affairs, and . . . liberate Native Americans to enjoy the privileges and rights guaranteed in the United States Constitution." To accomplish his goal of doing away with the Bureau of Indian Affairs, he looked to the state-level agencies to pick up the slack.

One glimpse into Myers personality and way of thinking is demonstrated in a seemingly relaxed interview he had years after leaving the BIA with an interviewer in Berkeley, California. [13] The interviewer asked him to reflect on his assignment with Indian Affairs. In his response he recalled one Indian group who made his life hard while he served at the BIA. This group, the Congress of American Indians, [14] were characterized, from his perspective, as harassing the BIA, digging up dirt and spreading rumors. Myer told the interviewer that he was offended these Indian people wanted the Federal Indian Bureau to run in a way that suited *them*. He recalled that at one meeting, representatives from the Congress of American Indians spoke out in strong support of the BIA continuing an Indian advisory council. Myer had not made up his mind if he wanted to have an Indian advisory council, but after this group expressed their views, he became determined *not* to incorporate one. Myer couldn't believe these Indian representatives had the *audacity* to tell him what he should do. This group had emphasized that he should have an Indian advisory council – and *not* make policy decisions without consulting with this council of Indians. Well, this was too much for Myer! He immediately responded that he would not handicap his job as Commissioner or limit his functions with such nonsense. *No one* was going to make his decisions for him!

Say it Simply!

"audacity" -- shameless boldness, daring

Dig Deeper

The interview mentioned above can be read online at the Harry S. Truman, online Library & Museum, *Oral History Interview with Dillon S. Myer*, Chapter XII, section 296-297 at: *http://www.trumanlibrary.org/oralhist/myerds3.htm#295*

The 83rd Congress

PL 280 is sometimes referred to as Public Law 83-280. The *"83"* is an indicator of the *83rd US Congress*.

The Termination Period covered fifteen years, from 1945 through 1960. The 83rd Congress, which convened between January 3, 1953, through January 3, 1955, heard more on Indian issues than prior Congresses. This Congress also acted on about one-sixth of the bills regarding Indian affairs that were introduced. [15] The 83rd Congress was the Congress who enacted both House Concurrent Resolution 108 and Public Law 83-280. [16]

"zenith" -- highest point

The timing of the 83rd Congress was also the beginning of the Eisenhower administration. [17] Upon entering into office, President Eisenhower faced several international issues that necessarily kept his focus. He depended on his Vice President and executive officers to help him accomplish his goals. Specifically regarding Native American issues, "the Eisenhower administration depended upon . . . its Indian experts." [18] While the 83rd Congress has the distinction of being the legislative assembly who sat at the Termination Period's *zenith*, the direction of Indian policy and legislation presented was actually monopolized by a handful of members of this Congress. As significant as HCR 108 was to Indian policy, it was passed with very little discussion. Many members of Congress were entrenched in the bigger issues of the day. [19]

The Bureau of Indian Affairs (BIA) worked closely with the Senate subcommittee on Indian Affairs (with acting chairman Senator Arthur Watkins), submitting a total of 162 reports. Many of these reports relayed an optimistic view of Indian *progress* into mainstream America. [20] Much to the dismay of the Indians, tribal communities were put on a schedule for termination.

There are several books that go into detail concerning stories of Indian tribes who were terminated during the Termination Period. The following are a suggested few:

1) *Termination and Relocation: Federal Indian Policy*, 1945-1960, by Donald L. Fixico
2) *Seeking Recognition: The Termination and Restoration of the Coos, Lower Umpqua, and Siuslaw Indians*, 1855-1984, by David R. M. Beck
3) *American Indian Nations from Termination to Restoration*, 1953-2006, by Roberta Ulrich
4) *Bartering with the Bones of Their Dead: The Colville Confederated Tribes and Termination*, by Laurie Arnold
5) *Termination Revisited: American Indians on the Trail to Self-Determination*, 1933-1953, by Kenneth R. Philp

On the List

There was actually a list made up by the BIA rating the period of time expected before a tribe could be terminated. These rating periods fell into three categories and every tribe was somewhere on that list. [21]

The three categories were:

1) Ready for immediate termination
2) Ready in ten years for termination
3) Ready in as long as fifty years for termination

Ten tribes were identified as falling into the first category of immediate termination. It was also made note that these terminations would save the federal government approximately five million dollars annually. That was music to the ears of legislators whose goal was to reduce the size of the federal bureaucracy during a time of great national debt. [22]

Dig Deeper

Kenneth R. Philp's book, *Termination Revisited*, has a copy of the list. Philp, Kenneth R., *Termination Revisited*, University of Nebraska Press 1999, pp. 72-75.

The Term "Termination"

We've used the word "termination" quite a bit, but what did termination really mean? If you had asked that question during the Termination Period, you would have gotten quite a variety of answers such as . . .

Termination is making the Indian a first-class citizen . . . It's the desegregation of the Indian race . . . *It's ending the unacceptable wardship or trust status of Indians* . . . It's bringing Indians into the one-American ideal melting pot . . . *It's the assumption by individual Indians of all the duties, obligations, and privileges of free citizens* . . . It's freedom from federal supervision and control . . . *It's escaping the over-supervision and over-regulation of the BIA* . . . It's breaking the limitations that only apply to Indians . . . *etc.*

There was a real problem with vague ideas expressed by people who were unaware of the historical background and political consequences of such ideas. They either did not understand the unique relationship of the Indian tribes and the federal government – or, perhaps, simply didn't care. To use just one example, saying *"ending the unacceptable wardship or trust status of Indians"* sounds easy enough, but how can it be done legally without discarding important trust obligations of the federal government? That's not to say it couldn't or shouldn't be done, it's just that there was a lot more involved legally than people indicated or even realized.

Various Indian groups brought to light a host of *unresolved* issues regarding termination. There were questions about the land, water and mineral rights, liens on properties and taxes, buildings needing to be brought up to code, medical and educational services, hunting and fishing rights guaranteed in treaties, irrigation on poor lands, correct land divisions drawn up, etc. How could there be meaningful discussions about terminating the federal supervision over Indians with these important concerns left unanswered? Certainly, it was the Indians' future, individually and as tribal units, that hung in the balance.

Quotes

"Dare we let Indians do their own thinking? *What to prune and what to retain of the Indian way of life must in the end be decided by Indians themselves. Like unwise parents, the Federal government and the church . . . have in the past often denied the Indians their right of self-determination by deciding many issues for them. This has been done frequently without understanding Indian purposes and tendencies and all unmindful of the full consequences the destruction of one element in Indian life may have on the total interrelated structure."*

Bronson, Ruth Muskrat, Indians Are People Too, Friendship Press, 1944, pp. 80-81

Nerdy Stuff

One archive that documents discussions before the Senate Interior and Insular Affairs Committee about the legal implications of termination, tells how the Associate Commissioner of Indian Affairs, H. Rex Lee, when asked, stated he had no idea how many treaties the United States had made with the Indian tribes. He also wasn't worried about getting tribal consent to adjust the treaties because, "… if they won't consent, some compromise will just have to be reached." His goal was to "get this thing wound up." See book: *Keeper of the Concentration Camps*, by Richard Drinnon, University of California Press 1987, p. 171.

Dig Deeper

The author of a book published during the Termination Period, *Indians Are People Too*, does an amazing job explaining the Indian perspective. Of course, this author, Ruth Muskrat Bronson, is only one individual, and she could not speak for all Indians, but she was an articulate voice of reason, helping, especially non-Indians, have a clearer picture of the issues at hand. See: Bronson, Ruth Muskrat, *Indians Are People Too*, Friendship Press 1944.

Merely Semantics?

Say it Simply!

"semantics" -- interpretation of a word or the meaning of a word or words

"polarizing" -- divide sharply into two extreme, opposite sides

"synonymous" -- equivalent in meaning, expressing the same idea

One may wonder, "Was the issue between those *for* termination and those *against* termination merely a matter of *semantics*? Were they really trying to accomplish the same things but they just didn't know how to express it correctly?" The answer is a most definite "no." It was an advantage to those supporting termination to keep their motives hidden. Yet, when all the nice-sounding words were stripped away to expose the true meaning of termination, it simply meant that the ***Indians were to go away and be no more***. Termination, from the government's perspective, was in no uncertain terms the ultimate and total assimilation of all Indians into society at-large. How could this not have a *polarizing* effect – *one way or another* – once it was understood?

Desegregation & Assimilation Synonyms?

A simple comparison of the two words, "desegregation" and "assimilation" will give you an idea of why Indian tribes were, in fact, almost completely opposed to termination. Racial desegregation was a hot topic of the day and termination was touted as being the government's method of desegregating the Indians. Yet, when you compare the two words – the implication of "desegregation" is a far cry from the implication of "assimilation." These two words are *not synonymous* terms.

(Racial) Desegregation = seeing all people equal; color-blind in regard to opportunities; no race superior and no race inferior to another race

Assimilation = implies one society is superior to another; forcing conformity to society's norms; no significant variations are to exist; non-conformity is not tolerated

As you see, the two words are very different. With desegregation there can still exist individuality. However, assimilation will not tolerate diversity and one must blend into the dominant society with no significantly unique distinctions.

Dig Deeper

According to the book entitled, *Indians Are People Too*, the author explains how Indian people wanted liberty, equality and freedom. Indians wanted the right to work with equal opportunity, political and social freedom. They never wanted someone else to carry their responsibilities or burdens – and they wanted the freedom to make their own mistakes and learn from them. Bronson, Ruth Muskrat, *Indians Are People Too*, Friendship Press, 1944, p. 180.

Nerdy Stuff

The immigration policy of the day revealed national intolerance of cultures that were too different, greatly favoring Western European immigration. The Immigration and Nationality Act of 1952 set forth immigration limitations primarily in the form of the national origins quota system. This immigration act passed both the House and the Senate, overriding the veto of President Truman who had declared, ". . . we have entered into an alliance, the North Atlantic Treaty, with Italy, Greece, and Turkey against one of the most terrible threats mankind has ever faced. We are asking them to join with us in protecting the peace of the world. We are helping them to build their defenses, and train their men, in the common cause. But, through this bill we say to their people: You are less worthy to come to this country than Englishmen or Irishmen . . ." US Immigration Law and Policy, 1952-1986, A report prepared for the use of the Subcommittee on Immigration and Refugee Affairs, Committee on the Judiciary, United States Senate, p.1.

Oscillating Policy

"oscillated" -- to swing back and forth, as a pendulum does

"periphery" -- the far edge, outskirts

Through the years the United States' federal Indian policy "*oscillated*," [23] going one way, and then another way. The allotment policy had shifted to the policy of reorganization, only to then move towards a termination policy. With the ending of treaty-making in the late 1800's, Congress often made decisions regarding Indian tribes without even talking to the people who were greatly affected by those decisions. Although the tribes had lost their formal government-to-government negotiating power through treaty-making, starting in the early to mid 1900's, Indian people found other ways to make their voices heard. Out of necessity, Indian groups united in order to speak up for the issues that were impacting their tribal communities.

The official website for one of these Indian groups who evolved out of these difficult times, the National Congress of American Indians, gives some history that you can look up at: *www.ncai.org*. The website states, "The National Congress of American Indians, founded in 1944, is the oldest, largest and most represented American Indian and Alaska Native organization serving the broad interests of tribal governments and communities."

Collectively, Indians were very concerned how the federal laws would affect them. Indians expressed their views and misgivings to legislators during the Termination Period. "Indians did not remain on the *periphery* of events during termination." [24] This was especially true during the days leading up to the enactment of PL 280. "The Public Law 280 legislation was approved by Congress in the face of strenuous Indian opposition and denied consent of the Indian tribes affected by the Act." [25]

Steps Towards PL 280

State agencies had become involved with tribal communities when Congress, in 1929, transferred some of the federal health and educational responsibilities to the states. This had been in response to the Meriam report's findings and recommendations. [26] Federal money was delegated to the states to fund these new responsibilities. Legislators additionally began looking at ways to transfer federal civil and/or criminal jurisdiction in Indian country to the states. This had also been recommended in the 1928 Meriam report because "the maintenance of order and the administration of justice among restricted Indians on the reservation" was *"unsatisfactory."* [27]

Say it Simply!

"feasible" -- able to be done or put into effect, possible

This criticism of law and order being unsatisfactory was attributed, in the report, to several factors. Remember, the purpose of the report was to logically analyze the situation of Indian affairs, collect and document factual data, and then present *feasible* solutions for any deficiencies found. With this in mind, consider the eight areas of concern that were specifically pointed out in the Meriam report as the reasons why the federal maintenance and administration of law and order was given the "unsatisfactory" grade.

Eight findings specific to federal jurisdictional issues in Indian country (All of these findings are contained within the Meriam report, Chapter 13 – "Legal Aspects of the Indian Problem", pp. 743 – 811):

Finding #1: Federal Indian Law was confusing, voluminous and complex.

Finding #2: Federal criminal Indian law was very specialized and incomplete.

Finding #3: There were jurisdictional gaps – It was a burden for US judges to deal with minor civil and misdemeanor cases that generally would fall to a local Justice of the Peace – US judges generally would not hear such cases.

Finding #4: No Federal Indian civil law existed.

Finding #5: The states expressed much uncertainty and confusion about jurisdiction on Indian lands. States did not get involved and acknowledged Indian reservations as the exclusive problem of the national government – "government in spots".

Finding #6: Federal US courts were often located far away from the reservations.

Finding #7: Areas such as California had tribes scattered throughout the state which made it virtually impossible for Indian Office agents to effectively maintain the order and administration of justice.

Finding #8: Some states were not yet willing to accept jurisdiction over Indian country or the local sentiment toward Indians was so hostile or indifferent that Indians would not get a fair trial – or perhaps no trial at all. Federal courts should remain a viable option for more serious cases where Indians would not otherwise receive justice at the local level. For the protection of the Indians, property rights needed to remain protected at the federal level.

As mentioned earlier, the scientific minds who drafted the Meriam report had ruled out, as a *long-term solution*, tribal governments' administration of their own justice. It was believed the tribes had gone through too much and were so broken down that independent tribal government would *eventually* be a moot point. Accompanying this assumption was the clear purpose of the federal government to "adjust" Indians "to the prevailing civilization of the state and nation." [28]

However, to say the report made recommendations for the tribal administration of justice and its courts to be totally eliminated would *not* be accurate. Total assimilation into the prevailing society was the ultimate goal – but until that time was properly and responsibly determined, there were valid reasons for supporting the tribal systems of justice. The report made special notice that the more remote Indian reservations especially depended on such a system and the development of a practical "non-technical" written code for the tribal courts was encouraged for all existing tribal courts. [29]

To read about the findings in the Meriam report more thoroughly, read Chapter 13 – "Legal Aspects of the Indian Problem", pp. 743 -811. Online you can download the report from: *http://www.eric.ed.gov/PDFS/ED087573.pdf*

Say it Simply!

"fragmented" -- not unified, disorganized, individual pieces

Make the Comparison

PL 280 is often read as an isolated piece of legislation -- causing PL 280 to appear a bit *fragmented*.

If PL 280 is read, instead, considering the findings of the Meriam report, it makes more sense why certain provisions were included. It would be reasonable and prudent for legislators to look to an authoritative source, such as the Meriam report, for guidance in drafting PL 280. Indeed, this report was the most comprehensive, exhaustive and impartial report to-date on Indian affairs.

See the chart (CH-4A) on the next page comparing the Meriam report's findings with the provisions that were included in PL 280. As you read PL 280 from this perspective, it seems evident that this law was written with very specific concerns in mind, and its provisions definitely were not pulled out of thin air.

The maintenance of order and the administration of justice = "unsatisfactory"

Meriam Report Findings	PL 280 Provisions
Finding #1: Federal Indian Law was confusing, voluminous and complex ***Finding #2:*** Federal criminal Indian law was very specialized and incomplete ***Finding #3:*** There were jurisdictional gaps – It was a burden for US judges to deal with minor civil and misdemeanor cases that generally would fall to a local Justice of the Peace – US judges generally would not hear such cases ***Finding #4:*** No Federal Indian civil law existed	In order to remove confusion and complexity, it was simply written that a State's criminal laws would be consistent on or off Indian country. Also, the same way a State dealt with civil causes of action of general applicability, was exactly the same way it was to be applied in Indian country. This addressed the issue of jurisdictional gaps and the problems associated with incomplete federal laws. *". . . such State has jurisdiction over offenses committed elsewhere within the State, and the criminal laws of such State shall have the same force and effect within such Indian country as they have elsewhere within the State."* *"States listed . . . shall have jurisdiction over civil causes of action between Indians or to which Indians are parties . . . to the same extent that such State has jurisdiction over other civil causes of action, and those civil laws of such State that are of general application to private persons or private property shall have the same force and effect within such Indian country as they have elsewhere within the State."*
Finding #5: The states expressed much uncertainty and confusion about jurisdiction on Indian lands. States did not get involved and acknowledged Indian reservations as the exclusive problem of the national government – "government in spots"	The two major laws which authorized federal criminal jurisdiction in Indian country, the General Crimes Act and the Major Crimes Act, were declared "not to be applicable" in the mandatory states. This provided clarity to these states that federal criminal jurisdiction was completely transferred to their jurisdictions. *"The provisions of sections 1152 and 1153 of this chapter shall not be applicable within the areas of Indian country listed . . ."*
Finding #6: US courts were often located far away from the reservations ***Finding #7:*** Areas such as California have tribes scattered throughout the state which made it virtually impossible for Indian Office agents to effectively maintain the order and administration of justice	Mandatory states were chosen for reasons that benefited the federal government more than consideration of how the law would affect the states. Reducing federal costs and conserving resources were considerations. "Congress, we are told, passed Pub. L. 280 not as a measure to benefit the States, but to reduce the economic burdens associated with federal jurisdiction on reservations." *Washington v. Confederate Bands and Tribes of the Yakima Indian Nation, 439 US 463, 498 (1979)*
Finding #8: Some states were not yet willing to accept jurisdiction over Indian country or the local sentiment toward Indians was so hostile or indifferent that Indians would not get a fair trial – or perhaps no trial at all. Federal courts should remain a viable option for more serious cases where Indians would not otherwise receive justice at the local level. For the protection of the Indians, property rights needed to remain protected at the federal level.	"The consent of the United States" was given to all other states to assume "criminal offenses or civil causes of action, or . . . both" when the people of the State bound themselves to this jurisdiction by legislative action. In these optional states, federal jurisdiction was *not* removed but remained *concurrent.* Regarding property rights, both the criminal and civil sections clearly protect the property right of "any Indian or any Indian tribe."

CH -4A

Not a Termination Statute

It must be noted that PL 280, in and of itself, is *not* a termination statute. [30] It specifically provided for the protection of lands, including water rights, belonging to any Indian or Indian tribe, held in trust by the United States. Additionally, it protected federal treaty, agreement or statute rights and provided for incorporation of tribal ordinances or customs into civil causes of action involving Indians in Indian country.

Quotes

> *"Pub. L. 280 was plainly not meant to effect total assimilation. Public L. 280 was only one of many types of assimilationist legislation under active consideration."*
>
> *Bryan v. Itasca County, 426 U.S. 373, 387 (1976)*

There were two other clear indications that PL 280 was not intended for total assimilation of the tribes. The first proof of this was the fact that Congress actually *did* enact several termination acts specifically spelling out their intent of total termination. If Congress had wanted PL 280 to terminate the tribes "Congress knew well how to express its intent" and "it would have expressly said so." [31]

Say it Simply!

"exempted" -- to be freed from an obligation others are subject to

"purview" -- control, authority

Secondly, "certain tribal reservations were completely *exempted* from the provisions of Pub. L. 280 precisely because each had 'a tribal law-and-order organization that function(ed) in a reasonably satisfactory manner.' Congress plainly meant only to allow state courts to decide criminal and civil matters arising on reservations not so organized." [32] In fact, when President Eisenhower eventually signed PL 280 into law he noted, "Three Indian tribes that have effective law and order organizations of their own, (have) asked to be excluded from the *purview* of the bill." One of Eisenhower's strong objections to the bill was that certain sections of PL 280 could unnecessarily, in some instances, remove the Indians from "effective *self-government*." [33]

Key Point

Even though PL 280 was enacted at the height of the Termination Period, it is *not* a termination statute.

Exempted from PL 280

The original version of PL 280 when it was enacted in 1953, (see copy in Appendix E, pgs. 366-367) contained three exemptions to PL 280 jurisdiction in the listed PL 280 states of 18 USC § 1162. The three tribes who were exempt were the Red Lake Reservation in Minnesota, the Warm Springs Reservation in Oregon, and the Menominee Reservation in Wisconsin. These tribes had specifically petitioned for an exemption of PL 280's jurisdiction on their lands: [34]

► *The Red Lake Band of Chippewa Indians in Minnesota*
This tribe unanimously opposed state jurisdiction because "State law would not be of any benefit to tribal members and . . . tribal members should (first) be given an opportunity by referendum to accept or reject the extension of State jurisdiction."

► *The Warm Springs Tribe of Oregon*
This tribe reportedly opposed state jurisdiction due to "fear that its members would not be treated fairly in the State courts."

► *The Menominee Tribe of Wisconsin*
This tribe expressed their reason for opposing state jurisdiction was because "its tribal organization was capable of maintaining order on the reservation and . . . its people are not yet ready to be subjected to State laws."

Say it Simply!

"mandate" -- an order or command

There were five states specifically listed: California, Minnesota, Nebraska, Oregon and Wisconsin (Alaska was included later after statehood). All Indian tribes within these States' boundaries were included in PL 280 jurisdiction except for the three exceptions. PL 280 was the express *mandate* from Congress to the states and the tribes to incorporate the specified state jurisdiction in Indian country. Congress had *passed the baton* –

and it wasn't optional. This is why these five states, and later six states, have been referred to as the *"Mandatory PL 280 States."* Unfortunately, this was an *unfunded mandate*, causing a financial strain upon these States' budgets. Lack of funding also created tensions between state and tribal governments regarding quantity and quality of services provided. State-level services were supposed to benefit the tribes, but with no monies designated for these responsibilities, the results were often quite the opposite of this goal. This lack of funding was one of the criticisms by the Indian communities who alleged PL 280 was "deficient in that it failed to fund the States who assumed jurisdiction and as a result vacuums of law enforcement protection have occurred in certain Indian reservations and communities." [35]

For any other state, the original version of PL 280 allowed each non-mandatory state to choose for themselves if they wanted to take over jurisdiction in Indian country. This was completely up to the states, requiring no consent of – or even consultation with – the Indian tribes that would be affected. These states are often called the *"Option States."*

Fix the Problem

Shortly before Congress' final approval of Public Law 280, a Congressional report had stated:

> "The States lack jurisdiction to prosecute Indians for most offenses committed on Indian reservations or other Indian country, with limited exceptions. The applicability of Federal criminal laws in States having Indian reservations is also limited . . . As a practical matter, the enforcement of law and order among the Indians in the Indian country has been left largely to the Indian groups themselves. In many States, tribes are not adequately organized to perform that function; consequently, there has been created a hiatus in law enforcement authority that could best be remedied by conferring criminal jurisdiction on States indicating an ability and willingness to accept such responsibility."
>
> *House Report No. 848, July 16, 1953*

Congress attempted to fix the problem of the *unsatisfactory maintenance of order and the administration of justice* on the reservations through legislation that eventually became known as PL 280 (pg. 194, Chart CH-4A). There was acknowledgement that "tribal law and order enforcement has completely broken down." [36] Legislators were of the opinion that the best plan of action was to rely on the states to take over criminal jurisdiction in Indian country. They also felt private civil litigation could be *completely* handled at the state level.

There had been earlier discussion about obtaining tribal consent before a state would assume jurisdiction in Indian country. Tribal spokespersons had clearly identified the point of tribal consent as a necessary element for any legislation affecting the tribes. At the hearings on "State Legal Jurisdiction in Indian Country," Indian Commissioner, Dillon S. Myer, suggested tribal consent would not be advisable because "tribes with 'a completely inadequate law and order code and ... policing system' might vote against state jurisdiction." [37]

Some representatives of Indian tribes and Indian groups were able to speak with the Senate subcommittee prior to the enactment of PL 280. They expressed how they generally favored state jurisdiction "in terms of escaping the 'oversupervision and overregulation' of (the) BIA." [38] One individual metaphorically spoke of the "iron rule of the Indian Bureau." [39] Nearly all stressed the importance of including tribal consent as a provision before any State jurisdiction would take place. Their concurrence with the proposed legislation was _contingent_ upon the requirement of a tribal referendum prior to the federal government's transfer of jurisdiction to any state. [40]

Say it Simply!

"contingent" -- conditional, subject to

Quotes "Q"

> *"Public Law 280 was the first jurisdictional bill of general applicability ever to be enacted by Congress. It reflected congressional concern over the law-and-order problems on Indian reservations and the financial burdens of continued federal jurisdictional responsibilities on Indian lands. It was also, however, without question reflective of the general assimilationist policy followed by Congress from the early 1950's through the late 1960's. The failure of Congress to write a tribal-consent provision into the transfer provision applicable to option States as well as its failure to consult with the tribes during the final deliberations on Pub. L. 280 provide ample evidence of this."*
>
> *Washington v. Confederated Bands and Tribes of the Yakima Indian Nation, 439 U.S. 463, 488, 489 (1979)*

Grave Doubts

PL 280 was approved by both the Senate and the House on the first day of August, 1953. This law was sent to the president for his final signature. President Eisenhower officially signed PL 280 into law on August 15, 1953. How fitting it was that the very first thing the president stated after signing PL 280 was that he had "grave doubts as to the wisdom of certain provisions contained" in it. He was not pleased PL 280 did not include "a requirement of full consultation" with the Indians "in order to ascertain" their "wishes and desires." He recommended "that at the earliest possible time in the next session of the Congress, the Act be amended to require such consultation with the tribes prior to the enactment of legislation subjecting them to state jurisdiction." [41]

Nerdy Stuff

President Eisenhower, who served the United States as a 5-Star General, stated, "Never did I hear a complaint about the battle conduct of the Native American Indian."

Meadows, William C., *The Comanche Code Talkers of World War II*, University of Texas Press 2002, p. 39.

Termination Repudiated

Although President Eisenhower strongly encouraged Congress to include tribal consent as a required element of PL 280, this provision would not become a reality until fifteen years later. During these many years, tribal groups and their supporters worked tirelessly informing both legislators and the public about why they were troubled, *even* alarmed, with the PL 280 legislation and the termination policy in general. [42]

As the devastating effects of termination were realized, legislators moved further and further away from supporting this federal policy. The tide began to turn regarding federal withdrawal during the Kennedy administration with the appointment of Dr. Philleo Nash as Commissioner of Indian Affairs. Dr. Nash, in his 1961 Annual Report, recommended a shift *away from* termination of federal trust relationships. Instead, he believed the emphasis in federal programs should be towards greater development of the human and natural resources on Indian reservations. [43]

Say it Simply!

"repudiated" -- rejected, renounced

President Johnson continued the momentum in his speech, *"The Forgotten American,"* where he stated, "We must assure the Indian people that it is our desire and intention that the special relationship between the Indian and his government grow and flourish. For, the first among us must not be last." [44] In this speech he publically *repudiated* the federal policy of termination. [45]

President Johnson then went on to encourage Congress to pass the Indian Civil Rights Act (ICRA) which included the provision of tribal consent prior to a state assuming PL 280 jurisdiction. He explained the ICRA would:

> "... remedy another matter of grave concern to the American Indian. Fifteen years ago, the Congress gave to the States authority to extend their criminal and civil jurisdictions to include Indian reservations – where jurisdiction previously was in the hands of the Indians themselves.
>
> Fairness and basic democratic principles require that Indians on the affected lands have a voice in deciding whether a State will assume legal jurisdiction on their land. I urge the Congress to enact legislation that would provide for tribal consent before such extensions of jurisdiction take place."
>
> *President Lyndon B. Johnson's Special Message to the Congress on the Problems of the American Indian: "The Forgotten American," March 6, 1968*

The president did not have to prod Congress too much, at this point in time, to support tribal consent, as many legislators were already moving in that direction. There were eighteen Senators who introduced a Senate Concurrent Resolution that stated the sense of Congress to be that:

> "the deplorable conditions [46] of American Indians and Alaska natives can only be alleviated through a sustained, positive, and dynamic Indian policy with the necessary constructive programs and services directed to the governing bodies of these groups for application in their respective communities, offering self-determination and self-help features for the people involved."
>
> *Senate Concurrent Resolution 11, 90th Congress, 2nd Session, p.2*

Of course, not everyone wanted to see the termination policy change. Termination's assimilation ideals had been deeply ingrained into the public mind-set. This was evidenced in a 1962 editorial in the Washington *Star*, which stated Indians needed to "join the rest of the country and stop stagnating as museum pieces." The writer of the editorial reasoned that the "average Indian was not stupid," therefore they should easily be able to assimilate into the dominant white society. [47]

Halls of Congress

We have made reference to the 83rd Congress many times through this chapter. It is this group who is infamous for their enactment of Public Law 83-280. Have you wondered though, "Exactly *who* made up the 83rd Congress?"

We invite you to take a minute to stroll down the halls of Congress to get acquainted with this group of legislators. As we open the doors to the chamber where they are assembled, many of you will be surprised by the familiar faces. Go ahead – walk down the aisle and rub shoulders with the 83rd Congress . . .

. . . Presiding as the President of the Senate is Vice President *Richard Nixon*. In approximately fifteen years he will be the 37th President of the United States.

. . . The Democratic House Minority Leader and Conference Chairman is a man named *Lyndon B. Johnson* who will become the 36th US President.

. . . You then glance over to see a young man of ruddy complexion who appears to be in his mid-thirties. Although he introduces himself to you as *Senator John F. Kennedy* from Massachusetts, you will always remember him as *President Kennedy*, who will soon serve as the 35th President of the United States.

. . . Next, you meet one of the House Representatives from the State of Michigan, *Gerald Ford*. He too will eventually become a United States President – the 38th President to be exact.

. . . You begin to walk towards the back of the room, as Congress is just about to convene, when you see one more familiar face before exiting. This man with thick eyebrows and broad chin smiles and gives a friendly nod. You return the smile and nod, knowing he will become the Vice President under President Johnson, *Hubert Humphrey* of Minnesota.

So, now you know some of the composition of the 83rd Congress. Quite an impressive group, wouldn't you say? We know these men would later reject the termination policy. As the ill effects of termination became known, these leaders said, *"no more!"* In repudiating the termination policy, these legislators were not the *new-kids-on-the-block* jumping on the latest political bandwagon. Rather, these were men who had been in the thick of events during the termination policy, and had seen first-hand its devastating results. When they renounced termination as a policy – they knew what they were talking about!

As *Vice President*, Richard Nixon was *Senate President* according to the US Constitution: "The Vice President of the United States shall be President of the Senate." Art. 1, sec. 3, cl. 4.

Termination to Self-Determination

It was President Richard Nixon's special message on Indian affairs to Congress on July 8, 1970, that became the national commencement of a new era in Indian policy. President Nixon started out this speech by saying:

"The first Americans – the Indians – are the most deprived and most isolated minority group in our nation. On virtually every scale of measurement – employment, income, education, health – the condition of the Indian people ranks at the bottom.

This condition is the heritage of centuries of injustice. From the time of their first contact with European settlers, the American Indians have been oppressed and brutalized, deprived of their ancestral lands and denied the opportunity to control their own destiny. Even the Federal programs which are intended to meet their needs have frequently proved to be ineffective and demeaning.

But the story of the Indian in America is something more than the record of the white man's frequent aggression, broken agreements, intermittent remorse and prolonged failure. It is a record also of endurance, of survival, of adaptation and creativity in the face of overwhelming obstacles."

President Richard Nixon's Special Message to the Congress on Indian Affairs, July 8, 1970

Say it Simply!

"demeaning" -- humiliating, to lower in dignity, honor or standing

These were powerful words spoken by a United States president. Remember, Nixon sat with the Congress who heard more about Indian affairs than any other Congress. He witnessed the whole progression of the policy of termination and the resulting reality of federal withdrawal of Indian communities. From the advantage of time and experience, he could now say with conviction – that US Indian policy must be that of self-determination without termination.

"Termination Is Wrong"

In clear and concise terms, President Nixon explained in his speech why the policy of forced termination was *"wrong."* He recapped the six "long-range" goals of the termination policy that had been embodied through Congress' *House Concurrent Resolution 108* declaration in 1953:

- Any special standing Indians had under federal law would cease
- The tax exempt status of Indian lands would discontinue
- Federal responsibility for the economic and social well-being for Indians would be stopped
- The Indian tribes would be dismantled
- Tribal property would be divided up among tribal members
- Individual tribal members must assimilate into the society at-large

It's interesting that here, after termination is officially rejected, the policy's goals are clearly articulated and openly stated for all to understand.

Implies, Forgets, Disregards

President Nixon invited his audience to see how the termination policy was fundamentally wrong:

- It implies the Federal trust responsibility is merely an act of generosity and therefore it can be withdrawn whenever the government sees fit to do so.

- It forgets the true historical and legal relationship for an Indian tribe's unique status – a status based on solemn obligations which the United States Government entered into with the tribes through treaties, and formal / informal agreements. [48]

- It disregards the fact that Indians have often surrendered vast tracts of land and accepted life on government reservations *in exchange* for the United States' agreement to provide community services of health, education and public safety. (These services were to "allow Indian communities to enjoy a standard of living comparable to that of other Americans.")

It is interesting to note that since PL 280's amendment including the provision of tribal consent for state jurisdiction, not one tribe has given such consent for state jurisdiction.

Severed Relationship

There were so many dynamics involved during the Termination Period. It was a time literally filled with *hundreds* of stories about individuals who became part of the flow of policy that drastically affected so many lives. As you saw, the Termination Period was the era that saw the birth of PL 280. Indeed, PL 280 entered a world that resented its existence from the very beginning. Through termination, an *historical relationship was severed* between the United States and the Indian tribes. PL 280 stood out as one of the strongest representations of the United States' broken promises. Although the termination policy was ultimately rejected, PL 280 survived. Yes, it was amended in 1968 to include the requirement of tribal consent, but this did not affect any PL 280 jurisdiction that had already been put in place.

"severed" -- separated, cut apart

Quotes

"Q"

"Historically, Indian territories were generally deemed beyond the legislative and judicial jurisdiction of the state governments . . . The pre-existing federal restrictions on state jurisdiction over Indian country were largely eliminated, however, in 1953 with Congress' enactment of the Act of Aug. 15, 1953 . . . which is commonly known as Pub. L. 280. Public Law 280 gave federal consent to the assumption of state civil and criminal jurisdiction over Indian country and provided the procedures by which such an assumption could be made . . . As originally enacted, Pub. L. 280 did not require the States to obtain the consent of affected Indian tribes before assuming jurisdiction over them, but Title IV of the Civil Rights Act of 1968 amended Pub. L. 280 to require that all subsequent assertions of jurisdiction be preceded by tribal consent."

Three Affiliated Tribes v. Wold Engineering, 476 US 877, 879 (1986)

Retrocession & Federal Assumption

Something called "retrocession" was another provision added to PL 280 in 1968. [49] Retrocession is a provision that allows the federal government to take back (completely or partially) PL 280 jurisdiction from a state. This action can *only* be initiated by the state and not by an Indian tribe. For this reason, PL 280 was amended in 2010 to include a provision for "United States Assumption of Concurrent Federal Criminal Jurisdiction." This action is initiated by the tribe and does *not* require state approval. [50] Essentially, this 2010 amendment to PL 280 permits an Indian tribe that is subject to Mandatory State PL 280 jurisdiction to request the United States to accept *concurrent* jurisdiction to prosecute violations of the General Crimes Act (18 USC § 1152) and the Major Crimes Act (18 USC § 1153). If authorized by the Attorney General, federal authorities can then investigate and prosecute offenses in Indian country that PL 280 otherwise prohibits. [51]

Federal v. State

We will end this section by making special notice that PL 280 is not a state law, but rather it is a *federal* law. The states never would have had the authority to make such a law – and more than likely – would not have enacted any such law without a guarantee of federal funding for the increase in responsibility created by PL 280. This had been the contention with PL 280 from the states' perspective from the very beginning. The legislation designed to ease the financial burden on the shoulders of the federal government, introduced a heavy weight on the several state governments who were suddenly faced with new and unique challenges. [52]

Knowing the historical context surrounding PL 280 gives one a fuller understanding of the intent of the law – and, perhaps as importantly, what it was *not* intended for. This knowledge will help one decipher what applies under PL 280 and what does not.

Endnotes - Chapter Four:

[1] *New Mexico v. Mescalero Apache Tribe*, 462 US 324, 332 (1983) quoting *Mescalero Apache Tribe v. Jones*, 411 US 145, 152 (1973)

[2] The Indian Reorganization period was between the years 1934 through 1944 "[A]fter receiving grim reports on the prevalence of depressed economic, educational, health conditions on the Indian reservations, Congress adopted the Indian Reorganization Act of 1934. The Act ended the allotment policy established in 1887 and attempted to stabilize and strengthen tribal organizations by encouraging a limited degree of self-government, under the supervision of the Department of Interior. The Act also established various assistance programs intended to help the Indian tribes to become economically self-sufficient." Ackerman, David M., *Background report on Public law 280 prepared at the request of Henry M. Jackson, chairman, Committee on Interior and Insular Affairs, United States Senate*, Committee print, 94th Congress, 1st session, US Government Printing Office 1975, pp. CRS-7, 8

[3] Watkins, Arthur V., *Termination of Federal Supervision: The Removal of Restrictions Over Indian Property and Person*, Annals of the American Academy of Political and Social Science, 311 (May 1957). The Emancipation Proclamation was an executive order proclaiming the freedom of slaves in the states that were part of the Confederacy.

[4] Cohen, Felix S., *Handbook of Federal Indian Law*, Washington, United States Government Printing Office, 1945, p.86, The vote for the IRA represented about 68.8% of the total Indians in the US and Alaska; See also Barnes, Dr. Ian, *The Historical Atlas of Native Americans*, Chartwell Books, Inc. 2009, p. 366-367 "Important tribes like the Crow, Navajo, Assiniboine, Fort Peck Lakota, Klamath, Crow Creek Lakota, and the Wyoming Arapaho voted against the IRA. The unfortunate outcome of this decision was that they now had no right to adopt a tribal constitution under an IRA protectorate, nor did they qualify for land-purchase and economic-development loans."

[5] President Theodore Roosevelt made note of the "mighty pulverizing" affect the General Allotment had on the tribes in his First Annual Message, December 3, 1901 "The General Allotment Act is a might pulverizing engine to break up the tribal mass . . ."

[6] Cohen, Felix S., *Handbook of Federal Indian Law*, Washington, United States Government Printing Office, 1945, p.86

[7] Fixico, Donald L., *Termination and Relocation*, Federal Indian Policy 1945-1960, University of New Mexico Press 1986, p. 93

[8] Id. at pp. 94, 96; See also

[9] Id. at p. 100

[10] Watkins, Arthur V., *Termination of Federal Supervision: The Removal of Restrictions Over Indian Property and Person*, Annals of the American Academy of Political and Social Science, 311 (May 1957)

[11] Lurie, Nancy Oestreich, *Wisconsin Indians* (2nd ed.), The Wisconsin Historical Society Press 2002, p. 53

[12] The Menominee Indian Termination Act; The status of this tribe as a federally recognized Indian tribe was restored on Dec. 22, 1973 signed into law by President Nixon, codified at 25 USC section 903a

[13] Harry S. Truman, Online Library & Museum, *Oral History Interview with Dillon S. Myer*, Berkeley, California, July 7, 1970, by the University of California Bancroft Library / Berkeley Regional Oral History Office (Helen S. Pryor interviewer), Chapter XII, sections 296-297 at: *http://www.trumanlibrary.org/oralhist/myerds3.htm#295*

[14] The National Congress of American Indians (NCAI) was instrumental in overturning the termination policy. They helped organize a seventy-nine tribe summit which produced a "Declaration of Indian Purpose." This declaration was officially presented to President John F. Kennedy in 1961.

[15] "The Eighty-third Congress introduced 288 public bills and resolutions on Indian affairs and 46 were to be enacted into law."

[16] PL 280 is also referred to as Public Law 83-280. The "83" signifies that is was enacted by the 83rd Congress.

[17] President Dwight D. Eisenhower served as President of the United States from January 20, 1953 through January 20th 1961; He immediately was involved with international issues (Iran and the Korean Conflict). Also worked towards nuclear deterrence and stopping the threat of Communism, while opposing the McCarthyism and the "red scare," shrinking the federal debt, racial desegregation of the military, etc.; See also Fixico, Donald L., *Termination and Relocation, Federal Indian Policy 1945-1960*, University of New Mexico Press 1986, p. 106, The Eisenhower administration had especially emphasized consultation with the tribes.

[18] Fixico, Donald L., *Termination and Relocation, Federal Indian Policy 1945-1960*, University of New Mexico Press 1986, p. 110; See also Institute for Government Research, Studies in Administration, *The Problem of Indian Administration (Meriam report)*, The Johns Hopkins Press, at p. 750, where it is pointed out that the great diversity and complexity of federal Indian law created a great burden on Congress to "consider a mass of detailed provisions regarding Indian affairs to which few Congressmen outside of the Committee on Indian Affairs can give much attention."

[19] Id. at p. 94

[20] Id. at pp. 91, 106

[21] Barsh, Russel L. & Henderson, James Youngblood, *The Road*, University of California Press 1980, p. 124

[22] Ackerman, David M., *Background report on Public law 280 prepared at the request of Henry M. Jackson, chairman, Committee on Interior and Insular Affairs, United States Senate*, Committee print, 94th Congress, 1st session, US Government Printing Office 1975, pp. CRS-9 "In 1947 the Senate Post office and Civil Service Committee, in hearings on how to reduce the size of the federal bureaucracy . . . prodded the Acting Commissioner into producing, apparently for the first time, a general timetable for the termination of federal services to particular tribes." See also Fixico, Donald L., *Termination and Relocation, Federal Indian Policy 1945-1960*, University of New Mexico Press 1986, p. 29 "Faced with an enormously inflated national debt, Congress sought the elimination of certain government programs and a reduction in the number of federal employees."

[23] Id. at p. CRS-7

[24] Philp, Kenneth R., Termination Revisited, University of Nebraska Press 1999, p. xii

[25] Ackerman, David M., *Background report on Public law 280 prepared at the request of Henry M. Jackson, chairman, Committee on Interior and Insular Affairs, United States Senate*, Committee print, 94th Congress, 1st session, US Government Printing Office 1975, at Memorandum of the Chairman

[26] Id. at p. CRS-5 "In 1929 it (Congress) authorized the states to enforce on Indian reservations their sanitation and quarantine laws, to make inspections for health and educational purposes, and to enforce compulsory school attendance." Federal funding was authorized for these state-run programs and services.

[27] Institute for Government Research, Studies in Administration, *The Problem of Indian Administration (Meriam report)*, The Johns Hopkins Press, at p. 743

[28] Id. at p.765 "If the Indian were left alone in his native ways, and if the government were not attempting to adjust him to the prevailing civilization of the state and nation, the problem might well be left to the Indian to solve by his own methods. The government, however, is attempting to do that very thing. In the schools it teaches the student to read and write the English language. to wear the clothes of our civilization, and to conform to most of our customs and habits."

[29] Id. at p. 778: See also p. 769 Although there actually was a Dept. of Interior book of limited regulations that were supposed to govern the rulings of the Indian courts – it was really not used by the Indian judges. "[I]t is doubtful whether one in ten of the judges has ever read any of it, and certain it is that it has little practical effect in governing their deliberations." These courts dealt with common cases found in many civil and misdemeanor courts: "drunkenness, sexual offenses, minor assaults, domestic troubles, and person property disputes involving small values." Interestingly, the Indian judges used "that subtle quality of mind called common sense" and also that which could only be understood through the knowledge of Indian culture and norms regarding property and justice.

[30] *Washington v. Confederated Bands and Tribes of the Yakima Indian Nation*, 439 U.S. 463, footnote 32 (1979) "In *Bryan v. Itasca County*, 426 U. S. 373, the Court emphasized that Pub. L. 280 was not a termination measure and should not be construed as such. Our discussion here is not to the contrary. The parties agree that Pub. L. 280 reflected an assimilationist philosophy. That Congress intended to facilitate assimilation when it authorized a transfer of jurisdiction from the Federal Government to the States does not necessarily mean, however, that it intended in Pub. L. 280 to terminate tribal self-government. Indeed, the Tribe has argued that even after the transfer tribal courts retain concurrent jurisdiction in areas in which they formerly shared jurisdiction with the Federal Government."

[31] *Bryan v. Itasca County*, 426 U.S. 373, 389, 411 (1976)

[32] Id. at 385

[33] *Public Papers of the Presidents of the United States: Dwight D. Eisenhower*, 1953 (Washington: Office of the Federal Register, National Archives and Records Service, n. d.), pp. 564-566 "My objection to the bill arises because of the inclusion in it of Sections 6 and 7. These Sections permit other states to impose on Indian tribes within their borders, the criminal and civil jurisdiction of the state, removing the Indians from Federal jurisdiction, and, in some instances, effective self-government." (p.565)

[34] Ackerman, David M., *Background report on Public law 280 prepared at the request of Henry M. Jackson, chairman, Committee on Interior and Insular Affairs, United States Senate*, Committee print, 94th Congress, 1st session, US Government Printing Office 1975, at p. CRS-22, Information relayed in House Report No. 848, 834d Congress, 1st Session (July 16,1953) The Department of Interior made notation that "the Colville and Yakima Tribes of Washington opposed state jurisdiction because of a 'fear of inequitable treatment in the State courts and fear that the extension of State law to their reservations would result in the loss of various rights.'"

[35] Id. at *Memorandum of the Chairman*

[36] Id. at p. CRS-13; Although the Meriam report stated the maintenance of law and order was unsatisfactory on the reservations, it referred to a broken system. Yet in regard to the Indians, it has a section in the report entitled, *"The Indians Not Generally Lawless"* where it states, "As a general statement it may be said that the Indians are peaceable, tractable individuals, not inclined to commit serious crimes. This is particularly true of those, who preserving a large measure of their tribal life and customs, live remote from white communities and have but little money to spend in acquiring the luxuries and vices of the white man." Institute for Government Research, Studies in Administration, *The Problem of Indian Administration (Meriam report)*, The Johns Hopkins Press, at p. 764; See also p. 776 "felony cases are not large in number."

[37] Id. at p. CRS-15 statement of Dillon S. Myer, Commissioner of Indian Affairs, Hearings on "State Legal Jurisdiction in Indian Country," Subcommittee on Indian Affairs of House Committee on Interior and Insular

and Insular Affairs, 82nd Congress, 2nd Session (Feb. 28-29, 1952); See also p. CRS-13 - Interestingly, this comment merely parrots what the Senate Subcommittee had said earlier. Although no actual example or specific concern is given, there is a belief that they should not allow Indian consent prior to a state taking jurisdiction because "any Indian reservation under the dominance of a criminal element would not be able to institute (State) police protection by majority vote." H. Rept. No. 1506

[38] Id. at p. CRS-17

[39] Id.

[40] Id.

[41] *Public Papers of the Presidents of the United States: Dwight D. Eisenhower*, 1953 (Washington: Office of the Federal Register, National Archives and Records Service, n. d.), pp. 564-566

[42] Ackerman, David M., *Background report on Public law 280 prepared at the request of Henry M. Jackson, chairman, Committee on Interior and Insular Affairs, United States Senate*, Committee print, 94th Congress, 1st session, US Government Printing Office 1975, at *Memorandum of the Chairman*, "The Indian community viewed the passage of Public Law 280 as an added dimension to the dreaded termination policy. Since the inception of its passage the statute has been criticized and opposed by tribal leaders throughout the Nation. The Indians allege that the Act is deficient in that it failed to fund the States who assumed jurisdiction and as a result vacuums of law enforcement protection have occurred in certain Indian reservations and communities. They contend further that the Act has resulted in complex jurisdictional problems for Federal, State and tribal governments; (see also p. CRS-36) Representative Reifel from South Dakota urged Congress to amend PL 280 stating, "I know of no Indian tribe in this country which has not bitterly resented the arbitrary authority invested in States under Public Law 280, and which does not now support the provision of tribal consent prior to such assumption of jurisdiction by States..."

[43] Annual Report, The Secretary of the Interior, Washington: Government Printing Office, 1961, pg. 277-279

[44] President Lyndon B. Johnson's Special Message to the Congress on the Problems of the American Indian: *"The Forgotten American,"* March 6, 1968

[45] Id., "I propose a new goal for our Indian programs; a goal that *ends* the old debate about *"termination"* of Indian programs and stresses self-determination; a goal that erases old attitudes of paternalism and promotes partnership and self-help . . . I propose, in short a policy of maximum choice for the American Indian: a policy expressed in programs of self-help, self-development, self-determination."

[46] Fixico, Donald L., *Termination and Relocation*, Federal Indian Policy 1945-1960, University of New Mexico Press 1986, pp. 113-114, 118, The Association on American Indian Affairs president, Oliver La Farge, called termination the "government's reckless abandonment of Indian responsibilities." A 1955 editorial in a widely read magazine, which had brought social awareness of the Japanese-American relocation and internment camps in earlier issues, now reported that the living conditions of Native Americans "were little better than those of former Korean refugees." (June 1955 editorial in The Christian Century, a 71-year established magazine)

[47] Fixico, Donald L., *Termination and Relocation*, Federal Indian Policy 1945-1960, University of New Mexico Press 1986, p. 193

[48] *Joint Tribal Council of the Passamaquoddy Tribe v. Morton*, 528 F.2d 370 (1st.Cir. 1975) showed how the 1790 Trade and Intercourse Act imposes a trust obligation on the US to protect the lands of all Indian tribes.

[49] 25 USC § 1323

[50] The Tribal Law & Order Act of 2010 (PL 111-211, enacted on July 29,2010) amended PL 280 by adding subsection (d) to 18 USC § 1162: (d) Notwithstanding subsection (c), at the request of an Indian tribe, and after consultation with and consent by the Attorney General—
(1) sections 1152 and 1153 shall apply in the areas of the Indian country of the Indian tribe; and
(2) jurisdiction over those areas shall be concurrent among the Federal Government, State governments, and, where applicable, tribal governments.

[51] 18 USC § 1162 (c) bars federal jurisdiction in the Mandatory States (listed in subsection (a)) areas: The provisions of sections 1152 and 1153 of this chapter shall not be applicable within the areas of Indian country listed in subsection (a) of this section as areas over which the several States have exclusive jurisdiction.

[52] " . . . the purposes underlying Pub. L. 280: promoting the gradual assimilation of Indians into the dominant American culture and easing the fiscal and administrative burden borne by the Federal Government by virtue of its control over Indian affairs." *Three Affiliated Tribes v. Wold Engineering*, 476 US 877, 886 (1986)

Chapter Five

This chapter will cover:

- *The three sections of PL 280*
- *How legal cases have clarified "scope of authority"*
- *Criminal/Prohibitory v. Civil/Regulatory*

Chapter Five

Analyzing PL 280

You Made It!

You have now come to the very point that everything in this book has led up to – Wow!

All the things you have become acquainted with thus far were intended to give you the broad historical context necessary for understanding PL 280. (If we have done our job right – we will have laid a strong foundation for you.)

The following chart (Chart CH-5A) recaps the jurisdictional events that have taken place throughout the history of the United States with the Indian tribes. All of these events have been brought to life through this resource guide. It is our hope, that as you now see the jurisdictional events on this chart, you will recall the stories that surround them and each will be alive with *meaning* for you.

Evolution of Criminal Jurisdiction in Indian Country

"Jurisdictional statutes are to be construed 'with precision and with fidelity to the terms by which Congress has expressed its wishes'." U.S. v. Cook, 922 F.2d 1026 at 29 (1991)

Page #	Year	Federal Act	Description	Scope of Authority
15, 21-25	1778 - 1871	Treaties	The United States of America followed the pattern of other foreign nations of treaty-making with the Indian tribes from the very beginning of our nation's existence until 1871 when Congress stopped this process. Over 370 treaties were formally negotiated between the US government and the various "domestic dependant nations" who retained sovereignty over their members and territories. [see *Cherokee Nation v. Georgia*, 30 US (5 Pet.) 1, 17, (1831)]	Quiver & Exparte. Doctrine of Discovery gave federal government exclusive right to deal with Indian tribes. This right is evidenced in the US Constitution in Art. 1, Sec. 8, cl. 3 regulates commerce with the Indian tribes.
91-94	1790	Trade & Intercourse Act 25 USC § 177	These acts were for the protection of the Indians and their property from non-Indian abuse. These acts gave the federal government jurisdiction to deal with crimes perpetrated against Indians on Indian lands.	For inter-racial crime only -- Non-Indian offender against Indian victim. The tribe continued to have criminal jurisdiction over their members and territory.
105-106	1817	Indian Country Crimes Act (General Crimes Act) 18 USC § 1152	The federal criminal laws designed for federal enclaves became applicable within Indian Country for all inter-racial crime. It established for the first time a system of criminal justice applied to Indians as well as non-Indians in Indian country. However, it safe-guarded tribal jurisdiction Indian vs. Indian.	The purpose was to deal with all inter-racial crime. *Non-Indian v. Indian and Indian v. Non-Indian:* The tribe continued to have exclusive jurisdiction over their members and territory. *Indian v. Indian criminal jurisdiction:* If the Indian offender had been punished by the tribe or there were treaty stipulations, the federal government had no criminal jurisdiction for the inter-racial crime.
107-110	1825	Assimilative Crimes Act (ACA) 18 USC § 13	This took the place of having to create an immense and complicated federal penal code for its federal enclaves. The ACA uses a state's criminal laws to fill-in-the-gap where laws/penalties were lacking. The US Supreme Court Case, *Williams v. US*, 327 US 711 (1946) brought clarity of ACA's aplication in Indian country. "[T]he ACA is a general law of the United States made applicable to Indian reservations by 18 USC 1152." US v. Marcyes, 557 F.2d 1361 (9th Cir. 1977)	Only a state's criminal laws are assimilated, not regulatory laws. "Congress did not intend to include the penal provisions of a state regulatory system within the ACA. The rationale for this arguement is obvious; a state could thereby enforce its regulatory system on the federal jurisdiciton by making criminal any failure to comply with those regulations (i.e. licenses, permits, etc.)." U.S. v. Marcyes, 557 F2d 1361 at 9 (Ninth Cir. 1977)
149-151	1885	Major Crimes Act 18 USC § 1153	Originally 7 major crimes (has since been expanded), giving federal jurisdiction over these criminal actions by an Indian offender that occurred in Indian Country.	First time Indian v. Indian crime-committed in Indian Country fell under federal jurisdicition. Tribal jurisdiction continued concurrently.

CH-5A

First-Of-Its-Kind

PL 280 was enacted in 1953. Think about that . . . and look at the chart again . . .

Doesn't it seem striking that the most *recent* criminal jurisdictional change within Indian country, prior to PL 280, was *all* the way back in 1885? Today as we consider PL 280, we generally think of it as a law that has been around for quite some time. Yet, as we look at it compared to the broader history of our Nation's relationship with Indian tribes, PL 280 is a relatively *brand new* thing.

Because PL 280 was something that had never been done before, there really was no way that the tribes, the states or the federal government could have foreseen all that would take place as a result of its enactment. It truly was a *first-of-its-kind*. There were a few select areas, prior to PL 280, where the federal government allowed *some* state jurisdiction, but until 1953 the federal government had guarded its exclusive jurisdiction as a *vigilant sentinel*. The enactment of PL 280 was the "first federal jurisdictional statute of general applicability to Indian reservation lands" authorizing state jurisdiction. [1]

"vigilant sentinel" -- a guard unwilling to give up ground

"expressly" -- clearly, specifically, directly

Say It Loud & Clear

The unwavering stance of the federal government had always been that, *absent clear congressional consent*, the states had no authority on Indian lands. [2] History shows "state jurisdiction over reservations" was "strongly disfavored." [3] Year after year, the actions of Congress revealed their "assumption that the States have no power to regulate the affairs of Indians on a reservation." [4] A reservation situated within what later became the boundaries of a state, was not under the jurisdictional authority of that state or its laws. The only way a state's laws could apply on a reservation was if Congress enacted a law that told a state, *loud and clear*, that they were allowing such jurisdiction. "[S]tate law is not to apply on Indian lands, unless *expressly* authorized by federal statute." [5]

Say it Simply!

"ambiguous" -- unclear

"omnibus" -- a collection from one source regarding the same theme

"scope of authority" -- the amount or extent authorized, the legal boundaries

In 1953, PL 280 became that express authorization and clear congressional consent for state jurisdictional authority. There was no shadow of a doubt that Congress wanted to transfer specific types of federal responsibility over to the states. Yet, even with Congress' clear intent on wanting to transfer such jurisdiction, the actual verbiage of PL 280 is poorly written and "admittedly *ambiguous*." [6] Of course, some of the ambiguity can be attributed to what we mentioned at the very beginning – PL 280 was a first-of-its-kind and there was no way to completely anticipate everything. It's like the saying, "The problem seems easy when you know the answer." It appears that Congress could have, and should have made their intentions for this law more clear – but we are also looking at it from this side of history.

Come One, Come All

With the enactment of PL 280, over a century and an half of federal exclusive jurisdictional authority was surrendered in an instant. What had never been allowed access before was now wide open: *Any* state could assume jurisdictional authority over Indian lands – and it was essentially offered to the states on a silver platter.

Every state *could* participate, and a few were even *required* to take on this new transfer of responsibility. This "first federal statute to attempt an *omnibus* transfer" [7] was brought to life by the 83rd Congress of the United States, embodied in the legal format of a public law.

Experience Under Its Belt

With over fifty years of legal cases under its belt, PL 280 is still far from being crystal clear in its application. Many reading this book are personally aware of the many issues PL 280 has created, some of which are yet to be resolved. Over the years, these legal cases have, however, clarified one important thing: The specific *scope of authority* Congress intended the states to have.

In order to understand this scope of authority, it is important to recognize that PL 280 consists of three parts. These three parts, or sections, serve as *road signs* for us, directing us on how to interpret their intent. The three sections are:

- ► A criminal section
- ► A civil section
- ► Informational sections

We usually read the text of PL 280 as one complete piece, not realizing there are three distinct sections. When the proper distinctions are not made, especially between the criminal and civil sections, it can become very confusing.

So, let's take at look at PL 280's three distinct sections . . .

PL 280 consists of three separate parts:

► A criminal section

► A civil section

► Informational sections

Public Law 83-280

CRIMINAL SECTION

18 U.S.C. § 1162

Title 18 is the federal penal code that covers crime and criminal procedure.

The criminal section of PL 280 is found within Title 18 of the United States Code. Title 18 is the *federal penal code* covering crime and criminal procedure. In the original 1953 statute, PL 280 explained exactly where to place the criminal section in the federal penal code:

PUBLIC LAW 280

18 U.S.C. § 1162. STATE JURISDICTION OVER OFFENSES COMMITTED BY OR AGAINST INDIANS IN THE INDIAN COUNTRY

(a) Each of the States or Territories listed in the following table shall have jurisdiction over offenses committed by or against Indians in the areas of Indian country listed opposite the name of the State or Territory to the same extent that such State or Territory has jurisdiction over offenses committed elsewhere within the State or Territory, and the criminal laws of such State or Territory shall have the same force and effect within such Indian country as they have elsewhere within the State or Territory:

State or Territory of	*Indian Country Affected*
Alaska	All Indian country within the State, except that on Annette Islands, the Metlakatla Indian community may exercise jurisdiction over offenses committed by Indians in the same manner in which such jurisdiction may be exercised by Indian tribes in Indian country over which State jurisdiction has not been extended.
California	All Indian country within the State.
Minnesota	All Indian country within the State, except the Red Lake Reservation.
Nebraska	All Indian country within the State
Oregon	All Indian country within the State, except the Warm Springs Reservation.
Wisconsin	All Indian country within the State.

(b) Nothing in this section shall authorize the alienation, encumbrance, or taxation of any real or personal property, including water rights, belonging to any Indian or any Indian tribe, band, or community that is held in trust by the United States or is subject to a restriction against alienation imposed by the United States; or shall authorize regulation of the use of such property in a manner inconsistent with any Federal treaty, agreement, or statute or with any regulation made pursuant thereto; or shall deprive any Indian or any Indian tribe, band, or community of any right, privilege, or immunity afforded under Federal treaty, agreement, or statute with respect to hunting, trapping, or fishing or the control, licensing, or regulation thereof.

(c) The provisions of sections 1152 and 1153 of this chapter shall not be applicable within the areas of Indian country listed in subsection *(a)* of this section as areas over which the several States have exclusive jurisdiction.

(d) Notwithstanding subsection (c), at the request of an Indian tribe, and after consultation with and consent by the Attorney General—
(1) sections 1152 and 1153 shall apply in the areas of the Indian country of the Indian tribe; and
(2) jurisdiction over those areas shall be concurrent among the Federal Government, State governments, and, where applicable, tribal governments.

To see full text, go to Appendix A, pgs. 346-349.

"State jurisdiction over offenses committed by or against Indians in the Indian country . . . Title 18, United States Code, is hereby amended by inserting . . . a new section, to be designated as 1162 . . ."

Original wording of PL 280 in 1953
(See Appendix E, pgs. 366 –367)

The criminal section is the main feature of PL 280. Its legislative history reveals that the primary concern in the minds of the legislators of the 83rd Congress was the need for adequate law enforcement on the reservations.

"The primary concern of Congress in enacting Pub. L. 280 that emerges from its sparse legislative history was with the problem of lawlessness on certain Indian reservations, and the absence of adequate tribal institutions for law enforcement."

Bryan v. Itasca County,
426 U.S. 373, 379 (1976)

PL 280's criminal section is the most important section to understand and yet needs the greatest clarification. We will be spending time explaining more of its details after we have presented each of PL 280's sections.

Public Law 83-280

CIVIL SECTION

28 U.S.C. § 1360

Title 28 involves non-criminal "Judiciary & Judicial Procedure."

Next, the civil section of PL 280 is located within Title 28 of the United States Code. Title 28 is dedicated to the federal *"Judiciary & Judicial Procedure."* The original 1953 statute of PL 280 also detailed where its civil section should be categorized:

PUBLIC LAW 280

28 U.S.C. § 1360. STATE CIVIL JURISDICTION IN ACTIONS TO WHICH INDIANS ARE PARTIES

(a) Each of the States listed in the following table shall have jurisdiction over civil causes of action between Indians or to which Indians are parties which arise in the areas of Indian country listed opposite the name of the State to the same extent that such State has jurisdiction over other civil causes of action, and those civil laws of such State that are of general application to private persons or private property shall have the same force and effect within such Indian country as they have elsewhere within the State:

State of	*Indian Country Affected*
Alaska	All Indian country within the State.
California	All Indian country within the State.
Minnesota	All Indian country within the State, except the Red Lake Reservation.
Nebraska	All Indian country within the State
Oregon	All Indian country within the State, except the Warm Springs Reservation.
Wisconsin	All Indian country within the State.

(b) Nothing in this section shall authorize the alienation, encumbrance, or taxation of any real or personal property, including water rights, belonging to any Indian or any Indian tribe, band, or community that is held in trust by the United States or is subject to a restriction against alienation imposed by the United States; or shall authorize regulation of the use of such property in a manner inconsistent with any Federal treaty, agreement, or statute or with any regulation made pursuant thereto; or shall confer jurisdiction upon the State to adjudicate, in probate proceedings or otherwise, the ownership or right to possession of such property or any interest therein.

(c) Any tribal ordinance or custom heretofore or hereafter adopted by an Indian tribe, band, or community in the exercise of any authority which it may possess shall, if not inconsistent with any applicable civil law of the State, be given full force and effect in the determination of civil causes of action pursuant to this section.

To see full text, go to Appendix A, pgs. 346-349.

"Title 28, United States Code, is hereby amended by inserting . . . a new section to be designated as 1360, as follows: State civil jurisdiction in actions to which Indians are parties . . ."

Original wording of PL 280 in 1953
(See Appendix E, pgs. 366-367)

The civil section of PL 280 would not naturally fall under Title 18 of the United States Code (the federal penal code) because it does not deal with crime. PL 280's civil section deals with providing reservation Indians access to the state courts for civil causes of action.

Providing a viable forum for Indians' civil cases was Congress' secondary concern in enacting PL 280. One court case explained how the civil section of PL 280 was "primarily intended to redress the lack of adequate Indian forums for resolving private legal disputes between reservation Indians, and between Indians and other private citizens, by permitting the courts of the States to decide such disputes." [8]

Unless specifically restricted by federal (guardian/trust) law, Indians, like other persons, had the right to acquire property and make contracts. Sometimes there was a need to settle issues that arose regarding personal matters. These civil cases could be heard in either US federal or state courts. However, many Indians would not choose to use state courts and the US federal courts failed to hear minor civil cases. [9] Also, there was great confusion about jurisdiction over Indian cases at the state level. This civil section of PL 280 clarified that *all* civil cases were to be heard in the courts of the specified States. This removed any doubt as to who would hear such cases, and for these areas, it eased the burden on the federal system. [10]

Say it Simply!

"adjudicatory" -- give a ruling, deliver a judgment, referee, umpire

> "The civil grant (in PL 280) is one of power over 'civil causes of action.' This language would appear to mean that the state simply acquired *adjudicatory* jurisdiction – the power to decide cases – *not the entire power to legislate and regulate in Indian country* . . .
>
> The Supreme Court . . . concluded that the primary purpose of the civil provisions of Public Law 280 was to *provide a state forum for the resolution of disputes*. Viewed in that light, the provision that the civil laws of the state should have effect in Indian country simply 'authorizes application by the state courts of their rules of decision to decide such disputes.'
>
> The effect of the Court's decision is to confine the civil grant of Public Law 280 to adjudicatory jurisdiction only."

Doe v. Mann, 415 F.3d 1038 (9th Cir. 2005) with quotes from William C. Canby, Jr., American Indian Law in a Nutshell (4th ed. 2004)

After PL 280 was enacted, Indians living in the affected areas now had clear access to State courts. For clarification to the States and to encourage Indian people to use the state court system a provision was included which stated:

> "Any tribal ordinance or custom heretofore or hereafter adopted by an Indian tribe, band, or community in the exercise of any authority which it may possess shall, if not inconsistent with any applicable civil law of the State, be given full force and effect in the determination of civil causes of action pursuant to this section."

Original wording of PL 280 in 1953
(See Appendix E, pgs. 366-367)

This provision also served to protect the inherent right of the tribes to govern themselves according to their customs and traditions. As you will remember in our earlier chapters, we discussed how traditional tribal governments were adversely affected as a result of various US policies. Yet, in spite of this, at least one authoritative document on Indian affairs indicated how Indian people, especially where culture and tradition remained intact, abided by lawful principles. [11] The lawlessness referred to by legislators prior to the enactment of PL 280 had to do with a *broken system*.

The civil provision in PL 280 did *not* eliminate existing tribal courts, but merely offered to reservation Indians who either had no tribal court available, or who preferred to use state court, to have their "civil causes of action" heard. [12] Although PL 280 was enacted by Congress during a time that reflected "an assimilationist slant in Federal policy . . . with an eye toward *eventual* termination of Federal supervision over Indian tribes and Indian trust territory, (it) is not itself a termination statute." [13] This is clearly indicated by section (c) of 28 USC 1360 which showed the congressional intent to wholly support a tribe's civil process and remedies by giving them "full force and effect" in state courts. Congress clearly contemplated "the continuing vitality of tribal government" which included the fundamental functions of government. [14]

The civil section for the Mandatory PL 280 States is often seen as "28 U.S.C. section 1360 -State civil jurisdiction in Actions to which Indians are Parties." Technically, it is:

28 USC > Part IV > Chapter 85 > Section 1360

Title 28 has six parts: Part I: Organization of Courts; Part II: Dept. of Justice; Part III: Court Officers & Employees; Part IV: Jurisdiction & Venue; Part V: Procedure; PartVI: Particular Proceedings

PL 280 did not eliminate concurrent tribal jurisdictional authority.

Public Law 83-280

INFORMATIONAL SECTIONS

25 U.S.C. § 1321 -1326

Title 25 is labeled "Indians" and contains any of the general information about PL 280.

The informational sections of PL 280 are all under *Title 25* of the United States Code. Title 25 is dedicated to the various statutes generally relating to Indians. There are six informational sections of PL 280:

PUBLIC LAW 280

25 U.S.C. § 1321. ASSUMPTION BY STATE OF CRIMINAL JURISDICTION

(a) Consent of United States

(1) In general

The consent of the United States is hereby given to any State not having jurisdiction over criminal offenses committed by or against Indians in the areas of Indian country situated within such State to assume, with the consent of the Indian tribe occupying the particular Indian country or part thereof which could be affected by such assumption, such measure of jurisdiction over any or all of such offenses committed within such Indian country or any part thereof as may be determined by such State to the same extent that such State has jurisdiction over any such offense committed elsewhere within the State, and the criminal laws of such State shall have the same force and effect within such Indian country or part thereof as they h[illegible]

PUBLIC LAW 280

25 U.S.C. § 1322. ASSUMPTION BY STATE OF CIVIL JURISDICTION

(a) Consent of United States; force and effect of civil laws

The consent of the United States is hereby given to any State not having jurisdiction over civil causes of action between Indians or to which Indians are parties which arise in the areas of Indian country situated within such State to assume, with the consent of the tribe occupying the particular Indian country or part thereof which would be affected by such assumption, such measure of jurisdiction over any or all such civil causes of action arising within such Indian country or any part thereof as may be determined by such State to the same extent that such State has jurisdiction over other civil causes of action, and those civil laws of such State that are of general application to private persons or private property shall have the same force and effect within such Indian country or part thereof as they have elsewhere within that State.

(b) Alienation, encumbrance, taxation, use, and probate of property

Nothing in this section shall authorize the alienation, encumbrance, or taxation of any real or personal property, including water rights, belonging to any Indian or any Indian tribe, band, or community that is held in trust by the United States or is subject to a restriction against alienation imposed by the United States; or shall authorize regulation of the use of such property in a manner inconsistent with any Federal treaty, agreement, or statute, or with any regulation made pursuant thereto; or shall confer jurisdiction upon the State to adjudicate, in probate proceedings or otherwise, the ownership or right to possession of such property or any interest therein.

(c) Force and effect of tribal ordinances or customs

Any tribal ordinance or custom heretofore or hereafter adopted by an Indian tribe, band, or community in the exercise of any authority which it may possess shall, if not inconsistent with any applicable civil law of the State, be given full force and effect in the determination of civil causes of action pursuant to this section.

To see full text, go to Appendix A, pgs. 346-349.

25 U.S.C. § 1321: Assumption by State of Criminal Jurisdiction

This section starts out by stating, *"The consent of the United States is hereby given to any State . . ."* Remember, for a state to have any jurisdictional authority, there must be *clear* permission from Congress. And so, here it is. This section contains the legal jargon giving congressional consent to the states (other than the Mandatory States) for PL 280 jurisdiction. This section is not a mandate requiring a state to assume jurisdiction in Indian country, but simply is an opportunity extended for any state to do so if they chose.

The provision requiring tribal consent, *"with the consent of the Indian tribe occupying the particular Indian country or part thereof which could be affected by such assumption,"* was not in the original draft of PL 280 when it was enacted. This was added later in 1968.

"Concurrent (federal) jurisdiction" to prosecute 1152 and 1153 violations at the request and after consultation with the Attorney General was added in 2010.

25 U.S.C. § 1322: Assumption by State of Civil Jurisdiction

Here is another section giving *"consent of the United States"* to any state (other than the Mandatory States) who wished to open their courts to private civil litigation for reservation Indians. And again, this is not a mandate, but simply an opportunity extended.

PUBLIC LAW 280

25 U.S.C. § 1323. RETROCESSION OF JURISDICTION BY STATE

(a) Acceptance by United States

The United States is authorized to accept a retrocession by any State of all or any measure of the criminal or civil jurisdiction, or both, acquired by such State pursuant to the provisions of section 1162 of title 18, section 1360 of title 28, or section 7 of the Act of August 15, 1953 (67 Stat. 588), as it was in effect prior to its repeal by subsection *(b)* of this section.

(b) Repeal of statutory provisions

Section 7 of the Act of August 15, 1953 (67 Stat. 588), is hereby repealed, but such repeal shall not affect any cession of jurisdiction made pursuant to such section prior to its repeal.

PUBLIC LAW 280

25 U.S.C. § 1324. AMENDMENT OF STATE CONSTITUTIONS OR STATUTES TO REMOVE LEGAL IMPEDIMENT; EFFECTIVE DATE

Notwithstanding the provisions of any enabling Act for the admission of a State, the consent of the United States is hereby given to the people of any State to amend, where necessary, their State constitution or existing statutes, as the case may be, to remove any legal impediment to the assumption of civil or criminal jurisdiction in accordance with the provisions of this subchapter. The provisions of this subchapter shall not become effective with respect to such assumption of jurisdiction by any such State until the people thereof have appropriately amended their State constitution or statutes, as the case may be.

PUBLIC LAW 280

25 U.S.C. § 1325. ABATEMENT OF ACTIONS

(a) Pending actions or proceedings; effect of cession

No action or proceeding pending before any court or agency of the United States immediately prior to any cession of jurisdiction by the United States pursuant to this subchapter shall abate by reason of that cession. For the purposes of any such action or proceeding, such cession shall take effect on the day following the date of final determination of such action or proceeding.

(b) Criminal actions; effect of cession

No cession made by the United States under this subchapter shall deprive any court of the United States of jurisdiction to hear, determine, render judgment, or impose sentence in any criminal action instituted against any person for any offense committed before the effective date of such cession, if the offense charged in such action was cognizable under any law of the United States at the time of the commission of such offense. For the purposes of any such criminal action, such cession shall take effect on the day following the date of final determination of such action.

PUBLIC LAW 280

25 U.S.C. § 1326. SPECIAL ELECTIONS

State jurisdiction acquired pursuant to this subchapter with respect to criminal offenses or civil causes of action, or with respect to both, shall be applicable in Indian country only where the enrolled Indians within the affected area of such Indian country accept such jurisdiction by a majority vote of the adult Indians voting at a special election held for that purpose. The Secretary of the Interior shall call such special election under such rules and regulations as he may prescribe, when requested to do so by the tribal council or other governing body, or by 20 per centum of such enrolled adults.

To see full text, go to Appendix A, pgs. 346-349.

25 U.S.C. § 1323: Retrocession of Jurisdiction by State

"The United States is authorized to accept a retrocession . . . " This section gives the legal authority for a PL 280 state to give jurisdiction back to the federal government. Retrocession can only be initiated by the state, and not the Indian tribe.

25 U.S.C. § 1324: Amendment of State Constitutions or Statutes to Remove Legal Impediment; Effective Date

Here is a bunch of legalese for eliminating anything standing in the way for a non-mandatory PL 280 state from taking on PL 280 jurisdiction if they so chose to do so.

25 U.S.C. § 1325: Abatement of Actions

This section makes sure there are no problems created for the courts during a jurisdictional transition between the federal government and the states.

25 U.S.C. § 1326: Special Election

"State jurisdiction . . . ONLY where . . ." It is clearly stated here that, only where consent is given by a tribe, will there be any state jurisdiction. This section was late-in-coming. When the US President originally signed PL 280 into law, he wanted tribal consent added ASAP. It took 15 years for this to happen – when in 1968, PL 280 was amended, through the Indian Civil Rights Act, to require tribal consent before any federal jurisdiction could be transferred to a state.

Two Choices

According to PL 280 then, it really comes down to two choices in determining state jurisdiction in Indian country. State jurisdiction, under the authority of PL 280, will either be for the purpose of dealing with crime, or for dealing with private "civil causes of action between Indians or to which Indians are parties." In other words, all state jurisdictional authority on Indian lands will fall within either:

- The criminal section of PL 280

  or

- The civil section of PL 280

There are no other options. As you saw, the rest of PL 280 is merely informational, having to do with federal or tribal consent and breaking down any legal issues or barriers.

> *"[W]hen a State seeks to enforce a law within an Indian reservation under the authority of Pub. L. 280, it must be determined whether the state law is criminal in nature, and thus fully applicable to the reservation, or civil in nature and applicable only as it may be relevant to private civil litigation in state court."*
>
> *California v. Cabazon Band of Mission Indians, 480 U.S. 202, 208 (1987)*

So Far, So Good . . .

Up to this point, PL 280 seems rather straight forward, huh? So far, it is!

Where it begins to get a bit tricky is when things do not fall into neat little compartments and are "not so easily categorized." [15] As promised, we are going to go back to the criminal section of PL 280 to remove the layers this law has hidden behind for years! Although the *criminal* section of PL 280 gives state criminal laws "the same force and effect" in Indian country as a state has "elsewhere within the State," this does not mean *everything* a state enforces is applicable within Indian country.

Only Intended To Transfer

The states are only to have jurisdictional authority over the things Congress clearly intended to transfer. It is this very point – the point of jurisdictional authority – that has been the focus of many a court case. The names and the places change from one legal battle to the next, but the storyline remains the same: A state exercising jurisdictional authority in Indian country on one side, with tribal folks protecting Indian sovereignty from state interference on the other side. Sometimes the state jurisdiction prevails, while other times a state's exercise of authority is found to be overreaching and beyond the scope of the authority Congress intended.

> *"In order for a state law to be fully applicable to a reservation under the authority of Public Law 280, it must be a criminal law."*
>
> *State v. Stone, 572 N.W.2d 725,729 (1997)*

If a *criminal* law is violated in a PL 280 jurisdictional area, the statute fully authorizes enforcement against such an offense. You may be thinking here, "Well, that easy . . . If the law is in a state's penal code … it's criminal – right?"

The answer is – *maybe*, but not necessarily.

To determine the legal application of PL 280, it's not enough to determine a "criminal offense" based *only* on the fact that the law is located in a state's criminal code and contains a criminal penalty. [16] This is where applying law "with precision and with *fidelity*" [17] according to Congress' intent is so important.

Say it Simply!

"fidelity" -- strict adherence, exactness, faithfulness

The historical jurisdiction established by the federal government through both the Indian Country Crimes Act (18 USC § 1152) and the Major Crimes Act (18 USC § 1153) was the jurisdiction Congress intended to transfer through the enactment of PL 280. 18 USC § 1162 (c) of the criminal section of PL 280 specifically mentions that PL 280 will *replace* both of these federal criminal statutes:

> "The provisions of sections 1152 and 1153 of this chapter shall not be applicable within the areas of Indian country listed in subsection (a) of this section as areas over which the several States have exclusive jurisdiction."
>
> *18 USC § 1162 (c)*

To make things extremely clear, Congress added the last phrase, "as areas over which the several States have exclusive jurisdiction" to subsection (c) in 1970 through Public Law 91-523.

No Alterations Here

Just as Congress unmistakably showed their intention of transferring their 1152 and 1153 jurisdiction to the states, they also unmistakably conveyed there would be no change to a tribe's unique government-to-government relationship with the United States. A state's new jurisdiction was not to alter anything protected through the early treaties or other legal obligations between the US government and the Indian tribes. Congress' intent for protecting the historic tribal treaties and the political status of Indians is demonstrated through these sections of PL 280:

- ▶ 18 USC § 1162 (b)
- ▶ 28 USC § 1360 (b)
- ▶ 25 USC § 1321 (b)
- ▶ 25 USC § 1322 (b)

"Indians stand in a special relationship to the federal government from which the States are excluded unless the Congress has manifested a clear purpose . . ."

Bryan v. Itasca County, citing Oklahoma Tax Comm'n v. U.S., 426 U.S. 373, 392 (1976)

Enclaves and Reservations

As we have discussed in earlier chapters, there has been common ground in the federal government's application of state law within areas under its exclusive jurisdiction – federal enclaves and Indian reservations. These areas have always been intended to only have *criminal* laws applied and not the "full *panoply* of civil regulatory" laws. [18]

Say it Simply!

"panoply" -- entire variety, splendid array

The landmark court case, *United States v. Marcyes*, [19] explains how Congress did not intend state regulatory laws to be enforced upon the federal enclaves or Indian lands. Concerning the federal enclaves, the logical reason for not applying state regulatory laws was that it was never the intent of the federal government to put itself in the position of being regulated by the states. If a state's regulatory laws were applied on a federal enclave, a state could essentially regulate the federal government through its penal provisions. This, of course, was never Congress' purpose for applying state law on federal enclaves. [20] Continuing with this rationale concerning Indian reservations, the reason for not applying a state's civil/ regulatory laws is "even stronger . . . because a state would thereby be able to implement all its regulatory provisions on Indian reservations and thereby destroy the strong concept of tribal sovereignty." [21]

Although there are unique differences between federal enclaves and federally recognized Indian reservations, federal courts have treated them with similarity when determining whether a state's criminal law is to be applied on their lands or not. When there is a question regarding whether a state's law can be applied in either of these areas, the solution is always determined by finding the answer to one important question:

- Does the action *violate a state's public **criminal** policy?*

Federal enclaves are also referred to as "federal reservations."

Public Policy

So, let's start with looking at what is meant by "public policy"

The formal definition says public policy "refers rather vaguely to matters regarded by the legislature or by the courts as being of *fundamental concern* to the state and the whole of society." [22]

Say it Simply!

"dichotomy" -- two separate parts

More *easily* stated . . . Public policy refers to the rules and regulations people of a community have set up for themselves. Public policy determines how a community functions and is implemented for the safety and welfare of everyone within that community. Public policy can be determined by a small local group or by an entire state. What we are concerned about, regarding the application of PL 280, is a *state's public policy*.

There are two *separate* parts of public policy. These two parts are the legs public policy stands upon. On one side of public policy is the civil/regulatory section, while the other side is the criminal/prohibitory section. Sometimes this is referred to as the public policy dichotomy.

Quotes "Q"

> *"[T]he criminal/prohibitory – civil/regulatory dichotomy was originally developed to aid in the interpretation of Public Law 280."*
>
> *U.S. v. Dakota, 796 F.2d 186 at 14 (6th Cir. 1986)*

Attention! It is very important *not* to get the "civil" used here regarding public policy mixed up with the civil section of PL 280 found in 28 U.S.C. § 1360. [23] This is a common mistake because the word *"civil"* is used in both places.

Say it Simply!

"**synthesis**" -- combination of separate parts into one

Breakin' It Down

Let's start breaking things down to get a clearer understanding of the public policy dichotomy. . . we will first start with defining the civil/regulatory section:

Civil = community of people, society in general

Regulatory = having to do with rules and regulations for the common good; safety concerns

The *synthesis* of these is *civil/regulatory* = Rules and regulation for a safe community; restrictions for the benefit of everyone, promoting the general health and welfare of society.

The bottom line is that people want to live in a community where they feel safe and secure. Public policy is the course of action the people in a certain area have established for maintaining a safe and secure environment.

Irony Behind Iron Bars

The following story is a great illustration showing how all people, no matter *where* they may reside, desire a safe and secure environment:

A personal story was told to us by a deputy sheriff working in a Los Angeles County Jail during the 1992 LA Riots. During the riots, the jail was packed to full capacity, especially due to a large number (literally hundreds) of looters who had been arrested.

When each of these inmates entered the jail, they were given a small "care package" by the jail staff. This package contained essential hygiene items such as a comb, deodorant, razor, toothbrush and toothpaste. This package was theirs to use during their short stay at the jail.

This deputy sheriff was working in one of the inmate dorms where almost all the inmates were there on charges of looting. As the day went on, several of these inmates approached the deputy, one after another, with complaints of their care packages being stolen by other inmates inside the dorm. They were angry their property was being taken and felt it was very unfair someone would steal anything that belonged to them.

The deputy sheriff was amazed at the irony of how they could see so clearly it was wrong for someone to steal from them but seemingly had very little conscience about their own theft.

This story reveals how people want to live in a safe and secure community – even if that community is within a county jail!

Pool Party

Say it Simply!

"myopic" -- narrow, limited

An extremely *myopic* example of public policy can be illustrated using the example of a swimming pool in an apartment complex. Of course, this swimming pool is sectioned off with definite boundaries. Within these boundaries are rules and regulations – usually clearly posted. These rules are not posted to stop people from having a good time, rather, quite the opposite. The purpose for the rules is for the general safety and welfare of the whole apartment's community. If the pool rules are disregarded, there are penalties – usually in the form of some type of personal privilege being taken away. Under the authority of the apartment's management, who legally represent the owners of the property, the pool's rules and regulations are enforced.

And so, on a vastly larger scale, cities, counties and states regulate the behavior of their citizens for the general safety and welfare of the community-at-large. Such rules and regulations fall under the branch of civil/regulatory within public policy. Civil/regulatory laws have some type of consequence or penalty if they are disregarded. The enforcement of civil/regulatory laws may begin with simple warnings, which can eventually lead to large and painful fines, privileges or freedoms taken away. City, county and state governments have ways of *encouraging* compliance with their civil/regulatory laws.

Prohibited Actions – Totally!

The other branch of public policy, *criminal/prohibitory*, is truly a completely separate section of the public policy dichotomy. These laws deal with violations that go *above and beyond* a general disregard for the safety and welfare of the community. While civil/regulatory laws restrict or regulate actions *only* to the point where it's necessary for the good of the community, criminal/prohibitory laws are designed to completely stop (prohibit) certain actions or activities.

"[T]he criminal/prohibitory -- civil/regulatory dichotomy was originally developed to aid in the interpretation of Public Law 280."
U.S. v. Dakota, 796 F.2d 186 at 14 (6th Cir.1986)

PL 280 -- 18 U.S.C. § 1162
PUBLIC POLICY

Civil / Regulatory	Criminal / Prohibitory
Something people are allowed to do, in accordance with the rules and regulations.	Something *totally prohibited*; not allowed or tolerated in society.

Breakin' It Down Some More

Let's break things down here and define *criminal/prohibitory* . . .

Criminal = actions of a crime; activity not tolerated in society

Prohibitory = not allowed, fully restricted

The *synthesis* of these is *criminal/prohibitory* = that which society elevates to a crime; behavior or action not allowed or tolerated in the community.

For the things which society labels "criminal," society also correspondingly penalizes. Actions not tolerated are generally classified as either *misdemeanor crimes* (lower level crimes with corresponding lesser punishments) or *felony crimes* (highest level crimes with corresponding greater punishments). The weight or seriousness of the penalty reveals how strongly society feels about the action. One can *usually* determine if something violates a state's public criminal policy by its classification as either a misdemeanor or a felony crime.

Authorized State Jurisdiction

When the word "crime" is mentioned, many criminal actions immediately come to mind – murder, assault, kidnapping, etc. These things are easily identified as criminal actions society completely prohibits. It is such criminal actions that PL 280 authorizes jurisdiction over and enforcement with "full force and effect" on Indian lands.

An informational bulletin authored by the United States Department of Justice, Office of Tribal Justice, discussed the basic intent for the criminal section of PL 280 by citing what they called "[t]he most authoritative text on federal Indian law." [24]

This authoritative text explains PL 280's intent:

> "The basic intent of the criminal law section was to substitute *state* for federal jurisdiction under the Indian Country Crimes Act and the Major Crimes Act . . . *the statute should only be interpreted to delegate to the states that jurisdiction which Congress clearly intended to transfer.*"

> *"Public Law 280 undermines the long-standing doctrine that federally recognized Indian tribes and their members are immune from the application of state law for on-reservation activities . . . the Supreme Court has narrowly construed the reach of the statute, holding that Public Law 280 does not authorize states generally to assert civil regulatory powers over Indian reservations."*
>
> *United States v. Dakota, 796 F.2d 186 (6th Cir. 1986)*

Criminal/Prohibitory v. Civil/Regulatory

We have established the fact that only a state's *criminal* laws (actions that a state categorizes as prohibited and not tolerated) are enforced within Indian country. It would be fantastic and extremely convenient if we could easily categorize all laws into either the *criminal* box or *regulatory* box. But, alas, this is not so and there are areas of law that "do not squarely fall under one category within the criminal/prohibitory – civil/regulatory dichotomy." [25]

Therefore, it takes a bit more work to figure things out by looking at the law closely *under a microscope*. When a law is focused upon, close examination will reveal the law's "nature and intent." [26] Such examinations into a law's intent can get really interesting . . . sometimes laws labeled "criminal" can really be "regulatory" under a state's public policy, and *vice versa*.

"vice versa" -- a Latin phrase meaning 'the other way round' or 'the position being reversed'

Under the Microscope

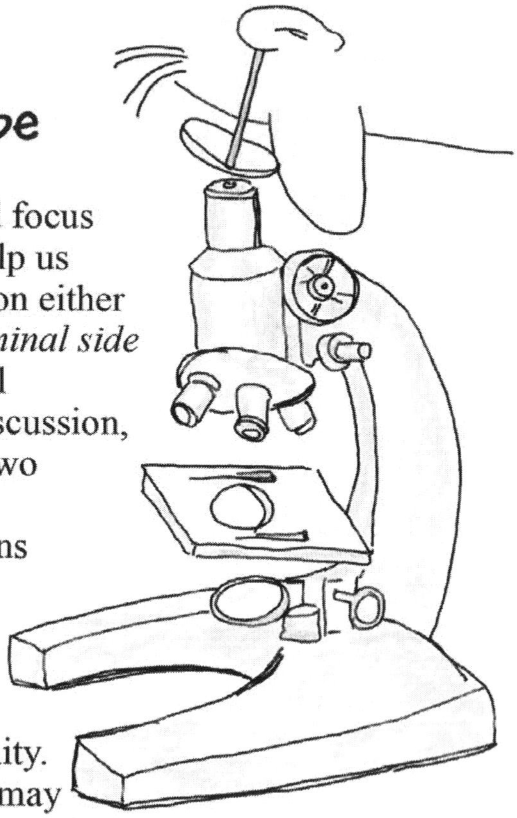

So let's take a closer look and focus on certain criteria that will help us determine a law's placement on either the *regulatory side* or the *criminal side* of public policy. [27] You will remember from our earlier discussion, public policy only has these two options. We gave the earlier example of the pool regulations at an apartment complex to illustrate civil/regulatory – how such rules and regulations are for the general welfare of the whole community. Violations of civil/regulatory may have penalties or consequences, but these violations are not criminal. So, what is it then that determines the public *criminal* policy of a state?

The essence of a state's criminal public policy is protection of the community from serious harm. As we have seen, "all laws implicate some public policy," [28] but "public *criminal* policy goes beyond merely promoting the public welfare. It seeks to protect society from *serious breeches* in the social fabric which threaten grave harm to persons or property." [29]

The Minnesota (a Mandatory PL 280 State) Supreme Court established a list of things to look at in determining if an action goes against a state's public policy "in a nature serious enough to be considered '*criminal*.'" [30] They used a series of four inquiries that were not meant to be the only things ever considered, but would be extremely helpful in *splitting hairs* over the intent of a state's public policy. [31]

Splitting Hairs

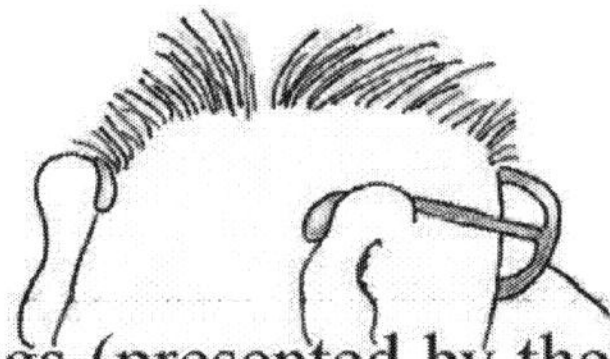

Here's the list of things (presented by the Minnesota Supreme Court) an action or activity should be filtered through to determine if it rises to the level of "criminal":

A State's *Criminal* Public Policy

"[A] nature serious enough to be considered 'criminal'." *State v. Stone, 572 N.W. 2d 725, 730 (1997)*

The Inquiry:	Posed as a Question:
1) The extent to which the activity directly threatens physical harm to persons or property or invades the rights of others.	1) *Is the action going to cause serious harm or violate human rights that are protected?*
2) The extent to which the law allows for exceptions and exemptions.	2) *Are there existing exceptions to this action or activity?*
3) The blameworthiness of the actor.	3) *Is this a repeat offense? How deliberate is the action of the individual?*
4) The nature and severity of the potential penalties for a violation of the law.	4) *What weight of importance did public policy give to the action through its corresponding penalty?*

No Sneakin' Around

Criminal actions on an Indian reservation cannot go around (or circumvent) the public criminal policy of the state in whose boundaries they are situated within. [32] Two outstanding examples of not circumventing a state's public criminal policy are *US v. Marcyes (1977)* and *California v. Cabazon (1987)*. [33] In one case, what appeared as *regulatory* was actually shown to be *prohibitory*. What came to light through this court case was that allowing the activity in question "would entirely circumvent" the state's "determination" that the activity was "dangerous to the general welfare of its citizens" (i.e. against the state's public criminal policy). [34] Interestingly, the *California v. Cabazon* case, on the other hand, revealed an opposite result. What was labeled *prohibitory* in the state's penal code was determined to be regulatory when applied on Indian lands. This case clarified that the tribes were certainly *not* trying to dodge around the state's public criminal policy. [35] They were merely doing something the state already allowed -- subject to regulation. Therefore, it did not violate the state's public criminal policy.

When everything was evaluated in these two cases, it all boiled down to whether the action was against the state's public *criminal* policy or not. Truly, this will be the deciding factor in every single situation that falls under PL 280's criminal section. For this is the bottom line: If it is determined a state's public criminal policy is *not* violated, it *cannot* be applied within Indian lands under the authority of PL 280. (Note: Every states' criminal public policy will not necessarily be exactly the same.)

Key Point

> **Only the criminal/prohibitory section of a state's public policy is enforced on a reservation. State laws that fall under civil/regulatory were never intended to apply on Indian lands under PL 280.**

Examples

PL 280's half a century of litigation provides us with situational examples of how a state's laws apply (or don't apply) in Indian country. The following chart shows examples of several court decisions:

Court Cases Determining Civil/Regulatory v. Criminal/Prohibitory

"[C]oncerns for protecting Indian sovereignty from state interference prompted courts to develop the criminal/prohibitory -- civil/regulatory test." US v. Dakota, 796 F.2d 186 (6th Cir. 1986)

Action or Activity within Indian country	Criminal / Prohibitory	Civil / Regulatory	Case Cite
1) Illegal Fireworks	X		1) *US v. Marcyes*
2) Gambling		X	2) *California v. Cabazon Band of Indians*
3) Illegal Gambling Business	X		3) *US v. Dakota*
4) Sale of California Class C Fireworks	X		4) *Quechan Indian Tribe v. McMullen*
5) Vehicle Law with Multiple Offenses	X		5) *St. Germaine v. Circuit Court for Vilas County*
6) Decriminalized Traffic Laws		X	6) *Confederated Tribes of the Colville Reservation v. State of Washington*
7) Dog Racing Track	X		7) *Pueblo of Santa Ana v. Hodel*
8) Traffic and Driving-Related Laws	X	X	8) *State v. Stone*
9) Underage Drinking	X		9) *State v. Robinson*
10) Driving While Intoxicated	X		10) *Bray v. Commissioner of Public Safety*
11) County and State Bingo Laws		X	11) *Barona Group v. Duffy*
12) Practicing Law without a License	X		12) *US v. Clark*
13) California Boxing Laws		X	13) *29 Palms Band of Mission Indians v. Wilson*
14) Outdoor Advertising Billboards		X	14) *People ex rel. Dept. of Transportation v. Naegele Outdoor Advertising Co.*
15) Slot Machines	X		15) *US v. Sosseur*
16) Zoning Ordinances & Building Codes		X	16) *Santa Rosa Band of Indians v. Kings County*
17) Personal Property Tax		X	17) *Bryan V. Itasca County*
18) Revoked Driver's License for failure to provide proof of insurance		X	18) *State v. Johnson*

CH-5B

1) Illegal Fireworks (criminal) - *U.S. v. Marcyes*, 557 F.2d 1361 (9th Cir. 1977)
Found: Possessing unmarked and unclassified and dangerous fireworks violated the public *criminal* policy of the state of Washington. Allowing this activity "would entirely circumvent Washington's determination that the possession of fireworks is dangerous to the general welfare of its citizens."

2) Gambling (regulatory) - *California v. Cabazon Band of Indians*, 480 U.S. 202 (1987)
Found: The State of California and the County of Riverside sought to apply laws governing the operation of bingo games on Indian reservations. "[I]f the intent of a state law is generally to prohibit certain conduct, it falls within Pub. L. 280's grant of criminal jurisdiction, but if the state law generally permits the conduct at issue, subject to regulation, it must be classified as civil/regulatory, and Pub. L. 280 does not authorize its enforcement on an Indian reservation."

3) Illegal Gambling Business (criminal) - *U.S. v. Dakota*, 796 F.2d 186 (6th Cir. 1986)
Found: Frederick and Sybil Dakota, enrolled tribal members of the Keweenaw Bay Indian Community, held a "gambling business for profit" license issued by their tribal council, but violated the public criminal policy of the State of Michigan by operating a commercial casino business. The State of Michigan did *not* regulate, but *prohibited* such activity. Therefore a federal law (the Organized Crime Control Act, 18 U.S.C. § 1955) was also violated. The decision of the court underscored "the supremacy of federal law."

4) Sale of California Class C Fireworks (criminal) –
***Quechan Indian Tribe v. McMullen*, 984 R.2d 304, Court of Appeals (9th Cir. 1993)**
Found: "California may restrict . . . the sale of fireworks on (a) reservation pursuant to Pub. L. 83-280 . . . because the intent of the California fireworks law is generally to prohibit the sale of Class C fireworks and because the sale of Class C fireworks violated the state's public policy to protect life and property." California has authority to regulate dangerous fireworks on Indian lands.

5) Vehicle Law with Multiple Offenses (criminal) –
***St. Germaine v. Circuit Court for Vilas County*, 938 F.2d 75 (7th Cir. 1991)**
Found: The State of Wisconsin statute for driving after a driver's license is revoked for operating a motor vehicle while intoxicated "is defined as criminal . . . by the state policy and purpose behind the prohibition . . . This prohibition reflects the state's public policy that certain individuals are dangerous drivers who must be prohibited from operating a motor vehicle to protect the health and safety of citizens." May be "considered merely regulatory" for a first offense, but elevates to a "public policy enforcement of high order" by the fourth conviction.

6) Decriminalized Traffic Laws (regulatory with distinctions of criminal) – *Confederated Tribes of the Colville Reservation v. State of Washington*, 938 F.2d 146 (9th Cir. 1991), cert. denied, 112 S. Ct. 1704 (1992)

Found: The State of Washington's decriminalized vehicle codes were unenforceable. The State of Washington could not assert jurisdiction over a civil/regulatory speeding law. "[T]he state's avowed public policy is served by treating speeding as a civil/regulatory offense . . . the state may not declare certain infractions as civil . . . and then insist the same infraction is criminal for purposes of expanding state jurisdiction and appropriating the revenue raised through enforcement of the speeding laws." However, it was clearly stated, "offenses like reckless driving or driving while intoxicated . . . remain criminal."

7) Dog Racing Track (criminal) – *Pueblo of Santa Ana v. Hodel*, 663 F. Supp. 1300 (D.D.C. 1987)

Found: Since dog racing was criminally prohibited by New Mexico, the Secretary of the Interior justifiably withheld approval of a dog track operation.

8) Traffic and Driving-related laws (regulatory for some, while prohibitory for others) – *State v. Stone*, 572 N.W.2d 725 (1997)

Found: "[T]he state lacked jurisdiction under Public Law 280 because the traffic and driving-related laws at issue were civil/regulatory rather than criminal/prohibitory . . . (and) lacked exceptional circumstances to justify enforcement of the laws . . ." The following were found to be unenforceable: "no motor vehicle insurance and no proof of insurance; driving with an expired registration; driving without a license; driving with an expired license; speeding; no seat belt; and failure to have child in a child restraint seat." However, traffic laws of "heighted public policy concerns include . . . drinking and driving and . . . reckless and careless driving."

9) Underage Drinking (criminal) – *State v. Robinson*, 572 N.W.2d 720 (1997)

Found: A tribal member of the Leech Lake Band of Chippewa Indians located in the State of Minnesota was charged with consumption of alcohol by a person under age 21. "While Minnesota generally permits the consumption of alcohol by adults, consumption by minors raises sufficiently increased policy concerns that the legislature proscribed (banished) this conduct outright . . . underage drinking is substantially different and heightened as compared to public policy concerns behind the regulation of alcohol consumption in general."

10) Driving While Intoxicated (criminal) – *Bray v. Commissioner of Public Safety*, 555 N.W.2d 757 (1996)

Found: "Minnesota does not seek merely to regulate driving while intoxicated: it categorically prohibits such driving." Therefore, consistent with "Minnesota's unequivocal policy of keeping intoxicated drivers off the road" gave authority to revoke a driver's license of a tribal member on a reservation pursuant to the implied consent law.

11) County and State Bingo Laws (regulatory) –
***Barona Group v. Duffy*, 694 F.2d 1185 (9th Cir. 1982)**

Found: The "public policy" test revealed this tribal activity was not "contrary to the 'public policy' of the state."

12) Practicing Law without a License (criminal) -
***U.S. v. Clark*, 195 F.3d 446 (9th Cir. 1999)**

Found: Virginia Clark was convicted for practicing law without a license on a federal enclave in violation of law found in the California Business and Professions Code. This law was shown to be "a prohibitory criminal statute" because it was a statute "intended to prohibit particular conduct in order to promote the general welfare, and (was) not primarily a licensing law aimed at regulating particular conduct." California's "determination that the unauthorized practice of law poses a threat to the general public" could not be circumvented by practicing law without a license on a federal enclave. "The unauthorized practice of law is flatly prohibited and criminally penalized." As certain certification is required for positions of public trust and safety, public policy concerns are heightened.

13) California Boxing Laws (regulatory) –
29 Palms Band of Mission Indians v. Wilson, 925 F.Supp. 1470 (1996)

Found: California boxing laws found in the CA Business & Professions Code did not apply on an Indian reservation over boxing events staged and promoted (or co-promoted) by the Tribe. California's history of boxing supported "the Tribe's position that California law and public policy do not generally condemn the activity but rather permit boxing subject to regulation."

14) Outdoor Advertising Billboards (regulatory) – *People ex rel. Dept. of Transportation v. Naegele Outdoor Advertising Co.*, 38 Cal.3d 509, 213 Cal. Rptr. 247; 698 P.2d 150 (1985)

Found: The State of California cannot regulate billboard displays on an Indian reservation or issue citations for compliance of California's Outdoor Advertising Act. Congress did not intend this Act to "apply to Indian reservations" and state enforcement of this Act "on Indian reservations is not authorized by Public Law 280."

15) Slot Machines (criminal) - *U.S. v Sosseur*, 181 F.2d 873 (7th Cir. 1950)

Found: This 1950's case determined the operation of slot machines on an Indian reservation within the boundaries of the State of Wisconsin, violated Wisconsin's public *criminal* policy.

16) Zoning Ordinances & Building Codes (regulatory) –
***Santa Rosa Band of Indians v. Kings County*, 532 F.2d 655 (1975)**

Found: Local zoning ordinances and building codes are not authorized or applicable on a Rancheria (Indian land). "P.L. 280 may reasonably be construed not to grant P.L. 280 states the jurisdiction to zone trust lands." U.S., Hoopa Valley Tribe v. County of Humboldt, 615 F.2d 1260 (9th Cir. 1980) followed the same vein of reasoning regarding local zoning and building codes concerning four Indian construction projects on Indian Trust Property within the Hoopa Valley Reservation.

17) Personal Property Tax (regulatory) – *Bryan v. Itasca County*, 426 U.S. 373 (1976)

Found: States cannot tax an Indian's personal property located on federal trust lands. PL 280 does not give states general civil regulatory power.

18) Revoked Driver's License for failure to provide proof of insurance (regulatory) –
***State v. Johnson*, 598 N.W.2d 680 (Minn. 1999)**

Found: A tribal member's driver's license was revoked for failure to provide proof of insurance. Driving on this revoked license was deemed civil/regulatory.

See US v. Marcyes, 557 F.2d 1361 (9th Cir. 1977)

"bright-line rule" -- a clearly defined rule or standard established by courts of law

"deference" -- the action of respectfully yielding or submitting to another

"prerogative" -- an exclusive right or privilege

Does It Apply?

As you see in chart CH-5B, determining what applies, or does not apply, in Indian country is not always cut-and-dry. Many court cases discuss how there is "not a *bright-line rule*" [36] when deciding whether a law is prohibitory versus regulatory. This lack of absolute and clear standard has its cons – but it also has its pros . . .

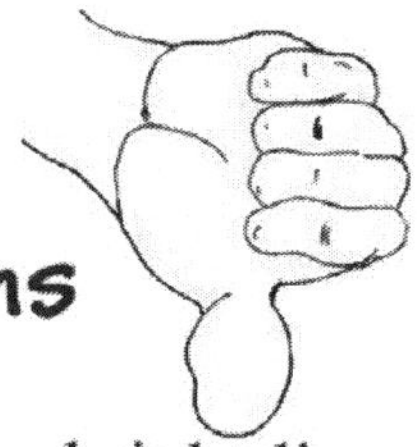

Let's Have It For the Cons

First of all, the con of not having a bright-line rule is that it leaves a lot of wiggle room for interpretation. This is why there is a large variation in the many legal cases having to do with the authorized application of a state's laws under PL 280. This variation is especially seen in cases involving things a state holds a strong interest in (e.g. traffic violations on a state-maintained roadway through a reservation). [37]

Let's Have It For the Pros

On the other hand, the pro for not having a bright-line rule is it allows the freedom of applying a *"balancing test."* A balancing test will weigh which government has the greatest or heaviest interest in a particular matter. A balancing test tends be more accurate in the broader scheme of things and gives *deference* to the government (i.e. tribal, federal or state) whose interest is strongest in a particular matter. If every decision was determined by a black and white rigid rule, it could easily minimize the complexity involved and deliver an overly harsh outcome.

My Prerogative

When Congress initially made the decision to enact a law where state laws would apply to federally exclusive areas, [38] it purposely chose to allow for the individual states' public policies to be a determining factor in a law's application. Congress, who represented the various states, recognized the importance of each state having the "*prerogative* to classify its laws as it sees fit". [39]

On the flip side of this, the very purpose of establishing the regulatory versus prohibitory regulation had to do with states, in some cases, overreaching the authority given to them by Congress.

Quotes "Q"

"[C]oncerns for protecting Indian sovereignty from state interference prompted courts to develop the criminal/ prohibitory – civil/regulatory test."

U.S. v. Dakota, 796 F.2d 186 (6th Cir. 1986)

Infringement Test

The court case, *Williams v. Lee*, [40] created a balancing test, which became known as the "infringement test." This infringement test weighed the state's interest against that of the tribe's. In this specific case, the state wanted to regulate tribal activity. However, through the balance test, it was shown that such regulation would infringe on the tribe. Therefore, the United States Supreme Court established that the state could not exercise their authority in Indian country.

The *Williams v. Lee* case declared [41] :

> "Congress has … acted consistently upon the assumption that the States have no power to regulate the affairs of Indians on a reservation."

Here is the balancing test from the case:

> "[A]bsent governing Acts of Congress, the question has always been whether the state action *infringed* on the right of reservation Indians to make their own laws and be ruled by them."

Say it Simply!

"infringed" -- violate or encroach

Tug-of-War

Sometimes it may seem more like a game of tug-of-war between state, tribal and federal governments. Certainly tensions will exist where conflicting interests also exist. This difference in views and priorities will always cause varying degrees of "abrasion" [42] between governments. This is inevitable and should not be seen as unusual because "precisely the same sort of conflicts often exist between non-Indian local communities with differing priorities." [43]

Say it Simply!

"trump card" -- to have the advantage; the "winning card"

Along with the discussion of the regulatory versus prohibitory test, the landmark case *California v. Cabazon* also discussed the balancing test. [44] This case noted state jurisdiction that "interferes or is incompatible with federal and tribal interests reflected in federal law" will get the federal *trump card* (be preempted). The only exception to this is if "the state interests at stake are *sufficient* to justify the assertion of state authority." [45]

Sufficient Interests

In considering the balance test between tribal, state and federal interests, when does a state's interest have the greater weight "sufficient to justify the assertion of state authority"? The answer is, where Congress expressly granted a state criminal and civil jurisdiction in Indian country. Also, where crime occurs *off* a reservation, yet the offender lives *on* the reservation, a state's interest is high. The weight of state interest provides authority to state agents to investigate criminal activity, serve search warrants and arrest warrants, and other state civil processes.

State Process

Where Congress has expressly authorized criminal and civil jurisdiction in Indian country, either through PL 280 or another statute, state courts may exercise jurisdiction over the same, including the exercise of state process. State process was defined in *Nevada v. Hicks*, a 2001 US Supreme Court case involving state officers serving state search warrants in Indian country. [46]

"'Process' is defined as 'any means used by a court to acquire or exercise its jurisdiction over a person or over specific property.'" [47]

In PL 280 states, state interest is strong. The balancing test of infringement will be implemented to consider all the facts involved if state process is contested. However, the weight of clear congressional intent to confer state jurisdiction is extremely heavy on that balancing scale.

Here are some examples:

1) *Kaul v. Stephan*, 83 f.3d 1208 (10th Cir. 1996)
A tribal member claimed the execution of search warrants and the subsequent seizure of property were against tribal sovereignty. This tribal member believed state officers should have been barred from entering the Indian reservation. However, clear congressional delegation of criminal jurisdiction had been authorized through the "Kansas Act," giving jurisdiction to execute the warrant.

2) *State v. Hook*, 476 N.W.2d 565 (ND 1991)
A tribal member was arrested on his reservation for driving under the influence of alcohol and attempting to flee from a peace officer. His driving privilege was subsequently revoked. Because a specific act of congress authorized state jurisdiction over misdemeanors committed by tribal members of the reservation, the peace officer was authorized to arrest the tribal member. The officer was not required to turn the tribal member over to a Bureau of Indian Affairs officer that worked on the reservation, nor was extradition needed in order to take the tribal member into custody.

3) *State ex rel. Lykins v. Steinhorst*, 197 Wis.2d 875 (1995)
This involved a writ of habeas corpus challenging a tribal member's arrest on Indian trust land in Wisconsin and detention pursuant to an extradition warrant. The warrant was based on crimes of which the tribal member was already convicted and sentenced. Wisconsin, a mandatory PL 280 state, was authorized to exercise criminal jurisdiction on Indian lands giving state officers authority to make an arrest pursuant to an extradition warrant. "Extradition is … intended … 'to bring offenders to trial as swiftly as possible'" and its "intent is to preclude states from becoming sanctuaries for fugitives of justice." [48] The extradition warrant was shown to fall under the state's public criminal policy.

On, Off ... On Again

As mentioned, in cases where an Indian lives on a reservation but commits a crime *off* the reservation, state interests are very high and a state's "interest in executing process is considerable." [49] Just because the tribal member returns to the reservation, the state's jurisdictional authority does not change. [50]

> "Congress has not stripped the states of their inherent jurisdiction on reservations with regard to off-reservation violations of state law. The federal statutory scheme neither prescribes nor suggests that state officers cannot enter a reservation to investigate or prosecute such violations." [51]

Interesting Twist

An interesting twist on authorized jurisdiction of a state search warrant is found in the case of *Sycuan Band of Mission Indians v. Roache*. [52] Through this case, it was determined that although California is a mandatory PL 280 state, its state process of a search warrant was *not* allowed because the state lacked jurisdiction.

You may be thinking, "Huh? That doesn't make sense!"

Remember the balancing test? In Indian country there are concurrent tribal, federal and state jurisdictions, sometimes with competing interests and priorities. In this specific case, San Diego County in the State of California was attempting to prohibit certain forms of Indian gaming on the reservations of the Barona, Sycuan and Viejas Bands of Mission Indians. San Diego County sheriff's deputies raided the gaming operations on the reservations, seizing gaming machines, cash and records pursuant to the search warrants.

However, this is where the tribal/federal interests were greater than those of the state. A federal law, the Indian Gaming Regulatory Act (IGRA) [53] authorizes *only* federal jurisdiction on such matters. What ended up happening was the State of California was shown the federal *trump card*. [54]

"scheme" --
a plan, design, program of action to be followed

It's a Wrap

As you have seen, PL 280's *scheme* is a bit different than the traditional city, county and state schemes – and it was meant to be. PL 280 is not guided simply by state statutes, rather its application (other than private civil litigation) is to fall in line with a state's public criminal policy.

Yes, it does sometimes take a bit of work to determine how PL 280 should be applied, but you now have the tools to accomplish this task! It all *starts* with asking the *right* question:

Does an act or action violate the state's public criminal policy?

Where it gets more tricky, the balancing test must also be used:

When everything is considered, which way does the balance tip? Which government has the heaviest or greatest interest?

To accurately apply PL 280,
you must first ask the right question:

"Does an act or action violate the state's public criminal policy?"

Endnotes - Chapter Five:

[1] *Washington v. Confederated Bands and Tribes of the Yakima Indian Nation*, 439 U.S. 463, 471 (1979)

[2] "From the commencement of our government, congress has passed acts to regulate trade and intercourse with the Indians; which treat them as nations, respect their rights, and manifest a firm purpose to afford that protection which treaties stipulate. All these acts . . . manifestly consider the several Indian nations as distinct political communities, having territorial boundaries, within which their authority is exclusive, and having a right to all the lands within those boundaries, which is not only acknowledged, but guarantied by the United States." *Worcester v. Georgia*, 31 U.S. 515, 557 (1832); "The policy of leaving Indians free from state jurisdiction and control is deeply rooted in the Nation's history." *Rice v. Olson*, 324 U.S. 786,789 (1945); "Significantly, when Congress has wished the States to exercise this power (criminal / civil jurisdiction over Indians) it has expressly granted them the jurisdiction which *Worcester v. Georgia* had denied." *Williams v. Lee*, 358 U.S. 217, 221 (1959)

[3] *Barona Group v. Duffy*, 694 F.2d 1185 (9th Cir. 1982)

[4] *Williams v. Lee*, 358 U.S. 217, 221 (1959)

[5] *United States v. Burns*, 529 F.2d 114 (9th Cir. 1975); See also *McClanahan v. Arizona State Tax Commission*, 411 U.S. 164, 170-171 (1973) quoting the US Department of the Interior, Federal Indian Law 845 (1958): "State laws generally are not applicable to tribal Indians on an Indian reservation except where Congress has expressly provided that State laws shall apply."

[6] *United States v. Dakota*, 796 F.2d 186 (6th Cir. 1986)

[7] Id. at fn. 8

[8] *Bryan v. Itasca County*, 426 U.S. 373, 383 (1976)

[9] See Institute for Government Research, Studies in Administration, *The Problem of Indian Administration (Meriam report)*, The Johns Hopkins Press, p. 761, 773

[10] Id. at p. 762 "Doubt as to the exact jurisdiction of the state and national governments leads, moreover, to uncertainty and confusion;" (Id. at pp. 768-769) "Even where the state has undoubted authority in law for assuming jurisdiction over the Indian, it will frequently refuse to exercise it, partly because the Indian escapes the payment of taxes for the support of the state and local governments and partly because he is considered the exclusive problem of the national government."

[11] Id. at p. 764 "The Indians Not Generally Lawless. As a general statement it may be said that the Indians are peaceable, tractable individuals, not inclined to commit serious crimes. This is particularly true of those, who preserving a large measure of their tribal life and customs, live remote from white communities . . ."

[12] *Confederated Tribes v. State of Washington*, 938 F.2d 146 (9th Cir. 1991) explained that PL 280, 28 U.S.C. Sec. 1360 was "essentially to afford Indians a forum to settle private disputes among themselves."

[13] *Santa Rosa Band of Indians v. Kings County*, 532 F.2d 655, 662 (1975)

[14] See *Bryan v. Itasca County*, 426 U.S. 373, 389 (1976). "[N]othing in its legislative history remotely suggests that Congress meant the Act's (PL 280's) extension of civil jurisdiction to the States should result in the undermining or destruction of such tribal governments as did exist and a conversion of the affected tribes into little more than 'private, voluntary organizations'." Id. at 388

[15] *State v. Burgess*, 262 Wis. 2d 354,368 (2003)

[16] See *State v. Stone*, 572 N.W.2d 725, fn. 4 (1997)

[17] "Jurisdictional statutes are to be construed 'with precision and with fidelity to the terms by which Congress has expressed its wishes.'" *U.S. v. Cook*, 922 F.2d 1026 at 29 (1991)

[18] See *Bryan v. Itasca County*, 426 U.S. 373, 388 (1976)

[19] *United States v. Marcyes,* 557 F.2d 1361 (9th Cir. 1977)

[20] Id. at 9 "Congress did not intend to include the penal provisions of a state regulatory system within the ACA."

[21] Id., The court agreed with the appellant's rationale here, but not in other areas of their argument. See also *Bryan v. Itasca County*, 426 U.S. 373, fn. 14 (1976) "[G]eneral regulatory control might relegate tribal governments to a level below that of counties and municipalities, thus essentially destroying them . . ."

[22] State v. Stone, 572 N.W.2d 725, fn.5 (1997)

[23] The "civil" in 28 U.S.C. § 1360 only deals with *non-criminal private civil litigation*. "Congress intended 'civil laws' to mean those laws which have to do with private rights and status. Therefore, 'civil laws . . . of general application to private persons or private property' would include the laws of contract, tort, marriage, divorce, insanity, descent, etc." See *Bryan v. Itasca County*, 426 U.S. 373, fn. 10 (1976)

[24] Felix Cohen's *Handbook of Federal Indian Law*, 1982 edition also states the fact that PL 280 was enacted primarily to address the problem of inadequate law enforcement in Indian country: "P.L. 280 conferred jurisdiction on certain states over most or all Indian country within their borders and suspended enforcement of the Major Crimes Act, 18 U.S.C. § 1153, and the General Crimes Act (or Inter-racial Crimes Act), 18 U.S.C. § 1152, in those areas. The statute also authorized other states to assume that jurisdiction."

[25] *State v. Burgess*, 262 Wis.2d 354, 369 (2003)

[26] Id.

[27] "[S]tate laws governing an activity must be examined in detail before they can be characterized as regulatory or prohibitory." *California v. Cabazon Band of Indians*, 480 U.S. 202, fn 10 (1987)

[28] *State v. Stone*, 572 N.W. 2d 725, 730 (1997)

[29] Id.

[30] Id.

[31] Id. "This list is not meant to be exhaustive, and no single factor is dispositive."

[32] This is true for all Indian territory, whether the lands are part of PL 280's criminal jurisdiction or not. If a state's public criminal policy is violated outside of a PL 280 area, criminal laws are enforced federally through the General Crimes Act together with the Assimilative Crimes Act (18 U.S.C. § 1152 & 13) and the Major Crimes Act (18 U.S.C. § 1153). The exception to this is where tribal jurisdiction is exclusive over Indian v. Indian offenses not covered by 1153. In PL 280 jurisdictional areas, state laws are enforced for violations of a state's public criminal policy.

[33] *United States v. Marcyes*, 557 R.2d 1361 (9th Cir. 1977) and *California v. Cabazon Band of Indians*, 480 U.S. 202 (1987)

[34] *United States v. Marcyes*, 557 R.2d 1361at 11 (9th Cir. 1977)

[35] Their argument was that the activity in question did not violate the state's public criminal policy, but activity such as "cockfighting, tattoo parlors, nude dancing and prostitution" would be violations and therefore were not 'permissible on Indian reservations' within the State." See California v. Cabazon Band of Indians, 480 U.S. 202, fn. 10 (1987)

[36] *California v. Cabazon Band of Indians*, 480 U.S. 202, 210 (1987)

[37] *State v. Robinson (1997); State v. Zornes (1997); State v. Shaugobay (1999); State v. R.M.H. (2000); State v. David (2009)*

[38] Indian Country Crimes Act (18 U.S.C. § 1152) along with the Assimilative Crimes Act (ACA 18 U.S.C. § 13)

[39] *U.S. v. Devenport*, 131 F.3d 604, 175 A.L.R. Fed. 709 (7th Cir. 1997)

[40] *Williams v. Lee*, 358 U.S. 217 (1959)

[41] Id. at 220-221

[42] *Santa Rosa Band of Indians v. King's County*, 532 F.2d 665, 664 (1975)

[43] Id.

[44] *California v. Cabazon Band of Indians*, 480 U.S. 202 (1987)

[45] Id. at 216

[46] *Nevada v. Hicks*, 533 U.S. 353 (2001)

[47] Id. at 364, citing Black's Law Dictionary 1084 (5th ed. 1979)

[48] *State ex rel. Lykins v. Steinhrost*, 197 Wis.2d 875, 880, 888 (1995)

[49] Nevada v. Hicks, 533 U.S. 353, 354 (2001)

[50] Id. at 364, service of a state's process is not prevented in Indian country and is necessary to prevent Indian reservations from becoming "an asylum for fugitives from justice;" See also: *Le Clair v. Powers*, 632 P.2d 370, 374 (Okla. 1981) "Indian country is not a federal enclave off limits to state process servers."

[51] Id. at 354

[52] *Sycuan Band of Mission Indians v. Roache*, 54 F.3d 535 (9th Cir. 1995)

[53] The Indian Gaming Regulatory Act (IGRA) became federal law in 1988 and is codified in 25 U.S.C. § 2701

[54] Federal trump card = federal pre-emption, "State jurisdiction in preempted by the operation of federal law if it interferes or is incompatible with federal and tribal interests reflected in federal law. Unless the state interests at stake are sufficient to justify the assertion of state authority." *New Mexico v. Mescalero Apache Tribe*, 462 U.S. 324, 334 (1983); See also *Lac du Flambeau Band of Lake Superior Chippewa Indians v. State of Wisconsin*, 743 F.Supp. 645 (1990) "[T]he state lacks authority to prosecute violations of the state's gambling laws on … reservations" either by PL 280 or IGRA. "[T]he United States has the exclusive authority to enforce violations of state gambling laws on … reservations."

Chapter Six ~ Part 1

This chapter will cover:

- *Powers of Indian tribes*
- *Limitations of powers by treaties or laws*
- *Criminal v. civil jurisdiction*

Chapter Six - Part 1

Tribal, Federal & State Jurisdictions

Concurrent Jurisdictions

Now that you have an understanding of how PL 280 is to be applied, let's look at the jurisdictions that exist in Indian country today. There are three jurisdictions: tribal, federal and state – that interact on tribal lands. Understanding these unique jurisdictions has always been important in PL 280 areas, but *even more so* with the most recent amendment to PL 280 – *Federal Assumption*. With the enactment of the 2010 Tribal Law and Order Act (TOLA), PL 280 was amended to include a new section within 18 USC § 1162 . . . section (d). This section gives Indian tribes within the mandatory PL 280 areas the opportunity to request the federal government to assume *concurrent* criminal jurisdiction. When PL 280 was originally enacted, it gave the Mandatory States exclusive jurisdiction over Indian country, therefore excluding federal jurisdiction of the General Crimes (18 USC § 1152) and Major Crimes (18 USC § 1153). However, the new amendment allows tribes, on an individual basis, to request federal jurisdiction of 1152 and 1153 to apply within their Indian country. If a tribe's request is accepted by the US Attorney General, there is no change to a state's responsibility under PL 280, but it allows for *federal* law enforcement to work concurrently in these areas, applying and prosecuting federal law as needed. A copy of the text of *Assumption of Concurrent Federal Criminal Jurisdiction in certain areas of Indian country* is included in the Appendix section (see Appendix F, pgs. 368-369).

Say it Simply!

"concurrent" -- existing side by side, at the same time, together

18 USC § 1162 (d) reads as follows:

> (d) Notwithstanding subsection (c), at the request of an Indian tribe, and after consultation with and consent by the Attorney General –
>
> (1) sections 1152 and 1153 shall apply in the areas of the Indian country of the Indian tribe; and
>
> (2) jurisdiction over those areas shall be concurrent among the Federal Government, State governments, and, where applicable, tribal governments.

Also, for clarity regarding concurrent federal prosecution in Indian country 25 USC 1321(a)(2) was added to PL 280: Concurrent jurisdiction – At the request of an Indian tribe, and after consultation with and consent by the Attorney General, the United States shall accept concurrent jurisdiction to prosecute violations of section 1152 and 1153 of title 18 within the Indian country of the Indian tribe.

One, Two, Three Jurisdictions

For tribal, federal and state jurisdictions to effectively work together there needs to be at least a *basic* understanding of the legal framework and authorization for each jurisdiction. You will remember how, all the way back in part 1 of Chapter Three, we discussed the frustrations you will experience while reading

Say it Simply!

"babble" -- to talk without meaning

the US Attorney's "Quick Reference Chart" for Indian country's criminal jurisdiction. These jurisdictional charts explain how tribal, federal and state jurisdictions work on tribal lands. Filled with confusing verbiage, these charts can appear as pure *babble*! Section by section they delineate jurisdiction depending on *who* the offender is, *what* crime(s) occurred and if the victim is either an Indian or non-Indian. In some situations, the charts tell us that one government has exclusive jurisdiction, yet while changing the variables in the columns, the charts now show a different government has exclusive jurisdiction, or at least concurrent jurisdiction.

These charts can make one so dizzy that, in our opinion, they ought to display hazardous health warning labels issued by the Surgeon General!

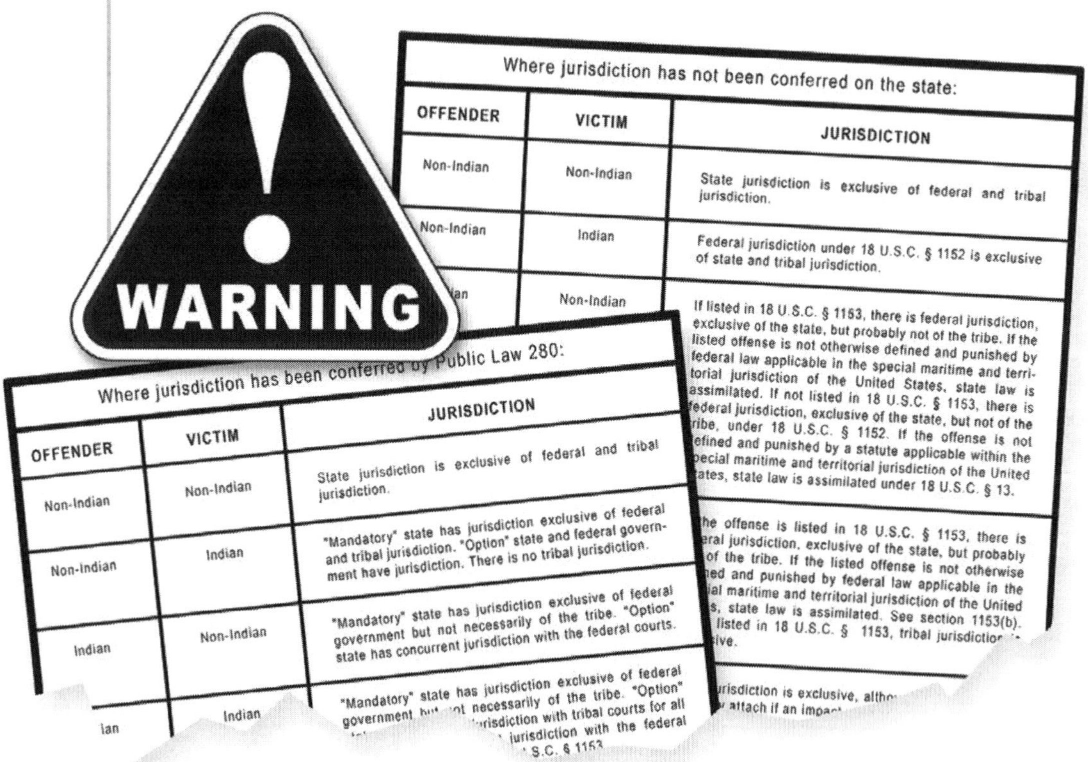

Seriously, those charts are bound to make *anyone* go cross-eyed! The truth is, the longer you stare at them, the more confusing they can appear unless you make the connection as to why the different jurisdictions are involved. And this is the beauty of what you have already become acquainted with through this resource guide . . . the jurisdictional events we have covered are the *pieces* for you to use in understanding tribal, federal and state jurisdictions.

Greatest Interest

In the previous chapter, we talked about what a *balancing test* is and how it helps determine who – or which government – has the *greatest* interest. As you learned, the government with the greatest interest is given deference over the other competing or conflicting governmental interests. It will be very helpful for you to keep such a balancing test in mind as we discuss jurisdiction, especially *criminal* jurisdiction, in Indian country.

In the tug-of-war between tribal, federal and state interests, the question must be asked, "Which of these three governments has the *strongest* interest in Indian country? What government has the *heaviest* weight on the balancing scale when it comes to things that take place on a reservation?" The answer, of course, is that tribal governments have the greatest interest regarding *their* own communities – over *their* own people and their own territories.

Golden Words of Margold

Back in 1934, the Solicitor for the US Department of the Interior, Nathan Margold, and his legal team, issued an opinion from the Office of the Solicitor regarding the "*Powers of Indian Tribes*." [1] We will spend some time reviewing his articulation of the "powers which are lawfully vested in an Indian tribe . . . powers of local self-government which have never been terminated by law or waived by treaty." Solicitor Margold categorized the powers of tribal governments into nine specific areas. He did all the hard work of organizing and outlining so that we can enjoy looking at these nine sections to understand tribal jurisdiction. His entire opinion is quite lengthy (actually, the size of a small book!) and you may want to dig deeper by reading it later. For the purposes of this resource guide, we will give you the "Reader's Digest" version. We will take time to discuss certain areas while skimming over others – depending on how it relates to or impacts the sphere of PL 280 jurisdiction.

Say it Simply!

"solicitor" (for the US Dept. of the Interior) -- the chief general counsel for Interior and represents the Department in administrative and judicial litigation and meetings, negotiations and other contracts with Congress, federal agencies, states, tribes and the public

Dig Deeper

The official website for the Office of the Solicitor, US Dept. of the Interior, has Solicitor Margold's lengthy opinion archived at: *http://www.doi.gov/solicitor/decisions.html*

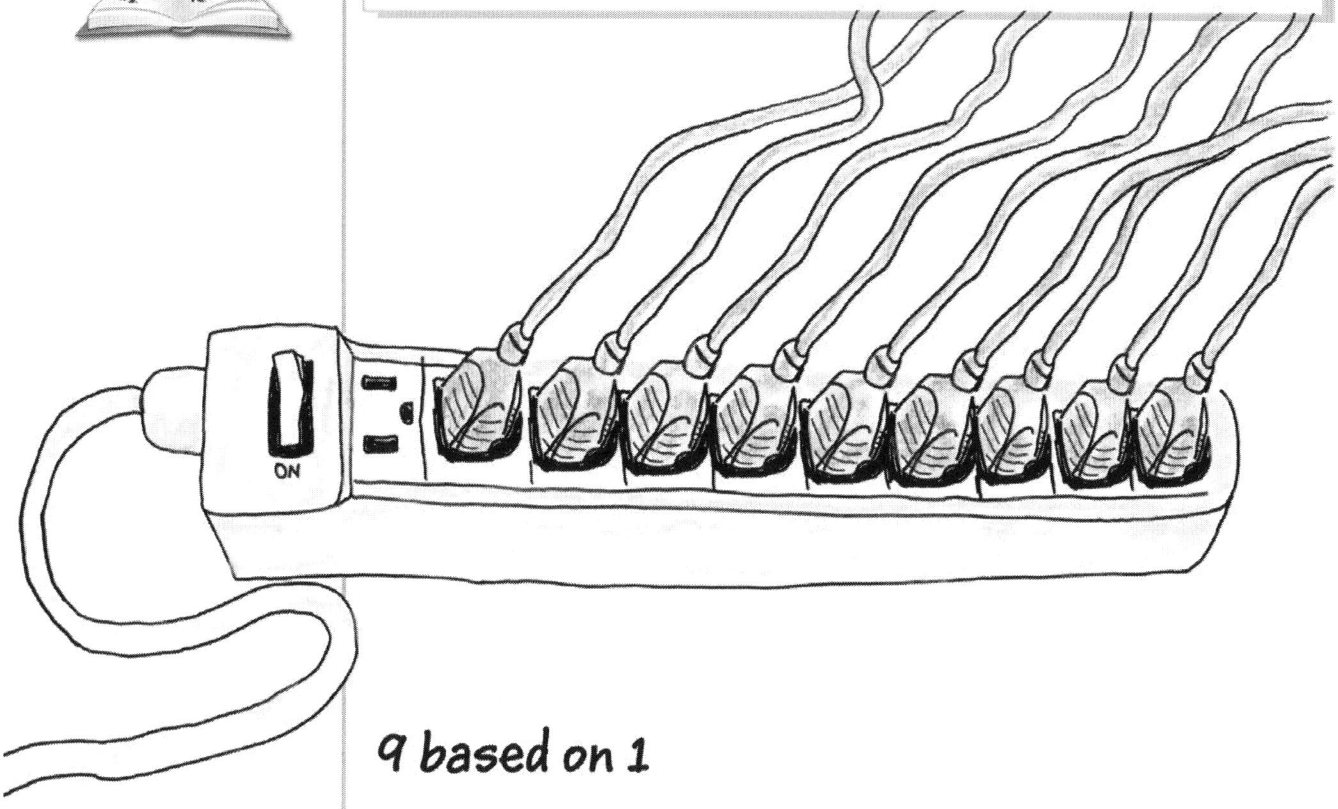

9 based on 1

Before going into the nine categories, it is very important to make note that these categorical powers are based upon what Solicitor Margold called *"the most basic principle of all Indian law."* This is what he explained:

> "[T]he most basic principle of all Indian law is the principle that *those powers which are lawfully vested in an Indian tribe are not*, in general, *delegated powers* granted by express acts of Congress, *but rather inherent powers* of a limited sovereignty which has never been extinguished. *Each Indian tribe begins its relationship with the Federal Government as a sovereign power*, recognized as such in treaty and legislation. The powers of sovereignty have been limited from time to time by special treaties and laws . . ." [2]

Let that soak in for a minute because these words are very powerful . . .

(One minute later…)

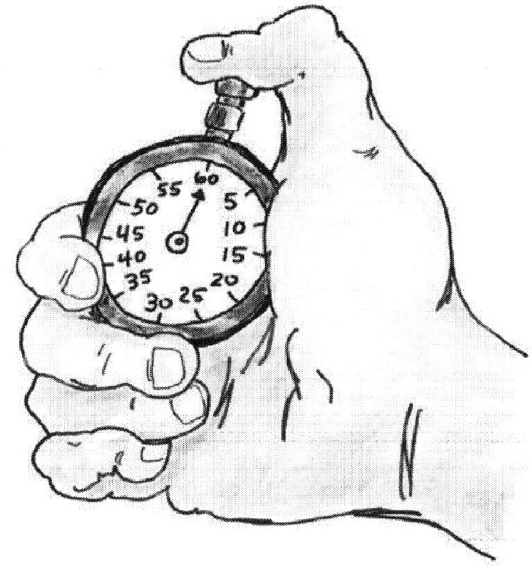

Indian tribal powers are not delegated, or given to them by Congress, but pre-exist the US Government. The sovereign powers of tribal nations, "although *recognized* by the Federal Government, were *not created* by the Federal Government." [3]

In order for us to grasp Indian law, and therefore understand how other governments interact with tribal governments, we must look at the legal powers that are vested in each Indian tribe. "It is illuminating to deal with the question of tribal criminal jurisdiction" by looking at "what the *original* Sovereign powers of the tribes were, and then, how far and in what respects these powers have been limited." [4] Because of tribal sovereignty, deference is given to tribal government unless Congress has *expressly* created a limitation to those powers.

As you view criminal jurisdiction in Indian country from this perspective, those corresponding criminal jurisdictional charts become less blurred and will actually come alive with meaning. Each area on those charts where state or federal jurisdiction is imposed on or limits tribal jurisdiction can (and must) be directly attributed to some type of historic jurisdictional event (i.e. treaty-making, federal legislation – or the interpretation of legislation through the courts).

The chart on the following pages (CH-6A) show how Solicitor Margold categorized the powers of tribal government:

POWERS OF INDIAN TRIBES

Opinion of the Solicitor, Department of the Interior, Solicitor Nathan Margold, Oct. 25, 1934

	POWER #1	POWER #2	POWER #3	POWER #4
POWERS OF TRIBAL GOVERNMENT (Tribal Council) "... powers of local self-government which have never been terminated by law or waived by treaty."	• Power to adopt a form of government • Power to create various offices and to prescribe the duties • Provide for the manner of election and removal of tribal officers • Prescribe the procedure of the tribal council and subordinate committees or councils • Provide for the salaries or expenses of tribal officers and other expenses of public business • Prescribe the forms through which the will of the tribe is to be executed.	• Define the conditions of membership within the tribe • Prescribe rules for adoption • Classify the members of the tribe • Grant or withhold the right of membership of the tribe	• Regulate the domestic relations of its members	• Prescribe rules of inheritance with respect to all personal property and all interests in real property
LIMITATIONS OF POWERS (by Treaties or laws) "It is illuminating to deal with the question of tribal criminal jurisdiction . . . by asking first, what the original sovereign powers of the tribes were, and then, how far and in what respects these powers have been limited."		". . . so far as may be consistent with existing acts of Congress governing the enrollment and property rights of members." ***Federal Law:*** The General Allotment Act		"... other than regular allotments of land." ***Federal Law:*** The General Allotment Act
LATER DECISIONS	***Indian Civil Rights Act*** 1968			

"[T]he most basic principle of all Indian law is the principle that **those powers which are lawfully vested in an Indian tribe are not**, in general, **delegated powers** granted by express acts of Congress, **but rather inherent powers** of a limited sovereignty which has never been extinguished. ***Each Indian tribe begins its relationship with the Federal Government as a sovereign power, recognized as such in treaty and legislation.*** The powers of sovereignty have been limited from time to time by special treaties and laws . . ."

POWER #5	POWER #6	POWER #7	POWER #8	POWER #9
• Levy dues, fees, or taxes upon the members of the tribe and upon nonmembers residing or doing any business of any sort with the reservation	• Remove or exclude from the limits of the reservation nonmembers of the tribe • Prescribe appropriate rules and regulations governing such removal and exclusion • Govern the conditions under which nonmembers of the tribe may come upon tribal land or have dealings with tribal members	• Regulate the use and disposition of all property within the jurisdiction of the tribe • Make public expenditures of tribal funds	• Administer justice with respect to all disputes and offenses of or among the members of the tribe	• Prescribe the duties of Federal employees on tribal lands • Regulate the conduct of Federal employees on tribal lands **The Exception:** Not an inherent power – but delegated by Congress.
". . . so far as may be consistent with the power of the Commissioner of Indian Affairs over licensed traders." ***Federal Law:*** Trade & Intercourse Acts	". . . excepting authorized Government officials and other persons now occupying reservation lands under lawful authority . . . providing such acts are consistent with Federal laws governing trade with the Indian tribes." ***Federal Law:*** Trade & Intercourse Acts	". . . where legal title to such funds lies in the tribe." ***Federal Law:*** Treaties & US Constitution	". . . other than the ten major crimes reserved to the Federal courts." (the tribes have concurrent jurisdiction over major crimes) ***Federal Law:*** The Major Crimes Act	". . . but only insofar as such powers of supervision may be expressly delegated by the Interior Department." ***Federal Law:*** 25 USC section 48
	Montana Decision 1981		***Oliphant Decision*** 1978	

CH-6A

#1 - The Power of an Indian Tribe to Define its Form of Government

> "The power to adopt a form of government, to create various offices and to prescribe the duties thereof, to provide for the manner of election and removal of tribal officers, to prescribe the procedure of the tribal council and subordinate committees or councils, to provide for the salaries or expenses of tribal officers and other expenses of public business, and, in general, to prescribe the forms through which the will of the tribe is to be executed."

Pre-existent Nations

Tribal nations, which pre-exist the nation of the United States, were recognized as sovereign through treaties with several European nations. As the US struggled to become an independent nation, they too made an official treaty with an Indian tribe. [5] After the US became a sovereign nation, over 370 government-to-government treaties were negotiated with various Indian tribes. The treaties were the vehicle for governmental agreements where each side had a voice. [6] In these mutual agreements the tribes placed themselves under the laws of the United States, therefore limiting their external sovereignty. A tribe's relinquishment of *external sovereignty* simply meant they agreed not to do anything contrary to or in conflict with the laws of the United States. Their inherent sovereignty – *internal sovereignty* – was not destroyed by their alliances with the United States "and the settled doctrine of the law of nations is that a weaker power does not surrender its independence – its right to self-government – by associating with a stronger, and taking its protection." [7]

Say it Simply!

"internal sovereignty" – a tribe's authority over their own people and territories

During the late 1880's, the language of a treaty, specifically the US – Sioux treaty, was a point of contention in the infamous case of *Ex Parte Crow Dog*. [8] The treaty stated: "Congress shall, by appropriate legislation, secure to them (the Sioux Indians) an orderly government: *they shall be subject to the laws of the United States*, and each individual shall be protected in his rights of property, person, and life." [9]

The US Supreme Court, in looking at the words of this treaty, clarified that such language was not intended to destroy a tribe's internal sovereignty, rather, quite the opposite:

> "The pledge to secure to these people (Indians), with whom the United States was contracting as a distinct political body, an orderly government, by appropriate legislation . . . necessarily implies . . . the highest and best of all, that of self-government, the regulation by themselves of their own domestic affairs, the maintenance of order and peace among their own members by the administration of their own laws and customs." [10]

Say it Simply!

"autonomy" -- the right of self-government, independent of another

Government Trespasses

The fact that tribal sovereignty has been disregarded at times, or as Solicitor Margold put it, "State governments and administrative officials have frequently trespassed upon the realm of tribal *autonomy* . . . These trespasses have not impaired the vested legal powers of local self-government." [11] Also, even though the tribes themselves have not always chosen to fully use their legal authority, "[p]ower and authority rightfully conferred do not necessarily cease to exist in consequence of a long nonuser." [12]

A more recent court case of the 20th Century makes a similar statement of fact:

Quotes "Q"

> *"The fact that the Tribe had not set up a system to punish certain of its members does not mean that it lacked the power to do so. It merely failed to exercise its jurisdiction."*
>
> *US v. Jackson, 600 F.2d 1283 (9th Cir. 1979)*

As we consider the inherent powers of an Indian tribe, it makes little difference if a tribe is currently flexing its jurisdictional authority. Their jurisdictional power will remain and can be exercised as the tribe sees fit. The only way these powers can be limited is by an *express* act of Congress.

Say it Simply!

"prescribe" --
to set rules or a course of action

"philosophy" --
a system of principles or beliefs

Tribal Government

In order for any group to exist there must be some type of form or system of government. "[A]n Indian tribe must, if it has any power at all, have the power to *prescribe* the forms through which its' will may be registered . . . to determine and define its own form of government." [13]

The form of government a tribe chooses is no less official if it is implemented via unwritten custom rather than wholly through written law. [14] Certainly, in this day and age, a tribe will face unique challenges through its choice to follow unwritten law; but if chosen, it is as legally viable as written law.

There are a few things to make note of though . . .

First of all, something we will be discussing soon is the Indian Civil Rights Act (ICRA) of 1968. Prior to Congress enacting the ICRA, a Senate subcommittee heard many complaints by tribal members about governmental abuse. One strong complaint voiced by tribal members during this time was regarding their unfair accountability to vague and unclear laws imposed by tribal governments. Many felt this was clearly a violation of their civil rights.

Another consideration for tribal governments regarding written law versus unwritten, is a stipulation in a recent amendment to the ICRA regarding a tribe's ability to implement stronger sentencing through their tribal court. This stipulation, now codified in 25 USC 1302(c)(4) states (with authors' emphasis):

> Prior to charging the defendant (accused), *make publicly available the criminal laws (including regulations and interpretative documents), rules of evidence, and rules of criminal procedure* (including rules governing the recusal of judges in appropriate circumstances) of the tribal government.

As you look at what we have emphasized here, you see that a tribe will need a written code, at least in the area of criminal law, if they want all options available for their tribal court.

Each tribal government will choose according to the will of the tribe, and may decide on a variation of both traditional and modern forms to fulfill the *philosophy* of their tribe.

Limitations

A limitation to "the power of an Indian tribe to define its form of government," [15] as previously mentioned, is that external sovereignty was necessarily relinquished through treaties of alliance with the United States government. The early treaties, agreements and statutes gave the framework for Indian tribes being defined as "domestic dependent nations." [16] Relinquished external sovereignty meant the tribe would no longer enter into treaties with foreign nations or operate in any way contrary to or in conflict with the United States government. The US federal government retains legislative authority over Indian tribes and has regulated or limited Indian tribes from time to time through such legislation. However, the "acts of Congress which appear to limit the powers of an Indian tribe are not to be unduly extended by doubtful *inference*." [17]

Say it Simply!

"inference" -- conclusion, assumption

One court case explained that tribal powers are not "implicitly divested (absolutely stripped of or taken away) by virtue of the tribes' dependent status." [18] Meaning, the fact an Indian tribe has relinquished its external sovereignty, does *not* mean all powers are relinquished. Only tribal power that would seek to impose external powers of government and override "interests of the national government" has been given up. [19]

Additionally, limitations were placed on tribal governments in 1968. An *express* act Congress imposed on the tribes was the Indian Civil Rights Act (ICRA). This Act sought to place on tribal governments the similar restrictions and limitations built into the US Constitution as safeguards against abusive or arbitrary actions of federal or state governments. Because of the uniqueness of tribal governments, and taking into account their ancient histories and cultures, Congress necessarily *modified* the individual protections from government found in the US Constitution when they were applied to tribal governments. In the third section of this chapter (Chapter 6, Part 3) we will look at this important piece of legislation in greater detail.

Application in PL 280 Areas

As you have seen through this resource guide, involvement at the state level is relatively a *new thing* in the area of criminal jurisdiction in Indian country. Keeping in mind how the Indian tribes have been around for a *long* time, we must also recognize that tribal governments may not *look* like state governments. Tribal governments reflect the culture and will of their people. Differences between tribal and state governments can present various challenges – to both governments.

Say it Simply!

"constituents" -- a person who authorizes another to act on his or her behalf. (Tribal members are the constituents of tribal council.)

A tribal government, often having a very different set of priorities than state and local governments, will operate on a different timetable and in accordance with the will of their *constituents*. When different governments necessarily interact with each other, there will not always be exactly the same interests or concerns. These differences can be compounded when cultural and philosophical diversity is additionally thrown into the *mix*. Also, on that note, we would be amiss not to mention the lack of trust many tribal communities have toward *any kind* of governmental agency. The historical relationship Indian tribes have experienced with federal and state governments, have left tribal folks with the need to remain vigilant in protecting their sovereignty and traditional cultures and values. [20]

Another thing to recognize, specifically in PL 280 areas, is the toll PL 280 took on a tribe's ability to build up their criminal justice system. A government's criminal justice system (i.e. the three elements: law enforcement, the courts and corrections) is very costly, yet each part is crucial for the effective operation of government. PL 280 did not *directly* take monies away from the tribes affected by its enactment. However, decisions were made at the federal level, through the Bureau of Indian Affairs, to stop funding toward criminal justice systems of PL 280 tribes. Federal authorities reasoned that tribal criminal justice needs could be met through the state systems. This reasoning disregarded the fact that a tribe retains concurrent jurisdiction over their people. It also gave little regard for the impact this would have on the state system which received no funding for added services that it would now need to provide. [21] Either way, it hurt the tribes because they were denied funding and state-level services were often lacking due to the financial strain added services had on state budgets.

Quotes

> *"Congress, we are told, passed Pub. L. 280 not as a measure to benefit the States . . ."*
>
> *Washington v. Confederated Bands & Tribes of the Yakima Indian Nation, 439 U.S.463, 498 (1979)*

Dig Deeper

> The book, ***Planting Tail Feathers: Tribal Survival and Public Law 280***, by Carole Goldberg-Ambrose contains a wealth of information regarding the history of PL 280 and the challenges tribal communities have faced since the enactment of this federal law.
>
> Goldberg-Ambrose, Carole, *Planting Tail Feathers*, McNaughton & Gunn, Inc. 1997.

One last thing to mention here . . .

The individual who sits as the leader of a tribal government will hold the title "Chairman," "Chairwoman" (or, "Chairperson"), "Governor" or "President." It is up to the tribe to define that specific title. Women often serve in leadership roles within tribal communities. This is important to make note of, because it can be a possible *cultural clash* that can easily be remedied through knowledge. One situation we were told of involved state law enforcement officers who, while addressing a safety issue with a tribal council, ignored the women sitting on the council (even though the women were the Chair and Vice-Chair of the tribe). The bottom line is respect. One can never go wrong by showing respect, especially in the political arena where governmental leaders rub shoulders with each other.

Say it Simply!

"anomalous" -- unusual, not fitting into a common or familiar classification

"quasi" -- having some, but not all of the features

Quotes

> *"Our relations with Indian tribes have 'always been . . .* ***anomalous****. . . and of a complex character'. . . 'we have also recognized that the tribes remain* ***quasi****-sovereign nations which, by governmental structure, culture, and source of sovereignty are in many ways foreign to the constitutional institutions of the Federal and State Governments.'"*
>
> *Santa Clara Pueblo v. Martinez, 436 U.S. 49, 71 (1978) citing US v. Kagama, 118 U.S. at 381 and Elk v. Wilkins, 112 U.S. 94 (1884)*

#2 - The Power of an Indian Tribe to Determine its Membership

> "To define the conditions of membership within the tribe, to prescribe rules for adoption, to classify the members of the tribe and to grant or withhold the right of tribal suffrage, and to make all other necessary rules and regulations governing the membership of the tribe so far as may be consistent with existing acts of Congress governing the enrollment and property rights of members."

Prerogative of the Tribe

It is the prerogative of each tribe to: set up their own rules for membership, decide if it allows for adoption into the tribe by non-Indians or Indians of another tribe, what type of memberships or citizenship the tribe will have, and if or when abandonment of membership will take place. *"In the absence of express legislation by Congress to the contrary, an Indian tribe has complete authority to determine all questions of its own membership."* [22] This right belongs to tribal governments "from the character of an Indian tribe as a distinct political entity." [23]

Solicitor Margold used the example of the *Waldron v. US* case [24] when explaining the inherent power of an Indian tribe to determine its membership. In this case, the Interior Department refused to recognize a certain woman as an Indian because she was only five-sixteenths Indian blood and her father was a white man. However, tribal custom recognized her as an Indian so the court directed the Interior Department to recognize her as an Indian as well.

Membership & ICRA

We will be presenting the Indian Civil Rights Act (ICRA) in Part 3 of this chapter. But for now, let's briefly look at how an important ICRA case, *Santa Clara Pueblo v. Martinez*, [25] involved a dispute about tribal membership. Here are the main points of the case:

► Santa Clara Pueblo is an Indian tribe located in New Mexico and has been in existence for over 600 years.

► Julia Martinez, a full-blood female member of the Santa Clara Pueblo married a Navajo man in 1941.

► They had several children that were raised on the Santa Clara Pueblo reservation who continued to live there as adults and who spoke the *Tewa* language of the tribe.

► The children were denied membership because a tribal ordinance enacted in 1939 only allowed membership to children of *male* tribal members who married non-members, but not to children of *female* tribal members who married non-members.

► Julia Martinez sued the Santa Clara Pueblo and its governor, stating the tribal rule discriminated against sex and ancestry and violated the Indian Civil Rights Act (ICRA).

► The ICRA provides that "No Indian tribe in exercising powers of self-government shall . . . deny any person within its jurisdiction the equal protection of its laws." (25 USC 1302)

► While this case was moving through the court system, a lower court commented, "To abrogate tribal decisions, particularly in the delicate area of membership, for whatever 'good' reasons, is to destroy cultural identity under the guise of saving it." [26]

► The US Supreme Court said the ICRA was designed to provide protection to "individual Indians from arbitrary and unjust actions of tribal governments." [27]

► In the final analysis, the court decided that interfering with how a tribe determines its membership would substantially be an interference of "a tribe's ability to maintain itself as a culturally and politically distinct entity." [28]

Limitations

The power of tribes in this area is limited by some statutes where Congress has defined an Indian as belonging to a certain tribe for the specific purpose of allotment assignment through a tribal roll (a list of tribal member names). Tribal rolls helped the Secretary of the Interior divide and distribute tribal funds and other property. [29]

Specific to PL 280 areas

Tribal membership is purely an internal tribal issue. State courts do not hear cases involving tribal membership in PL 280 areas and law enforcement will not get involved unless any actions elevate to criminal behavior.

#3 - The Power of an Indian Tribe to Regulate Domestic Relations

"To regulate the domestic relations of its members."

25 USC § 371 is a federal statute that recognizes the tribal "custom and manner" of marriage for the purposes of inheritance.

Domestic Relationships

Domestic relationships have to do with family and home relationships – husband, wife, father, mother, child, etc. "The Indian tribes have been accorded the *widest* possible latitude in regulating the domestic relations of their members." [30] Things such as: marriage, divorce, inheritance, and appointment of guardians for incompetents or minors, are all things which each tribe has the authority to regulate. Just as non-Indians can get married in one state and then file their divorce in another state, tribal jurisdiction is similar. Just because Indians can get a marriage license from a state official, "doesn't deprive the tribe of jurisdiction to issue a divorce where the parties are properly before tribal court." [31]

Specific to PL 280 areas

Regarding domestic relationships, many of the tribal courts in PL 280 areas (*where they exist*) [32] primarily hear child custody issues that fall under the Indian Child Welfare Act (ICWA). [33] The ICWA is an extremely important piece of legislation to tribal communities. ICWA was enacted as a response to a very real threat tribal communities faced – the loss of their children.

We mentioned early on about the government sanctioned Indian boarding schools where Indian children were taken from their homes. The taking of Indian children from their families and familiar surroundings to place them in far-away boarding schools began in the late 1870's and continued for decades. The boarding schools were guided by the philosophy of assimilation. A man named Richard Pratt founded the first Indian boarding school in 1879, seeing the boarding school system as an instrument to "kill the Indian . . . save the man." [34] This mode of education was made mandatory by Congressional legislation in 1891. In order to gain compliance of unwilling parents and tribal communities various methods were used – such as withholding food from the tribe or tribal members, or even threat of imprisonment.

During the height of the government's enforcement of compulsory attendance at Indian boarding schools, one group of Indians, the Hopi Tribe, resisted the will of the government for their children. (They also resisted the forced allotment of their lands that was aimed at destroying their social structure.) Nineteen of the Hopi "ringleaders" were arrested by the US Army on Nov. 25, 1894. They were escorted to Alcatraz to be "held in confinement, at hard labor, until . . . they shall show . . . they fully realize the error of their ways . . ." These Hopi "hostiles" were imprisoned at Alcatraz from January 3rd to August 7th, 1895. [35]

Nerdy Stuff

Senator Robert Kennedy chaired this special Senate Subcommittee on Indian Education until his death.

You will remember in our earlier discussion of the 1928 Meriam report, how this report revealed the deplorable conditions at many of the boarding schools. There were positive changes made in response to this revealing report, however, even by the year 1969, a special Senate subcommittee on Indian Education stated in their report:

Quotes

"Q"

"We are shocked at what we discovered."

Report on Indian Education, Nov. 3, 1969, Special Subcommitte on Indian Education, Senate Committee on Labor and Public Welfare, documented in Prucha, Francis Paul, Documents of United States Indian Policy, University of Nebraska Press 2000 p. 253

Dig Deeper

In his book, *Education for Extinction*, David Wallace Adams explains how the Meriam report revealed the poor diet the children of the boarding schools received, lacking basic nutrition because of the eleven-cents-a-day budget for each student. He also discusses the report's concern for the overcrowded and unsanitary conditions and how "Industrial Education" was really student labor for production work.

Adams, David Wallace, *Education for Extinction*, University Press of Kansas 1995, pp. 331-332.

This lengthy report of 4,077 pages, contained in seven volumes, spoke of "families which want to stay together but are forced apart . . . of 9-year old children who want a neighborhood school but are sent thousands of miles away to remote and alien boarding schools." [36] The report documented that there were seventy-seven boarding schools run by the Bureau of Indian Affairs in 1969, comprised of approximately 35,000 Indian children as resident students. The senate report made special notice that "nearly 9,000 of the boarding school children are under 9 years old." [37]

The Senate subcommittee lamented what they discovered:

> *"What concerned us most deeply . . . was the low quality of virtually every aspect of the schooling available to Indian children. The school buildings themselves; the course materials and books; the attitude of teachers and administrative personnel; the accessibility of school buildings – all these are of shocking quality."*
>
> *Report on Indian Education, Nov. 3, 1969, Special Subcommittee on Indian Education, Senate Committee on Labor and Public Welfare, documented in Prucha, Francis Paul, Documents of United States Indian Policy, University of Nebraska Press 2000 p. 255*

In response to this report, the *Indian Education Act* was passed three years later, in 1972. One provision in the Act was to make grants available to local educational agencies. Continued public awareness and Native American activism brought about the *Student Rights and Due Process Procedures* in 1974. This outlined students' rights and established due process procedures at the Bureau of Indian Affairs schools. [38]

Along with the need for reform in Indian education was the need for a drastic change in policy toward Native Americans in many public and private social agencies. Disregard for Indian culture and community had moved beyond the walls of the boarding schools. An ethnocentric way of thinking permeated various social agencies as they dealt with Native Americans. State courts also "failed" in Indian child custody hearings "to recognize the essential tribal relations of Indian people and the cultural and social standards prevailing in Indian communities and families." [39] Breaking up Indian families and removing Indian children (often permanently) from their reservations was seen as acceptable practice – even sometimes, preferable. Tribal communities lived under the fear of their children being taken away from them. ICWA was designed to reverse this philosophy by recognizing "that there is no resource that is more vital to the continued existence and integrity of Indian tribes than their children." [40] The Indian Child Welfare Act became a federal law in 1978 to *officially* prevent the breaking-up of Indian families and communities.

Quotes

"[A]n alarmingly high percentage of Indian families are broken up by the removal, often unwarranted, of their children from them by nontribal public and private agencies and that an alarmingly high percentage of such children are placed in non-Indian foster and adoptive homes and institutions."

Indian Child Welfare Act (ICWA), Congressional Findings, 25 USC § 1901(4)

Key Point

There are many Indian elders living on reservations today who experienced life at the Indian boarding schools. Indian people are very protective of their most valuable possession – their children.

Alex's & Mary's Story

Alex Tortes' * and Mary Belardo's story is one such illustration of the disregard for Indian culture and community that existed in state social services.

Social services have an important role to play in any community. In fact, many tribal communities have established their own social services on their reservations. The Indian Child Welfare Act (ICWA) was not designed to stop the needed work of social services but, rather, to halt the destructive policies of state social services and state courts in removing Indian children from their homes. Although many of you may be familiar with the fact that Indian children were taken from their families for an extensive amount of time through the boarding schools, or permanently through social services, you may not realize how recently these practices were implemented and condoned.

Alex and his sister, Mary, are living examples of the common and relatively recent practice of breaking up Indian families. When they were very young, circumstances brought state social services into their lives. As was played out in the lives of so many Indian children, Alex and Mary were transported away from their reservation, never to be returned back to their home and family.

They were taken to a city about two hours away and placed into foster care. They lived their formative years in a foster home having no knowledge of their Indian heritage. Although they grew up not too far from their immediate family and relatives, they were deprived of any connection with them. Alex and Mary faced many struggles and challenges growing up. They never felt they truly "belonged."

When Alex and Mary were teenagers, their older sister located them and told them of their Indian heritage and nearby family. Alex visited his mother twice. However, Mary never met her mother.

Mary eventually returned to the Torres-Martinez Desert Cahuilla Indian Reservation. She served with distinction as Tribal Chairwoman for many years. Mary continues to serve in leadership roles on her reservation.

Alex followed his own career path and when the opportunity arose for him to work with his tribe and other tribal communities he was very pleased. One of the greatest joys Alex now experiences is when he is able to reconnect with his extended tribal family and learn about his Indian heritage.

** This story relates to one of the co-authors of this book, Alex Tortes.*

Say it Simply!

"acronym" --
a word formed from the first letters in a phrase of series of words

"full faith and credit" --
one government recognizing the legal documents of another government as if it is their own

Another important *acronym* to be aware of is VAWA. This stands for Violence Against Women Act. This Act became federal law initially in 1994. VAWA is not specific to only Native American women, but it specifically includes Native American women. When VAWA was reenacted in 2005, *Title IX – Safety for Indian Women* was added, acknowledging the unique needs of Indian communities and the challenges facing Native American women. Under Title IX, there were listed six Congressional findings:

1) 1 out of every 3 Indian (including Alaska Native) women are raped in their lifetimes;

2) Indian women experience 7 sexual assaults per 1,000, compared with 4 per 1,000 among Black Americans, 3 per 1,000 among Caucasians, 2 per 1,000 among Hispanic women, and 1 per 1,000 among Asian women;

3) Indian women experience the violent crime of battering at a rate of 23.2 per 1,000, compared with 8 per 1,000 among Caucasian women;

4) During the period 1979 through 1992, homicide was the third leading cause of death of Indian females aged 15 to 34, and 75 percent were killed by family members or acquaintances;

5) Indian tribes require additional criminal justice and victim services resources to respond to violent assaults against women; and

6) The unique legal relationship of the United States to Indian tribes creates a federal trust responsibility to assist tribal governments in safeguarding the lives of Indian women.

An important provision within VAWA is its *Full Faith and Credit* section. Essentially, this provision directs all states, Indian tribes and US territories to honor each others' protection orders as if the order was their own. Because this is one important tool for keeping tribal communities safe, yet is generally not well-known, it is worthy of spending time showing you this section:

Full Faith and Credit Provision of the Violence Against Women Act:

"Any protection order issued that is consistent with subsection (b) of this section by the court of one State, Indian tribe, or territory (the issuing State, Indian tribe, or territory) shall be accorded full faith and credit by the court of another State, Indian tribe, or territory (the enforcing State, Indian tribe, or territory) and enforced by the court and law enforcement personnel of the other State, Indian tribal government or Territory as if it were the order of the enforcing State or tribe.

(b) Protection Order – A protection order issued by a State, tribal, or territorial court is consistent with this subsection if –

(1) such court has jurisdiction over the parties and matter under the law of such State, Indian tribe, or territory; and

(2) reasonable notice and opportunity to be heard is given to the person against whom the order is sought sufficient to protect that person's right to due process. In the case of ex parte orders, notice and opportunity to be heard must be provided within the time required by State, tribal, or territorial law, and in any event within a reasonable time after the order is issued, sufficient to protect the respondent's due process rights."

18 USC § 2265

In addition to domestic violence protective orders being given recognition, honor and enforcement, federal law requires the same for child custody orders and child support orders. [41]

The Full Faith and Credit provision does not come with an enforcement section saying if a state, tribe or US territory does not comply, then the law will make them comply. Or, in legal terms, full faith and credit for foreign protection orders is not *self-executing*. This means, although it is a federal mandate, it is up to each state, tribe and US territory to establish their own laws and procedures for honoring foreign protection orders as if the order is their own. Many states have, in fact, created their own enabling acts for this provision. It would be extremely prudent for anyone working in Indian country, especially law enforcement and the courts, to know their State's enabling acts and set procedures for recognizing foreign protection orders. And, for those who are working *boots on the ground*, it is important for them to recognize that tribal protection orders may look different than state protection orders. Therefore, it would be wise to be familiar with what various tribal protection orders look like. Protection orders are meant to protect the individual(s) wherever they are (home – even if it's a temporary shelter or living with a helping family member, work, school, etc.) from their abuser. This means protection orders must be enforced *on* or *off* Indian reservations.

Key Point

Tribal protection orders are to be enforced *on or off* Indian reservation.

Dig Deeper

An excellent resource for digging deeper regarding VAWA provisions is the Battered Women's Justice Project, National Center on Protection Orders and Full Faith and Credit (www.fullfaithandcredit.org). There are several helpful resources that are free to download off their site. One tool you may find very useful is a pocket guide for enforcing foreign protection orders which you can download at: *http://www.fullfaithandcredit.org/publications.aspx*

#4 - The Power of an Indian Tribe to Govern the Descent and Distribution of Property

"To prescribe rules of inheritance with respect to all personal property and all interests in real property other than regular allotments of land."

Supremely the Tribe's Authority

"With respect to all property other than allotments of land made under the General Allotment Act, the inheritance laws and customs of the Indian tribe are still of supreme authority." [42]

#5 - The Taxing Power of an Indian Tribe

"To levy dues, fees, or taxes upon the members of the tribe and upon nonmembers, residing or doing any business of any sort within the reservation, so far as may be consistent with the power of the Commissioner of Indian Affairs over licensed traders."

Maintenance & Effectiveness

An essential power of any government is its taxing power. Governmental taxes allow for the maintenance and effectiveness of that government. "Among the powers of sovereignty vested in an Indian tribe is the power to tax members of the tribe and nonmembers accepting privileges of trade or residence, to which taxes may be attached as conditions." [43]

Limitations

" . . . so far as may be consistent with the power of the Commissioner of Indian Affairs over licensed traders." [44]

Congress expressly granted authority to the Commissioner of Indian Affairs to appoint traders on Indian reservations and set the regulations and terms for their involvement with tribes. [45] Indian tribes could not tax contrary to these regulations.

A 1980 US Supreme Court case, while determining an issue about taxing, used a quote from this taxing section of the Solicitor's opinion. This case, *Washington v. Confederated Tribes of the Colville Indian Reservation*, [46] stated a tribe's "power to tax transactions occurring on trust lands and significantly involving a tribe or its members is a fundamental attribute of sovereignty which the tribes retain." [47]

#6 - The Power of an Indian Tribe to Exclude Nonmembers from its Jurisdiction

> "To remove or to exclude from the limits of the reservation nonmembers of the tribe, excepting authorized Government officials and other persons now occupying reservation lands under lawful authority, and to prescribe appropriate rules and regulations governing such removal and exclusion, and governing the conditions under which nonmembers of the tribe may come upon tribal land or have dealings with tribal members, providing such acts are consistent with Federal laws governing trade with the Indian tribes."

Exclusion

Solicitor Margold explained how an earlier, 1821 Attorney General opinion, stated: "So long as a tribe exists and remains in possession of its lands, its title and possession are sovereign and exclusive; and there exists no authority to enter upon their lands, for any purpose whatever, without their consent." [48]

Limitations

"... excepting authorized Government officials and other persons now occupying reservation lands under lawful authority ... providing such acts are consistent with Federal laws governing trade with the Indian tribes." [49]

Specific to PL 280 Areas

An important court case in 1990, *Duro v. Reina*, [50] explained how Indian tribes ...

> "possess their traditional and undisputed power to exclude persons whom they deem to be undesirable from tribal lands ... Tribal law enforcement authorities have the power to restrain those who disturb public order on the reservation, and if necessary, to eject them. Where jurisdiction to try and punish an offender rests outside the tribe, tribal officers may exercise their power to detain the offender and transport him to the proper authorities." [51]

In the next sections of this chapter we will discuss more about the role of tribal law enforcement on a reservation and present more details regarding their responsibilities and scope of authority. We will look closer at jurisdiction as it pertains to tribal law enforcement and review several important legal decisions that define this jurisdiction. But for now, keep in mind that a tribe has inherent power to exclude nonmembers from their tribal lands just as a landowner may remove someone off their property. Although a tribe may open some areas of their reservation for public use, tribal lands are *not* public property.

#7 - Tribal Powers Over Property

> "To regulate the use and disposition of all property within the jurisdiction of the tribe, and to make public expenditures of tribal funds, where legal title to such funds lies in the tribe."

The Tribe Rules

A tribe prescribes the rules concerning all property within their jurisdiction. Although the tribal members rightly occupy tribal lands, this "does not create any vested rights in the occupant as against the tribe." [52] Also, the "extent of any individual's interest in tribal property is subject to such limitations as the tribe may see fit to impose." [53] Therefore, a tribe has the authority to regulate the use of all property within its jurisdiction. [54]

Limitations

The tribe cannot go against any acts of Congress restricting the alienation or leasing of tribal property, designed to control the disposition of particular funds or lands. Also, under the Indian Civil Rights Act (ICRA), a tribal law cannot be enforced after-the-fact. The ICRA (Prohibition #9) states an Indian tribe, "Shall not pass any . . . ex post facto law." (see chart, pg. 327)

Specific to PL 280 Areas

Similar to what we mentioned regarding tribal membership, this area is also an internal tribal issue. In PL 280 areas, law enforcement will not get involved in a dispute regarding tribal property regulation unless any actions elevate to criminal behavior.

Quotes "Q"

> *"Federal and state courts have declined to interfere with the decisions of tribal authorities on property disputes internal to the tribe."*
>
> *Bennett, Elmer (2008), Federal Indian Law, The Lawbook Exchange, p. 443*

#8 - The Powers of an Indian Tribe in the Administration of Justice

> "To administer justice with respect to all disputes and offenses of or among the members of the tribe, other than the ten major crimes reserved to the Federal courts."

Equal Judicial Powers

In each of the executive and legislative powers of Indian tribes, which we've discussed in Powers #1-#7, there equally exists judicial powers. "If an Indian tribe has power to regulate marriage relationships of its members, it necessarily has power to adjudicate, through tribunals established by itself, controversies involving such relationships. So, too, with other fields of local government . . . according to the form of law or custom recognized by the tribe ..." [55]

Well-Settled Principle

Tribal administration of justice in the area of *civil law* "has a force that State courts and Federal courts will respect." [56] On the other hand, tribal judicial powers – when it comes to *criminal* law and order over its people and territories – must be enforced by the tribe itself. The reason for this, Solicitor Margold points out, is due to "the well-settled principle that one sovereign will not enforce the criminal laws of another sovereign . . ." [57]

" . . . State courts and Federal courts alike must decline to enforce *penal* provisions of tribal law. *Responsibility for the maintenance of law and order is therefore squarely upon the Indian tribe*, unless this field of jurisdiction has been taken over by the State or the Federal government." [58]

Specific to PL 280 Areas

Say it Simply!

"lacunae" -- gaps, missing parts, deficiencies

"prevalence" -- widespread, of wide extent of occurrence

It is important to note how the Solicitor emphasized what he called *"lacunae"* in law and order on tribal lands. Gaps in criminal jurisdiction . . . now here's an issue that is like the proverbial "broken record" – it just keeps jumping back and repeating again and again. Jurisdictional gaps were the very concern of Congress back in 1825 when they enacted the Assimilative Crimes Act (ACA). It was a concern to the Solicitor in the 1930's and even today we recognize that jurisdictional chasms are a major concern throughout Indian country.

You will notice in Chart CH-6A (pages 258-259) the Solicitor had stated a limitation to a tribe's administration of justice was "other than the . . . major crimes reserved to the Federal courts." [59] Yet, when he discussed things more thoroughly in his opinion, he stated it was his belief that the Major Crimes Act gave "only a *concurrent* jurisdiction upon the federal courts" and "this statute does not expressly terminate tribal jurisdiction over the enumerated crimes." [60] Legal decisions have since clarified that his belief was correct.

Even though the Indian tribes have concurrent criminal jurisdiction, the Indian Civil Rights Act of 1968 (ICRA) initially specified that tribal courts could only impose punishment for any one criminal conviction with a fine of $500 and/or six months in jail. The result of this federal law imposed on tribal courts was to create an ineffective system of consequences in relation to criminal acts. Such a *minimal* consequence for a *major* offense did not take seriously the tremendous impact violent crime had on victims as well as the entire tribal community. The federal restrictions specified in the ICRA communicated disrespect to the victim(s) regarding the level of crime committed when tribal sentencing power was so limited.

The sentencing power for tribal courts was eventually increased, 18 years later (1986), to a fine of $5,000 and/or one year in jail. The US Supreme Court also acknowledged, in 1978, the high volume of non-Indian crime that takes place on Indian reservations.

Quotes "Q"

> *"[W]e are not unaware of the prevalence of non-Indian crime on today's reservations . . . "*
>
> *Oliphant v. Suquamish Indian Tribe, 435 US 191, 212 (1978)*

The *2010 Tribal Law and Order Act (TLOA)* was essentially enacted in response to public safety concerns (jurisdictional gaps) within Indian country. The day TLOA was legally put in place, the statement from the US President stated:

> *"Today's passage of the Tribal Law and Order Act is an important step to help the federal government better address the unique public safety challenges that confront tribal communities. The fact is, American Indians and Alaska Natives are victimized by violent crime at far higher rates than Americans as a whole. Native communities have seen increased gang and drug activity, with* ***some tribes experiencing violent crime rates at more than ten times the national average****. And one in three Native women will be the victim of rape in her lifetime.*
>
> *The federal government's relationship with tribal governments, its obligations under treaty and law, and our values as a nation require that we do more to improve public safety in tribal communities. And this Act will help us achieve that. It will strengthen the relationship between the federal government and tribal governments. It will improve our ability to work with tribal communities in the investigation and prosecution of crime, and* ***it authorizes resources for tribes to fight crime more effectively****."*
>
> *Statement by President Obama on the passage of the Tribal Law and Order Act, July 21, 2010*

The Tribal Law and Order Act amended the ICRA, allowing tribal sentencing power to increase to $15,000 and/or one to three years imprisonment with a nine year cap on consecutive sentencing. (If there is a possibility for the accused to receive more than one year imprisonment, there are specific mandates a tribe must adhere to.) Even with this recent increase, tribal courts still are not allowed to prosecute comparable to the sentencing power in federal and state courts for violent crimes, leaving tribes with the need to rely on federal and state attorneys/courts for assistance in *sentencing justice*.

#9 - The Powers of an Indian Tribe to Supervise Government Employees

> "To prescribe the duties and to regulate the conduct of Federal employees, but only insofar as such powers of supervision may be expressly delegated by the Interior Department."

Not an Inherent Power

In concluding his opinion of the *Powers of Indian Tribes*, Solicitor Margold made it clear that the only power, amongst the nine, that "is certainly *not* an inherent power of tribal sovereignty" [61] is the power to supervise governmental employees who work for the benefit of a tribe. These governmental employees were individuals with an expertise promised to the tribes through the original treaties and subsequent statutes: teachers, blacksmiths, mechanics, farmers, etc. Congress specifically granted tribes this authority under 25 USC Sect. 48. [62] The supervision of the tribe over these governmental employees is limited to that which is expressly delegated by the Secretary of the Interior Department.

Chart CH-6B Illuminates It

We've now covered all the *Powers of Indian Tribes* Solicitor Margold categorized. Through this overview, you have become familiar with the whole gamut of internal sovereign powers Indian tribes possess. These powers have not diminished except where, either by treaties or by laws, specific authority has been limited. Since jurisdiction in Indian country must be clearly and explicitly authorized by Congress, every area where either federal or state agencies exercise jurisdictional authority must be connected to a specific act of Congress.

One authority on federal Indian law stated that an important key to understanding tribal powers of administration of justice is to keep in mind that federal courts are courts of *limited jurisdiction*. Essentially, this means federal courts have no *common law* jurisdiction and can *only* exercise jurisdiction over what Congress has *specifically* granted through laws. And this is also true for state courts – they can *only* exercise jurisdiction over Indians where Congress has so authorized.

"Common Law" is law that is based on customs and unwritten law of a society that has universal consent and goes way back in time. The legal decisions that were based on societal customs were developed over many years and were part of ancient English law. Prior to the American Revolution, common law was incorporated into the governing of the early American colonies. In the present day, most common law has been integrated into various statutes with contemporary purposes and application. Common law is considered opposite of statutory law which derives its force and authority from legislative enactments.

"gamut" -- extent, breadth, entire range or scale of

Quotes "Q"

> *"State law does not apply to Indian affairs except so far as, and to the extent that, the United States gives or has given its consent."*
>
> *Bennett, Elmer, Federal Indian Law, The Lawbook Exchange (2008), p. 501*

The following chart (CH-6B) illustrates the sovereign powers of tribal governments in their maintenance of criminal law and order (see center column). On each side are the two other governments who are involved in Indian country: federal and state governments. Federal statutes that grant criminal jurisdictional power to federal and state authorities are relatively few in number, showing Congressional intent to leave Indian tribes "considerable latitude" for the administration of justice over their people and territories. [63] This chart will be helpful to you as the Solicitor explained "It is illuminating to deal with the question of tribal criminal jurisdiction" by looking at "what the original sovereign powers of the tribes were, and then, how far and in what respects these powers have been limited." [64] Chart CH-6B indicates where either treaties or laws – and interpretations of the laws in court decisions – have been imposed upon the tribes. This chart shows the laws enacted by Congress authorizing federal, and (much) later state, jurisdiction. In the earlier chapters of this resource guide we have gone into detail about each of these laws. As you digest the information you may want to flip back to these earlier sections to refresh your memory.

Key Point

PL280 is a federal law that is to be applied "so far as, and to the extent" that has been authorized by Congress.

Criminal Jurisdiction: It is a "well-settled principle that one sovereign will not enforce the criminal laws of another sovereign." (Margold, pg. 57) *

* All page numbers in the chart refer to pages from Solicitor Margold's legal opinion.

Refer to historical background for fuller explanation of the specific laws.

Limited Sovereignty beginning 1783
STATE GOVERNMENTS
Maintenance of Law & Order

Authority: US Constitution & State Constitution

FEDERAL JURISDICTION, Exclusive of the States
US-Indian Treaties created a government-to-government relationship with the tribes and a "duty of protection" to dependent nations who owed "no allegiance to the States, and received from them no protection. Because of the local ill feeling, the people of the States where they are found are often their deadliest enemies."

US v. Kagama, 118 US 375, 384 (1886)

NO STATE CRIMINAL JURISDICTION OVER TRIBES
(Written by Solicitor Margold 1934) "It is clear that the original criminal jurisdiction of the Indian tribes has never been transferred to the States. Sporadic attempts of the States to exercise jurisdiction over offenses between Indians, or between Indians and whites, committed on an Indian reservation, have been held invalid usurpation of authority. The principle that a State has no criminal jurisdiction over offenses involving Indians committed on an Indian reservation is ... well estabished ... reaches back to the earlier years of the Republic." (the Solicitor lists 17 cases of proof -- pg. 57)

STATE JURISDICTION

- Over Non-Indian v. Non-Indian committed on an Indian reservation. — US v. McBratney 104 US 621 (1881)
- Over Indian off the reservation. — Pablo v. People 23 Colo. 134 (1896)

Sovereign since time immemorial
TRIBAL GOVERNMENTS
Maintenance of Law & Order

Authority: Tribal Customs/Constitution

"What is not expressly limited remains within the domain of tribal sovereignty" (pg. 19)

ORIGINAL SOVEREIGN POWERS -- COMPLETE & INDEPENDENT CIVIL & CRIMINAL JURISDICTION (pg. 57)

- Punish its subjects for offenses against each other or against aliens and for public offenses against the peace and dignity of the tribe.
- Punish aliens within its jurisdiction according to its own laws and customs.

Early treaties, such as the Treaty of July 2, 1791 with the Cherokees provided: "If any citizen of the United States, or other person not being an Indian, shall settle on any of the Cherokee lands, such person shall forfeit the protection of the United States, and the Cherokees may punish him or not as they please."

Later treaties provided for the offender to be delivered up to the United States for prosecution.

Treaties
US Constitution
Art. 2, Sec 2, cl 2 & Art. 6

Sovereign since 1783
FEDERAL GOVERNMENT
Maintenance of Law & Order

Authority: US Constitution

"[T]he constitutional authority of the Federal Government to prescribe laws and administer justice upon the Indian reservation is plenary." (pg 58)

"[T]he settled doctrine of the law of nations is, that a weaker power does not surrender its independance -- its right to self-government, by associating with a stronger, in taking its protection."

Worcester v. Georgia, 31 US 515, 520 (1832)

TREATY-MAKING AUTHORITY
Power of President with advice of 2/3rds consent of Senate.

SUPREMEACY OF TREATIES
"... all treaties made, or which shall be made, under the authority of the United States, shall be the supreme law of the land."

"The relations of Indians, among themselves -- the conduct of one towards another -- is to be controlled by the customs and laws of the tribe, save when Congress expressly or clearly directs otheriwise."

US v. Quiver, 241 US 602, 605-6 (1916)

In the absence of an explicit Congressional directive, Indian tribes have exclusive criminal jurisdiction over offenses committed by one Indian against another Indian. "The tribes (are) semi-independent . . . our government has always recognized as exempt from our laws . . . and in regard to their domestic government, left to their own rules and traditions, in whom we have recognized the capacity to make treaties, and with whom the governments, state and nations, deal with few exceptions only . . ."

Ex Parte Crow Dog, 109 US 556, 572 (1883)

Trade & Intercourse Act 1790

Express authorization by Congress to deal with inter-racial crime.

"Congress' concern was with providing effective protection for the Indians 'from the violence of the lawless part of our frontier inhabitants.' (Quote from

President George Washington's Seventh Annual Address) Without such protection, . . .'all the exertions of the Government to prevent destructive retaliations by the Indians will prove fruitless and all our present agreeable prospects illusory.' Beginning with the Trade & Intercourse Act of 1790 . . . Congress assumed federal jurisdiciton over offenses by non-Indians against Indians . . . In 1817, Congress went one step further and extended federal enclave law to Indian Country; the only exception was for 'any offense committed by one Indian against another.'"
Oliphant V. Suquamish Indian Tribe, 435 US 191, 201 (1978)

Tribal Self-Government -- Indian v. Indian. Also, if Indian v. Non-Indian had already been prosecuted by local law of tribe.

Federal Enclave Law Indian Country Crimes Act 1817
18 USC 1152

Works in tandum with 18 USC 1152 and never functions by itself.

1825 Assimilative Crimes Act (ACA)
18 USC 13

The fill-in-the-gap act where federal laws were lacking. Federal law crawls into the skin of state law and is federally prosecuted.

1885 Major Crimes Act
18 USC 1153

FEDERAL FIRST
Federal jurisdiction over certain 'major' crimes committed on an Indian reservation, Indian v. Indian.

Tribal concurrent jurisdiction

"As a general rule, tribal courts retain exclusive jurisdiction over all crimes committed by Native Americans against Native Americans in Indian Country . . . However, . . . federal courts have concurrent jurisdiction over the offenses listed in the Major Crimes Act."
US v. Young, 936 F. 2d 1050 (9th Cir. 1991)

IMPORTANCE OF TRIBAL JURISDICTION (pg. 60, 64)
"The lacunae (gaps) in this brief code of ten commandments (more added now) are serious, and indicate the importance of tribal jurisdiction in the field of law and order. . .Indian tribes retain sovereignty and jurisdiction over a vast area of ordinary offenses over which the Federal Government has never presumed to legislate and over which the State governments have not the authority to legislate."

PL 280 gave State authority over all violations of a state's criminal public policy -- but no regulatory authority.

Public Law 83-280 1953

"[A] state is not absolutely barred from exercising jurisdiction over activities of tribal members on their reservation, but the exercise of state jurisdiction is limited and must be based on a specific grant of authority by Congress . . . Indian tribes retain attributes of sovereignty over their members and the reservation territory, but that tribal sovereignty was dependent on and subordinate to only the federal government and not the states. A **major exception** was set forth which provided that state laws may be applied to tribal Indians on their reservations but only if Congress has expressly so provided. The relevant federal statute is if Congress has expressly so provided. The relevant federal statute is Public Law 280."
St. Germaine v. Circuit Court for Vilas County, 938 F. 2d 75 (7th Cir. 1991)

- Indian Civil Rights Act (ICRA) - **1968**
- The Oliphant Decision - **1978**
- Indian Gaming Regulatory Act (IGRA) - **1988**

Back to the Future

When Solicitor Margold wrote his opinion, there were some significant court cases that had not yet taken place, but are important in our discussion of the *Powers of Indian Tribes*. Two of these cases we would like to discuss are referred to as the *Oliphant Decision* [65] and the *Montana Decision*. [66] The first case involves tribal *criminal* jurisdiction, while the other defined the *civil* jurisdiction of Indian tribes.

The Oliphant Decision

The *Oliphant Decision* is a controversial court case. We have discussed how the powers of tribal sovereignty have been limited from time to time by special treaties and laws that clearly and expressly define such limitations. In the *Oliphant Decision*, the US Supreme Court stated, "While Congress never *expressly* forbade Indian tribes to impose criminal penalties on non-Indians, *we now make express* our implicit conclusion of nearly a century ago that Congress consistently believed this to be the necessary result of its repeated legislative actions." [67] Therefore, the result of this case was the determination that tribal courts may not exercise *criminal* jurisdiction over non-Indians unless specifically authorized to do so by Congress.

Say it Simply!

"emphatically" -- strongly expressed

The Court's majority was very conscious that Congressional intent to limit tribal sovereignty must be clearly stated. This is why it was *emphatically* pointed out that they believed Congress indicated Indian tribes did not have inherent criminal jurisdiction over non-Indians through consistent and repetitive legislative acts.

Here is the gist of the case:

► Two non-Indians, Mark David Oliphant and Daniel Belgarde, were arrested by Suquamish Indian tribal authorities for committing offenses, while on reservation lands, against *the Tribe's Law and Order Code*. These offenses were committed during the Suquamish tribe's annual Chief Seattle Days celebration. Notices had been displayed in prominent places at the entrances to the reservation informing the public that entry onto the reservation would be considered implied consent to the criminal jurisdiction of the Suquamish tribal court.

► Oliphant was charged, under the authority of the Tribe's Law and Order Code, with assaulting a tribal officer and resisting arrest. Belgarde was arrested after a high-speed chase ended with Belgarde colliding into a tribal police vehicle. He was charged under the tribal penal code with recklessly endangering another person and injuring tribal property.

► Both filed a writ of habeas corpus, arguing that tribal court does not have criminal jurisdiction over non-Indians. The US District Court declined the petitions. The US Supreme Court chose to review the case.

► The Suquamish Tribe claimed authority to try non-Indians based on their retained national sovereignty. The US Supreme Court determined that consistent legislative acts indicated Indian tribes lacked criminal jurisdiction over non-Indians, and it was the intent of Congress for the tribes to deliver the offender to the proper authorities rather than punish the non-Indian themselves.

► The US Supreme Court stated: "While Congress never expressly forbade Indian tribes to impose criminal penalties on non-Indians, we now express our implicit conclusion of nearly a century ago that Congress consistently believed this to be the necessary result of its repeated legislative actions." The Court also noted that when treaties and legislation are not totally clear, they may "be clear from the surrounding circumstances and legislative history." [68]

► The Court's conclusion was that "Indian tribes do not have inherent jurisdiction to try and to punish non-Indians." [69] Two Supreme Court judges submitted a dissenting opinion. There were a few briefs in support of Oliphant and Belgarde. Many, including the National Congress for American Indians, wrote briefs of *amici curiae* (friend of the court) in support of the Suquamish Indian Tribe.

A Huge Impact

This decision had a huge impact upon tribal communities. A major concern, for those who knew the realities of the non-Indian crime statistics on Indian reservations, was the concern regarding gaps in criminal jurisdiction. Sound familiar? Even the US Supreme Court acknowledged this concern: "We are not unaware of the prevalence of *non-Indian crime* on today's reservations which the tribes forcefully argue requires the ability to try non-Indians." [70]

Congress clarified tribal criminal jurisdiction is over all Indians, through the "Duro Fix" in 1991. This amended the ICRA's definition of a tribe's "power of self-government" to include "the inherent power of Indian tribes, hereby recognized and affirmed (by Congress) to exercise criminal jurisdiction over all Indians" (see 25 US 1301(2)). The Duro Fix was upheld in the 2004 US Supreme Court case, US v. Lara.

Although the *Oliphant Decision* established that Indian tribes cannot exercise *criminal* jurisdiction over non-Indians, this did not mean *civil* tribal administration of justice was eliminated. The *Oliphant Decision* had discussed how treaties and statues articulated how the tribes were to deliver non-Indian offenders to the proper authorities for trial. Indeed, many US–Indian treaties had specific provisions where the tribe agreed to deliver "offenders against the laws of the United States" to the US authorities. [71] One court case pointed out the distinction between tribal criminal and civil jurisdiction over non-Indians. This case stated that even if Indian tribes may not exercise criminal jurisdiction over non-Indians, this does not take away "from the sovereign power of tribal authorities to exclude trespassers who have violated state or federal law by delivering the offenders to the appropriate authorities." [72]

Montana Decision

Three years after the *Oliphant Decision*, the *Montana Decision* articulated the powers of Indian tribal government in the realm of *civil* jurisdiction over non-Indians. These powers were defined as falling within three scenarios:

1) Where Congress has expressly delegated such power to the tribal government.

2) When non-members have entered consensual (voluntary) relationships with the tribes or its members (commercial dealings, contracts, leases or other arrangements), the tribe may regulate activities through taxes, license requirements, etc.

3) If the conduct of a non-Indian threatens or has some direct effect on the political integrity, the economic security, or the health or welfare of the tribe – the tribe may exercise its civil jurisdiction.

Safety & Welfare Laws

Ways in which tribal governments carry out their responsibilities for the safety and welfare of their tribal community – tribal members, tribal residents, and all who enter their tribal lands – is through their civil jurisdictional powers (i.e. their "civil-regulatory" laws). You will remember in our discussion in Chapter 5 that "civil-regulatory" has to do with rules and regulations for a safe community. Yes, there are restrictions imposed and consequences for violations, but these are for the benefit of everyone, promoting the general health and welfare of society.

Say it Simply!

"decriminalized" -- to eliminate criminal penalties for the action

A good example of how public safety concerns are addressed through civil codes of conduct is seen where various states have *decriminalized* many of their traffic laws, treating actions like speeding "as a civil, not a criminal, offense." [73] By decriminalizing certain laws, public safety and welfare can be promoted, while implementing an effective civil-regulatory system for government. Similar to the way state or city governments regulate the behavior of all who are within their jurisdiction, tribal governments also regulate through civil codes of conduct.

An Indian tribe may use civil remedies such as warning citations, fines or exclusion to enforce their civil-regulatory laws. The tribes themselves can:

- ► enact laws for their community's welfare and safety;
- ► employ tribal enforcement officers;
- ► maintain tribal courts to deal with violations.

Endnotes - Chapter Six, Part 1:

[1] *"Powers of Indian Tribes"* Opinion of Solicitor Margold, U.S. Dept. Of the Interior, Office of the Solicitor, Oct. 25, 1934, accessible on the Office of the Solicitor's website, archives of the decisions of the Dept. of the Interior dating from July 1881 to Dec. 1994 at *http://www.doi.gov/solicitor/decisions.html*

[2] Id at pg. 19; The phrase "in general" notes the exception of the ninth area Solicitor Margold categorized which is not inherent, but a delegated power by an act of Congress

[3] Id. at pg 22, Also at pg 23 "It cannot be doubted . . . that prior to the formation of the Constitution, treaties were made with . . . tribes by which their autonomous existence was recognized." See also *Talton v. Mayes*, 163 U.S. 376 (1898) Tribal nations are not subject to the limitations imposed by the Bill of Rights because these were created to have limitations upon the General Government "which the Constitution called into being." Tribal governments pre-exist the Constitution and were not created by it.

[4] Id at pg. 57

[5] The first official treaty the US negotiated with an Indian Tribe was with the Delawares in 1778

[6] Tribes first negotiated from a position of strength. This changed over the years. See Chapt. 3, Part 3 of this resource guide for more details.

[7] *Worcester v. Georgia*, 31 U.S. 515, 520 (1832)

[8] *Ex Parte Crow Dog*, 109 U.S. 556 (1883)

[9] *"Powers of Indian Tribes"* Opinion of Solicitor Margold, supra fn.1, at 25 citing Ex Parte Crow Dog (at 568)

[10] Id.

[11] Id. at 28; see also Bennett, Elmer, *Federal Indian Law*, The Lawbook Exchange 2008, p. 395, "(Tribal) self-government ... has been consistently protected by the courts, was frequently recognized and intermittently ignored by treaty makers and legislators, and sometimes disregarded by administrative officials."

[12] Id.

[13] Id. at 30

[14] Id., "...to define the powers and duties of its officials, the manner of their appointment or election, the manner of their removal, and rules they are to observe in their capacity as officials, and the forms and procedures ... are matters which may be determined even in a modern civilized nation by unwritten custom as well as by written law."

[15] *"Powers of Indian Tribes"* Opinion of Solicitor Margold, supra fn.1, at 30

[16] *Cherokee Nation v. Georgia*, 30 U.S. 1, 2 (1831)

[17] *"Powers of Indian Tribes"* Opinion of Solicitor Margold, supra fn.1, at 19

[18] *Washington v. Confederated Tribes of the Colville Indian Reservation*, 447 US 134, at 153 (1980)

[19] Id. at 153-154, Examples of overriding government given in this case are: 1) Engage in foreign relations with other nations 2) Sell their lands to non-Indians without federal approval and 3) Prosecute non-Indians in tribal court (that do not accord the full protections of the Bill of Rights).

[20] The author of the book, *Tribal Policing*, discusses the "historical distrust" of Indian communities, Luna-Firebaugh, Eileen, *Tribal Policing*, The University of Arizona Press 2007, p. 47

[21] On author talks about the "dilemma" states experienced when handed the responsibility of jurisdiction without any funding, Goldberg-Ambrose, Carole, *Planting Tail Feathers*, McNaughton & Gunn, Inc. 1997, p. 56; See also *Williams v. Lee*, 358 US 217, 223 (1959) where it was noted how one State had not accepted PL 280 jurisdiction because "the people of the State anticipate that the burdens accompanying such power might be considerable."

[22] *"Powers of Indian Tribes"* Opinion of Solicitor Margold, supra fn.1, at 32

[23] Id. at 33

[24] Id. at 34

[25] *Santa Clara Pueblo v. Martinez*, 436 U.S. 49 (1978)

[26] Id. at 54

[27] Id. at 61

[28] Id. at 72

[29] Id. at 33 & 39

[30] Id. at 40

[31] Bennett, Elmer, *Federal Indian Law*, The Lawbook Exchange 2008, p. 427

[32] Tribal criminal justice systems, especially in PL 280 areas, are underdeveloped. This is due to the fact that federal funding and support was little to none for many years in the PL 280 areas. It was reasoned that the tribes within the PL 280 areas could use the state criminal justice systems as needed (i.e. law enforcement, courts and corrections). Many tribes still lack necessary funding and even the tribes who have been able to generate monies from tribal enterprises are faced with the high costs of establishing and building up their criminal justice systems.

[33] The Indian Child Welfare Act was enacted on Nov. 8, 1978 and is codified at 25 USC § 1901 – 1903

[34] Pratt, Richard H., *The Advantage of Mingling Indians with Whites*, Proceedings of the National Conference of Charities and Corrections, 1892, 46

[35] Official website for the National Park Service, Alcatraz Island, CA, on-line article by Park Ranger Craig Glassner, *The Army and American Indian Prisoners on the Rock*, at:
http://www.nps.gov/alca/historyculture/the-army-and-american-indian-prisoners.htm

[36] Report on Indian Education, Nov. 3, 1969, Special Subcommitte on Indian Education, Senate Committee on Labor and Public Welfare, documented in Prucha, Francis Paul, Documents of United States Indian Policy, University of Nebraska Press 2000 p. 254

[37] Id.

[38] Federal Register, 39:32741-42 (Sept. 11, 1974); codified in 25 Code of Federal Regulations 35, documented in Prucha, Francis Paul, *Documents of United States Indian Policy*, University of Nebraska Press 2000 p. 272

[39] 25 USC § 1901(5)

[40] 25 USC § 1901(3)

[41] child custody orders (25 USC 1911), child support orders (28 USC 1738B), domestic violence protective orders (18 USC 2265)

[42] *"Powers of Indian Tribes"* Opinion of Solicitor Margold, supra fn.1, at 43

[43] Id. at 15, See also *Merrion v. Jicarilla Apache Tribe*, 455 U.S. 130, 145 (1982) "The fact the tribe chooses not to exercise its power to tax when it initially grants a non-Indian entry onto the reservation does not permanently divest the tribe of its authority to impose such a tax."

[44] Id. at 17

[45] 25 USC Sec. 261 – Power to appoint traders with Indians – "The Commissioner of Indian Affairs shall have the sole power and authority to appoint traders to the Indian tribes and to make such rules and regulations as he may deem just and proper specifying the kind and quantity of goods and the prices at which such goods shall be sold to the Indians" ; 25 USC Sec. 262 – Persons permitted to trade with Indians – "Any person desiring to trade with the Indians on any Indian reservation shall, upon establishing the fact, to the satisfaction of the Commissioner of Indian Affairs, that he is a proper person to engage in such trade, be permitted to do so under such rules and regulations as the Commissioner of Indian Affairs may prescribe for the protection of said Indians."

[46] *Washington v. Confederated Tribes of the Colville Indian Reservation*, 447 US 134 (1980)

[47] *"Powers of Indian Tribes"* Opinion of Solicitor Margold, supra fn.1, at 152

[48] *"Powers of Indian Tribes"* Opinion of Solicitor Margold, supra fn.1, at 48, See also *New Mexico v. Mescalero Apache Tribe*, 462 U.S. 324, 333 (1983) "A tribe's power to exclude non-members entirely or to condition their presence on the reservation is . . . well established."

[49] Id. at 17

[50] *Duro v. Reina*, 495 U.S. 676, (1990)

[51] Id. at 696, 697, The Supreme Court recognized that in spite of federal jurisdiction of 18 USC § 1153 in this particular case (because it involved an alleged murder), "the tribes also possess their . . . power to exclude;" See also Bennett, Elmer (2008), *Federal Indian Law*, The Lawbook Exchange, p. 438, The power of a tribe to exclude non-members is "clearly stated in a series of authorities running back to the earliest days of the Republic."

[52] *"Powers of Indian Tribes"* Opinion of Solicitor Margold, supra fn.1, at 51

[53] Id. at 52

[54] See *Settler v. Lameer*, 507 F.2d 231, 238 (9th Cir. 1974) "The power to regulate is only meaningful when combined with the power to enforce."

[55] *"Powers of Indian Tribes"* Opinion of Solicitor Margold, supra fn.1, at 56

[56] Id. at 57

[57] Id.

[58] Id.

[59] Id. at 17

[60] Id. at 59, See also *US v. Young*, 936 F. 2d 1050 at 23 (1991), "As a general rule, tribal courts retain exclusive jurisdiction over all crimes committed by Native Americans against other Native Americans in Indian country…However, there are exceptions. First, federal courts have concurrent jurisdiction over the offenses listed in the major crimes act." See also *Wetsit v. Stafane*, 44 F. 3d 823 (9th Cir. 1995), "A tribal court, which is in compliance with the Indian Civil Rights Acts is competent to try a tribal member for a crime also prosecutable under the Major Crimes Act. That the tribes retain jurisdiction over crimes within the Major Crimes Act is the conclusion already reached by distinguished authorities on the subject. It has been noted for example that 'the great majority of tribes have for many years exercised jurisdiction over the crime of theft, which duplicates larceny, a crime rather surprisingly included in the original Major Crimes Act.' Canby, *American Indian Law in a Nutshell* 135 (2d Ed. 1988). Such a practice was, indeed, necessary because federal prosecution of the crime of theft on reservations was 'virtually non-existent'. Id at 106. Without the exercise of this jurisdiction by a tribe many crimes on a reservation would still go unpunished…Retention of this jurisdiction by the tribes can only increase their responsibility for efficient and fair justice."

[61] *"Powers of Indian Tribes"* Opinion of Solicitor Margold, supra fn.1, at 64

[62] 25 USC Sect. 48 – Right of tribes to direct employment of persons engaged for them – "Where any of the tribes are, in the opinion of the Secretary of Interior, competent to direct the employment of their blacksmiths, mechanics, teachers, farmers, or other persons engaged for them, the direction of such persons may be given to the proper authority of the tribe."

[63] Bennett, Elmer, *Federal Indian Law*, The Lawbook Exchange 2008, p. 449

[64] *"Powers of Indian Tribes"* Opinion of Solicitor Margold, supra fn.1, at 57

[65] *Oliphant v. Suquamish Indian Tribe*, 435 US 191 (1978)

[66] *Montana v. United States*, 450 US 544 (1981)

[67] *Oliphant v. Suquamish Indian Tribe*, 435 US 191, 204 (1978)

[68] Id. at footnote 17

[69] Id. at 212

[70] Id.

[71] Example in *State v. Schmuck*, 121 Wash. 2d (1993), quoting the treaty between the US and the Dwamish, Suquamish, and other allied and subordinate tribes of Indians in Washington Territory, Jan. 22, 1855, art. IX

[72] *Ex parte Kenyon*, 14 Fed. Cas. No. 7720 (1878) Cited in *Ortiz-barraza v. US*, 512 F. 2d 1176 (9th Cir. 1975)

[73] *Confederated Tribes of the Colville Reservation v. State of Washington*, 938 F. 2d 146 (9th Cir. 1991)

Chapter Six ~ Part 2

This chapter will cover:

- Criminal jurisdiction with & without PL 280
- Peculiarly federal laws
- Fact Sheets

Chapter Six - Part 2

Tribal, Federal & State Jurisdictions

Keeping Our Promise

At the very beginning of this resource guide (in the introduction), we promised you that by the end of this book, you should be able to navigate comfortably through PL 280 and have a clearer understanding of the US Attorneys' criminal jurisdictional charts for Indian country. Chapter 5 was dedicated to analyzing PL 280 but we still need to get you comfortable with those seemingly convoluted jurisdictional charts. So, here is where we deliver on the last part of our promise…

Simply Ain't Legal

The last two charts (CH-6A & CH-6B) *set you up* for making the final connections needed to clearly understand criminal jurisdiction between tribal, federal and state governments. As we have already discussed, there can be no *arbitrary* criminal jurisdiction imposed in Indian country by either the federal government or state governments. This means that in the area of criminal law, if you can't connect federal or state criminal jurisdiction to a specific treaty or law (or interpretation of the law) – it simply *ain't legal.*

With that thought in mind, let's look at the US Attorneys' criminal jurisdictional charts. We will go over the charts showing criminal jurisdiction in Indian country *without* PL 280, and then *with* PL 280. Often, in PL 280 areas, law enforcement only focuses on the second chart (jurisdiction with PL 280). Yet, understanding PL 280 jurisdiction is so much easier when you first understand jurisdiction *without* PL 280. The reason for this is because PL 280 is really a new thing in Indian country and stands as an *aberration.* If we presented you only with the PL 280 criminal jurisdictional chart, we would do you a disservice and leave you with *gaping* Swiss cheese holes in your understanding of criminal jurisdiction. Of course, we would never do that to you.

Say it Simply!

"arbitrary" -- unsupported, random, subjective

"aberration" -- irregularity, departing from the normal or usual course

"gaping" -- a wide opening, large breach

No Gaping Holes

Below are thumbnails of the two criminal jurisdiction charts for Indian country we will review:

1) Criminal jurisdiction *without* PL 280
2) Criminal jurisdiction *with* PL 280

These charts are simply a reference – a map – of where jurisdiction exists in Indian country. Even a quick glance of these charts shows you just how specific jurisdiction is regarding *who, what* and *where*. This is because federal criminal laws must be strictly adhered to.

Without **PL 280 jurisdiction**
(view larger chart, p. 301)

With **PL 280 jurisdiction**
(view larger chart, p. 306)

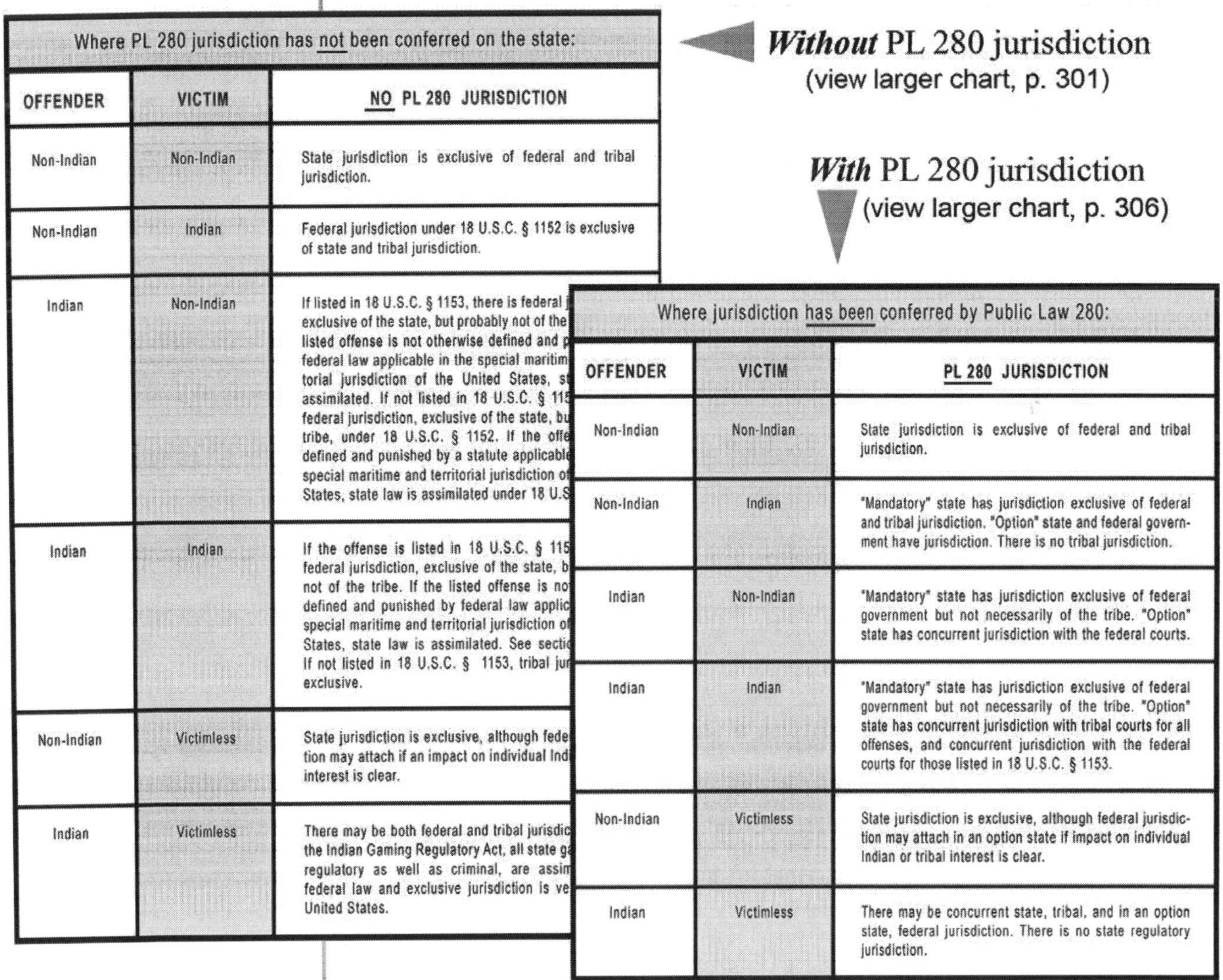

Where PL 280 jurisdiction has not been conferred on the state:

OFFENDER	VICTIM	NO PL 280 JURISDICTION
Non-Indian	Non-Indian	State jurisdiction is exclusive of federal and tribal jurisdiction.
Non-Indian	Indian	Federal jurisdiction under 18 U.S.C. § 1152 is exclusive of state and tribal jurisdiction.
Indian	Non-Indian	If listed in 18 U.S.C. § 1153, there is federal j exclusive of the state, but probably not of the listed offense is not otherwise defined and p federal law applicable in the special maritim torial jurisdiction of the United States, st assimilated. If not listed in 18 U.S.C. § 115 federal jurisdiction, exclusive of the state, bu tribe, under 18 U.S.C. § 1152. If the offe defined and punished by a statute applicabl special maritime and territorial jurisdiction o States, state law is assimilated under 18 U.S
Indian	Indian	If the offense is listed in 18 U.S.C. § 115 federal jurisdiction, exclusive of the state, b not of the tribe. If the listed offense is no defined and punished by federal law applic special maritime and territorial jurisdiction o States, state law is assimilated. See secti If not listed in 18 U.S.C. § 1153, tribal ju exclusive.
Non-Indian	Victimless	State jurisdiction is exclusive, although fede tion may attach if an impact on individual Ind interest is clear.
Indian	Victimless	There may be both federal and tribal jurisdic the Indian Gaming Regulatory Act, all state g regulatory as well as criminal, are assim federal law and exclusive jurisdiction is ve United States.

Where jurisdiction has been conferred by Public Law 280:

OFFENDER	VICTIM	PL 280 JURISDICTION
Non-Indian	Non-Indian	State jurisdiction is exclusive of federal and tribal jurisdiction.
Non-Indian	Indian	"Mandatory" state has jurisdiction exclusive of federal and tribal jurisdiction. "Option" state and federal government have jurisdiction. There is no tribal jurisdiction.
Indian	Non-Indian	"Mandatory" state has jurisdiction exclusive of federal government but not necessarily of the tribe. "Option" state has concurrent jurisdiction with the federal courts.
Indian	Indian	"Mandatory" state has jurisdiction exclusive of federal government but not necessarily of the tribe. "Option" state has concurrent jurisdiction with tribal courts for all offenses, and concurrent jurisdiction with the federal courts for those listed in 18 U.S.C. § 1153.
Non-Indian	Victimless	State jurisdiction is exclusive, although federal jurisdiction may attach in an option state if impact on individual Indian or tribal interest is clear.
Indian	Victimless	There may be concurrent state, tribal, and in an option state, federal jurisdiction. There is no state regulatory jurisdiction.

Know Your "A", "B", "C" & "D"s

Say it Simply!

"rudimentary" -- fundamental, elementary, first principles

As we review the charts and give explanations, keep in mind that you may need to review the information several times while it all soaks in! Being able to go back and see the broad historical context of the various laws and court cases will be helpful. Therefore, we have provided you with the page numbers where you can quickly look back, as desired. If you keep in mind your "A", "B", "C"s . . . and "D"s, it will help you decipher criminal jurisdiction in Indian country. The *rudimentary* points to keep in mind are:

Always federal for inter-racial

Federal jurisdiction is always involved in *inter-racial* crime in Indian country, whether Non-Indian v. Indian, or the other way around. (The exception to this is the Mandatory PL 280 areas because this is the jurisdiction that was transferred to the states.)

Because of McBratney

US v. McBratney (1881) clarified that the state would have jurisdiction if there was *no* Indian involvement.

Concurrent with the tribe

When the offender is Indian there is *always* concurrent tribal jurisdiction.

Determined by Oliphant

The Oliphant decision determined that tribes have no *criminal* jurisdiction over non-Indians.

So, let's take a look at the criminal jurisdictional charts . . .

Where PL 280 jurisdiction has not been conferred on the state:			
OFFENDER	**VICTIM**	**NO PL 280 JURISDICTION**	
Non-Indian	Non-Indian	State jurisdiction is exclusive of federal and tribal jurisdiction.	1
Non-Indian	Indian	Federal jurisdiction under 18 U.S.C. § 1152 is exclusive of state and tribal jurisdiction.	2
Indian	Non-Indian	If listed in 18 U.S.C. § 1153, there is federal jurisdiction, exclusive of the state, but probably not of the tribe. If the listed offense is not otherwise defined and punished by federal law applicable in the special maritime and territorial jurisdiction of the United States, state law is assimilated. If not listed in 18 U.S.C. § 1153, there is federal jurisdiction, exclusive of the state, but not of the tribe, under 18 U.S.C. § 1152. If the offense is not defined and punished by a statute applicable within the special maritime and territorial jurisdiction of the United States, state law is assimilated under 18 U.S.C. § 13.	3
Indian	Indian	If the offense is listed in 18 U.S.C. § 1153, there is federal jurisdiction, exclusive of the state, but probably not of the tribe. If the listed offense is not otherwise defined and punished by federal law applicable in the special maritime and territorial jurisdiction of the United States, state law is assimilated. See section 1153(b). If not listed in 18 U.S.C. § 1153, tribal jurisdiction is exclusive.	4
Non-Indian	Victimless	State jurisdiction is exclusive, although federal jurisdiction may attach if an impact on individual Indian or tribal interest is clear.	5
Indian	Victimless	There may be both federal and tribal jurisdiction. Under the Indian Gaming Regulatory Act, all state gaming laws, regulatory as well as criminal, are assimilated into federal law and exclusive jurisdiction is vested in the United States.	6

Source: US Attorneys > Criminal Resource Manual

Follow the numbers with explanations on the next pages . . .

Navigation Key

Legislation

18 USC § 1152 = General Crimes Act
18 USC § 13 = Assimilative Crimes Act (ACA)
18 USC § 1153 = Major Crimes Act
18 USC § 1162 = Public Law 83-280
18 USC § 1166 = Indian Gaming Regulatory Act (IGRA)

Court Decisons:

US v. McBratney, 104 US 621 (1881)
Oliphant v. Suquamish Tribe, 435 US 191 (1978)

Non-PL 280 Criminal Jurisdictional Chart Explained:

1

OFFENDER	VICTIM	NO PL 280 JURISDICTION
Non-Indian	Non-Indian	State jurisdiction is exclusive of federal and tribal jurisdiction.

Legal justification: *US v. McBratney,* 104 US 621 (1881)

Explanation: When the crime does not involve an Indian, criminal jurisdiction falls to the state unless there is any significant federal interest involved. This was clarified through the *US v. McBratney* court case.

Page(s) in Resource Guide: 138-139

2

OFFENDER	VICTIM	NO PL 280 JURISDICTION
Non-Indian	Indian	Federal jurisdiction under 18 U.S.C. § 1152 is exclusive of state and tribal jurisdiction.

Legal justification: *18 USC § 1152; Oliphant v. Suquamish Tribe, 435 US 191 (1978)*

Explanation: Inter-racial crime will always involve federal jurisdiction in the non-PL 280 areas. Inter-racial crime in Indian country, regardless of whether the victim is Indian or non-Indian, falls to federal jurisdiction (exclusive of the state). This began in 1790 with the first Trade and Intercourse Act and expanded in 1817 with the General Crimes Act (18 USC § 1152). Federal jurisdiction involving a non-Indian offender is also exclusive of the tribes because the *Oliphant Decision* determined that Indian tribes have no jurisdiction over non-Indians.

Page(s) in Resource Guide: 105-106; 288-290

3

OFFENDER	VICTIM	NO PL 280 JURISDICTION
Indian	Non-Indian	If listed in 18 U.S.C. § 1153, there is federal jurisdiction, exclusive of the state, but probably not of the tribe. If the listed offense is not otherwise defined and punished by federal law applicable in the special maritime and territorial jurisdiction of the United States, state law is assimilated. If not listed in 18 U.S.C. § 1153, there is federal jurisdiction, exclusive of the state, but not of the tribe, under 18 U.S.C. § 1152. If the offense is not defined and punished by a statute applicable within the special maritime and territorial jurisdiction of the United States, state law is assimilated under 18 U.S.C. § 13.

Legal justification: *Inherent sovereignty; 18 USC § 1153; 18 USC § 1152*

Explanation: Inter-racial crime will always involve federal jurisdiction in the non-PL 280 areas. Inter-racial crime in Indian country, when the offender is Indian, falls to federal jurisdiction (exclusive of the state). If an Indian commits any of the crimes listed in the Major Crimes Act (18 USC § 1153) prosecution will use the federal penal codes that apply to federal enclaves (i.e. "special maritime and territorial jurisdiction of the United States"). If the crime is not part of the federal penal code for its enclaves, federal law crawls into the skin of state law (assimilates) and is used for federal prosecution.

If an Indian commits any of the crimes listed in the General Crimes Act (18 USC § 1152) federal prosecution will use the federal penal codes that apply to federal enclaves (i.e. "special maritime and territorial jurisdiction of the United States"). If the crime is not part of the federal penal code for its enclaves, federal law crawls into the skin of state law (assimilates) and is used for federal prosecution according to the fill-in-the-gap act, the Assimilative Crimes Act (18 USC § 13).

Federal jurisdiction is shared concurrently with the tribe when an Indian commits any crime within their Indian country.

Page(s) in Resource Guide: 16-19; 149-151; 105-106

"The fact that the Tribe had not set up a system to punish certain of its members does not mean that it lacked the power to do so. It merely failed to exercise its jurisdiction."

US v. Jackson, 600 F.2d 1238 (9th Cir. 1979)

4

OFFENDER	VICTIM	NO PL 280 JURISDICTION
Indian	Indian	If the offense is listed in 18 U.S.C. § 1153, there is federal jurisdiction, exclusive of the state, but probably not of the tribe. If the listed offense is not otherwise defined and punished by federal law applicable in the special maritime and territorial jurisdiction of the United States, state law is assimilated. See section 1153(b). If not listed in 18 U.S.C. § 1153, tribal jurisdiction is exclusive.

Legal justification: *Inherent sovereignty; 18 USC § 1153; 18 USC § 1152*

Explanation: When a crime involves only Indians, federal jurisdiction is imposed only for the Major Crimes (18 USC § 1153). If an Indian commits a Major Crime, federal prosecution will use the federal penal code that applies to federal enclaves (i.e. "special maritime and territorial jurisdiction of the United States"). If the crime is not part of the federal penal code for its enclaves, federal law crawls into the skin of state law (assimilates) and is used for federal prosecution according to 18 USC § 1153(b) which mimics the ACA.

The federal jurisdiction of the listed crimes within the Major Crimes Act is not shared with the state.

Federal jurisdiction is shared concurrently with the tribe when an Indian commits any crime within their Indian country. Any crime not listed in the Major Crimes Act falls to tribal jurisdiction and is not shared with either federal or state jurisdictions.

Page(s) in Resource Guide: 16-19; 149-151; 105-106

18 USC § 1153 - Major Crimes Act was enacted 60 years after the Assimilative Crimes Act (ACA). Section (b) of the Major Crimes Act mimics the concept of assimilating state law. (The same concept of assimilating state law was also incorporated many years later in the criminal section of the Indian Gaming Regulatory Act 18 USC § 1166).

18 USC s 1153(b) reads:

(b) Any offense referred to in subsection (a) of this section that is not defined and punished by Federal law in force within the exclusive jurisdiction of the United States shall be defined and punished in accordance with the laws of the State in which such offense was committed as are in force at the time of such offense.

5

OFFENDER	VICTIM	NO PL 280 JURISDICTION
Non-Indian	Victimless	State jurisdiction is exclusive, although federal jurisdiction may attach if an impact on individual Indian or tribal interest is clear.

Legal justification: *US v. McBratney,* 104 US 621 (1881)

Explanation: When a victimless crime occurs (no Indian victim), the criminal jurisdiction falls to the state. Since there is no Indian involvement it is completely a non-Indian crime and the same rationale used in non-Indian v. non-Indian crime is applied.

The exception to this is if the crime significantly impacts either an individual Indian or an Indian tribe. If so, federal jurisdiction will be exclusive of the state because it would no longer be a completely non-Indian crime and would be viewed as an inter-racial crime.

Page(s) in Resource Guide: 138-139

6

OFFENDER	VICTIM	NO PL 280 JURISDICTION
Indian	Victimless	There may be both federal and tribal jurisdiction. Under the Indian Gaming Regulatory Act, all state gaming laws, regulatory as well as criminal, are assimilated into federal law and exclusive jurisdiction is vested in the United States.

Legal justification: *Inherent Sovereignty; 18 USC § 1166*

Explanation: The tribe has criminal jurisdiction when an Indian commits any crime within their Indian country.

The criminal provisions of the Indian Gaming Regulatory Act (IGRA) codified at 18 USC § 1166 gives federal criminal jurisdiction over the state for gambling in Indian country. All state gaming laws are assimilated into federal law.

Page(s) in Resource Guide: 16-19

Where jurisdiction has been conferred by Public Law 280:

OFFENDER	VICTIM	PL 280 JURISDICTION	
Non-Indian	Non-Indian	State jurisdiction is exclusive of federal and tribal jurisdiction.	7
Non-Indian	Indian	"Mandatory" state has jurisdiction exclusive of federal and tribal jurisdiction. "Option" state and federal government have jurisdiction. There is no tribal jurisdiction.	8
Indian	Non-Indian	"Mandatory" state has jurisdiction exclusive of federal government but not necessarily of the tribe. "Option" state has concurrent jurisdiction with the federal courts.	9
Indian	Indian	"Mandatory" state has jurisdiction exclusive of federal government but not necessarily of the tribe. "Option" state has concurrent jurisdiction with tribal courts for all offenses, and concurrent jurisdiction with the federal courts for those listed in 18 U.S.C. § 1153.	10
Non-Indian	Victimless	State jurisdiction is exclusive, although federal jurisdiction may attach in an option state if impact on individual Indian or tribal interest is clear.	11
Indian	Victimless	There may be concurrent state, tribal, and in an option state, federal jurisdiction. There is no state regulatory jurisdiction.	12

Source: US Attorneys > Criminal Resource Manual

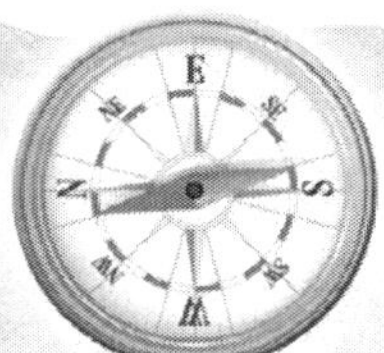

Navigation Key

Legislation

18 USC § 1152 = General Crimes Act
18 USC § 13 = Assimilative Crimes Act (ACA)
18 USC § 1153 = Major Crimes Act
18 USC § 1162 = Mandatory PL 280 States
25 USC § 1321 = Optional PL 280 States
18 USC § 1166 = Indian Gaming Regulatory Act (IGRA)

Court Decisons:

US v. McBratney, 104 US 621 (1881)
Oliphant v. Suquamish Tribe, 435 US 191 (1978)

Follow the numbers with explanations on the next pages . . .

PL 280 Criminal Jurisdictional Chart Explained:

7

OFFENDER	VICTIM	PL 280 JURISDICTION
Non-Indian	Non-Indian	State jurisdiction is exclusive of federal and tribal jurisdiction.

Legal justification: *US v. McBratney,* 104 US 621 (1881)

Explanation: When the crime does not involve an Indian, criminal jurisdiction falls to the state. This was clarified through the *US v. McBratney* court case.

Page(s) in Resource Guide: 138-139

8

OFFENDER	VICTIM	PL 280 JURISDICTION
Non-Indian	Indian	"Mandatory" state has jurisdiction exclusive of federal and tribal jurisdiction. "Option" state and federal government have jurisdiction. There is no tribal jurisdiction.

Legal justification: *18 USC § 1162; 25 USC § 1321; Oliphant v. Suquamish Tribe, 435 US 191 (1978)*

Explanation: Mandatory states have exclusive criminal jurisdiction. PL 280 specifies that the General Crimes (18 USC § 1152) and the Major Crimes (18 USC § 1153) do not apply in the mandatory PL 280 areas. (The new amendment to PL 280, Federal Assumption, would change this – allowing concurrent federal jurisdiction on a tribe-by-tribe basis. See *18 USC § 1162 (d)*)

Optional states share concurrent criminal jurisdiction with the federal government and federal prosecution of both the General Crimes (18 USC § 1152) and the Major Crimes (18 USC § 1153) does apply in the optional PL 280 areas.

The Oliphant Decision determined that Indian tribes have no jurisdiction over non-Indians.

Page(s) in Resource Guide: 219; 223; 288-290

9

OFFENDER	VICTIM	PL 280 JURISDICTION
Indian	Non-Indian	"Mandatory" state has jurisdiction exclusive of federal government but not necessarily of the tribe. "Option" state has concurrent jurisdiction with the federal courts.

Legal justification: Inherent sovereignty; *18 USC § 1162; 25 USC § 1321*

Explanation: Mandatory states have concurrent criminal jurisdiction with the tribe. Optional states share concurrent criminal jurisdiction with the tribes and with federal prosecution of the Major Crimes (18 USC § 1153) and the General Crimes (18 USC § 1152) for inter-racial crime.

Any state and federal criminal jurisdiction is shared concurrently with the tribe when an Indian commits any crime within a tribe's Indian country.

Page(s) in Resource Guide: 16-19; 219; 223

10

OFFENDER	VICTIM	PL 280 JURISDICTION
Indian	Indian	"Mandatory" state has jurisdiction exclusive of federal government but not necessarily of the tribe. "Option" state has concurrent jurisdiction with tribal courts for all offenses, and concurrent jurisdiction with the federal courts for those listed in 18 U.S.C. § 1153.

Legal justification: *Inherent sovereignty; 18 USC § 1162; 25 USC § 1321; 18 USC § 1152; 18 USC § 1153*

Explanation: Mandatory states have concurrent criminal jurisdiction with the tribe. Optional states share concurrent criminal jurisdiction with the tribes and with federal prosecution of the Major Crimes (18 USC § 1153). The General Crimes (18 USC § 1152) do apply in Indian v. Indian crime.

Any state and federal criminal jurisdiction is shared concurrently with the tribe when an Indian commits any crime within their Indian country.

Page(s) in Resource Guide: 16-19; 219; 223; 105-106; 149-151

11

OFFENDER	VICTIM	PL 280 JURISDICTION
Non-Indian	Victimless	State jurisdiction is exclusive, although federal jurisdiction may attach in an option state if impact on individual Indian or tribal interest is clear.

Legal justification: 18 USC § 1162; 25 USC § 1321; US v. McBratney, 104 US 621 (1881); Oliphant v. Suquamish Tribe, 435 US 191 (1978)

Explanation: When a victimless crime occurs (no Indian victim), the criminal jurisdiction falls to the state. Since there is no Indian involvement it is completely a non-Indian crime and the same rationale used in non-Indian v. non-Indian crime is applied.

The exception to this is if, in an Optional state, the crime significantly impacts either an individual Indian or an Indian tribe. If so, federal jurisdiction will be concurrent with the Optional state because it would no longer be a completely non-Indian crime and would be viewed as an inter-racial crime.

The Oliphant decision determined that Indian tribes have no jurisdiction over non-Indians.

Page(s) in Resource Guide: 219; 223; 138-139; 288-290

12

OFFENDER	VICTIM	PL 280 JURISDICTION
Indian	Victimless	There may be concurrent state, tribal, and in an option state, federal jurisdiction. There is no state regulatory jurisdiction.

Legal justification: *Inherent sovereignty; 18 USC § 1162; 25 USC § 1321*

Explanation: PL 280 authorized all criminal laws to be enforced in Indian country in the same way they are elsewhere enforced in the state or territory.

No state regulatory laws may be applied in Indian country.

Optional states share concurrent criminal jurisdiction with federal and tribal jurisdictions. The General Crimes (18 USC § 1152) and the Assimilative Crimes Act (18 USC § 13) do apply in the optional PL 280 areas.

Any state and federal criminal jurisdiction is shared concurrently with the tribe when an Indian commits any crime within their Indian country.

Page(s) in Resource Guide: 16-19; 219; 223

Make An Impression

Well, now you can impress your peers with your knowledge of the criminal jurisdictional charts for Indian country. Your associates will be awed as you explain to them what all the confusing verbiage means. No more mystifying babble! Doesn't that feel good . . . even empowering? Most importantly, you have learned an awful lot through this resource guide about:

- ► The inherent sovereign powers of each individual Indian tribe,
- ► How relinquishment of external sovereignty, along with treaties and federal laws have limited the original sovereignty of tribal governments, and
- ► The specific acts of Congress that have been enacted and impact criminal jurisdiction in Indian country.

Peculiarly Federal

We have previously talked about the differences between internal sovereignty versus external sovereignty. Although an Indian tribe has the authority to govern their people and their territory (internal sovereignty), they may not exercise external sovereignty by declaring laws or following a course of action contrary to the laws of the United States government.

This is also true of any state within the Union. Along with this, all individuals within the Unites States, no matter where they happen to be – are subject to certain federal laws. Federal criminal laws of general applicability have full force throughout the *entire* United States. This means, if a federal crime of general applicability is committed, it doesn't matter if the person is Indian or non-Indian, or if it was done on or off a reservation.

There are certain "crimes that are peculiarly Federal" [1] which "make actions criminal *wherever* committed … crimes which are generally applicable throughout the United States to *all* persons." [2]

These peculiarly Federal laws that apply to all people and all places within the United States are not affected in any way by PL 280. This fact was made clear in a court case in one of the Mandatory PL 280 States (Wisconsin).

> *". . . by the provisions of 18 USC 1162 (Mandatory PL 280 States) jurisdiction over offenses within Indian country has been delegated to the State of Wisconsin, and thus 1152 (General Crimes) and 1153 (Major Crimes) are no longer applicable. This is true. 1162 says that the state may apply its own laws to Indians on Indian lands as it can to the rest of its citizens, i.e. state law is to apply instead of federal enclave law. However, this section does not eliminate federal jurisdiction over persons committing crimes in violation of the federal statutes of general applicability."*
>
> *US V. Burns, 529 F. 2d 114 (9th Cir. 1975) in footnote referring to US v. Three Winchester, 30-30 Caliber Lever Action Carbines, etc., 504 F. 2d 1288 (7th Cir. 1974)*

The *US v. Burns* case quoted here illustrates how tribal self-governments, just as state governments, are subject to federal criminal laws of general applicability.

Here is a super-quick synopsis of what happened in the *US v. Burns* case:

► Tribal council appointed tribal officers and authorized them to carry firearms while on duty.

► One particular individual was appointed by tribal council to serve as their Tribal Game Warden.

► The court found this Tribal Game Warden, in the performance of his duties of keeping unauthorized persons off reservation lands, used unnecessary and unreasonable force.

► Violations of the Indian Civil Rights were not addressed but this Tribal Game Warden (an ex-felon) was found to have violated a federal law of general applicability: Unlawful possession of a firearm by a felon. He was convicted for violating this federal law.

Federal Supremacy

The supremacy of federal law of nationwide application extends "federal criminal jurisdiction over Indians … to offenses as to which there is an independent, federal interest to be protected." [3]

The following are some examples of acts which are criminal no matter where they are committed:

- Assaulting a federal officer
- Federal narcotics statutes
- Federal firearm violations
- Federal mail fraud
- Treason
- Terrorism
- Racketeering
- Bank Robberies
- Counterfeiting US currency

Other than nationwide federal criminal laws which the federal government enforces throughout the United States, the remaining administration of justice in Indian country is shared by tribal, federal and state jurisdictions.

Tribal governments retain the authority over their people and their territory which has not been specifically limited by treaty or Congress, and all that falls consistently with their relinquishment of external sovereignty.

Federal and State governments are granted specific jurisdictional authority through enactments of Congress (federal law).

Federal Jurisdiction in Indian Country

The historical government-to-government relationship the United States has with Indian tribes is rooted in the US Constitution where Indian tribes were clearly recognized as separate political entities. The treaty and commerce clauses of the US

Constitution not only acknowledge tribal sovereignty, but also create a legal and political relationship with the Indian tribes. The United States' relationship with Indian tribes is "rooted in the unique status of Indians as 'a separate people' with their own political institutions, and is not to be viewed as legislation of a 'racial' group consisting of 'Indians.'" [4] Federal criminal jurisdiction over Indians is not based on individuals being of the "Indian race," but rather, based on the fact they are members of a federally recognized tribe. [5]

Historic governmental actions on the part of the United States with the Indian tribes through treaties, federal legislation, executive orders and court decisions, have established a federal trust responsibility. This trust responsibility involves the preservation of *public safety* within Indian country. [6]

The BIA

As far back as 1775, the Continental Congress actually established a Committee on Indian Affairs which was headed by – none other than – Benjamin Franklin. [7] The Bureau of Indian Affairs (BIA), was originally under the War Department, but is now under the Interior Department. The BIA could have been called the "IO," "IB," "ID" or "IS." At different times it was referred to as the "Indian Office," the "Indian Bureau," the "Indian Department" and the "Indian Service." The "Bureau of Indian Affairs" is what stuck and became the formal title for this bureau in 1947. [8]

The BIA, Office of Justice Services (BIA – OJS) helps fulfill the federal government's responsibility for law enforcement and public safety in Indian country. The Law Enforcement division of BIA-OJS provides or supplements tribal governments with police and/or investigators *(not necessarily federally funded)* who, with the consent of the tribe, can investigate both tribal and federal violations. These services are directed by the BIA and its day-to-day operations are governed by BIA administrators.

BIA officers receive standardized training at the Indian Police Academy. This federal academy is located in Artesia, New Mexico at the Department of Homeland Security's Federal Law Enforcement Training Center (FLETC). At this location sits an impressive *Indian Country Law Enforcement Officers Memorial*, honoring law enforcement officers who have died in the line of duty while working in Indian country. The first of these fallen officers recognized dates back to the year 1852. [9]

FACT SHEET

US Department of the Interior (DOJ), Bureau of Indian Affairs (BIA)

The Bureau of Indian Affairs (BIA) is one of the nine technical bureaus within the Department of the Interior.

DOI Head: Secretary of Interior

Oversees the BIA: Assistant Secretary – Indian Affairs

Included within the BIA: The Office of Justice Services (BIA – OJS) has 5 divisions:

1) Division of Law Enforcement

2) Division of Corrections

3) The Indian Police Academy

4) Division of Professional Standards

5) Division of Tribal Justice Support

Statutory Authority: The BIA derives its jurisdictional authority for the management of Indian affairs from the congressional delegation of a federal agency (initially the War Dept. in 1789, then transferred to the Dept. of the Interior in 1849) to oversee Indian affairs based on the treaty and commerce clauses of the US Constitution.

Scope of Authority: Federal law enforcement responsibility / jurisdiction is shared concurrently with the Federal Bureau of Investigations (FBI).

The DOJ - FBI

The US Department of Justice (DOJ) was not established until 1870 ("Act to Establish the Department of Justice" bill was signed into law by President Ulysses S. Grant). Since its establishment, the DOJ has been responsible for enforcing federal law and administering justice at the federal level. The top official of this department is the US Attorney General. [10] The Federal Bureau of Investigations (FBI) is part of the DOJ and was established on March 16, 1909.

FBI Special Agents, along with the Indian Country Special Crimes Unit (ICSCU), are assigned to work investigations of serious crimes that take place within Indian country. The FBI works together with the BIA-OJS and tribal officers to deal with crime on reservations. Sometimes combating crime in Indian country involves other federal agencies for assistance in their areas of expertise. The United States may utilize any federal agency it deems necessary for its fulfillment of the federal trust responsibility. Other federal agencies that assist with law enforcement in Indian country include:

- Bureau of Alcohol, Tobacco, Firearms & Explosives (ATF)
- Drug Enforcement Administration (DEA)
- United States Marshals Service (USMS)
- Immigration & Customs Enforcement (ICE)

In the Mandatory PL 280 areas, federal jurisdiction is limited as 18 USC 1152 and 18 USC 1153 do not apply. The exception to this would be where an individual tribe requests and is granted concurrent federal assumption in their Indian country.

FACT SHEET

US Department of Justice (DOJ), Federal Bureau of Investigation (FBI)

The Department of Justice (DOJ) was established in 1870

DOJ Head: US Attorney General

Included within DOJ: Primary divisions involved in Indian country criminal jurisdiction

1) Federal Bureau of Investigations (FBI)
2) Executive Office for US Attorneys (EOUSA)
3) United States Attorney Offices

Other agencies within DOJ include:
- United States Marshal Service (USMS)
- Bureau of Alcohol, Tobacco, Firearms & Explosives (ATF)
- Drug Enforcement Administration (DEA)
- Office of Inspector General (OIG)
- Federal Bureau of Prisons (BOP)

And other offices include:
- Office of Justice Programs (OJP), National Institute of Justice (NIJ)
- Office of Tribal Justice (OTJ)
- Office of Community Oriented Policing Services (COPS)
- Office of Violence Against Women (OVAW)

Statutory Authority: The FBI with US Attorneys derive jurisdictional authority to investigate and prosecute crime in Indian country from 28 USC § 533 which states the US Attorney General may appoint officials to "detect and prosecute crimes" against the United States and other official matters under the control of DOJ (and also the Dept. of State).

FBI's Scope of Authority: Federal law enforcement responsibility / jurisdiction is shared concurrently with the Bureau of Indian Affairs, Office of Justice Services (BIA-OJS).

The **Indian Country Crimes Unit (FBI-ICCU)** manages programs and policies aimed at crime problems in Indian country. ICCU's implementation and management include:
- Training of Indian country law enforcement officers
- Gang assessments
- Domestic violence & sex offense initiatives
- Support forensic operational expenses
- Updated reporting on the Tribal Law & Order Act (TLOA)
- Support the multi-agency task force, Safe Trails Task Force (STTF)

Safe Trails Task Force (STTF) is a multi-agency task force (federal, tribal, state & local law enforcement agencies) working together to combat crime in Indian country.

FBI Agents and US Attorneys investigate and prosecute the most serious crimes in Indian country, such as: death investigations, physical abuse of a child, sexual abuse of a child, violent felony assaults and rape.

US Attorneys

The Executive Office for United States Attorneys (EOUSA) serves as the liaison between the US attorneys throughout the United States with Department of Justice (DOJ) headquarters in Washington, D.C.

US Attorneys are federal prosecutors who represent the United States government throughout the United States in US District Courts (there are 9 districts). Congress appoints each district court judge.

In prosecuting a crime that has taken place in Indian country, a US Attorney can request FBI to investigate where deemed necessary. It is not uncommon though, for a US Attorney to receive reports from BIA officers or tribal police and not require the involvement of the FBI. [11] (However, FBI involvement is mandated in cases involving death(s), sexual abuse, rape, kidnapping, arson, assault, and crimes involving weapons.)

Due to the fact that US Attorneys will prioritize criminal prosecutions, it is rare for them to prosecute a federal misdemeanor as they focus on felony offenses. This has created gaps in criminal jurisdiction where tribal criminal jurisdiction is restricted from prosecuting non-Indian criminal offenses against members of their tribe.

As mentioned earlier, in the Mandatory PL 280 areas, federal jurisdiction is limited as 18 USC 1152 and 18 USC 1153 do not apply. The exception to this would be where an individual tribe requests and is granted concurrent federal assumption in their Indian country.

Federal Courts

The authorization for federal courts is found in the US Constitution. Article III, Section 1 says:

"The judicial power of the United States, shall be vested in one Supreme Court, and in such inferior courts as the Congress may from time to time ordain and establish. . ."

Article III, Section 2 continues:

"The judicial power shall extend to all cases, in law and equity, arising under this Constitution, the laws of the United States, and treaties made, or which shall be made . . ."

Supreme and Inferior

The US Constitution established one "Supreme Court" and left the decision about any other courts up to Congress. In the eyes of the Constitution, any federal court other than the Supreme Court, is considered "inferior." Of course this is only in relation to the nation's highest court – all other courts are situated under it. If you ever have to testify in a federal court, you will most likely be awed by the experience and ***not*** be too inclined to tell the federal judge that you think his court is inferior!

Endnotes - Chapter Six, Part 2:

[1] *US v. Smith*, 562 F. 2d 453 (1977)

[2] *Stone v. US*, 506 F. 2nd 561 (1975) See also *US v. Young*, 936 F. 2d 1050 (9th Cir. 1991) "... federal courts continue to retain jurisdiction over violations of federal laws of general, non-territorial applicability." In this case an individual Indian, John Young, appealed his conviction of three federal crimes. "Each of the three offenses of which Young was convicted were violations of federal laws of general applicability... Accordingly, the Major Crimes Act is no way impugned (attacked or challenged as false) by charges lodged against Young."

[3] *US v. Markiewicz*, 978 F. 2d 786, 76 (1992) "[A]cts which are criminal regardless of their location in the United States apply of their own force to Indian territories." Id. at 67

[4] See beginning case summary for *US v. Antelope*, 430 US 641 (1977)

[5] Id. at 646; See also footnote 7, quoting *United States v. Heath*, 509 F.2d 16, 19 (CA9 1974) ". . . members of tribes whose official status has been terminated by congressional enactment are no longer subject, by virtue of their status, to federal criminal jurisdiction under the Major Crimes Act . . . ('While anthropologically a Klamath Indian even after the Termination Act obviously remains an Indian, his unique status vis-a-vis the Federal Government no longer exists')."

[6] "Indian country" has a legal definition which is found in 18 USC § 1151 (and is intended to include all reservations whether established by treaty, executive order, or act of Congress): (a) all land within the limits of any Indian reservation under the jurisdiction of the United States Government, notwithstanding the issuance of any patent, and, including rights-of-way running through the reservation, (b) all dependent Indian communities within the borders of the United States whether within the original or subsequently acquired territory thereof, and whether within or without the limits of a state, and (c) all Indian allotments, the Indian titles to which have not been extinguished, including rights-of-way running through the same.

[7] See the Bureau of Indian Affairs' official website on the FAQS page under "What is the BIA's history?" at *http://www.bia.gov/FAQs/index.htm*

[8] Id.

[9] A picture of the *Indian Country Law Enforcement Officers Memorial*, along with the names of the fallen officers can be seen online at *http://www.fletc.gov/about-fletc/locations/artesia/indian-country-law-enforcement-officers-memorial.html*

[10] 28 USC § 503:The President shall appoint, by and with the advice and consent of the Senate, an Attorney General of the United States; The Attorney General is the head of the Department of Justice.

[11] If there is an established multi-jurisdictional drug task force made up of tribal, state and/or local law enforcement investigators, this task force may present cases for federal prosecution.

Chapter Six ~ Part 3

This chapter will cover:

- *The Indian Civil Rights Act (ICRA)*
- *How the exclusionary rule works*
- *Laws of arrest compared*

Chapter Six - Part 3

Tribal, Federal & State Jurisdictions

Indian Civil Rights Act (ICRA)

The mid 1950's through the mid 1960's was a time period known as the Civil Rights era. This period is memorialized by brave men and women who spoke out against abuses of government. Native Americans were also among those who spoke out. During this period of time, a Senate subcommittee was created to hear issues involving civil rights violations of American Indians. This subcommittee heard allegations regarding abusive tribal governments in such matters as: membership and voting practices, free speech / press infringements, discrimination, vague criminal statutes, arrest and search procedures, and jail conditions. "In addition . . . the subcommittee also . . . received complaints concerning deprivation of constitutional rights through illegal detention of reservation Indians by State and tribal officials, arbitrary decision-making by the Bureau of Indian Affairs, denial of various State welfare services to Indians living off the reservation, discrimination by government officials in health services, mistreatment and brutality of Indians by State and tribal law enforcement officers, and job discrimination by Federal and State agencies and private businesses." [1]

Some of the Senators on the subcommittee were rather surprised to learn during the hearings, that many of the constitutional provisions for US citizens were not applicable to on-reservation Indians. As you remember, this was due to the fact that tribal governments predate the US Constitution. [2] Indian sovereign nations were recognized as distinctly separate entities from the United States when the US Constitution was written. Senator Roman L. Hruska of Nebraska, who sat on the Senate subcommittee, expressed to his peers:

> "As the hearings developed and as the evidence and testimony was taken, I believe all of us who were students of the law were jarred and shocked by the conditions as far as constitutional rights for members of the Indian tribes were concerned. There was found to be unchecked and unlimited authority over many facets of Indian rights . . . The Constitution simply was not applicable." [3]

Therefore, "to 'secure for the American Indian the broad constitutional rights afforded to other Americans,' and thereby to 'protect individual Indians from arbitrary and unjust actions of tribal governments,'" the Indian Civil Rights Act (ICRA) was enacted by Congress in 1968. [4] Yet, this "protection against tribal authority" [5] purposed *also* to "protect tribal sovereignty from undue interference." [6] This is why, even though it was initially suggested by some members of Congress, that the constitutional provisions in the *Bill of Rights* be extended in "wholesale fashion" to create the ICRA, it was instead "modified." These modifications were to "fit the unique political, cultural, and economic needs of tribal governments." [7] *(See full text of ICRA in Appendix G, p. 370)*

Say it Simply!

"Bill of Rights" -- the first ten amendments to the US Constitution

"red tape" -- excessive regulation and rigid rules that hinder or prevent some action from taking place; usually applied to governments or large corporations

Also, very important to the ICRA are sections 1321, 1322 and 1326 (under Title 25 of the United States Code). These sections amended PL 280 to include "consent of the Indian tribe occupying the particular Indian country or part thereof which could be affected by such assumption" before any state could assume criminal or civil jurisdiction in Indian Country. This was a provision President Eisenhower, who signed PL 280 into law in 1953, had asked Congress to implement as soon as possible. Many tribal leaders had worked hard over the years to get the provision of tribal consent included in PL 280.

The ICRA did reveal Congress' intent and "commitment to the goal of tribal self-determination" by providing for "strengthening certain tribal courts through training of Indian judges" and by reducing some of the frustrating *red tape* tribes had been experiencing from the Federal Bureau of Indian Affairs. [8]

Key Point

PL280 was amended in 1968 through the ICRA to include tribal consent before PL 280 jurisdiction could be implemented on tribal lands.

Dig Deeper

> The book, *Partial Justice* by Petra T. Shattuck and Jill Norgren, (Berg Publishers Inc. 1991, p. 167) explains how the chief sponsor of the ICRA, Senator Sam Irvine (N. Dakota) was "astounded to learn that ... reservation Indians do not possess the same Constitutional rights which are conferred upon all other Americans..."

As we have already indicated, although the ICRA was modeled generally after the Bill of Rights, it was not meant to be identical, and there were specific reasons for this. The landmark ICRA case, *Santa Clara Pueblo v. Martinez*, while outlining the legislative history of the ICRA, explained how individual rights were weighed in relation to the ancient governments and communities tribal members were a part of. To put things in perspective, think about this . . .

The *Santa Clara Pueblo* case was heard by the US Supreme Court – a court that had been in existence for less than 200 years (being created by the US Constitution through Art. 3, Sec. 1). The government and community of the Santa Clara Pueblo Indian Tribe was not only twice the age of the US Supreme Court, it was more than three times older. [9] Therefore, the Court established that it was not seeking to "undermine the authority of the tribal court . . . and hence . . . infringe on the right of the Indians to govern themselves." [10] The Supreme Court was careful to "tread lightly" as it reviewed a "tribal government's ability to maintain authority (sovereignty)." [11]

One Remedy Only

Say it Simply!

> **"writ of habeas corpus"** -- a challenge to the legality of a person's detention -- literally means in Latin to "have the body"

The Indian Civil Rights Act is a federal law. Compliance with the ICRA, therefore, is consistent with an Indian tribe's relinquishment of *external sovereignty* (doing nothing contrary or in conflict with the laws of the United States). It must be remembered though that alleged violations of the ICRA can only be addressed through tribal court. The only exception to this is if someone contests their detention, believing they are being illegally detained by tribal court (*writ of habeas corpus*). Placing habeas corpus relief as the *only* federal remedy for alleged ICRA violations, was consistent with Congress' intent of "avoiding undue or *precipitous* interference in the affairs of Indian people." [12] Congress was aware that as tribal members addressed issues regarding their civil rights, federal courts would be less prepared to evaluate tribal tradition and custom than tribal courts. "[T]hose issues likely to arise in a civil context, will frequently depend on questions of tribal tradition and custom which tribal forums may be in a better position to evaluate than federal courts." [13] The fact Congress provided *only* habeas corpus relief in the ICRA revealed that it was Congress' intent for solutions for civil rights violations to be found through tribal court proceedings.

There have been mixed feelings about the ICRA since its inception. On one hand, it exposed abuses that had taken place and it sought to protect an individual's rights without undermining a tribal government's power to be self-governing. Yet, many saw the ICRA as an intrusion by the federal government into matters tribes hold sacred – their tribal cultures and ways. Indeed, the ICRA gave federal courts the authority, through writ of habeas corpus, to *arbitrate* regarding internal affairs of a tribe.

Fit & Mod ICRA

The Indian Civil Rights Act was purposely designed to "fit the unique political, cultural, and economic needs of tribal governments." [14] Assimilation was not the Congressional intent of the ICRA and the specific modifications made to the ICRA reveal Congressional concern for showing respect for tribal history and culture.

So, what exactly does ICRA say? In what ways is it similar to the civil rights provisions found in the US Constitution? And – in which ways is it different . . . and, why?

The following chart puts the ICRA side-by-side with the Bill of Rights. This will help you see where there are similarities. Where there are differences or modifications, we will briefly discuss why this is so . . .

"precipitous" -- hasty, abrupt or sudden

"arbitrate" -- decide between opposing sides

Although the ICRA is often compared only to the Bill of Rights (the first 10 Amendments to the U.S. Constitution) it actually implements a few sections that are found in other areas: One of the ICRA's provisions is comparable to the 14th Amendment's "equal protection of the law," while another provision has a prohibition against passing either "bill of attainder or ex post facto law" which is found in Art. 1, sec. 9, cl. 3 of the original body of the Constitution.

BILL OF RIGHTS / US CONSTITUTION v. INDIAN CIVIL RIGHTS ACT (ICRA)

A Side-by-Side Comparison

BILL OF RIGHTS PROVISIONS (Amendments 1-10)	INDIAN CIVIL RIGHTS ACT (ICRA) PROVISIONS (All are prohibitions)
#1 - Congress shall make no law respecting an establishment of religion, or prohibiting the free exercise thereof; or abridging the freedom of speech, or of the press; or the right of the people peaceably to assemble, and to petition the Government for a redress of grievances.	**#1** - SHALL NOT: make or enforce any law prohibiting the free exercise of religion, or abridging the freedom of speech, or of the press, or the right of the people peaceably to assemble and to petition for a redress of grievances;
#2 - A well regulated Militia, being necessary to the security of a free State, the right of the people to keep and bear Arms, shall not be infringed.	
#3 - No Soldier shall, in time of peace be quartered in any house, without the consent of the Owner, nor in time of war, but in a manner to be prescribed by law.	
#4 - The right of the people to be secure in their persons, houses, papers, and effects, against unreasonable searches and seizures, shall not be violated, and no Warrants shall issue, but upon probable cause, supported by Oath or affirmation, and particularly describing the place to be searched, and the persons or things to be seized.	**#2** - SHALL NOT: violate the right of the people to be secure in their persons, houses, papers, and effects against unreasonable search and seizures, nor issue warrants, but upon probable cause, supported by oath or affirmation, and particularly describing the place to be searched and the person or thing to be seized;
#5 - No person shall be held to answer for a capital, or otherwise infamous crime, unless on a presentment or indictment of a Grand Jury, except in cases arising in the land or naval forces, or in the Militia, when in actual service in time of War or public danger; nor shall any person be subject for the same offence to be twice put in jeopardy of life or limb; nor shall be compelled in any criminal case to be a witness against himself, nor be deprived of life, liberty, or property, without due process of law; nor shall private property be taken for public use, without just compensation.	**#3** - SHALL NOT: subject any person for the same offense to be twice put in jeopardy; **#4** - SHALL NOT: compel any person in any criminal case to be a witness against himself; **#5** - SHALL NOT: take any private property for a public use without just compensation;
#6 - In all criminal prosecutions, the accused shall enjoy the right to a speedy and public trial, by an impartial jury of the State and district wherein the crime shall have been committed, which district shall have been previously ascertained by law, and to be informed of the nature and cause of the accusation; to be confronted with the witnesses against him; to have compulsory process for obtaining witnesses in his favor, and to have the Assistance of Counsel for his defence.	**#6** - SHALL NOT: deny to any person in a criminal proceeding the right to a speedy and public trial, to be informed of the nature and cause of the accusation, to be confronted with the witnesses against him, to have compulsory process for obtaining witnesses in his favor, and at his own expense to have the assistance of counsel for his defense; **#10** - SHALL NOT: deny to any person accused of an offense punishable by imprisonment the right, upon request, to a trial by jury of not less than six persons.
#7 - In Suits at common law, where the value in controversy shall exceed twenty dollars, the right of trial by jury shall be preserved, and no fact tried by a jury, shall be otherwise reexamined in any Court of the United States, than according to the rules of the common law.	
#8 - Excessive bail shall not be required, nor excessive fines imposed, nor cruel and unusual punishments inflicted.	**#7** - SHALL NOT: (A) require excessive bail, impose excessive fines, or inflict cruel and unusual punishments; (B) except as provided in subparagraph (C), impose for conviction of any 1 offense any penalty or punishment greater than imprisonment for a term of 1 year or a fine of $5,000, or both; (C) subject to subsection (b), impose for conviction of any 1 offense any penalty or punishment greater than imprisonment for a term of 3 years or a fine of $15,000, or both; or (D) impose on a person in a criminal proceeding a total penalty or punishment greater than imprisonment for a term of 9 years;
#9 - The enumeration in the Constitution, of certain rights, shall not be construed to deny or disparage others retained by the people.	
#10 - The powers not delegated to the United States by the Constitution, nor prohibited by it to the States, are reserved to the States respectively, or to the people.	CH-6D

UNITED STATES CONSTITUTION with AMMENDMENTS	INDIAN CIVIL RIGHTS ACT (ICRA) PROVISIONS (All are prohibitions)
14th Amendment, sec. 1 - 1) All persons born or naturalized in the United States, and subject to the jurisdiction thereof, are citizens of the United States and of the State wherein they reside. No State shall make or enforce any law which shall abridge the privileges or immunities of citizens of the United States; nor shall any State deprive any person of life, liberty, or property, without due process of law; nor deny to any person within its jurisdiction the equal protection of the laws.	**#8** - SHALL NOT: deny to any person within its jurisdiction the equal protection of its laws or deprive any person of liberty or property without due process of law;
Art. 1, sec. 9, cl.3 - No Bill of Attainder or ex post facto Law shall be passed.	**#9** - SHALL NOT: pass any bill of attainder or ex post facto law;

CH-6D

Over 8,000 American Indian soldiers served in World War I (6,000 of whom were volunteers). In WWII 25,000 American Indian and Alaska Native men and women fought on all fronts in Europe and the South Pacific. At least 71 Air Medals, 51 Silver Stars, 47 Bronze Stars, 34 Distinguished Flying Crosses, and 2 Congressional Medals of Honor were collectively obtained by American Indians and Alaska Natives. American Indians and Alaska Natives served in subsequent conflicts. Veterans are considered to be among the tribe's most honored members. [15]

"indigent" -- poor, needy (cannot afford to hire an attorney)

Modifications

► The prohibition against making a law establishing a religion (the Establishment Clause of the First Amendment) is not found in the ICRA. This was an important modification for tribal communities as often a tribe's religion cannot be separated from tribal government. A tribe's governmental leaders can also be the tribe's religious leaders – and often are in traditional tribal governments.

► A provision regarding professional soldiers and a regulated militia would not apply directly to tribal governments as this would be contrary to their relinquishment of external sovereignty. Indian tribes do not have professional soldiers or tribal armies subject to their government. However, a very large proportion of Native Americans have honorably served as soldiers in the US armed forces.

► Any person in a criminal proceeding has the right to have the assistance of counsel for his defense – but the ICRA states "at his own expense." This modification was made because, for many tribal governments, it would be a financial hardship if they were required to pay for the legal defense of the accused. If the accused is unable to pay for a defense attorney, he or she simply represent themselves. The exception to this is a new amendment to the ICRA which stipulates that, if there is a possibility of prosecuting someone for a criminal offense subject to greater than 1 year imprisonment, the tribe must provide a licensed defense attorney for an *indigent* defendant (the accused), at the tribe's expense.

► A right to a jury trial for a civil case is not a requirement of the ICRA. Also, for a criminal trial, the jury number is only six persons. For cost savings and simplicity, a Grand Jury is not necessary to initiate a criminal proceeding.

► Not part of the Bill of Rights, but certainly a major US civil rights provision outlined in the 15th Amendment of the US Constitution is the right of US citizens to not be denied a vote due to race, color, or previous condition of servitude. The reason this provision is not included in the ICRA is due to the unique nature and history of tribal communities which often have large populations of non-Indians living on reservations. A good example of the uniqueness of such tribal communities is the Port Madison Indian Reservation in the State of Washington. A "substantial non-Indian population" reside on this reservation as a result of the Allotment Act. [16] If the non-members of the tribe residing within the geographical limits of the reservation were able to vote in tribal elections and hold office, tribal leadership could possibly be removed and replaced with non-Indian governmental leadership. This would not follow the intent of Congress.

"Due Process"- A person who has been accused of wrongdoing has the right to be notified in ample and reasonable time to know the circumstances and tell his/her side of the story. Government process that has the possibility of denying someone of their liberty or property must be applied with fair notification that is equally administered to all.

"Bill of Attainder"- is any legislative act used to declare a person or any group guilty of a criminal act and subsequently render a punishment without the privilege of a trial. (This method was often used in England in the 18th Century.)

"Ex post facto law"- is a law that makes illegal an act that, when committed, was legal. Someone cannot be punished for an action which was not illegal when they committed the act - even if a law is passed later making that action illegal.

PL 280 and ICRA

It would seem the non-tribal side of PL 280 areas (state law enforcement and state courts) would have nothing to do with the ICRA. We have seen how the ICRA is imposed on *tribal* governments and violations are to be addressed in *tribal* court. Even the habeas corpus appeal is to the *federal* courts, not state courts.

So, PL 280 areas don't have to be concerned about the ICRA – right?

Well, not exactly. The truth is, PL 280 areas actually have the potential of seeing cases involving the ICRA. You may be asking, "How is that possible?" Let us explain . . .

Bill of Rights' 4 is ICRA's 2

Remember, the purpose of the Indian Civil Rights Act (ICRA) was to impose on tribal governments the same restrictions imposed on federal and state governments under the US Constitution. The only difference was the ICRA allowed for modifications as Congress considered the "unique political, cultural and economic needs of tribal governments." [17]

For this reason, the ICRA's 1302 (2) prohibition of "unreasonable search and seizures" has been seen as equal with the fourth amendment's protection "against unreasonable search and seizures." As we have mentioned, the individual protections provided in the US Constitution are not applicable to tribal governments. However, "tribal power to investigate violations in Indian country is constrained by the limits contained in the Indian Civil Rights Act, which was enacted to secure the right to be free of arbitrary and unjust actions by tribal governments." [18] The ICRA's ten listed civil rights extend to *anyone*, Indian or non-Indian, while on tribal lands. [19]

Criminal Jurisdictional Authority:
Tribal government has jurisdiction over all Indians who violate enacted tribal codes and tribal officers may arrest/prosecute accordingly. Refer to the Indian Civil Rights Act "powers of self-government" 25 USC 1301 (2).
In non-PL 280 areas, violations of 1152 (General Crimes) and 1153 (Major Crimes) fall to federal jurisdiction and tribal officers will deliver the offender to federal authorities. The exception to this is Indian v. Indian crime other than 1153 violations.
In PL 280 areas, violators of a state's criminal public policy will fall to state jurisdiction and tribal officers will deliver the offender to state authorities. Mandatory PL 280 areas have exclusive jurisdiction over federal jurisdiction (other than the exception to Federal Concurrent Assumption under 18 USC 1162(d)), and Option PL 280 areas will share concurrent jurisdiction with federal authorities for violations of 1152 and 1153.
*It is possible for an Indian to be arrested under tribal law violations and additionally under state or federal law violations. This would not be considered double-jeopardy because the violation(s) would be against separate sovereigns. Refer to US v. Lara, 541 US 193 (2004).

Tribal Officers and ICRA

You have seen in Part 1 of this chapter, the powers vested in Indian tribes and how tribal governments have the authority to set up any type of official or officer to enforce the will of the tribe. These officers may be given the title of tribal "police", "patrol," "rangers," "security," etc. It is up to the tribe to determine such label as they want for their law and order officers. The tribe, in accordance with its internal sovereignty, will choose to regulate and enact laws that reflect the values and philosophy of their community. Each tribe will determine what authority it will extend to their designated officers through their internal policies and procedures.

"[A]n Indian tribe may employ police officers to aid in the enforcement of tribal law and in the exercise of tribal power." [20] If a tribe has an ordinance in place and has authorized officers to enforce such ordinance, tribal officers will investigate when they believe an individual is violating that law. If, in fact, there is a violation the officer is responsible to take action – *reasonable action*, that is.

This is where PL 280 areas have the potential to see cases involving the ICRA. This is true, especially with tribes who have a casino business enterprise or other type of large public venue. Public interaction with tribal officers and the need for public safety increases wherever there is a high volume of people in one area. As one court case put it, "Unfortunately, more people on Indian land means a greater potential for crime on Indian land . . ." [21]

When a tribal officer acts in accordance with the will of the tribe by enforcing law and order, this can involve both Indian and non-Indian violators. If the violation is civil-regulatory, tribal officers will follow the tribe's civil code of conduct and issue warnings, citations, or exclusions. If a criminal violation occurs, tribal government has criminal jurisdiction over all Indians. If the violator is non-Indian, and the violation is against a state's public criminal policy, the tribal officer can detain the individual and deliver him or her to the proper authorities. The tribe always has the authority to exclude any individual from their lands who disturbs the public peace. If an individual will not willing leave their lands, tribal officers may use *reasonable* force to restrain and remove them.

> *"Tribal police officers do not lack authority to detain non-Indians whose conduct disturbs the public order of their reservation . . . The Supreme Court has recognized that tribal law enforcement authorities possess 'traditional and undisputed power to exclude persons whom they deem undesirable from tribal lands,' and therefore have 'the power to restrain those who disturb public order on the reservation, and if necessary to eject them.'"*
>
> *United States v. Terry, 400 F. 3d 575, 579 (2005) quoting Duro v. Reina, 495 US 676, 696-97*

Binding Law

Laws of the United States are "binding upon Indian nations only where it expressly binds them, or is made binding by treaty or some acts of Congress." [22]

> "Section 1302 of the Indian Civil Rights Act is one such (binding) act of Congress. That statute provides in relevant part as follows: 'No Indian tribe in exercising powers of self-government shall . . . violate the right of people to be secure in their persons, houses, papers, and effects against unreasonable search and seizures . . .' This language is, for all intents and purposes, identical to the language of the Fourth Amendment . . . and thus evidences a congressional intent to extend, as against the Indian tribes, '[t]he security of one's privacy against arbitrary intrusion by the police -- which is the core of the Fourth Amendment.'"
>
> *People v. Ramirez, 148 Cal. App. 4th 1467, 1470 (2007)*

> One case defined "search and seizure" as: "prying into hidden places for that which is concealed and that the object searched for has been hidden or intentionally put out of the way." *State v. Cundy. 301 N.W. 2d 236, 239 (1972)*

The Exclusionary Rule

We want to introduce you to something called the "exclusionary rule." The exclusionary rule stems from the 4th Amendment's protection and security against "unreasonable searches and seizures" by government officials. If someone is accused of a crime and there is evidence against them, such evidence found in a search and seizure must have been obtained legally. If it is shown the evidence was illegally obtained by an *unreasonable* search and seizure, the exclusionary rule purposely excludes such evidence from the criminal proceedings. This is done even though it may hinder the prosecution of a crime. This is adhered to because the US Constitutional provision must be strictly followed – or its protection would be meaningless. The exclusionary rule was intended to stop governmental officials (most commonly law enforcement officers) from abusing their authority.

"integral" -- necessary part of the whole; essential

"jurisprudence" -- system or development of laws

Remember, absent habeas corpus the remedy or solution for an individual who believes their civil rights have been violated by a tribal government must be addressed in a tribal court. The exclusionary rule, which evolved through the United States' legal system, will have no bearing on tribal court proceedings. However, because of specific federal statutes, federal and state agencies sometimes interact with a tribal government's administration of justice. In PL 280 areas this is especially true – either with concurrent jurisdiction or exclusive criminal jurisdiction with non-Indians. The exclusionary rule will be considered in cases that are heard in federal and state trial courts. The exclusionary rule has evolved through the years and become an *integral* part of US trial courts' judicial processes.

> *"The exclusionary rule has been a part of the Fourth Amendment search and seizure jurisprudence for nearly a century."*
>
> *People v. Ramirez, 148 Cal. App. 4th 1467, 1470 (2007)*

Quick History of the Exclusionary Rule (outlined in *People v. Ramirez*)

1914 – Supreme Court announced the basic rule: Evidence obtained by federal officers in violation of the Fourth Amendment must be excluded on proper objection in a federal prosecution. *Weeks v. United States 232 US 383 (1914)*

1949 – Supreme Court determined the Fourth Amendment's prohibition against unreasonable searches and seizures was applicable to the states through the due process clause of the Fourteenth Amendment, but the court refused to extend the exclusionary rule to the states at that time. *Wolf v. Colorado, 338 US 25 (1949)*

1960 – Supreme Court expanded the exclusionary rule to prohibit the use in federal courts of evidence illegally seized by state agents, thus putting an end to what had been known as the "silver platter" doctrine. *Elkins v. United States, 364 US 206 (1960)*

1961 – Supreme Court partially overruled *Wolf* (the above 1949 case) and extended the exclusionary rule to cover evidence obtained by state officers used in state criminal prosecutions. *Mapp v. Ohio, 367 US 643 (1961)*

1968 – Congress passed the ICRA a few years after an important court case (*Mapp v. Ohio*) involving the exclusionary rule declaring it was an *"essential part"* of the Fourth and Fourteenth Amendments and applicable to both federal and state governmental actions.

This understanding of the exclusionary rule in relation to the Fourth and Fourteen Amendments was the mindset and understanding of Congress at that time the ICRA was enacted. Legislative history shows Congress wanted all protections included in the ICRA except those necessarily excluded or modified due to the *"unique political, cultural, and economic needs of tribal government."* [23]

> *"Because Congress acted against this background, we take it as given that Congress expected this well-established common law principle – the exclusionary rule – to be as much a part of the prohibition against unreasonable search and seizures in section 1302(2) as it was then considered a part of the identical prohibition in the federal Constitution."*
>
> *People v. Ramirez, 148 Cal. App. 4th 1464, 1473 (2007)*

1973 – Supreme Court described the rule as "judicially created remedy designed to safeguard Fourth Amendment rights generally through its deterrent effect, rather than a personal constitutional right of the party aggrieved. *United States v. Calandra, 414 US 338 (1973)*

1984 – Supreme Court went even further reiterating its characterization of the exclusionary rule as a judicially created remedy but also specifically rejecting any implication from *Mapp* "that the exclusionary rule is a necessary corollary of the Fourth Amendment". *United States v. Leon, 468 US 897 (1984)*

The Exclusion to the Exclusionary Rule

As certain cases legally come before federal or state trial courts, there is an exclusion or exception to the Exclusionary Rule. This exception has to do with private citizens. "The constitutional provision prohibiting unreasonable searches and seizures only protect against actions by the government, its officials and agents, *and have no application to the wrongful or unauthorized acts of private individuals*." *State V. Cundy*, 201 N.W. 2d 236, 239 (1972)

Say it Simply!

"auspices" -- sanction, authority of

So, as we consider PL 280 areas, tribal law enforcement officers are not classified as state "peace officers." [24] (Even federal officers are not state peace officers and have limited powers of arrests within a state's jurisdiction. [25]) In fact, if a tribal police/security officer makes an arrest for a violation of state law in a PL 280 area, they arrest under the *auspices* of a "Private Person's Arrest." With this said, it appears that tribal police/security would fall under the "no application ... of private individuals" exception to the exclusionary rule. For power of arrest, tribal officers are treated as private persons in the eyes of the law, similar to security guards.

Government Agents

There is a major legal difference between officers who are working for a tribal government, as opposed to officers working as security guards for a department store or office building. The difference is in the fact that tribal officers are agents or representatives of tribal *government*. In this capacity they are obligated to not violate the civil rights of anyone subject to the authority of tribal government. When tribal officers enforce tribal law and order, "tribal officers must avoid effecting a constitutionally unreasonable search or seizure. *See 25 USC 1302 (2)*." [26]

The exclusionary rule is often thought of only in reference to peace officer action. However, more accurately, it should be thought of broadly in reference to *governmental action* (employees' or agents' actions). "[T]he Fourth Amendment prohibition against unreasonable searches and seizures has never been limited exclusively to the conduct of law enforcement officers." [27] The exclusionary rule has also been held to apply to the following:

1. State-run hospital employees
2. Public school officials
3. City building inspectors
4. Occupational Safety & Health Act inspectors
5. Firemen

As you see, the common thread is the fact that the individuals are working in a *governmental* capacity. Therefore, the exclusionary rule applies.

Tribal police/security not being classified as state peace officers has no bearing on the application of the ICRA over their actions. However, their classification as agents of tribal government obligates tribal police/security to act in a way that does not violate the individual rights of anyone who is on tribal lands.

LAWS OF ARREST COMPARED

Arrest = The lawful taking of someone into custody (not free to leave).

An arrest can be made by a police officer or a private person.

"PROBABLE CAUSE" = That which would lead a reasonable and prudent person to have a strong suspicion of guilt (also called "reasonable cause").

"REASONABLE SUSPICION" = A police officer in the same circumstances could reasonably believe a person has been, is or is about to be engaged in criminal activity.

POLICE OFFICER'S POWER OF ARREST	PRIVATE PERSON'S POWER OF ARREST
Warrant: Police officer may make an arrest with a warrant.	**Warrant:** A private person has no warrant arrest power.
Felony: A police officer may arrest without a warrant if the officer has probable cause to believe the person they are arresting committed a felony.	**Felony:** A private person may arrest if a felony has actually been committed. The private person must have knowledge the felony *did* in fact occur as well as probable cause to believe the person he/she is arresting committed the felony. Without unnecessary delay, they are to turn the arrested person over to the magistrate or to a police officer.
Misdemeanor: Police officer may make arrest if officer has probable cause to believe the person they are arresting committed a misdemeanor crime in their presence.	**Misdemeanor:** A private person may make an arrest if they have direct knowledge of the misdemeanor crime and it was committed in their presence.
Detain & Investigate: If the police officer has a reasonable *suspicion* (less than probable cause) that a suspect committed a felony or a misdemeanor crime, the **officer can detain to investigate**.	**Detain & Investigate:** A private person has **no power to detain** and investigate *based on* reasonable suspicion or even probable cause.

Source: California Penal Code, Powers of Arrest sections.

CH-6E

Reasonable Search & Seizure

You may be asking, "Well, how do I know what the court will see as a reasonable search and seizure?" As you see in Chart CH-6E, the laws of arrest are a bit different between a peace officer's lawful arrest and a private person's lawful arrest. This will also affect what is determined reasonable regarding search and seizure. Since tribal security/police are classified as private persons for powers of arrest, it would be best to look at a state's guidelines for security guards. Private security guards arrest under the auspices of a private person's arrest, just as tribal security/police do. Each state has the responsibility for regulating private security within their state and providing guidelines. Such guidelines explain how the state views reasonable search and seizure for a private person's arrest which are available through each state's Attorney General's Office.

As an example of one state's guidelines for private security, California's Dept. of Consumer Affairs, Bureau of Security and Investigative Services provides a training manual covering power of arrest. To access this training manual go to: http://www.bsis.ca.gov/forms_pubs/poa.pdf

Exception to Private Person's Arrest

Many states have an exception to the private person's arrest which allows for certain private persons to stop and detain for investigation. Using California's penal code as an example, we see in CA Penal Code 490.5 something referred to as the "Merchant's Privilege." The essential key points to this exception for a private person's arrest are that a private person as an owner or agent of a store may:

- Stop and detain to investigate for a reasonable amount of time to recover merchandise if one has probable cause that the person has unlawfully taken merchandise or attempted to do so.

- Examine/search for merchandise in plain view and in property in immediate possession of person (packages, shopping bags, handbags, etc.) BUT CANNOT SEARCH clothing worn by the suspect.

- Can request the suspect to show identification, but cannot demand it.

- Applies also to persons employed by a library or theater. Libraries will protect their books and materials and theater owners will protect from someone operating a video recording device within the premises.

► During the detention, a merchant, theater owner or person employed by a library may use a reasonable amount of non-deadly force necessary to protect himself or herself and to prevent escape of the person detained or the loss of property.

► When a private person transfers custody to a peace officer, the officer who accepts custody will search the person and his/her immediate possessions.

A library facility shall post at all entrances/exits a conspicuous sign to read: "IN ORDER TO PREVENT THE THEFT OF BOOKS AND LIBRARY MATERIALS, STATE LAW AUTHORIZES THE DETENTION FOR A REASONABLE PERIOD OF ANY PERSON USING THESE FACILITIES SUSPECTED OF COMMITTING 'LIBRARY THEFT' (PENAL CODE SECTION 490.5)."

In the area of criminal justice, this exception serves as an example of how state laws can evolve according to specific needs. Many states have recognized the need for merchants, along with libraries and theaters to protect their assets. If state laws provide for store and theater owners and their agents – heck, even librarians – to use reasonable force to detain, it shouldn't seem strange for sovereign nations to implement similar powers. As a balance, the ICRA provides the safeguard against unreasonable or abusive governmental action.

Endnotes - Chapter Six, Part 3:

[1] Hearings on constitutional rights of the American Indian before the Subcommittee on Constitutional Rights of the Committee on the Judiciary, U.S. Senate, 88th Cong., 2d Sess., p. 22

[2] *Santa Clara Pueblo v. Martinez*, 436 U.S. 49, 56 (1978), "As separate sovereigns pre-existing the Constitution, tribes have historically been regarded as unconstrained by those constitutional provisions framed specifically as limitations on federal or state authority. Thus, in *Talton v. Mayes*, 163 U.S. 376 (1896), this Court held that the Fifth Amendment did not 'operat[e] upon' 'the powers of local self-government enjoyed' by the tribes. In ensuing years the lower federal courts have extended the holding of *Talton* to other provisions of the Bill of Rights, as well as to the Fourteenth Amendment."

[3] 113 Cong. Rec. part 26, p. 35473, 90th Cong., 1st Session (Dec. 7, 1967)

[4] *Santa Clara Pueblo v. Martinez*, 436 U.S. 49, 61 (1978) citing the central purpose of the ICRA from its legislative history, S. Rep. No. 841, 90th Cong., 1st Sess., 5-6 (1967)

[5] Id. at 55

[6] Id. at 63

[7] Id. at 62

[8] Id. at 62-64, see also fn. 15-18 "At exploratory hearings . . . it became apparent that the Interior Department had engaged in inordinate delays . . . "

[9] Id. at 51 "Santa Clara Pueblo is an Indian tribe that has been in existence for over 600 years."

[10] Id. at 59

[11] Id. at 60

[12] *Santa Clara Pueblo v. Martinez*, 436 US 49, 67 (1978)

[13] Id. at 71

[14] *Santa Clara Pueblo v. Martinez*, 436 US 49, 62 (1978)

[15] See the Bureau of Indian Affairs' official website on the FAQS page under "Do American Indians and Alaska Natives serve in the Armed Forces?" at *http://www.bia.gov/FAQs/index.htm*

[16] See Footnote 1 in the US Supreme Court's case of *Oliphant v. Suquamish Indian Tribe*, 435 US 191 (1978), "The substantial non-Indian population on the Port Madison Reservation is primarily the result of the sale of Indian allotments to non-Indians by the Secretary of the Interior."

[17] *Santa Clara Pueblo v. Martinez*, 436 US 49, 61 (1978)

[18] *State v. Madsen*, 760 N.W. 2d 370, 375 (2009)

[19] Id. at 376

[20] *Ortiz-Barraza v. US*, 512 F. 2d 1176, 1179 (1975)

[21] *People v. Ramirez*, 148 Cal. App. 4th 1467 (2007)

[22] *Native American Church v. Navajo Tribal Council*, 272 F. 2d 131, 134-135 (10th Cir. 1959)

[23] *Santa Clara Pueblo v. Martinez*, 436 US 49, 62 (1978)

[24] Sometimes such an officer is additionally trained and certified through a state agency in order to obtain the status (legal privileges and responsibilities) of a cross-sworn peace officer, with the permission of the Sheriff/Chief of Police.

[25] For example, see California Penal Code, Sect. 830.8(a) "Federal criminal investigators and law enforcement officers are not California peace officers, but may exercise the powers of arrest of a peace officer in any of the following circumstances ..." See PC 830.8(a)(1)-(4) for limitations.

[26] *United States v. Terry*, 400 F. 3d 575, 580 (2005)

[27] *State v. Madsen*, 760 N.W. 2d 370, 379 (2009)

Chapter Seven

This chapter will cover:

- *Strong foundation and effective tools*
- *Ready reference and guide*
- *Dog-eared copies in the hands of readers*

Chapter Seven

Conclusion

In Conclusion . . .

The fact that we are bringing this resource guide to a conclusion, certainly does not mean we have exhausted the material – far from it. We packed as much as we could into this book's hefty body! We believe we have laid a strong foundation and given you effective tools for understanding PL 280.

It has been our desire that the compilation of this material will serve as a road map for the many individuals who live and work within Indian country where PL 280 jurisdiction applies. The hope is that,

instead of feeling stuck inside the maze of confusion surrounding PL 280, you will now have direction and confidence in maneuvering through the legal areas of this federal law.

If we have fulfilled our goal, many barriers that have been created through PL 280 jurisdictional issues between Native American communities and public safety and service providers will be broken down, allowing for a common ground of understanding. Where there is common ground, there is also the opportunity to work together and build strong relationships for the benefit of the whole community.

Your broad understanding of PL 280 will now serve you well. This resource guide is intended to be a ready reference and to guide you where you specifically may want to dig deeper.

What will be a joy to us as authors is when dog-eared copies of *A User-friendly PL 280 Resource Guide* are seen in the hands of readers.

Our most sincere wishes for
your prosperous future,

Alex Tortes & Cindy Pierce

The End

APPENDIX

Appendix A

Public Law 83-280

(18 USC § 1162, 28 USC § 1360, 25 USC § 1321, § 1322, § 1323, § 1324, § 1325, § 1326)

18 U.S.C. § 1162. STATE JURISDICTION OVER OFFENSES COMMITTED BY OR AGAINST INDIANS IN THE INDIAN COUNTRY

(a) Each of the States or Territories listed in the following table shall have jurisdiction over offenses committed by or against Indians in the areas of Indian country listed opposite the name of the State or Territory to the same extent that such State or Territory has jurisdiction over offenses committed elsewhere within the State or Territory, and the criminal laws of such State or Territory shall have the same force and effect within such Indian country as they have elsewhere within the State or Territory:

State or Territory of	***Indian country affected***
Alaska	All Indian country within the State, except that on Annette Islands, the Metlakatla Indian community may exercise jurisdiction over offenses committed by Indians in the same manner in which such jurisdiction may be exercised by Indian tribes in Indian country over which State jurisdiction has not been extended.
California	All Indian country within the State
Minnesota	All Indian country within the State, except the Red Lake Reservation
Nebraska	All Indian country within the State
Oregon	All Indian country within the State, except the Warm Springs Reservation
Wisconsin	All Indian country within the State

(b) Nothing in this section shall authorize the alienation, encumbrance, or taxation of any real or personal property, including water rights, belonging to any Indian or any Indian tribe, band, or community that is held in trust by the United States or is subject to a restriction against alienation imposed by the United States; or shall authorize regulation of the use of such property in a manner inconsistent with any Federal treaty, agreement, or statute or with any regulation made pursuant thereto; or shall deprive any Indian or any Indian tribe, band, or community of any right, privilege, or immunity afforded under Federal treaty, agreement, or statute with respect to hunting, trapping, or fishing or the control, licensing, or regulation thereof.

(c) The provisions of sections 1152 and 1153 of this chapter shall not be applicable within the areas of Indian country listed in subsection (a) of this section as areas over which the several States have exclusive jurisdiction.

(d) Notwithstanding subsection (c), at the request of an Indian tribe, and after consultation with and consent by the Attorney General—
(1) sections 1152 and 1153 shall apply in the areas of the Indian country of the Indian tribe; and
(2) jurisdiction over those areas shall be concurrent among the Federal Government, State governments, and, where applicable, tribal governments.

28 U.S.C. § 1360. STATE CIVIL JURISDICTION IN ACTIONS TO WHICH INDIANS ARE PARTIES

(a) Each of the States listed in the following table shall have jurisdiction over civil causes of action between Indians or to which Indians are parties which arise in the areas of Indian country listed opposite the name of the State to the same extent that such State has jurisdiction over other civil causes of action, and those civil laws of such State that are of general application to private persons or private property shall have the same force and effect within such Indian country as they have elsewhere within the State:

State of	***Indian country affected***
Alaska	All Indian country within the State
California	All Indian country within the State
Minnesota	All Indian country within the State, except the Red Lake Reservation
Nebraska	All Indian country within the State
Oregon	All Indian country within the State, except the Warm Springs Reservation
Wisconsin	All Indian country within the State

(b) Nothing in this section shall authorize the alienation, encumbrance, or taxation of any real or personal property, including water rights, belonging to any Indian or any Indian tribe, band, or community that is held in trust by the United States or is subject to a restriction against alienation imposed by the United States; or shall authorize regulation of the use of such property in a manner inconsistent with any Federal treaty, agreement, or statute or with any regulation made pursuant thereto; or shall confer jurisdiction upon the State to adjudicate, in probate proceedings or otherwise, the ownership or right to possession of such property or any interest therein.

(c) Any tribal ordinance or custom heretofore or hereafter adopted by an Indian tribe, band, or community in the exercise of any authority which it may possess shall, if not inconsistent with any applicable civil law of the State, be given full force and effect in the determination of civil causes of action pursuant to this section.

25 U.S.C. § 1321. ASSUMPTION BY STATE OF CRIMINAL JURISDICTION

(a) Consent of United States
(1) In general
The consent of the United States is hereby given to any State not having jurisdiction over criminal offenses committed by or against Indians in the areas of Indian country situated within such State to assume, with the consent of the Indian tribe occupying the particular Indian country or part thereof which could be affected by such assumption, such measure of jurisdiction over any or all of such offenses committed within such Indian country or any part thereof as may be determined by such State to the same extent that such State has jurisdiction over any such offense committed elsewhere within the State, and the criminal laws of such State shall have the same force and effect within such Indian country or part thereof as they have elsewhere within that State.

(2) Concurent jurisdiction
At the request of an Indian tribe, and after consultation with and consent by the Attorney General, the United States shall accept concurrent jurisdiction to prosecute violations of sections 1152 and 1153 of title 18 within the Indian country of the Indian tribe.

(b) *Alienation, encumbrance, taxation, and use of property; hunting, trapping, or fishing*
Nothing in this section shall authorize the alienation, encumbrance, or taxation of any real or personal property, including water rights, belonging to any Indian or any Indian tribe, band, or community that is held in trust by the United States or is subject to a restriction against alienation imposed by the United States; or shall authorize regulation of the use of such property in a manner inconsistent with any Federal treaty, agreement, or statute or with any regulation made pursuant thereto; or shall deprive any Indian or any Indian tribe, band, or community of any right, privilege, or immunity afforded under Federal treaty, agreement, or statute with respect to hunting, trapping, or fishing or the control, licensing, or regulation thereof.

25 U.S.C. § 1322. ASSUMPTION BY STATE OF CIVIL JURISDICTION

(a) *Consent of United States; force and effect of civil laws*
The consent of the United States is hereby given to any State not having jurisdiction over civil causes of action between Indians or to which Indians are parties which arise in the areas of Indian country situated within such State to assume, with the consent of the tribe occupying the particular Indian country or part thereof which would be affected by such assumption, such measure of jurisdiction over any or all such civil causes of action arising within such Indian country or any part thereof as may be determined by such State to the same extent that such State has jurisdiction over other civil causes of action, and those civil laws of such State that are of general application to private persons or private property shall have the same force and effect within such Indian country or part thereof as they have elsewhere within that State.

(b) *Alienation, encumbrance, taxation, use, and probate of property*
Nothing in this section shall authorize the alienation, encumbrance, or taxation of any real or personal property, including water rights, belonging to any Indian or any Indian tribe, band, or community that is held in trust by the United States or is subject to a restriction against alienation imposed by the United States; or shall authorize regulation of the use of such property in a manner inconsistent with any Federal treaty, agreement, or statute, or with any regulation made pursuant thereto; or shall confer jurisdiction upon the State to adjudicate, in probate proceedings or otherwise, the ownership or right to possession of such property or any interest therein.

(c) *Force and effect of tribal ordinances or customs*
Any tribal ordinance or custom heretofore or hereafter adopted by an Indian tribe, band, or community in the exercise of any authority which it may possess shall, if not inconsistent with any applicable civil law of the State, be given full force and effect in the determination of civil causes of action pursuant to this section.

25 U.S.C. § 1323. RETROCESSION OF JURISDICTION BY STATE

(a) *Acceptance by United States*
The United States is authorized to accept a retrocession by any State of all or any measure of the criminal or civil jurisdiction, or both, acquired by such State pursuant to the provisions of section 1162 of title 18, section 1360 of title 28, or section 7 of the Act of August 15, 1953 (67 Stat. 588), as it was in effect prior to its repeal by subsection (b) of this section.

(b) *Repeal of statutory provisions*
Section 7 of the Act of August 15, 1953 (67 Stat. 588), is hereby repealed, but such repeal shall not affect any cession of jurisdiction made pursuant to such section prior to its repeal.

25 U.S.C. § 1324. AMENDMENT OF STATE CONSTITUTIONS OR STATUTES TO REMOVE LEGAL IMPEDIMENT; EFFECTIVE DATE

Notwithstanding the provisions of any enabling Act for the admission of a State, the consent of the United States is hereby given to the people of any State to amend, where necessary, their State constitution or existing statutes, as the case may be, to remove any legal impediment to the assumption of civil or criminal jurisdiction in accordance with the provisions of this subchapter. The provisions of this subchapter shall not become effective with respect to such assumption of jurisdiction by any such State until the people thereof have appropriately amended their State constitution or statutes, as the case may be.

25 U.S.C. § 1325. ABATEMENT OF ACTIONS

(a) *Pending actions or proceedings; effect of cession*
No action or proceeding pending before any court or agency of the United States immediately prior to any cession of jurisdiction by the United States pursuant to this subchapter shall abate by reason of that cession. For the purposes of any such action or proceeding, such cession shall take effect on the day following the date of final determination of such action or proceeding.

(b) *Criminal actions; effect of cession*
No cession made by the United States under this subchapter shall deprive any court of the United States of jurisdiction to hear, determine, render judgment, or impose sentence in any criminal action instituted against any person for any offense committed before the effective date of such cession, if the offense charged in such action was cognizable under any law of the United States at the time of the commission of such offense. For the purposes of any such criminal action, such cession shall take effect on the day following the date of final determination of such action.

25 U.S.C. § 1326. SPECIAL ELECTION

State jurisdiction acquired pursuant to this subchapter with respect to criminal offenses or civil causes of action, or with respect to both, shall be applicable in Indian country only where the enrolled Indians within the affected area of such Indian country accept such jurisdiction by a majority vote of the adult Indians voting at a special election held for that purpose. The Secretary of the Interior shall call such special election under such rules and regulations as he may prescribe, when requested to do so by the tribal council or other governing body, or by 20 per centum of such enrolled adults.

Treaties

Treaty with the Delawares (1778)

Articles of agreement and confederation, made and, entered; into by, Andrew and Thomas Lewis, Esquires, Commissioners for, and in Behalf of the United States of North-America of the one Part, and Capt. White Eyes, Capt. John Kill Buck, Junior, and Capt. Pipe, Deputies and Chief Men of the Delaware Nation of the other Part.

ARTICLE I.
That all offences or acts of hostilities by one, or either of the contracting parties against the other, be mutually forgiven, and buried in the depth of oblivion, never more to be had in remembrance.

ARTICLE II.
That a perpetual peace and friendship shall from henceforth take place, and subsist between the contracting: parties aforesaid, through all succeeding generations: and if either of the parties are engaged in a just and necessary war with any other nation or nations, that then each shall assist the other in due proportion to their abilities, till their enemies are brought to reasonable terms of accommodation: and that if either of them shall discover any hostile designs forming against the other, they shall give the earliest notice thereof that timeous measures may be taken to prevent their ill effect.

ARTICLE III.
And whereas the United States are engaged in a just and necessary war, in defence and support of life, liberty and independence, against the King of England and his adherents, and as said King is yet possessed of several posts and forts on the lakes and other places, the reduction of which is of great importance to the peace and security of the contracting parties, and as the most practicable way for the troops of the United States to some of the posts and forts is by passing through the country of the Delaware nation, the aforesaid deputies, on behalf of themselves and their nation, do hereby stipulate and agree to give a free passage through their country to the troops aforesaid, and the same to conduct by the nearest and best ways to the posts, forts or towns of the enemies of the United States, affording to said troops such supplies of corn, meat, horses, or whatever may be in their power for the accommodation of such troops, on the commanding officer's, &c. paying, or engageing to pay, the full value of whatever they can supply them with. And the said deputies, on the behalf of their nation, engage to join the troops of the United States aforesaid, with such a number of their best and most expert warriors as they can spare, consistent with their own safety, and act in concert with them; and for the better security of the old men, women and children of the aforesaid nation, whilst their warriors are engaged against the common enemy, it is agreed on the part of the United States, that a fort of sufficient strength and capacity be built at the expense of the said States, with such assistance as it may be in the power of the said Delaware Nation to give, in the most convenient place, and advantageous situation, as shall be agreed on by the commanding officer of the troops aforesaid, with the advice and concurrence of the deputies of the aforesaid Delaware Nation, which fort shall be garrisoned by such a number of the troops of the United States, as the commanding officer can spare for the present, and hereafter by such numbers, as the wise men of the United States in council, shall think most conducive to the common good.

ARTICLE IV.
For the better security of the peace and friendship now entered into by the contracting parties, against all infractions of the same by the citizens of either party, to the prejudice of the other, neither party shall proceed to the infliction of punishments on the citizens of the other, otherwise than by securing the offender or offenders by imprisonment, or any other competent means, till a fair and impartial trial can be had by judges or juries of both parties, as near as can be to the laws, customs and usages of the contracting parties and natural justice. The mode of such trials to be hereafter fixed by the wise men of the United States in Congress assembled, with the assistance of such deputies of the Delaware nation, as may be appointed to act in concert with them in adjusting this matter to their mutual liking. And it is further agreed between the parties aforesaid, that neither shall entertain or give countenance to the enemies of the other, or protect in their respective states, criminal fugitives, servants or slaves, but the same to apprehend, and secure and deliver to the State or States, to which such enemies, criminals, servants or slaves respectively belong.

ARTICLE V.
Whereas the confederation entered into by the Delaware nation and the United States, renders the first dependent on the latter for all the articles of clothing, utensils and implements of war, and it is judged not only reasonable, but indispensably necessary, that the aforesaid Nation be supplied with such articles from time to time, as far as the United States may have it in their power, by a well-regulated trade, under the conduct of an intelligent, candid agent, with an adequate salary, one more influenced by the love of his country, and a constant attention to the duties of his department by promoting the common interest, than the sinister purposes of converting and binding all the duties of his office to his private emolument: Convinced of the necessity of such measures, the Commissioners of the United States, at the earnest solicitation of the deputies aforesaid, have engaged in behalf of the United States, that such a trade shall be afforded said nation conducted on such principles of mutual interest as the wisdom of the United States in Congress assembled shall think most conducive to adopt for their mutual convenience.

ARTICLE VI.
Whereas the enemies of the United States have endeavored, by every artifice in their power, to possess the Indians in general with an opinion, that it is the design of the States aforesaid, to extirpate the Indians and take possession of their country to obviate such false suggestion, the United States do engage to guarantee to the aforesaid nation of Delawares, and their heirs, all their territorial rights in the fullest and most ample manner, as it bath been bounded by former treaties, as long as they the said Delaware nation shall abide by, and hold fast the chain of friendship now entered into. And it is further agreed on between the contracting parties should it for the future be found conducive for the mutual interest of both parties to invite any other tribes who have been friends to the interest of the United States, to join the present confederation, and to form a state whereof the Delaware nation shall be the head, and have a representation in Congress: Provided, nothing contained in this article to be considered as conclusive until it meets with the approbation of Congress. And it is also the intent and meaning of this article, that no protection or countenance shall be afforded to any who are at present our enemies, by which they might escape the punishment they deserve.

In witness whereof, the parties have hereunto interchangeably set their hands and seals, at Fort Pitt, September seventeenth, anno Domini one thousand seven hundred and seventy-eight.
Andrew Lewis, [L. S.]
Thomas Lewis, [L. S.]
White Eyes, his x mark, [L. S.]
The Pipe, his x mark, [L. S.]
John Kill Buck, his x mark, [L. S.]

In presence of-
Lach'n McIntosh, brigadier-general, commander the Western Department.
Daniel Brodhead, colonel Eighth Pennsylvania Regiment,
W. Crawford, colonel,
John Campbell,
John Stephenson,
John Gibson, colonel Thirteenth Virginia Regiment,
A. Graham, brigade major,
Lach. McIntosh, jr., major brigade,
Benjamin Mills,
Joseph L. Finley, captain Eighth Pennsylvania Regiment,
John Finley, captain Eighth Pennsylvania Regiment.

Source: http://avalon.law.yale.edu/subject_menus/ntreaty.asp
Indian Affairs : Laws and Treaties, Vol. II (Treaties), Compiled and Edited By Charles J. Kappler LL. M. Clerk to the Senate Committee on Indian Affairs, Washington, DC : Government Printing Office, 1904

The Treaty of Greenville (1795)

A treaty of peace between the United States of America, and the tribes of Indians called the Wyandots, Delawares, Shawanees, Ottawas, Chippewas, Pattawatimas, Miamis, Eel Rivers, Weas, Kickapoos, Piankeshaws, and Kaskaskias.

To put an end to a destructive war, to settle all controversies, and to restore harmony and friendly intercourse between the said United States and Indian tribes, Anthony Wayne, major general commanding the army of the United States, and sole commissioner for the good purposes above mentioned, and the said tribes of Indians, by their sachems, chiefs, and warriors, met together at Greenville, the head quarters of the said army, have agreed on the following articles, which, when ratified by the President, with the advice and consent of the Senate of the United States, shall be binding on them and the said Indian tribes.

Art. 1:
Henceforth all hostilities shall cease; peace is hereby established, and shall be perpetual; and a friendly intercourse shall take place between the said United States and Indian tribes.

Art. 2:
All prisoners shall, on both sides, be restored. The Indians, prisoners to the United States, shall be immediately set at liberty. The people of the United States, still remaining prisoners among the Indians, shall be delivered up in ninety days from the date hereof, to the general or commanding officer at Greenville, fort Wayne, or fort Defiance; and ten chiefs of the said tribes shall remain at Greenville as hostages, until the delivery of the prisoners shall be effected.

Art. 3:
The general boundary line between the lands of the United States and the lands of the said Indian tribes, shall begin at the mouth of Cayahoga river, and run thence up the same to the portage, between that and the Tuscarawas branch of the Muskingum, thence down that branch to the crossing place above fort Lawrence, thence westerly to a fork of that branch of the Great Miami river, running into the Ohio, at or near which fork stood Loromie's store, and where commences the portage between the Miami of the Ohio, and St. Mary's river, which is a branch of the Miami which runs into lake Erie; thence a westerly course to fort Recovery, which stands on a branch of the Wabash; thence southwesterly in a direct line to the Ohio, so as to intersect that river opposite the mouth of Kentucke or Cuttawa river. And in consideration of the peace now established; of the goods formerly received from the United States; of those now to be delivered; and of the yearly delivery of goods now stipulated to be made hereafter; and to indemnify the United States for the injuries and expenses they have sustained during the war, the said Indian tribes do hereby cede and relinquish forever, all their claims to the lands lying eastwardly and southwardly of the general boundary line now described: and these lands, or any part of them, shall never hereafter be made a cause or pretence, on the part of the said tribes, or any of them, of war or injury to the United States, or any of the people thereof.

And for the same considerations, and as an evidence of the returning friendship of the said Indian tribes, of their confidence in the United States, and desire to provide for their accommodations, and for that convenient intercourse which will be beneficial to both parties, the said Indian tribes do also cede to the United States the following pieces of land, to wit:

1) One piece of land six miles square, at or near Loromie's store, before mentioned.
2) One piece two miles square, at the head of the navigable water or landing, on the St. Mary's river, near Girty's town.
3) One piece six miles square, at the head of the navigable water of the Auglaize river.
4) One piece six miles square, at the confluence of the Auglaize and Miami rivers, where fort Defiance now stands.
5) One piece six miles square, at or near the confluence of the rivers St. Mary's and St. Joseph's, where fort Wayne now stands, or near it.
6) One piece two miles square, on the Wabash river, at the end of the portage from the Miami of the lake, and about eight miles westward from fort Wayne.
7) One piece six miles square, at the Ouatanon, or Old Wea towns, on the Wabash river.
8) One piece twelve miles square, at the British fort on the Miami of the lake, at the foot of the rapids.
9) One piece six miles square, at the mouth of the said river, where it empties into the lake.

10) One piece six miles square, upon Sandusky lake, where a fort formerly stood.
11) One piece two miles square, at the lower rapids of Sandusky river.
12) The post of Detroit, and all the land to the north, the west and the south of it, of which the Indian title has been extinguished by gifts or grants to the French or English governments: and so much more land to be annexed to the district of Detroit, as shall be comprehended between the river Rosine, on the south, lake St. Clair on the north, and a line, the general course whereof shall be six miles distant from the west end of lake Erie and Detroit river.
13) The post of Michilimackinac, and all the land on the island on which that post stands, and the main land adjacent, of which the Indian title has been extinguished by gifts or grants to the Frewnch or English governments; and a piece of land on the main to the north of the island, to measure six miles, on lake Huron, or the strait between lakes Huron and Michigan, and to extend three miles back from the water of the lake or strait; and also, the Island De Bois Blane, being an extra and voluntary gift of the Chippewa nation.
14) One piece of land six miles square, at the mouth of Chikago river, emptying into the southwest end of lake Michigan, where a fort formerly stood.
15) One piece twelve miles square, at or near the mouth of the Illinois river, emptying into the Mississippi.
16) One piece six miles square, at the old Piorias fort and village near the south end of the Illinois lake, on said Illinois river. And whenever the United States shall think proper to survey and mark the boundaries of the lands hereby ceded to them, they shall give timely notice thereof to the said tribes of Indians, that they may appoint some of their wise chiefs to attend and see that the lines are run according to the terms of this treaty.

And the said Indian tribes will allow to the people of the United States a free passage by land and by water, as one and the other shall be found convenient, through their country, along the chain of posts hereinbefore mentioned; that is to say, from the commencement of the portage aforesaid, at or near Loromie's store, thence along said portage to the St. Mary's, and down the same to fort Wayne, and then down the Miami, to lake Erie; again, from the commencement of the portage at or near Loromie's store along the portage from thence to the river Auglaize, and down the same to its junction with the Miami at fort Defiance; again, from the commencement of the portage aforesaid, to Sandusky river, and down the same to Sandusky bay and lake Erie, and from Sandusky to the post which shall be taken at or near the foot of the Rapids of the Miami of the lake; and from thence to Detroit. Again, from the mouth of Chikago, to the commencement of the portage, between that river and the Illinois, and down the Illinois river to the Mississippi; also, from fort Wayne, along the portage aforesaid, which leads to the Wabash, and then down the Wabash to the Ohio. And the said Indian tribes will also allow to the people of the United States, the free use of the harbors and mouths of rivers along the lakes adjoining the Indian lands, for sheltering vessels and boats, and liberty to land their cargoes where necessary for their safety.

Art. 4:
In consideration of the peace now established, and of the cessions and relinquishments of lands made in the preceding article by the said tribes of Indians, and to manifest the liberality of the United States, as the great means of rendering this peace strong and perpetual, the United States relinquish their claims to all other Indian lands northward of the river Ohio, eastward of the Mississippi, and westward and southward of the Great Lakes and the waters, uniting them, according to the boundary line agreed on by the United States and the King of Great Britain, in the treaty of peace made between them in the year 1783. But from this relinquishment by the United States, the following tracts of land are explicitly excepted:

1st. The tract on one hundred and fifty thousand acres near the rapids of the river Ohio, which has been assigned to General Clark, for the use of himself and his warriors.

2nd. The post of St. Vincennes, on the River Wabash, and the lands adjacent, of which the Indian title has been extinguished.

3rd. The lands at all other places in possession of the French people and other white settlers among them, of which the Indian title has been extinguished as mentioned in the 3d article; and

4th. The post of fort Massac towards the mouth of the Ohio. To which several parcels of land so excepted, the said tribes relinquish all the title and claim which they or any of them may have.

And for the same considerations and with the same views as above mentioned, the United States now deliver to the said Indian tribes a quantity of goods to the value of twenty thousand dollars, the receipt whereof they do hereby acknowledge; and henceforward every year, forever, the United States will deliver, at some convenient place northward of the river Ohio, like useful goods, suited to the circumstances of the Indians, of the value of nine thousand five hundred dollars; reckoning that value at the first cost of the goods in the city or place in the United States where they shall be procured. The tribes to which those goods are to be annually delivered, and the proportions in which they are to be delivered, are the following:

1st. To the Wyandots, the amount of one thousand dollars.

2nd. To the Delawares, the amount of one thousand dollars.

3rd. To the Shawanees, the amount of one thousand dollars.

4th. To the Miamis, the amount of one thousand dollars.

5th. To the Ottawas, the amount of one thousand dollars.

6th. To the Chippewas, the amount of one thousand dollars.

7th.To the Pattawatimas, the amount of one thousand dollars, and

8th. To the Kickapoo, Wea, Eel River, Piankeshaw, and Kaskaskia tribes, the amount of five hundred dollars each.

Provided, that if either of the said tribes shall hereafter, at an annual delivery of their share of the goods aforesaid, desire that a part of their annuity should be furnished in domestic animals, implements of husbandry, and other utensils convenient for them, and in compensation to useful artificers who may reside with or near them, and be employed for their benefit, the same shall, at the subsequent annual deliveries, be furnished accordingly.

Art. 5:
To prevent any misunderstanding about the Indian lands relinquished by the United States in the fourth article, it is now explicitly declared, that the meaning of that relinquishment is this: the Indian tribes who have a right to those lands, are quietly to enjoy them, hunting, planting, and dwelling thereon, so long as they please, without any molestation from the United States; but when those tribes, or any of them, shall be disposed to sell their lands, or any part of them, they are to be sold only to the United States; and until such sale, the United States will protect all the said Indian tribes in the quiet enjoyment of their lands against all citizens of the United States, and against all other white persons who intrude upon the same. And the said Indian tribes again acknowledge themselves to be under the protection of the said United States, and no other power whatever.

Art. 6:
If any citizen of the United States, or any other white person or persons, shall presume to settle upon the lands now relinquished by the United States, such citizen or other person shall be out of the protection of the United States; and the Indian tribe, on whose land the settlement shall be made, may drive off the settler, or punish him in such manner as they shall think fit; and because such settlements, made without the consent of the United States, will be injurious to them as well as to the Indians, the United States shall be at liberty to break them up, and remove and punish the settlers as they shall think proper, and so effect that protection of the Indian lands herein before stipulated.

Art. 7:
The said tribes of Indians, parties to this treaty, shall be at liberty to hunt within the territory and lands which they have now ceded to the United States, without hindrance or molestation, so long as they demean themselves peaceably, and offer no injury to the people of the United States.

Art. 8:
Trade shall be opened with the said Indian tribes; and they do hereby respectively engage to afford protection to such persons, with their property, as shall be duly licensed to reside among them for the purpose of trade; and to their agents and servants; but no person shall be permitted to reside among them for the purpose of trade; and to their agents and servants; but no person shall be permitted to reside at any of their towns or hunting camps, as a trader, who is not furnished with a license for that purpose, under the hand and seal of the superintendent of the department northwest of the Ohio, or such other person as the President of the United States shall authorize to grant such licenses; to the end, that the said Indians may not be imposed on in their trade.* And if any licensed trader shall abuse his privilege by unfair dealing, upon complaint and proof thereof, his license shall be taken from him, and he shall be further punished according to the laws of the United States. And if any person shall intrude himself as a trader, without such license, the said Indians shall take and bring him before the superintendent, or his deputy, to be dealt with according to law. And to prevent impositions by forged licenses, the said Indians shall, at lease once a year, give information to the superintendent, or his deputies, on the names of the traders residing among them.

Art. 9:
Lest the firm peace and friendship now established, should be interrupted by the misconduct of individuals, the United States, and the said Indian tribes agree, that for injuries done by individuals on either side, no private revenge or retaliation shall take place; but instead thereof, complaint shall be made by the party injured, to the other: by the said Indian tribes or any of them, to the President of the United States, or the superintendent by him appointed; and by the superintendent or other person appointed by the President, to the principal chiefs of the said Indian tribes, or of the tribe to which the offender belongs; and such prudent measures shall then be taken as shall be necessary to preserve the said peace and friendship unbroken, until the legislature (or great council) of the United States, shall make other equitable provision in the case, to the satisfaction of both parties. Should any Indian tribes meditate a war against the United States, or either of them, and the same shall come to the knowledge of the before mentioned tribes, or either of them, they do hereby engage to give immediate notice thereof to the general, or officer commanding the troops of the United States, at the nearest post. And should any tribe, with hostile intentions against the United States, or either of them, attempt to pass through their country, they will endeavor to prevent the same, and in like manner give information of such attempt, to the general, or officer commanding, as soon as possible, that all causes of mistrust and suspicion may be avoided between them and the United States. In like manner, the United States shall give notice to the said Indian tribes of any harm that may be meditated against them, or either of them, that shall come to their knowledge; and do all in their power to hinder and prevent the same, that the friendship between them may be uninterrupted.

Art. 10:
All other treaties heretofore made between the United States, and the said Indian tribes, or any of them, since the treaty of 1783, between the United States and Great Britain, that come within the purview of this treaty, shall henceforth cease and become void.

In testimony whereof, the said Anthony Wayne, and the sachems and war chiefs of the before mentioned nations and tribes of Indians, have hereunto set their hands and affixed their seals. Done at Greenville, in the territory of the United States northwest of the river Ohio, on the third day of August, one thousand seven hundred and ninety five.

WYANDOTS.
Tarhe, or Crane, his x mark L.S. J. Williams, jun. his x mark, L.S. Teyyaghtaw, his x mark, L.S. Haroenyou, or half king's son, his x mark, L.S. Tehaawtorens, his x mark, L.S. Awmeyeeray, his x mark, L.S. Stayetah, his x mark L.S. Shateyyaronyah, or Leather Lips, his x mark, L.S. Daughshuttayah, his x mark L.S. Shaawrunthe, his x mark L.S.

DELAWARES.
Tetabokshke, or Grand Glaize King, his x mark, L.S. Lemantanquis, or Black King, his x mark, L.S. Wabatthoe, his x mark, L.S. Maghpiway, or Red Feather, his x mark, L.S. Kikthawenund, or Anderson, his x mark, L.S. Bukongehelas, his x mark, L.S. Peekeelund, his x mark, L.S. Wellebawkeelund, his x mark, L.S. Peekeetelemund, or Thomas Adams, his x mark, L.S. Kishkopekund, or Captain Buffalo, his x mark, L.S. Amenahehan, or Captain Crow, his x mark, L.S. Queshawksey, or George Washington, his x mark, L.S. Weywinquis, or Billy Siscomb, his x mark, L.S. Moses, his x mark, L.S.

SHAWANEES.
Misquacoonacaw, or Red Pole, his x mark, L.S. Cutthewekasaw, or Black Hoof, his x mark, L.S. Kaysewaesekah, his x mark, L.S. Weythapamattha, his x mark, L.S. Nianysmeka, his x mark, L.S. Waytheah, or Long Shanks, his x mark, L.S. Weyapiersenwaw, or Blue Jacket, his x mark, L.S. Nequetaughaw, his x mark, L.S. Hahgoosekaw, or Captain Reed, his x mark, L.S.

OTTAWAS.
Augooshaway, his x mark, L.S. Keenoshameek, his x mark, L.S. La Malice, his x mark, L.S. Machiwetah, his x mark, L.S. Thowonawa, his x mark, L.S. Secaw, his x mark, L.S.

CHIPPEWAS.
Mashipinashiwish, or Bad Bird, his x mark, L.S. Nahshogashe, (from Lake Superior), his x mark, L.S. Kathawasung, his x mark, L.S. Masass, his x mark, L.S. Nemekass, or Little Thunder, his x mark, L.S. Peshawkay, or Young Ox, his x mark, L.S. Nanguey, his x mark, L.S. Meenedohgeesogh, his x mark, L.S. Peewanshemenogh, his x mark, L.S. Weymegwas, his x mark, L.S. Gobmaatick, his x mark, L.S.

OTTAWA.
Chegonickska, an Ottawa from Sandusky, his x mark, L.S.

PATTAWATIMAS OF THE RIVER ST. JOSEPH.
Thupenebu, his x mark, L.S. Nawac, for himself and brother Etsimethe,
his x mark, L.S. Nenanseka, his x mark, L.S. Keesass, or Run, his x mark, L.S. Kabamasaw, for himself and brother Chisaugan, his x mark, L.S. Sugganunk, his x mark, L.S. Wapmeme, or White Pigeon, his x mark, L.S. Wacheness, for himself and brother Pedagoshok, his x mark, L.S. Wabshicawnaw, his x mark, L.S. La Chasse, his x mark, L.S. Meshegethenogh, for himself and brother, Wawasek, his x mark, L.S. Hingoswash, his x mark, L.S. Anewasaw, his x mark, L.S. Nawbudgh, his x mark, L.S. Missenogomaw, his x mark, L.S. Waweegshe, his x mark, L.S. Thawme, or Le Blanc, his x mark, L.S. Geeque, for himself and brother Shewinse, his x mark, L.S.

PATTAWATIMAS OF HURON.
Okia, his x mark, L.S. Chamung, his x mark, L.S. Segagewan, his x mark, L.S. Nanawme, for himself and brother A. Gin, his x mark, L.S. Marchand, his x mark, L.S. Wenameac, his x mark, L.S.

MIAMIS.
Nagohquangogh, or Le Gris, his x mark, L.S. Meshekunnoghquoh, or Little Turtle, his x mark, L.S.

MIAMIS AND EEL RIVERS.
Peejeewa, or Richard Ville, his x mark, L.S. Cochkepoghtogh, his x mark, L.S.

EEL RIVER TRIBE.
Shamekunnesa, or Soldier, his x mark, L.S.

MIAMIS.
Wapamangwa, or the White Loon, his x mark, L.S.

WEAS, FOR THEMSELVES AND THE PIANKESHAWS.
Amacunsa, or Little Beaver, his x mark, L.S. Acoolatha, or Little Fox, his x mark, L.S. Francis, his x mark, L.S.

KICKAPOOS AND KASKASKIAS.
Keeawhah, his x mark, L.S. Nemighka, or Josey Renard, his x mark, L.S. Paikeekanogh, his x mark, L.S.

DELAWARES OF SANDUSKY.
Hawkinpumiska, his x mark, L.S. Peyamawksey, his x mark, L.S. Reyntueco, (of the Six Nations, living at Sandusky), his x mark, L.S. H. De Butts, first A.D.C. and Sec'ry to Major Gen. Wayne, Wm. H. Harrison, Aid de Camp to Major Gen. Wayne, T. Lewis, Aid de Camp to Major Gen. Wayne, James O'Hara, Quartermaster Gen'l. John Mills, Major of Infantry, and Adj. Gen'l. Caleb Swan, P.M.T.U.S. Gen. Demter, Lieut. Artillery, Vigo, P. Frs. La Fontaine, Ast. Lasselle, Sworn interpreters. H. Lasselle, Wm. Wells, Js. Beau Bien, Jacques Lasselle, David Jones, Chaplain U.S.S. M. Morins, Lewis Beaufait, Bt. Sans Crainte, R. Lachambre, Christopher Miller, Jas. Pepen, Robert Wilson, Baties Coutien, Abraham Williams, his x mark P. Navarre. Isaac Zane, his x mark

Source: http://avalon.law.yale.edu/subject_menus/ntreaty.asp
Indian Affairs : Laws and Treaties, Vol. II (Treaties), Compiled and Edited By Charles J. Kappler LL. M.
Clerk to the Senate Committee on Indian Affairs, Washington, DC : Government Printing Office, 1904

Fort Laramie Treaty (1868)

ARTICLES OF A TREATY MADE AND CONCLUDED BY AND BETWEEN Lieutenant General William T. Sherman, General William S. Harney, General Alfred H. Terry, General O. O. Augur, J. B. Henderson, Nathaniel G. Taylor, John G. Sanborn, and Samuel F. Tappan, duly appointed commissioners on the part of the United States, and the different bands of the Sioux Nation of Indians, by their chiefs and headmen, whose names are hereto subscribed, they being duly authorized to act in the premises.

ARTICLE I.

From this day forward all war between the parties to this agreement shall for ever cease. The government of the United States desires peace, and its honor is hereby pledged to keep it. The Indians desire peace, and they now pledge their honor to maintain it.

If bad men among the whites, or among other people subject to the authority of the United States, shall commit any wrong upon the person or property of the Indians, the United States will, upon proof made to the agent, and forwarded to the Commissioner of Indian Affairs at Washington city, proceed at once to cause the offender to be arrested and punished according to the laws of the United States, and also reimburse the injured person for the loss sustained.

If bad men among the Indians shall commit a wrong or depredation upon the person or property of nay one, white, black, or Indian, subject to the authority of the United States, and at peace therewith, the Indians herein named solemnly agree that they will, upon proof made to their agent, and notice by him, deliver up the wrongdoer to the United States, to be tried and punished according to its laws, and, in case they willfully refuse so to do, the person injured shall be reimbursed for his loss from the annuities, or other moneys due or to become due to them under this or other treaties made with the United States; and the President, on advising with the Commissioner of Indian Affairs, shall prescribe such rules and regulations for ascertaining damages under the provisions of this article as in his judgment may be proper, but no one sustaining loss while violating the provisions of this treaty, or the laws of the United States, shall be reimbursed therefor.

ARTICLE II.

The United States agrees that the following district of country, to wit, viz: commencing on the east bank of the Missouri river where the 46th parallel of north latitude crosses the same, thence along low-water mark down said east bank to a point opposite where the northern line of the State of Nebraska strikes the river, thence west across said river, and along the northern line of Nebraska to the 104th degree of longitude west from Greenwich, thence north on said meridian to a point where the 46th parallel of north latitude intercepts the same, thence due east along said parallel to the place of beginning; and in addition thereto, all existing reservations of the east back of said river, shall be and the same is, set apart for the absolute and undisturbed use and occupation of the Indians herein named, and for such other friendly tribes or individual Indians as from time to time they may be willing, with the consent of the United States, to admit amongst them; and the United States now solemnly agrees that no persons, except those herein designated and authorized so to do, and except such officers, agents, and employees of the government as may be authorized to enter upon Indian reservations in discharge of duties enjoined by law, shall ever be permitted to pass over, settle upon, or reside in the territory described in this article, or in such territory as may be added to this reservation for the use of said Indians, and henceforth they will and do hereby relinquish all claims or right in and to any portion of the United States or Territories, except such as is embraced within the limits aforesaid, and except as hereinafter provided.

ARTICLE III.

If it should appear from actual survey or other satisfactory examination of said tract of land that it contains less than 160 acres of tillable land for each person who, at the time, may be authorized to reside on it under the provisions of this treaty, and a very considerable number of such persons shall be disposed to comnence cultivating the soil as farmers, the United States agrees to set apart, for the use of said Indians, as herein provided, such additional quantity of arable land, adjoining to said reservation, or as near to the same as it can be obtained, as may be required to provide the necessary amount.

ARTICLE IV.

The United States agrees, at its own proper expense, to construct, at some place on the Missouri river, near the centre of said reservation where timber and water may be convenient, the following buildings, to wit, a warehouse, a store-room for the use of the agent in storing goods belonging to the Indians, to cost not less than $2,500; an agency building, for the residence of the agent, to cost not exceeding

$3,000; a residence for the physician, to cost not more than $3,000; and five other buildings, for a carpenter, farmer, blacksmith, miller, and engineer-each to cost not exceeding $2,000; also, a school-house, or mission building, so soon as a sufficient number of children can be induced by the agent to attend school, which shall not cost exceeding $5,000.

The United States agrees further to cause to be erected on said reservation, near the other buildings herein authorized, a good steam circular saw-mill, with a grist-mill and shingle machine attached to the same, to cost not exceeding $8,000.

ARTICLE V.
The United States agrees that the agent for said Indians shall in the future make his home at the agency building; that he shall reside among them, and keep an office open at all times for the purpose of prompt and diligent inquiry into such matters of complaint by and against the Indians as may be presented for investigation under the provisions of their treaty stipulations, as also for the faithful discharge of other duties enjoined on him by law. In all cases of depredation on person or property he shall cause the evidence to be taken in writing and forwarded, together with his findings, to the Commissioner of Indian Affairs, whose decision, subject to the revision of the Secretary of the Interior, shall be binding on the parties to this treaty.

ARTICLE VI.
If any individual belonging to said tribes of Indians, or legally incorporated with them, being the head of a family, shall desire to commence farming, he shall have the privilege to select, in the presence and with the assistance of the agent then in charge, a tract of land within said reservation, not exceeding three hundred and twenty acres in extent, which tract, when so selected, certified, and recorded in the "Land Book" as herein directed, shall cease to be held in common, but the same may be occupied and held in the exclusive possession of the person selecting it, and of his family, so long as he or they may continue to cultivate it.

Any person over eighteen years of age, not being the head of a family, may in like manner select and cause to be certified to him or her, for purposes of cultivation, a quantity of land, not exceeding eighty acres in extent, and thereupon be entitled to the exclusive possession of the same as above directed.

For each tract of land so selected a certificate, containing a description thereof and the name of the person selecting it, with a certificate endorsed thereon that the same has been recorded, shall be delivered to the party entitled to it, by the agent, after the same shall have been recorded by him in a book to be kept in his office, subject to inspection, which said book shall be known as the "Sioux Land Book."

The President may, at any time, order a survey of the reservation, and, when so surveyed, Congress shall provide for protecting the rights of said settlers in their improvements, and may fix the character of the title held by each. The United States may pass such laws on the subject of alienation and descent of property between the Indians and their descendants as may be thought proper. And it is further stipulated that any male Indians over eighteen years of age, of any band or tribe that is or shall hereafter become a party to this treaty, who now is or who shall hereafter become a resident or occupant of any reservation or territory not included in the tract of country designated and described in this treaty for the permanent home of the Indians, which is not mineral land, nor reserved by the United States for special purposes other than Indian occupation, and who shall have made improvements thereon of the value of two hundred dollars or more, and continuously occupied the same as a homestead for the term of three years, shall be entitled to receive from the United States a patent for one hundred and sixty acres of land including his said improvements, the same to be in the form of the legal subdivisions of the surveys of the public lands. Upon application in writing, sustained by the proof of two disinterested witnesses, made to the register of the local land office when the land sought to be entered is within a land district, and when the tract sought to be entered is not in any land district, then upon said application and proof being made to the Commissioner of the General Land Office, and the right of such Indian or Indians to enter such tract or tracts of land shall accrue and be perfect from the date of his first improvements thereon, and shall continue as long as be continues his residence and improvements and no longer. And any Indian or Indians receiving a patent for land under the foregoing provisions shall thereby and from thenceforth become and be a citizen of the United States and be entitled to all the privileges and immunities of such citizens, and shall, at the same time, retain all his rights to benefits accruing to Indians under this treaty.

ARTICLE VII.
In order to insure the civilization of the Indians entering into this treaty, the necessity of education is admitted, especially of such of them as are or may be settled on said agricultural reservations, and they, therefore, pledge themselves to compel their children, male and female, between the ages of six and sixteen years, to attend school, and it is hereby made the duty of the agent for said Indians to see that this stipulation is strictly complied with; and the United States agrees that for every thirty children between said ages, who can be induced or compelled to attend school, a house shall be provided, and a teacher competent to teach the elementary branches of an English education shall be furnished, who will reside among said Indians and faithfully discharge his or her duties as a teacher. The provisions of this article to continue for not less than twenty years.

ARTICLE VIII.
When the head of a family or lodge shall have selected lands and received his certificate as above directed, and the agent shall be satisfied that he intends in good faith to commence cultivating the soil for a living, he shall be entitled to receive seeds and agricultural implements for the first year, not exceeding in value one hundred dollars, and for each succeeding year he shall continue to farm, for a period of three years more, he shall be entitled to receive seeds and implements as aforesaid, not exceeding in value twenty-five dollars. And it is further stipulated that such persons as commence farming shall receive instruction from the farmer herein provided for, and whenever more than one hundred persons shall enter upon the cultivation of the soil, a second blacksmith shall be provided, with such iron, steel, and other material as may be needed.

ARTICLE IX.
At any time after ten years fro the making of this treaty, the United States shall have the privilege of withdrawing the physician, farmer, blacksmith, carpenter, engineer, and miller herein provided for, but in case of such withdrawal, an additional sum thereafter of ten thousand dollars per annum shall be devoted to the education of said Indians, and the Commissioner of Indian Affairs shall, upon careful inquiry into their condition, make such rules and regulations for the expenditure of said sums as will best promote the education and moral improvement of said tribes.

ARTICLE X.
In lieu of all sums of money or other annuities provided to be paid to the Indians herein named under any treaty or treaties heretofore made, the United States agrees to deliver at the agency house on the reservation herein named, on or before the first day of August of each year, for thirty years, the following articles, to wit:

For each male person over 14 years of age, a suit of good substantial woollen clothing, consisting of coat, pantaloons, flannel shirt, hat, and a pair of home-made socks.

For each female over 12 years of age, a flannel shirt, or the goods necessary to make it, a pair of woollen hose, 12 yards of calico, and 12 yards of cotton domestics.

For the boys and girls under the ages named, such flannel and cotton goods as may be needed to make each a suit as aforesaid, together with a pair of woollen hose for each.

And in order that the Commissioner of Indian Affairs may be able to estimate properly for the articles herein named, it shall be the duty of the agent each year to forward to him a full and exact census of the Indians, on which the estimate from year to year can be based.

And in addition to the clothing herein named, the sum of $10 for each person entitled to the beneficial effects of this treaty shall be annually appropriated for a period of 30 years, while such persons roam and hunt, and $20 for each person who engages in farming, to be used by the Secretary of the Interior in the purchase of such articles as from time to time the condition and necessities of the Indians may indicate to be proper. And if within the 30 years, at any time, it shall appear that the amount of money needed for clothing, under this article, can be appropriated to better uses for the Indians named herein, Congress may, by law, change the appropriation to other purposes, but in no event shall the amount of the appropriation be withdrawn or discontinued for the period named. And the President shall annually detail an officer of the army to be present and attest the delivery of all the goods herein named, to the Indians, and he shall inspect and report on the quantity and quality of the goods and the manner of their delivery. And it is hereby expressly stipulated that each Indian over the age of four years, who shall have removed to and settled permanently upon said reservation, one pound of meat and one pound of flour per day, provided the Indians cannot furnish their own subsistence at an earlier date. And it is further stipulated that the United States will furnish and deliver to each lodge of Indians or family of persons legally incorporated with the, who shall remove to the reservation herein described and commence farming, one good American cow, and one good well-broken pair of American oxen within 60 days after such lodge or family shall have so settled upon said reservation.

ARTICLE XI.
In consideration of the advantages and benefits conferred by this treaty and the many pledges of friendship by the United States, the tribes who are parties to this agreement hereby stipulate that they will relinquish all right to occupy permanently the territory outside their reservations as herein defined, but yet reserve the right to hunt on any lands north of North Platte, and on the Republican Fork of the Smoky Hill river, so long as the buffalo may range thereon in such numbers as to justify the chase. And they, the said Indians, further expressly agree:

1st. That they will withdraw all opposition to the construction of the railroads now being built on the plains.

2d. That they will permit the peaceful construction of any railroad not passing over their reservation as herein defined.

3d. That they will not attack any persons at home, or travelling, nor molest or disturb any wagon trains, coaches, mules, or cattle belonging to the people of the United States, or to persons friendly therewith.

4th. They will never capture, or carry off from the settlements, white women or children.

5th. They will never kill or scalp white men, nor attempt to do them harm.

6th. They withdraw all pretence of opposition to the construction of the railroad now being built along the Platte river and westward to the Pacific ocean, and they will not in future object to the construction of railroads, wagon roads, mail stations, or other works of utility or necessity, which may be ordered or permitted by the laws of the United States. But should such roads or other works be constructed on the lands of their reservation, the government will pay the tribe whatever amount of damage may be assessed by three disinterested commissioners to be appointed by the President for that purpose, one of the said commissioners to be a chief or headman of the tribe.

7th. They agree to withdraw all opposition to the military posts or roads now established south of the North Platte river, or that may be established, not in violation of treaties heretofore made or hereafter to be made with any of the Indian tribes.

ARTICLE XII.
No treaty for the cession of any portion or part of the reservation herein described which may be held in common, shall be of any validity or force as against the said Indians unless executed and signed by at least three-fourths of all the adult male Indians occupying or interested in the same, and no cession by the tribe shall be understood or construed in such manner as to deprive, without his consent, any individual member of the tribe of his rights to any tract of land selected by him as provided in Article VI of this treaty.

ARTICLE XIII.
The United States hereby agrees to furnish annually to the Indians the physician, teachers, carpenter, miller, engineer, farmer, and blacksmiths, as herein contemplated, and that such appropriations shall be made from time to time, on the estimate of the Secretary of the Interior, as will be sufficient to employ such persons.

ARTICLE XIV.
It is agreed that the sum of five hundred dollars annually for three years from date shall be expended in presents to the ten persons of said tribe who in the judgment of the agent may grow the most valuable crops for the respective year.

ARTICLE XV.
The Indians herein named agree that when the agency house and other buildings shall be constructed on the reservation named, they will regard said reservation their permanent home, and they will make no permanent settlement elsewhere; but they shall have the right, subject to the conditions and modifications of this treaty, to hunt, as stipulated in Article XI hereof.

ARTICLE XVI.
The United States hereby agrees and stipulates that the country north of the North Platte river and east of the summits of the Big Horn mountains shall be held and considered to be unceded. Indian territory, and also stipulates and agrees that no white person or persons shall be permitted to settle upon or occupy any portion of the same; or without the consent of the Indians, first had and obtained, to pass through the same; and it is further agreed by the United States, that within ninety days after the conclusion of peace with all the bands of the Sioux nation, the military posts now established in the territory in this article named shall be abandoned, and that the road leading to them and by them to the settlements in the Territory of Montana shall be closed.

ARTICLE XVII.

It is hereby expressly understood and agreed by and between the respective parties to this treaty that the execution of this treaty and its ratification by the United States Senate shall have the effect, and shall be construed as abrogating and annulling all treaties and agreements heretofore entered into between the respective parties hereto, so far as such treaties and agreements obligate the United States to furnish and provide money, clothing, or other articles of property to such Indians and bands of Indians as become parties to this treaty, but no further. In testimony of all which, we, the said commissioners, and we, the chiefs and headmen of the Brule band of the Sioux nation, have hereunto set our hands and seals at Fort Laramie, Dakota Territory, this twenty-ninth day of April, in the year one thousand eight hundred and sixty-eight.

N. G. TAYLOR,
W. T. SHERMAN,
Lieutenant General
WM. S. HARNEY,
Brevet Major General U.S.A.
JOHN B. SANBORN,
S. F. TAPPAN,
C. C. AUGUR,
Brevet Major General
ALFRED H. TERRY,
Brevet Major General U.S.A.
Attest:
A. S. H. WHITE, Secretary.

Executed on the part of the Brule band of Sioux by the chiefs and headman whose names are hereto annexed, they being thereunto duly authorized, at Fort Laramie, D. T., the twenty-ninth day of April, in the year A. D. 1868.
MA-ZA-PON-KASKA, his X mark, Iron Shell.
WAH-PAT-SHAH, his X mark, Red Leaf.
HAH-SAH-PAH, his X mark, Black Horn.
ZIN-TAH-GAH-LAT-WAH, his X mark, Spotted Tail.
ZIN-TAH-GKAH, his X mark, White Tail.
ME-WAH-TAH-NE-HO-SKAH, his X mark, Tall Man.
SHE-CHA-CHAT-KAH, his X mark, Bad Left Hand.
NO-MAH-NO-PAH, his X mark, Two and Two.
TAH-TONKA-SKAH, his X mark, White Bull.
CON-RA-WASHTA, his X mark, Pretty Coon.
HA-CAH-CAH-SHE-CHAH, his X mark, Bad Elk.
WA-HA-KA-ZAH-ISH-TAH, his X mark, Eye Lance.
MA-TO-HA-KE-TAH, his X mark, Bear that looks behind.
BELLA-TONKA-TONKA, his X mark, Big Partisan.
MAH-TO-HO-HONKA, his X mark, Swift Bear.
TO-WIS-NE, his X mark, Cold Place.
ISH-TAH-SKAH, his X mark, White Eye.
MA-TA-LOO-ZAH, his X mark, Fast Bear.
AS-HAH-HAH-NAH-SHE, his X mark, Standing Elk.
CAN-TE-TE-KI-YA, his X mark, The Brave Heart.
SHUNKA-SHATON, his X mark, Day Hawk.
TATANKA-WAKON, his X mark, Sacred Bull.
MAPIA SHATON, his X mark, Hawk Cloud.
MA-SHA-A-OW, his X mark, Stands and Comes.
SHON-KA-TON-KA, his X mark, Big Dog.
Attest:
ASHTON S. H. WHITE, Secretary of Commission.
GEORGE B. WITHS, Phonographer to Commission.
GEO. H. HOLTZMAN.
JOHN D. HOWLAND.
JAMES C. O'CONNOR.
CHAR. E. GUERN, Interpreter.
LEON T. PALLARDY, Interpreter.
NICHOLAS JANIS, Interpreter.

Executed on the part of the Ogallalla band of Sioux by the chiefs and headmen whose names are hereto subscribed, they being thereunto duly authorized, at Fort Laramie, the 25th day of May, in the year A. D. 1868.
TAH-SHUN-KA-CO-QUI-PAH, his mark, Man-afraid-of-his-horses.
SHA-TON-SKAH, his X mark, White Hawk.
SHA-TON-SAPAH, his X mark, Black Hawk.
EGA-MON-TON-KA-SAPAH, his X mark, Black Tiger
OH-WAH-SHE-CHA, his X mark, Bad Wound.
PAH-GEE, his X mark, Grass.
WAH-NON SAH-CHE-GEH, his X mark, Ghost Heart.
COMECH, his X mark, Crow.

OH-HE-TE-KAH, his X mark, The Brave.
TAH-TON-KAH-HE-YO-TA-KAH, his X mark, Sitting Bull.
SHON-KA-OH-WAH-MEN-YE, his X mark, Whirlwind Dog.
HA-KAH-KAH-TAH-MIECH, his X mark, Poor Elk.
WAM-BU-LEE-WAH-KON, his X mark, Medicine Eagle.
CHON-GAH-MA-HE-TO-HANS-KA, his X mark, High Wolf.
WAH-SECHUN-TA-SHUN-KAH, his X mark, American Horse.
MAH-KAH-MAH-HA-MAK-NEAR, his X mark, Man that walks under the ground.
MAH-TO-TOW-PAH, his X mark, Four Bears.
MA-TO-WEE-SHA-KTA, his X mark, One that kills the bear.
OH-TAH-KEE-TOKA-WEE-CHAKTA, his X mark, One that kills in a hard place.
TAH-TON-KAH-TA-MIECH, his X mark, The Poor Bull.
OH-HUNS-EE-GA-NON-SKEN, his X mark, Mad Shade.
SHAH-TON-OH-NAH-OM-MINNE-NE-OH-MINNE, his X mark, Whirling hawk.
MAH-TO-CHUN-KA-OH, his X mark, Bear's Back.
CHE-TON-WEE-KOH, his X mark, Fool Hawk.
WAH-HOH-KE-ZA-AH-HAH, his X mark,
EH-TON-KAH, his X mark, Big Mouth.
MA-PAH-CHE-TAH, his X mark, Bad Hand.
WAH-KE-YUN-SHAH, his X mark, Red Thunder.
WAK-SAH, his X mark, One that Cuts Off.
CHAH-NOM-QUI-YAH, his X mark, One that Presents the Pipe.
WAH-KE-KE-YAN-PUH-TAH, his X mark, Fire Thunder.
MAH-TO-NONK-PAH-ZE, his X mark, Bear with Yellow Ears.
CON-REE-TEH-KA, his X mark, The Little Crow.
HE-HUP-PAH-TOH, his X mark, The Blue War Club.
SHON-KEE-TOH, his X mark, The Blue Horse.
WAM-BALLA-OH-CONQUO, his X mark, Quick Eagle.
TA-TONKA-SUPPA, his X mark, Black Bull.
MOH-TOH-HA-SHE-NA, his X mark, The Bear Hide.
Attest:
S. E. WARD.
JAS. C. O'CONNOR.
J. M. SHERWOOD.
W. C. SLICER.
SAM DEON.
H. M. MATHEWS.
JOSEPH BISS
NICHOLAS JANIS, Interpreter.
LEFROY JOTT, Interpreter.
ANTOINE JANIS, Interpreter.

Executed on the part of the Minneconjou band of Sioux by the chiefs and headmen whose names are hereunto subscribed, they being thereunto duly authorized.
HEH-WON-GE-CHAT, his X mark, One Horn.
OH-PON-AH-TAH-E-MANNE, his X mark, The Elk that Bellows Walking.
HEH-HO-LAH-ZEH-CHA-SKAH, his X mark, Young White Bull.
WAH-CHAH-CHUM-KAH-COH-KEEPAH, his X mark, One that is Afraid of Shield.
HE-HON-NE-SHAKTA, his X mark, The Old Owl.
MOC-PE-A-TOH, his X mark, Blue Cloud.
OH-PONG-GE-LE-SKAH, his X mark, Spotted Elk.
TAH-TONK-KA-HON-KE-SCHUE, his X mark, Slow bull.
SHONK-A-NEE-SHAH-SHAH-ATAH-PE, his X mark, The Dog Chief.
MA-TO-TAH-TA-TONK-KA, his X mark, Bull Bear.
WOM-BEH-LE-TON-KAH, his X mark, The Big Eagle.
MATOH, EH-SCHNE-LAH, his X mark, The Lone Bear.
MA-TOH-OH-HE-TO-KEH, his X mark, The Brave Bear.
EH-CHE-MA-KEH, his X mark, The Runner.
TI-KI-YA, his X mark, The Hard.
HE-MA-ZA, his X mark, Iron Horn.
Attest:
JAS. C O'CONNOR,
WM. D. BROWN,
NICHOLAS JANIS,
ANTOINE JANIS,
Interpreters.

Executed on the part of the Yanctonais band of Sioux by the chiefs and headmen whose names are hereto subscribed, they being thereunto duly authorized:
MAH-TO-NON-PAH, his X mark, Two Bears.
MA-TO-HNA-SKIN-YA, his X mark, Mad Bear.
HE-O-PU-ZA, his X mark, Louzy.
AH-KE-CHE-TAH-CHE-KA-DAN, his X mark, Little Soldier.
MAH-TO-E-TAN-CHAN, his X mark, Chief Bear.
CU-WI-TO-WIA, his X mark, Rotten Stomach.
SKUN-KA-WE-TKO, his X mark, Fool Dog.
ISH-TA-SAP-PAH, his X mark, Black Eye.

IH-TAN-CHAN, his X mark, The Chief.
I-A-WI-CA-KA, his X mark, The One who Tells the Truth.
AH-KE-CHE-TAH, his X mark, The Soldier.
TA-SHI-NA-GI, his X mark, Yellow Robe.
NAH-PE-TON-KA, his X mark, Big Hand.
CHAN-TEE-WE-KTO, his X mark, Fool Heart.
HOH-GAN-SAH-PA, his X mark, Black Catfish.
MAH-TO-WAH-KAN, his X mark, Medicine Bear.
SHUN-KA-KAN-SHA, his X mark, Red Horse.
WAN-RODE, his X mark, The Eagle.
CAN-HPI-SA-PA, his X mark, Black Tomahawk.
WAR-HE-LE-RE, his X mark, Yellow Eagle.
CHA-TON-CHE-CA, his X mark, Small Hawk, or Long Fare.
SHU-GER-MON-E-TOO-HA-SKA, his X mark, Fall Wolf.
MA-TO-U-TAH-KAH, his X mark, Sitting Bear.
HI-HA-CAH-GE-NA-SKENE, his X mark, Mad Elk.
Arapahoes.
LITTLE CHIEF, his X mark.
TALL BEAR, his X mark.
TOP MAN, his X mark.
NEVA, his X mark.
THE WOUNDED BEAR, his X mark.
WHIRLWIND, his X mark.
THE FOX, his X mark.
THE DOG BIG MOUTH, his X mark.
SPOTTED WOLF, his X mark.
SORREL HORSE, his X mark.
BLACK COAL, his X mark.
BIG WOLF, his X mark.
KNOCK-KNEE, his X mark.
BLACK CROW, his X mark.
THE LONE OLD MAN, his X mark.
PAUL, his X mark.
BLACK BULL, his X mark.
BIG TRACK, his X mark.
THE FOOT, his X mark.
BLACK WHITE, his X mark.
YELLOW HAIR, his X mark.
LITTLE SHIELD, his X mark.
BLACK BEAR, his X mark.
WOLF MOCASSIN, his X mark.
BIG ROBE, his X mark.
WOLF CHIEF, his X mark.
Witnesses:
ROBERT P. MCKIBBIN,
Captain 4th Infantry, and Bvt. Lieut. Col. U. S. A.,
Commanding Fort Laramie.
WM. H. POWELL,
Brevet Major, Captain 4th Infantry.
HENRY W. PATTERSON,
Captain 4th Infantry.
THEO E. TRUE,
Second Lieutenant 4th Infantry.
W. G. BULLOCK.
FORT LARAMIE, WYOMING TERRITORY
November 6, 1868.
MAH-PI-AH-LU-TAH, his X mark, Red Cloud.
WA-KI-AH-WE-CHA-SHAH, his X mark, Thunder Man.
MA-ZAH-ZAH-GEH, his X mark, Iron Cane.
WA-UMBLE-WHY-WA-KA-TUYAH, his X mark, High Eagle.
KO-KE-PAH, his X mark, Man Afraid.
WA-KI-AH-WA-KOU-AH, his X mark, Thunder Flying Running.
Witnessess:
W. MCE. DYE,
Brevet Colonel U. S. Army,
Commanding.
A. B. CAIN,
Captain 4th Infantry, Brevet Major U. S. Army.
ROBT. P. MCKIBBIN,
Captain 4th Infantry, Bvt. Lieut. Col. U. S. Army.
JNO. MILLER,
Captain 4th Infantry.
G. L. LUHN,
First Lieutenant 4th Infantry, Bvt. Capt. U. S. Army.
H. C. SLOAN,
Second Lieutenant 4th Infantry.

Assimilative Crimes Act

18 USC § 13

18 USCS § 13. Laws of States adopted for areas within Federal jurisdiction

(a) Whoever within or upon any of the places now existing or hereafter reserved or acquired as provided in section 7 of this title [18 USCS § 7], or on, above, or below any portion of the territorial sea of the United States not within the jurisdiction of any State, Commonwealth, territory, possession, or district is guilty of any act or omission which, although not made punishable by any enactment of Congress, would be punishable if committed or omitted within the jurisdiction of the State, Territory, Possession, or District in which such place is situated, by the laws thereof in force at the time of such act or omission, shall be guilty of a like offense and subject to a like punishment.

(b) (1) Subject to paragraph (2) and for purposes of subsection (a) of this section, that which may or shall be imposed through judicial or administrative action under the law of a State, territory, possession, or district, for a conviction for operating a motor vehicle under the influence of a drug or alcohol, shall be considered to be a punishment provided by that law. Any limitation on the right or privilege to operate a motor vehicle imposed under this subsection shall apply only to the special maritime and territorial jurisdiction of the United States.

(2) (A) In addition to any term of imprisonment provided for operating a motor vehicle under the influence of a drug or alcohol imposed under the law of a State, territory, possession, or district, the punishment for such an offense under this section shall include an additional term of imprisonment of not more than 1 year, or if serious bodily injury of a minor is caused, not more than 5 years, or if death of a minor is caused, not more than 10 years, and an additional fine under this title, or both, if--

(i) a minor (other than the offender) was present in the motor vehicle when the offense was committed; and

(ii) the law of the State, territory, possession, or district in which the offense occurred does not provide an additional term of imprisonment under the circumstances described in clause (i).

(B) For the purposes of subparagraph (A), the term "minor" means a person less than 18 years of age.

(c) Whenever any waters of the territorial sea of the United States lie outside the territory of any State, Commonwealth, territory, possession, or district, such waters (including the airspace above and the seabed and subsoil below, and artificial islands and fixed structures erected thereon) shall be deemed, for purposes of subsection (a), to lie within the area of the State, Commonwealth, territory, possession, or district that it would lie within if the boundaries of such State, Commonwealth, territory, possession, or district were extended seaward to the outer limit of the territorial sea of the United States.

History of the Assimilative Crimes Act (ACA):

The first **Assimilative Crimes Act** was passed as § 3 of the **Crimes Act of 1825**.

Sec. 3. And be it further enacted, that, if any offence shall be committed in any of the places aforesaid, the punishment of which offence is not specially provided for by any law of the United States, such offence shall, upon a conviction in any court of the United States having cognisance thereof, by liable to, and receive the same punishment as the laws of the state in which such fort, dock-yard, navy-yard, arsenal, armory, or magazine, or other place, ceded as aforesaid, is situated, provide for the like offence when committed within the body of any county of such state.

Appendix D

House Concurrent Resolution 108

Passed August 1953

Whereas it is the policy of Congress, as rapidly as possible, to make the Indians within the territorial limits of the United States subject to the same laws and entitled to the same privileges and responsibilities as are applicable to other citizens of the United States, to end their status as wards of the United States, and to grant them all of the rights and prerogatives pertaining to American citizenship; and

Whereas the Indians within the territorial limits of the United States should assume their full responsibilities as American citizens:

Now, therefore, be it resolved by the House of Representatives (the Senate concurring), That it is declared to be the sense of Congress that, at the earliest possible time, all of the Indian tribes and the individual members thereof located within the States of California, Florida, New York, and Texas, and all of the following named Indian tribes and individual members thereof, should be freed from Federal supervision and control and from all disabilities and limitations specially applicable to Indians: The Flathead Tribe of Montana, the Klamath Tribe of Oregon, the Menominee Tribe of Wisconsin, the Potowatamie Tribe of Kansas and Nebraska, and those members of the Chippewa Tribe who are on the Turtle Mountain Reservation, North Dakota. It is further declared to be the sense of Congress that, upon the release of such tribes and individual members thereof from such disabilities and limitations, all offices of the Bureau of Indian Affairs in the States of California, Florida, New York, and Texas and all other offices of the Bureau of Indian Affairs whose primary purpose was to serve any Indian tribe or individual Indian freed from Federal supervision should be abolished. It is further declared to be the sense of Congress that the Secretary of the Interior should examine all existing legislation dealing with such Indians, and treaties between the Government of the United States and each such tribe, and report to Congress at the earliest practicable date, but not later than January 1, 1954, his recommendations for such legislation as, in his judgment, may be necessary to accomplish the purposes of this resolution.

Appendix E

Public Law 280 as Adopted in 1953

An Act to confer jurisdiction on the States of California, Minnesota, Nebraska, Oregon, and Wisconsin, with respect to criminal offenses and civil causes of action committed or arising on Indian reservations within such States, and for other purposes.

Be it enacted by the Senate and House of Representatives of the United States of America in Congress assembled, that:

Chapter 53 of title 18, United States Code, is hereby amended by inserting at the end of the chapter analysis preceding section 1151 of such title the following new item:

1162. State jurisdiction over offenses committed by or against Indians in the Indian country.

Sec. 2. Title 18, United States Code, is hereby amended by inserting in chapter 53 thereof immediately after section 1161 a new section, to be designated as section 1162, as follows:

§ 1162. State jurisdiction over offenses committed by or against Indians in the Indian country.
(a) Each of the States listed in the following table shall have jurisdiction over offenses committed by or against Indians in the areas of Indian country listed opposite the name of the State to the same extent that such State has jurisdiction over offenses committed elsewhere within the State, and the criminal laws of such state shall have the same force and effect within such Indian country as they have elsewhere within the State:

State of	***Indian country affected***
California	All Indian country within the State
Minnesota	All Indian country within the State, except the Red Lake Reservation
Nebraska	All Indian country within the State
Oregon	All Indian country within the State, except the Warm Springs Reservation
Wisconsin	All Indian country within the State, except the Menominee Reservation

(b) Nothing in this section shall authorize the alienation, encumbrance, or taxation of any real or personal property, including water rights, belonging to any Indian or any Indian tribe, band, or community that is held in trust by the United States or is subject to a restriction against alienation imposed by the United States; or shall authorize regulation of the use of such property in a manner inconsistent with any Federal treaty, agreement, or statute or with any regulation made pursuant thereto; or shall deprive any Indian or any Indian tribe, band, or community of any right, privilege or immunity afforded under Federal treaty, agreement, or statute with respect to hunting, trapping, or fishing or the control, licensing, or regulation thereof.

(c) The provisions of sections 1152 and 1153 of this chapter shall not be applicable within the areas of Indian country listed in subsection (a) of this section.

Sec. 3. Chapter 85 of title 28, United States Code, is hereby amended by inserting at the end of the chapter analysis preceding section 1331 of such title the following new item:

1360. State civil jurisdiction in actions to which Indians are parties.
(a) Each of the States listed in the following table shall have jurisdiction over civil causes of action between Indians or to which Indians are parties which arise in the areas of Indian country listed opposite the name of the State to the same extent that such State has jurisdiction over other civil causes of action, and those civil laws of such State that are of general application to private persons or private property shall have the same force and effect within such Indian country as they have elsewhere within the State:

State of	***Indian country affected***
California	All Indian country within the State
Minnesota	All Indian country within the State, except the Red Lake Reservation
Nebraska	All Indian country within the State
Oregon	All Indian country within the State, except the Warm Springs Reservation
Wisconsin	All Indian country within the State, except the Menominee Reservation

(b) Nothing in this section shall authorize the alienation, encumbrance, or taxation of any real or personal property, including water rights, belonging to any Indian or any Indian tribe, band, or community that is held in trust by the United States or is subject to a restriction against alienation imposed by the United States; or shall authorize regulation of the use of such property in a manner inconsistent with any Federal treaty, agreement, or statute or with any regulation made pursuant thereto; or shall confer jurisdiction upon the State to adjudicate, in probate proceedings or otherwise, the ownership or right to possession of such property or any interest therein.

(c) Any tribal ordinance or custom heretofore or hereafter adopted by an Indian tribe, band, or community in the exercise of any authority which it may possess shall, if not inconsistent with any applicable civil law of the State, be given full force and effect in the determination of civil causes of action pursuant to this section.

Sec. 5. Section 1 of the Act of October, 1949 (63 Stat. 705, ch. 604), is hereby repealed, but such repeal shall not affect any proceedings heretofore instituted under that section.

Sec. 6. Notwithstanding the provisions of any Enabling Act for the admission of a State, the consent of the United States is hereby given to the people of any State to amend, where necessary, their State constitution or existing statutes, as the case may be, to remove any legal impediment to the assumption of civil and criminal jurisdiction in accordance with the provisions of this Act; Provided, that the provisions of this Act shall not become effective with respect to such assumption of jurisdiction by any such State until the people thereof have appropriately amended their State constitution or statutes as the case may be.

Sec. 7. The consent of the United States is hereby given to any other State not having jurisdiction with respect to criminal offenses or civil causes of action, or with respect to both, as provided for in this Act, to assume jurisdiction at such time and in such manner as the people of the State shall, by affirmative legislative action, obligate and bind the State to assumption thereof.

Approved August 15, 1953.

Appendix F

Assumption of concurrent Federal criminal jurisdiction

Administrative practice and procedure, Crime, Indians.
Accordingly, for the reasons set forth in the preamble, part 50 of chapter I of title 28 of the Code of Federal Regulations is amended as follows:

1.The authority citation for part 50 is revised to read as follows:

5 U.S.C. 301; 18 U.S.C. 1162; 28 U.S.C. 509, 510; 42 U.S.C. 1921 et seq., 1973c; and Public Law 107-273, 116 Stat. 1758, 1824. 2. Section 50.25 is added to read as follows:

§ 50.25 Assumption of concurrent Federal criminal jurisdiction in certain areas of Indian country.
(a) Assumption of concurrent Federal criminal jurisdiction. (1) Under 18 U.S.C. 1162(d), the United States may accept concurrent Federal criminal jurisdiction to prosecute violations of 18 U.S.C. 1152 (the General Crimes, or Indian Country Crimes, Act) and 18 U.S.C. 1153 (the Major Crimes, or Indian Major Crimes, Act) within areas of Indian country in the States of Alaska, California, Minnesota, Nebraska, Oregon, and Wisconsin that are subject to State criminal jurisdiction under Public Law 280, 18 U.S.C. 1162(a), if the tribe requests such an assumption of jurisdiction and the Attorney General consents to that request. Once the Attorney General has consented to an Indian tribe's request for assumption of concurrent Federal criminal jurisdiction, the General Crimes and Major Crimes Acts shall apply in the Indian country of the requesting tribe that is located in any of these "mandatory" Public Law 280 States, and criminal jurisdiction over those areas shall be concurrent among the Federal Government, the State government, and (where applicable) the tribal government. Assumption of concurrent Federal criminal jurisdiction under 18 U.S.C. 1162(d) does not require the agreement, consent, or concurrence of any State or local government.
(2) Under 25 U.S.C. 1321(a)(2), the United States may exercise concurrent Federal criminal jurisdiction in other areas of Indian country as to which States have assumed "optional" Public Law 280 criminal jurisdiction under 25 U.S.C. 1321(a), if a tribe so requests and after consultation with and consent by the Attorney General. The Department's view is that such concurrent Federal criminal jurisdiction exists under applicable statutes in these areas of Indian country, even if the Federal Government does not formally accept such jurisdiction in response to petitions from individual tribes. This rule therefore does not establish procedures for processing requests from tribes under 25 U.S.C. 1321(a)(2).
(b) Request requirements. (1) A tribal request for assumption of concurrent Federal criminal jurisdiction under 18 U.S.C. 1162(d) shall be made by the chief executive official of a federally recognized Indian tribe that occupies Indian country listed in 18 U.S.C. 1162(a). For purposes of this section, a chief executive official may include a tribal chairperson, president, governor, principal chief, or other equivalent position.
(2) The tribal request shall be submitted in writing to the Director of the Office of Tribal Justice at the Department of Justice. The first page of the tribal request shall be clearly marked: "Request for United States Assumption of Concurrent Federal Criminal Jurisdiction." The tribal request shall explain why the assumption of concurrent Federal criminal jurisdiction will improve public safety and criminal law enforcement and reduce crime in the Indian country of the requesting tribe. The tribal request shall also identify each local or State agency that currently has jurisdiction to investigate or prosecute criminal violations in the Indian country of the tribe and shall provide contact information for each such agency.
(c) Process for handling tribal requests. (1) Upon receipt of a tribal request, the Office of Tribal Justice shall:
(i) Acknowledge receipt; and
(ii) Open a file.
(2) Within 30 days of receipt of a tribal request, the Office of Tribal Justice shall:
(i) Publish a notice in the Federal Register, seeking comments from the general public;
(ii) Send written notice of the request to the State and local agencies identified by the tribe as having criminal jurisdiction over the tribe's Indian country, with a copy of the notice to the governor of the State in which the agency is located, requesting that any comments be submitted within 45 days of the date of the notice;
(iii) Seek comments from the relevant United States Attorney's Offices, the Federal Bureau of Investigation, and other Department of Justice components that would be affected by consenting to the request; and
(iv) Seek comments from the Department of the Interior (including the Bureau of Indian Affairs), the Department of Homeland Security, other affected Federal departments and agencies, and Federal courts.
(3) As soon as possible but not later than 30 days after receipt of a tribal request, the Office of Tribal Justice shall initiate consultation with the requesting tribe, consistent with applicable Executive Orders and Presidential Memoranda on tribal consultation.

(4) To the extent appropriate and consistent with applicable laws and regulations, including requirements of the Privacy Act of 1974, as amended, 5 U.S.C. 552a, governing personally identifiable information, and with the duty to protect law enforcement sensitive information, the Office of Tribal Justice may share with the requesting tribe any comments from other parties and provide the tribe with an opportunity to respond in writing.
(5) An Indian tribe may submit a request at any time after the effective date of this rule. However, requests received by February 28 of each calendar year will be prioritized for decision by July 31 of the same calendar year, if feasible; and requests received by August 31 of each calendar year will be prioritized for decision by January 31 of the following calendar year, if feasible. The Department will seek to complete its review of prioritized requests within these time frames, recognizing that it may not be possible to do so in each instance.
(d) Factors. Factors that will be considered in determining whether or not to consent to a tribe's request for assumption of concurrent Federal criminal jurisdiction include the following:
(1) Whether consenting to the request will improve public safety and criminal law enforcement and reduce crime in the Indian country of the requesting tribe.
(2) Whether consenting to the request will increase the availability of law enforcement resources for the requesting tribe, its members, and other residents of the tribe's Indian country. (3) Whether consenting to the request will improve access to judicial resources for the requesting tribe, its members, and other residents of the tribe's Indian country.
(4) Whether consenting to the request will improve access to detention and correctional resources for the requesting tribe, its members, and other residents of the tribe's Indian country.
(5) Other comments and information received from the relevant United States Attorney's Offices, the Federal Bureau of Investigation, and other Department of Justice components that would be affected by consenting to the request.
(6) Other comments and information received from the Department of the Interior (including the Bureau of Indian Affairs), the Department of Homeland Security, other affected Federal departments and agencies, and Federal courts.
(7) Other comments and information received from tribal consultation.
(8) Other comments and information received from other sources, including governors and State and local law enforcement agencies.
(e) Decision. (1) The decision whether to consent to a tribal request for assumption of concurrent Federal criminal jurisdiction shall be made by the Deputy Attorney General after receiving written recommendations from the Office of Tribal Justice, the Executive Office for United States Attorneys, and the Federal Bureau of Investigation.
(2) The Deputy Attorney General will:
(i) Consent to the request for assumption of concurrent Federal criminal jurisdiction, effective as of some future date certain within the next twelve months (and, if feasible, within the next six months), with or without conditions, and publish a notice of the consent in the Federal Register;
(ii) Deny the request for assumption of concurrent Federal criminal jurisdiction; or
(iii) Request further information or comment before making a final decision.
(3) The Deputy Attorney General shall explain the basis for the decision in writing.
(4) The decision to grant or deny a request for assumption of concurrent Federal criminal jurisdiction is not appealable. However, at any time after a denial of such a request, a tribe may submit a renewed request for assumption of concurrent Federal criminal jurisdiction. A renewed request shall address the basis for the prior denial. The Office of Tribal Justice may provide appropriate technical assistance to any tribe that wishes to prepare and submit a renewed request.
(f) Retrocession of State criminal jurisdiction. Retrocession of State criminal jurisdiction under Public Law 280 is governed by 25 U.S.C. 1323(a) and Executive Order 11435 of November 21, 1968. The procedures for retrocession do not govern a request for assumption of concurrent Federal criminal jurisdiction under 18 U.S.C. 1162(d).

Dated: November 28, 2011.
Eric H. Holder, Jr.,
Attorney General.

[FR Doc. 2011-31313 Filed 12-5-11; 8:45 am]

Appendix G

Indian Civil Rights Act of 1968

25 USC §§ 1301-03

25 USC § 1301. Definitions

For purposes of this subchapter, the term -

1."Indian tribe" means any tribe, band, or other group of Indians subject to the jurisdiction of the United States and recognized as possessing powers of self-government;

2."powers of self-government" means and includes all governmental powers possessed by an Indian tribe, executive, legislative, and judicial, and all offices, bodies, and tribunals by and through which they are executed, including courts of Indian offenses; and means the inherent power of Indian tribes, hereby recognized and affirmed, to exercise criminal jurisdiction over all Indians;

3."Indian court" means any Indian tribal court or court of Indian offense.

4."Indian" means any person who would be subject to the jurisdiction of the United States as an Indian under section 1153, Title 18, if that person were to commit an offense listed in that section in Indian country to which that section applies.

25 USC § 1302. Constitutional rights

(a) In General -- No Indian tribe in exercising powers of self-government shall -

1.make or enforce any law prohibiting the free exercise of religion, or abridging the freedom of speech, or of the press, or the right of the people peaceably to assemble and to petition for a redress of grievances;

2.violate the right of the people to be secure in their persons, houses, papers, and effects against unreasonable search and seizures, nor issue warrants, but upon probable cause, supported by oath or affirmation, and particularly describing the place to be searched and the person or thing to be seized;

3.subject any person for the same offense to be twice put in jeopardy;

4.compel any person in any criminal case to be a witness against himself;

5.take any private property for a public use without just compensation;

6.deny to any person in a criminal proceeding the right to a speedy and public trial, to be informed of the nature and cause of the accusation, to be confronted with the witnesses against him, to have compulsory process for obtaining witnesses in his favor, and at his own expense to have the assistance of counsel for his defense (except as provided in subsection (b);

7. (A) require excessive bail, impose excessive fines, or inflect cruel and unusual punishments;

(B) except as provided in subparagraph (C), impose for conviction of any 1 offense any penalty or punishment greater than imprisonment for a term of 1 year or a fine of $5,000, or both;

(C) subject to subsection (b), impose for conviction of any 1 offense any penalty or punishment greater than imprisonment for a term of 3 years or a fine of $15,000, or both; or

(D) impose on a person in a criminal proceeding a total penalty or punishment greater than imprisonment for a term of 9 years;

8.deny to any person within its jurisdiction the equal protection of its laws or deprive any person of liberty or property without due process of law;

9.pass any bill of attainder or ex post facto law; or

10. deny to any person accused of an offense punishable by imprisonment the right, upon request, to a trial by jury of not less than six persons.

(b) OFFENSES SUBJECT TO GREATER THAN 1-YEAR IMPRISONMENT OR A FINE GREATER THAN $5,000.—A tribal court may subject a defendant to a term of imprisonment greater than 1 year but not to exceed 3 years for any 1 offense, or a fine greater than $5,000 but not to exceed $15,000, or both, if the defendant is a person accused of a criminal offense who—

(1) has been previously convicted of the same or a comparable offense by any jurisdiction in the United States; or

(2) is being prosecuted for an offense comparable to an offense that would be punishable by more than 1 year of imprisonment if prosecuted by the United States or any of the States.

(c) RIGHTS OF DEFENDANTS.—In a criminal proceeding in which an Indian tribe, in exercising powers of self-government, imposes a total term of imprisonment of more than 1 year on a defendant, the Indian tribe shall—

(1) provide to the defendant the right to effective assistance of counsel at least equal to that guaranteed by the United States Constitution; and

(2) at the expense of the tribal government, provide an indigent defendant the assistance of a defense attorney licensed to practice law by any jurisdiction in the United States that applies appropriate professional licensing standards and effectively ensures the competence and professional responsibility of its licensed attorneys;

(3) require that the judge presiding over the criminal proceeding—

(A) has sufficient legal training to preside over criminal proceedings; and

(B) is licensed to practice law by any jurisdiction in the United States;

(4) prior to charging the defendant, make publicly available the criminal laws (including regulations and interpretative documents), rules of evidence, and rules of criminal procedure (including rules governing the recusal of judges in appropriate circumstances) of the tribal government; and

(5) maintain a record of the criminal proceeding, including an audio or other recording of the trial proceeding.

(d) SENTENCES.—In the case of a defendant sentenced in accordance with subsections (b) and (c), a tribal court may require the defendant—

(1) to serve the sentence—

(A) in a tribal correction center that has been approved by the Bureau of Indian Affairs for long-term incarceration, in accordance with guidelines to be developed by the Bureau of Indian Affairs (in consultation with Indian tribes) not later than 180 days after the date of enactment of the Tribal Law and Order Act of 2010;

(B) in the nearest appropriate Federal facility, at the expense of the United States pursuant to the Bureau of Prisons tribal prisoner pilot program described in section 304(c) of the Tribal Law and Order Act of 2010;

(C) in a State or local government-approved detention or correctional center pursuant to an agreement between the Indian tribe and the State or local government; or

(D) in an alternative rehabilitation center of an Indian tribe; or

(2) to serve another alternative form of punishment, as determined by the tribal court judge pursuant to tribal law.

(e) DEFINITION OF OFFENSE.—In this section, the term 'offense' means a violation of a criminal law.

(f) EFFECT OF SECTION.—Nothing in this section affects the obligation of the United States, or any State government that has been delegated authority by the United States, to investigate and prosecute any criminal violation in Indian country.

25 USC § 1303. Habeas corpus

The privilege of the writ of habeas corpus shall be available to any person, in a court of the United States, to test the legality of his detention by order of an Indian tribe.

July 29, 2010 - Indian Civil Rights Act (ICRA) as amended by the Tribal Law and Order Act (TLOA)

"Pop Quiz"

Quiz A ~ Chapter 1 - Chapter 2, Part 1

1. "Legislative History" is the historical background of a law:
   T or F

2. "Sovereignty" is exercising independent and self-governing authority:
   T or F

3. The tribal nations originally stayed out of the "family feud" between Mother England and her children of the American colonies.
   T or F

4. A treaty is legally binding.
   T or F

5. When the North American content was discovered by Europeans, it was not inhabited.
   T or F

6. The two ways tribal sovereignty is unique from most other sovereigns is:
   a. That it is self-governing and gave recognition for power of treaty-making.
   b. It existed from time immemorial and is inherent, not given.

7. The treaty contracts the US made with Indian tribes were often broken.
   T or F

8. The first US president, George Washington, and the first Secretary of War, Henry Knox, were both very concerned about land encroachments and the lawlessness of non-Indians on the frontier.
   T or F

9. Helen Jackson Hunt wrote a book in 1881 about US violations of Indian treaties.
   T or F

Quiz B ~ Chapter 2, Part 2

1. A tribe's political relationship with the US is based on:
   a. Individual ethnicity.
   b. Historical dealings between the US and Indian tribes.
   c. There is no political relationship.

2. Title 25 of the United States Code (USC) is entitled "Indians".
   T or F

3. Years of written treaties along with formal and informal agreements that the US government has made with Indian tribes has created a special political relationship between the two.
T or F

4. The federal trust responsiblity is clearly defined.
T or F

5. Every US president since Nixon has acknowledged the federal government-to-government relationship between the United States and Indian tribes.
T or F

6. Tribal sovereignty gives a tribe authority to manage their territories and their people.
T or F

Quiz C - Chapter 3, Part 1 - Chapter 3, Part 2

1. The legal framework that exists in Indian country today:
   a. Was built piece by piece throughout history.
   b. Has an unknown history.
   c. Was developed by the tribes only.

2. Indian tribes were, and still are, all alike and really one big tribe.
T or F

3. The Doctrine of Discovery was only acknlowledged by the European Powers.
T or F

4. When the American colonists won the Revolutionary War, the Doctrine of Discovery was passed on through the 1783 Treaty of Paris.
T or F

5. The Continental Congress stated in the Northwest Ordinance that ____________________ shall always be observed toward the Indians.:
   a. They said nothing.
   b. utmost good faith
   c. trading

6. It became necessary for the federal government to create laws to protect Indians from non-Indian abuses.
T or F

7. The Pennsylvania Mutiny of 1783 was influencial in creating:
   a. The California gold rush.
   b. Indian country.
   c. Federal enclaves.

8. Indians are mentioned in the US Constition.
T or F

Quiz D - Chapter 3, Part 3 - Chapter 3, Part 4

1. Indian affairs were placed under which US federal department in 1798?
   a. War Department.
   b. Treasury Department.
   c. State Department.

2. Trading with Indians was important to the economy of early America.
   T or F

3. The first federal Indian law enacted by Congress made offenses by non-Indians against Indians a federal crime.
   T or F

4. The General Crimes Act is also referred to as:
   a. The Trade and Intercourse Act.
   b. The Indian Country Crimes Act and 18 USC 1152.
   c. None of the above.

5. The Indian Removal Act authorized the US president to force tribes off their ancestral lands.
   T or F

6. Treaty-making with Indians officially stopped in:
   a. 1783.
   b. 1953.
   c. 1871.

7. There is no difference with Congress' dealing with the Indians by way of treaty or by legislation.
   T or F

Quiz E - Chapter 3, Part 5

1. The philosophy of assimilation assumes one culture is better or more civilized than another.
   T or F

2. Many Indian children were forced to attend off-reservation boarding schools.
   T or F

3. Jurisdiction over crime between non-Indians in Indian country was generally enforced by:
   a. The federal government.
   b. The state.
   c. The tribe.

4. The 1883 US Supreme Court case, *Ex Parte Crow Dog*, involved a crime between two Indians.
   T or F

5. The Major Crimes Act was enacted by Congress in response to the *Ex Parte Crow Dog* court decision.
T or F

6. The federal government had criminal jurisdiction over Indian v. Indian crimes on Indian land before the Major Crimes Act.
T or F

7. The General Allotment Act had a debilitating effect on tribal governments.
T or F

8. A report was written showing "The Problem of Indian Administration". This report is referred to as:
a. The Smith Report.
b. The Life and Times of Spotted Tail.
c. The Meriam Report.

9. The 1934 Indian Reorganization Act stopped the selling of Indian lands.
T or F

Quiz F ~ Chapter 4

1. The federal government has always shared criminal jurisdiction with the states.
T or F

2. The Indian Reorganization Act was just starting to take root when it felt the impact of WWII.
T or F

3. Native Americans and Alaska Natives did not contribute to the war efforts of WWII.
T or F

4. The "83" in PL 83-280 indicates the 83rd Congress.
T or F

5. "Desegregation" and "assimilation" imply the same thing.
T or F

6. PL 280 is a termination statute.
T or F

7. Some tribes were exempted from PL 280 jurisdiction in the Mandatory States.
T or F

8. President Eisenhower's response to the enactment of PL 280 was:
a. He was very happy and satisfied with all its provisions.
b. He was not pleased that there was no tribal consent provision included.
c. He did not read it.

9. Termination was eventually rejected.
T or F

10. Tribal consent was added to PL 280 in 1968.
T or F

11. PL 280 is a:
a. Tribal law.
b. State law.
c. Federal law.

Quiz G - Chapter 5

1. The unwavering stance of the federal government had always been that, absent clear Congressional consent, the states had no authority on Indian lands.
T or F

2. PL 280 was a first-of-its-kind.
T or F

3. PL 280 can be categorized into three sections.
T or F

4. The federal Penal Code is:
a. 28 USC.
b. 18 USC.
c. 10 USC.

5. PL 280 eliminated tribal concurrent jurisdiction.
T or F

6. Every state law that applies off the reservation also applies on the reservation.
T or F

7. The two parts of a state's public policy are civil/regulatory and criminal/prohibitory.
T or F

8. Civil/regulatory laws are for the common good and safety of the community.
T or F

9. Criminal/prohibitory laws are usually classified as misdemeanors and felonies.
T or F

10. It is always totally clear what laws violate a state's criminal policy.
T or F

11. Only a state's criminal/prohibitory laws apply on Indian lands under PL 280.
T or F

12. If an Indian violates a state's public policy off the reservation he/she is safe from state prosecution once on the reservation.
T or F

Quiz H - Chapter 6

1. "Concurent jurisdiction" means jurisdictions work:
   a. In opposition to each other.
   b. Side-by-side.

2. Indian tribes have the greatest interest in their people and their territories.
   T or F

3. The sovereign powers of Indian tribes were given to them by the federal government.
   T or F

4. If an Indian tribe does not excercise their inherent jurisdictional power, they eventally lose it.
   T or F

5. Tribal governments always look exactly like federal and state governments.
   T or F

6. There are elders living on Indian reservations today who experienced life at Indian boarding schools.
   T or F

7. Jurisdiction in Indian country must be connected to a federal law, treaty or interpretation of law.
   T or F

8. The *Oliphant Decision of 1978* determined that Indian tribes have no criminal jurisdiction over non-Indians.
   T or F

9. There are federal laws which apply on or off the reservation regardless if one is an Indian or a non-Indian.
   T or F

10. The Indian Civil Rights Act (ICRA) protects both Indians and non-Indians against arbitrary and/or abusive actions by tribal governments.
    T or F

11. The Indian Civil Rights Act is exactly like the US Constitution's Bill of Rights.
    T or F

"Pop Quiz" Answer Key

Quiz A - 1. True; 2. True; 3. True; 4. True; 5. False; 6. b; 7. True; 8. True; 9. True

Quiz B - 1. b; 2. True; 3. True; 4. False; 5. True; 6. True

Quiz C - 1. a; 2. False; 3. True; 4. True; 5. b; 6. True; 7. c; 8. True

Quiz D - 1. a; 2. True; 3. True; 4. b; 5. False; 6. c; 7. False

Quiz E - 1. True; 2. True; 3. b; 4. True; 5. True; 6. False; 7. True; 8. c; 9. True

Quiz F - 1. False; 2. True; 3. False; 4. True; 5. False; 6. False; 7. True; 8. b; 9. True; 10. True; 11. c

Quiz G - 1. True; 2. True; 3. True; 4.b; 5. False; 6. False; 7. True; 8. True; 9. True; 10. False; 11. True; 12. False

Quiz H - 1. b; 2. True; 3. False; 4. False; 5. False; 6. True; 7. True; 8. True; 9. True; 10. True; 11. False

Index

5764204R00207

Made in the USA
San Bernardino, CA
24 November 2013